VIDEO GAMES
AND GAMING CULTURE

Critical Concepts in Media and Cultural Studies

Other titles in this series:

Advertising
Edited with a new introduction by Iain MacRury
4-volume set

Bollywood
Edited with a new introduction by Rachel Dwyer
4-volume set

Book Publishing
Edited with a new introduction by John Feather
4-volume set

British Cinema
Edited with a new introduction by Robert Murphy
4-volume set

Chinese Cinema
Edited with a new introduction by Chris Berry
4-volume set

Communication Theories
Edited with a new introduction by Paul Cobley
4-volume set

Cybercultures
Edited with a new introduction by David Bell
4-volume set

Cultural Heritage
Edited with a new introduction by Laurajane Smith
4-volume set

Documentary Film
Edited with a new introduction by Ian Aitken
4-volume set

Everyday Life
Edited with a new introduction by Ben Highmore
4-volume set

Fashion
Edited with a new introduction by Malcolm Barnard
4-volume set

Film and Gender
Edited with a new introduction by Sue Thornham and Niall Richardson
4-volume set

Film Theory
Edited with a new introduction by Philip Simpson,
Andrew Utterson and K. J. Shepherdson
4-volume set

French Cinema
Edited with a new introduction by Phil Powrie
4-volume set

Hollywood
Edited with a new introduction by Thomas Schatz
4-volume set

Information Science
Edited with a new introduction by David Nicholas and Eti Herman
4-volume set

International Librarianship
Edited with a new introduction by Ravindra N. Sharma
4-volume set

Japanese Cinema
Edited with a new introduction by Nikki J. Y. Lee and Julian Stringer
4-volume set

Journalism
Edited with a new introduction by Howard Tumber
4-volume set

Mobile Technologies
Edited with a new introduction by Gerard Goggin,
Rich Ling and Larissa Hjorth
4-volume set

Media in China
Edited with a new introduction by Michael Keane and Wanning Sun
4-volume set

Popular Culture
Edited with a new introduction by Chris Rojek
4-volume set

Popular Music
Edited with a new introduction by Simon Frith
4-volume set

Public Relations
Edited with a new introduction by Robert Heath
4-volume set

Radio
Edited with a new introduction by Andrew Crisell
3-volume set

Sound Studies
Edited with a new introduction by Michael Bull
4-volume set

Subcultures
Edited with a new introduction by Ken Gelder
4-volume set

Television
Edited with a new introduction by Toby Miller
5-volume set

Visual Culture
Edited with a new introduction by Joanne Morra and Marquard Smith
4-volume set

Visual Culture and Gender
Edited with a new introduction by Annette Burfoot
4-volume set

War and Conflict Communication
Edited with a new introduction by Philip Seib
2-volume set

Forthcoming:

Animation
Edited with a new introduction by Paul Wells
4-volume set

Cultural Policy
Edited with a new introduction by Dave O'Brien and Kate Oakley
4-volume set

Disability and the Media
Edited with a new introduction by Katie Ellis and Mike Kent
4-volume set

Gender and the Media
Edited with a new introduction by Kaitlynn Mendes
4-volume set

Gender and Popular Culture
Edited with a new introduction by Katie Milestone and Anneke Meyer
4-volume set

Silent Cinema
Edited with a new introduction by Andrew Higson
4-volume set

VIDEO GAMES AND GAMING CULTURE

Critical Concepts in Media and Cultural Studies

Edited by
Mark J. P. Wolf

Volume I
Foundations

Routledge
Taylor & Francis Group

LONDON AND NEW YORK

First published 2016
by Routledge
2 Park Square, Milton Park, Abingdon, Oxon OX14 4RN

and by Routledge
711 Third Avenue, New York, NY 10017

Routledge is an imprint of the Taylor & Francis Group, an informa business

British Library Cataloguing in Publication Data
A catalogue record for this book is available from the British Library

Library of Congress Cataloging in Publication Data
A catalog record for this book has been requested

ISBN: 978-1-138-81125-6 (Set)
ISBN: 978-1-138-81126-3 (Volume I)

Typeset in Times New Roman
by Book Now Ltd, London

Publisher's Note
References within each chapter are as they appear in the original complete work

CONTENTS

VOLUME I FOUNDATIONS

Acknowledgements xix
Chronological table of reprinted articles and chapters xxiii

General introduction 1
MARK J. P. WOLF

Introduction to Volume I 4
MARK J. P. WOLF

PART 1
Defining video game studies 9

1 **Defining games** 11
KATIE SALEN AND ERIC ZIMMERMAN

2 **Defining game mechanics** 29
MIGUEL SICART

3 **The gaming situation** 46
MARKKU ESKELINEN

4 **Simulation versus narrative: introduction to ludology** 59
GONZALO FRASCA

5 **Games telling stories? A brief note on games and narratives** 73
JESPER JUUL

6 **Introduction: videogames and storytelling** 86
SOUVIK MUKHERJEE

7 Games, the new lively art   105
   HENRY JENKINS

8 Manifesto for a Ludic century   128
   ERIC ZIMMERMAN

PART 2
Game studies classics   133

9 Nature and significance of play as a cultural phenomenon   135
   JOHAN HUIZINGA

10 The play-element in contemporary civilization   *   155
    JOHAN HUIZINGA

11 'The definition of play' and 'The classification of games'   169
    ROGER CAILLOIS

12 Deep play: notes on the Balinese cockfight   196
    CLIFFORD GEERTZ

13 Play and ambiguity   213
    BRIAN SUTTON-SMITH

14 The lessons of Lucasfilm's *Habitat*   227
    F. RANDALL FARMER AND CHIP MORNINGSTAR

15 Hearts, clubs, diamonds, spades: players who suit MUDs   249
    RICHARD BARTLE

16 Environmental storytelling: creating immersive 3D worlds
    using lessons learned from the theme park industry   278
    DON CARSON

PART 3
History and historiographical concerns   287

17 The history of video games   289
    STEVEN D. BRISTOW

CONTENTS

18 Video games caught up in history: accessibility, teleological
    distortion, and other methodological issues   303
    CARL THERRIEN

19 Strategic simulations and our past: the bias of computer
    games in the presentation of history   321
    KEVIN SCHUT

20 Mainframe games and simulations   344
    DAVID H. AHL

21 Videogames in Computer Space: the complex history of Pong   348
    HENRY LOWOOD

22 *BattleZone* and the origins of first-person shooting games   371
    MARK J. P. WOLF

VOLUME II DESIGN AND THEORY

Acknowledgements   ix

Introduction to Volume II   1
MARK J. P. WOLF

PART 4
Video game design and formal aspects   5

23 I have no words & I must design   7
    GREG COSTIKYAN

24 Formal abstract design tools   23
    DOUG CHURCH

25 Tools for creating dramatic game dynamics   36
    MARC LeBLANC

26 MDA: a formal approach to game design and
    game research   54
    ROBIN HUNICKE, MARC LeBLANC, AND ROBERT ZUBEK

27 An introduction to the participatory and non-linear
    aspects of video games audio   64
    KAREN COLLINS

28 In the loop: creativity and constraint in 8-bit video
    game audio   89
    KAREN COLLINS

29 *Pac-Man*   109
    NICK MONTFORT AND IAN BOGOST

30 Game design as narrative architecture   123
    HENRY JENKINS

31 Theorizing navigable space in video games   139
    MARK J. P. WOLF

32 Gamic action, four moments   159
    ALEXANDER R. GALLOWAY

33 In defense of cutscenes   191
    RUNE KLEVJER

34 Fear of failing? The many meanings of difficulty in
    video games   202
    JESPER JUUL

PART 5
Video game theory, methodology, and analysis   217

35 Changing the game   219
    BERNARD DeKOVEN

36 Computer game semiotics   235
    DAVID MYERS

37 Computer game criticism: a method for computer
    game analysis   248
    LARS KONZACK

38 Playing research: methodological approaches to game analysis   259
    ESPEN AARSETH

CONTENTS

39 Towards the definition of a framework and grammar for
   game analysis and design   274
   ROBERTO DILLON

40 Bombs, barbarians, and backstories: meaning-making within
   Sid Meier's Civilization   285
   DAVID MYERS

41 Genre and game studies: toward a critical approach to
   video game genres   302
   THOMAS H. APPERLEY

42 Camera-eye, CG-eye: videogames and the "cinematic"   321
   WILL BROOKER

43 Color-cycled space fumes in the pixel particle shockwave:
   the technical aesthetics of *Defender* and the Williams
   arcade platform, 1980–82   328
   BRETT CAMPER

44 Procedural rhetoric   346
   IAN BOGOST

VOLUME III PLAY AND PLAYERS

   Acknowledgements   ix

   Introduction to Volume III   1
   MARK J. P. WOLF

PART 6
Embodiment and identity   5

45 Stories for eye, ear, and muscles: video games, media, and
   embodied experiences   7
   TORBEN GRODAL

46 Embodiment and interface   32
   ANDREAS GREGERSEN AND TORBEN GRODAL

47 The myth of the ergodic videogame: some thoughts on
   player-character relationships in videogames   49
   JAMES NEWMAN

48 Playing at being: psychoanalysis and the avatar   61
    BOB REHAK

49 Lara Croft: feminist icon or cyberbimbo? On the limits of
    textual analysis   86
    HELEN W. KENNEDY

50 Theorizing gender and digital gameplay: oversights, accidents
    and surprises   99
    JENNIFER JENSON AND SUZANNE DE CASTELL

51 Serious play: playing with race in contemporary gaming culture   110
    ANNA EVERETT

52 The power of play: the portrayal and performance of
    race in video games   132
    ANNA EVERETT AND S. CRAIG WATKINS

53 Race   157
    ANNA EVERETT

PART 7
Play, control, and the magic circle   171

54 The assemblage of play   173
    T. L. TAYLOR

55 Coming to play at frightening yourself: welcome to
    the world of horror video games   181
    BERNARD PERRON

56 I fought the law: transgressive play and the implied player   197
    ESPEN AARSETH

57 Video games and the pleasures of control   205
    TORBEN GRODAL

58 Allegories of control   222
    ALEXANDER R. GALLOWAY

59 The magic circle   241
    KATIE SALEN AND ERIC ZIMMERMAN

CONTENTS

60 There is no magic circle   250
   MIA CONSALVO

61 Jerked around by the magic circle – clearing the air
   ten years later   259
   ERIC ZIMMERMAN

62 Fundamental components of the gameplay experience:
   analysing immersion   269
   LAURA ERMI AND FRANS MÄYRÄ

63 Emersion as an element of gaming experience   286
   PIOTR KUBIŃSKI

PART 8
Threat, aggression, and violence   301

64 A rape in cyberspace: how an evil clown, a Haitian
   trickster spirit, two wizards, and a cast of dozens turned
   a database into a society   303
   JULIAN DIBBELL

65 Ephemeral games: is it barbaric to design videogames
   after Auschwitz?   319
   GONZALO FRASCA

66 Video games and aggressive thoughts, feelings, and behavior
   in the laboratory and in life   327
   CRAIG A. ANDERSON AND KAREN E. DILL

67 Effects of violent video games on aggressive behavior, aggressive
   cognition, aggressive affect, physiological arousal, and prosocial
   behavior: a meta-analytic review of the scientific literature   371
   CRAIG A. ANDERSON AND BRAD J. BUSHMAN

68 Violent video game effects on aggression, empathy, and
   prosocial behavior in Eastern and Western countries:
   a meta-analytic review   385
   CRAIG A. ANDERSON, AKIKO SHIBUYA, NOBUKO IHORI,
   EDWARD L. SWING, BRAD J. BUSHMAN, AKIRA SAKAMOTO,
   HANNAH R. ROTHSTEIN, AND MUNIBA SALEEM

69 Sign of a threat: the effects of warning systems in survival
horror games 435
BERNARD PERRON

70 The motivating role of violence in video games 455
ANDREW K. PRZYBYLSKI, RICHARD M. RYAN, AND C. SCOTT RIGBY

VOLUME IV CULTURAL CONTEXTS

Acknowledgements ix

Introduction to Volume IV 1
MARK J. P. WOLF

PART 9
Video games and education 5

71 The educational benefits of videogames 7
MARK GRIFFITHS

72 What video games have to teach us about learning and literacy 16
JAMES PAUL GEE

73 Video games in education 20
KURT SQUIRE

74 From content to context: videogames as designed experience 37
KURT SQUIRE

75 Game design and learning: a conjectural analysis of how
massively multiple online role-playing games (MMORPGs)
foster intrinsic motivation 60
MICHELE D. DICKEY

76 Video games and the future of learning 82
DAVID WILLIAMSON SHAFFER, KURT R. SQUIRE,
RICHARD HALVERSON, AND JAMES P. GEE

PART 10
Video games and culture 95

77 What is video game culture? Cultural studies and game studies 97
ADRIENNE SHAW

CONTENTS

78 Productive play: game culture from the bottom up 118
CELIA PEARCE

79 Material culture and Angry Birds 124
HEIKKI TYNI AND OLLI SOTAMAA

80 Nintendo® and new world travel writing: a dialogue 141
MARY FULLER AND HENRY JENKINS

81 *Civilization* and its discontents: simulation, subjectivity, and space 158
TED FRIEDMAN

82 Social play 173
DAVID MYERS

83 Gaining advantage: how videogame players define and
negotiate cheating 187
MIA CONSALVO

84 Girl gamers and their relationship with the gaming culture 207
GARETH R. SCHOTT AND KIRSTY R. HORRELL

85 Introduction (excerpt) to *Video Games around the World* 224
MARK J. P. WOLF

86 Balancing the tensions between rationalization and creativity
in the video games industry 237
F. TED TSCHANG

87 Convergence and globalization in the Japanese videogame industry 269
MIA CONSALVO

88 Videology: video-games as postmodern sites/sights of ideological
reproduction 276
SIMON GOTTSCHALK

89 Too many cooks: media convergence and self-defeating adaptations 294
TREVOR ELKINGTON

90 The centrality of play 314
JAMES NEWMAN

Index 329

xvii

ACKNOWLEDGEMENTS

The Publishers would like to thank the following for permission to reprint their material:

Katie Salen and Eric Zimmerman, 'Defining Games', *Rules of Play: Game Design Fundamentals* (Cambridge, MA: The MIT Press, 2003), pp. 71–83.

Miguel Sicart for permission to include Miguel Sicart, 'Defining Game Mechanics', *Game Studies: The International Journal of Computer Game Research*, 8(2), December 2008.

Markku Eskelinen, 'The Gaming Situation', *Game Studies: The International Journal of Computer Game Research*, 1(1), July 2001.

Routledge for permission to reprint Gonzalo Frasca, 'Simulation versus Narrative: Introduction to Ludology', in Mark J. P. Wolf and Bernard Perron (eds), *The Video Game Theory Reader* (New York, NY: Routledge, 2003), pp. 221–235.

Jesper Juul, 'Games Telling Stories? A Brief Note on Games and Narratives', in Joost Raessens and Jeffrey Goldstein (eds), *Handbook of Computer Game Studies* (Cambridge, MA: The MIT Press, 2005), pp. 219–226.

Palgrave MacMillan for permission to reprint Souvik Mukherjee, 'Introduction: Videogames and Storytelling', *Video Games and Storytelling: Reading Games and Playing Books* (New York: Palgrave MacMillan, 2015), pp. 1–20.

Henry Jenkins, 'Games, The New Lively Art', in Joost Raessens and Jeffrey Goldstein (eds), *Handbook of Computer Game Studies* (Cambridge, MA: The MIT Press, 2005), pp. 175–189.

Eric Zimmerman, 'Manifesto for a Ludic Century', *Kotaku.com*, 2013, available at http://kotaku.com/manifesto-the-21st-century-will-be-defined-by-games-1275355204, and republished in Steffen Walz and Sebastian Detering (eds), *The Gameful World: Approaches, Issues, Applications* (Cambridge, MA: The MIT Press, 2015), pp. 19–22.

Johan Huizinga, 'Nature and Significance of Play as a Cultural Phenomenon', *Homo Ludens: A Study of the Play-Element in Culture* (Original Dutch edition, 1938; New York, NY: Routledge, 1949), pp. 1–27.

Johan Huizinga, 'The Play-Element in Contemporary Civilization', *Homo Ludens: A Study of the Play-Element in Culture* (Original Dutch edition, 1938; New York, NY: Routledge, 1949), pp. 195–213.

Roger Caillois, 'The Definition of Play' and 'The Classification of Games', *Man, Play and Games* (Paris: Librairie Gallimard, 1958), pp. 3–11; 11–37.

Clifford Geertz, 'Deep Play: Notes on the Balinese Cockfight', *Daedalus*, 101(1), *Myth, Symbol, and Culture* (Winter, 1972), 1–37.

Brian Sutton-Smith, 'Play and Ambiguity', *The Ambiguity of Play* (Cambridge, MA: Harvard University Press, 1997), pp. 1–17.

F. Randall Farmer and Chip Morningstar, 'The Lessons of Lucasfilm's *Habitat*', in Michael Benedikt (ed.), *Cyberspace: First Steps* (Cambridge, MA: The MIT Press, 1990), pp. 273–301.

The author for permission to reprint Richard Bartle, 'Hearts, Clubs, Diamonds, Spades: Players Who Suit MUDs', *Journal of MUD Research*, 1(1), 1996.

Don Carson, 'Environmental Storytelling: Creating Immersive 3D Worlds Using Lessons Learned from the Theme Park Industry', *Gamasutra*, March 1, 2000, available at http://www.gamasutra.com/features/20000301/carson_pfv.htm.

IEEE for permission to reprint Steven D. Bristow, 'The History of Video Games', *IEEE Transactions on Consumer Electronics*, (1), February 1977, 58–68.

Wayne State University Press for permission to reprint Carl Therrien, 'Video Games Caught Up in History: Accessibility, Teleological Distortion, and Other Methodological Issues', in Mark J. P. Wolf (ed.), *Before the Crash: Early Video Game History* (Detroit, MI: Wayne State University Press, 2012), pp. 9–29. © 2012 Wayne State University Press, with the permission of Wayne State University Press.

Sage for permission to reprint Kevin Schut, 'Strategic Simulations and Our Past: The Bias of Computer Games in the Presentation of History', *Games and Culture*, 2(3), 2007, 213–235.

Greenwood Press for permission to reprint David H. Ahl, 'Mainframe Games and Simulations', in Mark J. P. Wolf (ed.), *The Video Game Explosion: A History from PONG to PlayStation and Beyond* (Westport, CT: Greenwood Press, 2007), pp. 31–34.

IEEE for permission to reprint Henry Lowood, 'Videogames in Computer Space: The Complex History of Pong', *IEEE Annals in the History of Computing*, July–September 2009, 5–19.

Bloomsbury for permission to reprint Mark J. P. Wolf, '*BattleZone* and the Origins of First-Person Shooting Games', in Gerald Voorhees, Joshua Call, and Katie Whitlock (eds), *Guns, Grenades and Grunts: First Person Shooter Games* (New York, NY: Continuum, 2012), pp. 25–40.

Disclaimer

The publishers have made every effort to contact authors/copyright holders of works reprinted in *Video Games and Gaming Culture* (Critical Concepts in Media and Cultural Studies). This has not been possible in every case, however, and we would welcome correspondence from those individuals/companies whom we have been unable to trace.

Chronological table of reprinted articles and chapters

Date	Author	Article/chapter	Source	Vol.	Chap.
1938	Johan Huizinga	Nature and significance of play as a cultural phenomenon	*Homo Ludens: A Study of the Play-Element in Culture* (New York: Routledge, 1949), pp. 1–27. Originally published in Dutch, 1938.	I	9
1938	Johan Huizinga	The play-element in contemporary civilization	*Homo Ludens: A Study of the Play-Element in Culture* (New York: Routledge, 1949), pp. 195–213. Originally published in Dutch, 1938.	I	10
1958	Roger Caillois	'The definition of play' and 'The classification of games'	*Man, Play and Games* (Paris: Librairie Gallimard), pp. 3–11; 11–37.	I	11
1972	Clifford Geertz	Deep play: notes on the Balinese cockfight	*Daedalus*, 101(1), *Myth, Symbol, and Culture* (Winter), 1–37.	I	12
1977	Steven D. Bristow	The history of video games	*IEEE Transactions on Consumer Electronics*, (1), February, 58–68.	I	17
1978	Bernard DeKoven	Changing the game	*The Well-Played Game* (New York: Doubleday), pp. 39–59. Reprinted in Katie Salen and Eric Zimmerman (eds), *The Game Design Reader: A Rules of Play Anthology* (Cambridge, MA: The MIT Press, 2006), pp. 518–537.	II	35
1990	F. Randall Farmer and Chip Morningstar	The lessons of Lucasfilm's *Habitat*	Michael Benedikt (ed.), *Cyberspace: First Steps* (Cambridge, MA: The MIT Press), pp. 273–301.	I	14
1991	David Myers	Computer game semiotics	*Play & Culture*, 4(4), 334–345.	II	36
1993	Julian Dibbell	A rape in cyberspace: how an evil clown, a Haitian trickster spirit, two wizards, and a cast of dozens turned a database into a society	*The Village Voice*, December 23, 36–42.	III	64
1994	Greg Costikyan	I have no words & I must design	*Interactive Fantasy: The Journal of Role-Playing and Story-Making Systems*, 2 (London: Hogshead Publishing, 1994), pp. 192–211.	II	23

Chronological table continued

Date	Author	Article/chapter	Source	Vol.	Chap.
1995	Mary Fuller and Henry Jenkins	Nintendo® and new world travel writing: a dialogue	Steven G. Jones (ed.), *Cybersociety: Computer-Mediated Communication and Community* (Thousand Oaks, CA: Sage Publications), pp. 57–72.	IV	80
1995	Simon Gottschalk	Videology: video-games as postmodern sites/sights of ideological reproduction	*Symbolic Interaction*, 18(1), Spring, 1–18.	IV	88
1996	Richard Bartle	Hearts, clubs, diamonds, spades: players who suit MUDs	*Journal of MUD Research*, 1(1) (available online).	I	15
1997	Brian Sutton-Smith	Play and ambiguity	*The Ambiguity of Play* (Cambridge, MA: Harvard University Press), pp. 1–17.	I	13
1999	Doug Church	Formal abstract design tools	*Game Developer*, August, 44–50. Reprinted in Katie Salen and Eric Zimmerman (eds), *The Game Design Reader: A Rules of Play Anthology* (Cambridge, MA: The MIT Press, 2006), pp. 366–380.	II	24
1999	Ted Friedman	*Civilization* and its discontents: simulation, subjectivity, and space	Greg M. Smith (ed.), *On a Silver Platter: CD-ROMs and the Promises of a New Technology* (New York, NY: New York University Press), pp. 132–150.	IV	81
1999	Marc LeBlanc	Tools for creating dramatic game dynamics	Game Developer's Conference (GDC), pp. 438–459. Reprinted in Katie Salen and Eric Zimmerman (eds) *The Game Design Reader: A Rules of Play Anthology* (Cambridge, MA: The MIT Press, 2006), pp. 438–459.	II	25
2000	Craig A. Anderson and Karen E. Dill	Video games and aggressive thoughts, feelings, and behavior in the laboratory and in life	*Journal of Personality and Social Psychology*, 78(4), April, 772–790.	III	66
2000	Don Carson	Environmental storytelling: creating immersive 3D worlds using lessons learned from the theme park industry	*Gamasutra*, March, available at http://www.gamasutra.com/features/20000301/carson_pfv.htm.	I	16

Year	Author	Title	Source	Part	Page
2000	Gonzalo Frasca	Ephemeral games: is it barbaric to design videogames after Auschwitz?	*Cybertext Yearbook 2000* (Saarijärvi, Finland: University of Jyväskayla), pp. 172–182.	III	65
2000	Torben Grodal	Video games and the pleasures of control	Dolf Zillmann and Peter Vorderer (eds), *Media Entertainment: The Psychology of its Appeal* (Mahwah, NJ: Lawrence Erlbaum Associates), pp. 197–213.	III	57
2000	Gareth R. Schott and Kirsty R. Horrell	Girl gamers and their relationship with the gaming culture	*Convergence*, 6(4), December, 36–53.	IV	84
2001	Craig A. Anderson and Brad J. Bushman	Effects of violent video games on aggressive behavior, aggressive cognition, aggressive affect, physiological arousal, and prosocial behavior: a meta-analytic review of the scientific literature	*Psychological Science*, 12(5), September, 353–359.	III	67
2001	Markku Eskelinen	The gaming situation	*Game Studies: The International Journal of Computer Game Research*, 1(1), July, available at http://www.gamestudies.org/0101/eskelinen.	I	3
2002	Mark Griffiths	The educational benefits of videogames	*Education and Health*, 20(3), 47–51.	IV	71
2002	Helen W. Kennedy	Lara Croft: feminist icon or cyberbimbo? On the limits of textual analysis	*Game Studies: The International Journal of Computer Game Research*, 2(2), December, available at http://www.gamestudies.org/0202/kennedy/.	III	49
2002	Rune Klevjer	In defense of cutscenes	Frans Mäyrä (ed.), *Proceedings of Computer Games and Digital Cultures Conference* (Tampere: Tampere University Press), pp. 191–202.	II	33
2002	Lars Konzack	Computer game criticism: a method for computer game analysis	Frans Mäyrä (ed.), *Proceedings of Computer Games and Digital Cultures Conference* (Tampere: Tampere University Press), pp. 89–100.	II	37
2002	James Newman	The myth of the ergodic videogame: some thoughts on player-character relationships in videogames	*Game Studies: The International Journal of Computer Game Research*, 2(1), July, available at http://www.gamestudies.org/0102/newman/.	III	47

Chronological table continued

Date	Author	Article/chapter	Source	Vol.	Chap.
2003	Espen Aarseth	Playing research: methodological approaches to game analysis	Digital Art and Culture conference, Melbourne, Australia, May 19–23, and also published in *Fine Art Forum*, 17(8), August 2003, available at hypertext.rmit.edu.au/dac/papers/Aarseth.pdf.	II	38
2003	Gonzalo Frasca	Simulation versus narrative: introduction to ludology	Mark J. P. Wolf and Bernard Perron (eds), *The Video Game Theory Reader* (New York, NY: Routledge), pp. 221–235.	I	4
2003	James Paul Gee	What video games have to teach us about learning and literacy	*Computers in Entertainment (CIE) – Theoretical and Practical Computer Applications in Entertainment*, 1(1), October.	IV	72
2003	Torben Grodal	Stories for eye, ear, and muscles: video games, media, and embodied experiences	Mark J. P. Wolf and Bernard Perron (eds), *The Video Game Theory Reader* (New York, NY: Routledge), pp. 129–155.	III	45
2003	Bob Rehak	Playing at being: psychoanalysis and the avatar	Mark J. P. Wolf and Bernard Perron (eds), *The Video Game Theory Reader* (New York, NY: Routledge), pp. 103–127.	III	48
2003	Katie Salen and Eric Zimmerman	Defining games	*Rules of Play: Game Design Fundamentals* (Cambridge, MA: The MIT Press), pp. 71–83.	I	1
2003	Katie Salen and Eric Zimmerman	The magic circle	*Rules of Play: Game Design Fundamentals* (Cambridge, MA: The MIT Press), pp. 93–99.	III	59
2003	Kurt Squire	Video games in education	*International Journal of Intelligent Games & Simulation*, 2(1), 49–62.	IV	73
2004	Robin Hunicke, Marc LeBlanc, and Robert Zubek	MDA: a formal approach to game design and game research	*19th National Conference of Artificial Intelligence*, San Jose, California.	II	26
2004	Henry Jenkins	Game design as narrative architecture	Noah Wardrip-Fruin and Pat Harrigan (eds), *First Person: New Media as Story; Performance, and Game* (Cambridge, MA: The MIT Press), pp. 118–130.	II	30

Year	Author	Title	Source	Part	Page
2004	Bernard Perron	Sign of a threat: the effects of warning systems in survival horror games	*COSIGN 2004 Proceedings*, Art Academy, University of Split (Croatia), pp. 132–141.	III	69
2005	Anna Everett	Serious play: playing with race in contemporary gaming culture	Joost Raessens and Jeffrey Goldstein (eds), *Handbook of Computer Game Studies* (Cambridge, MA: The MIT Press), pp. 311–325.	III	51
2005	Henry Jenkins	Games, the new lively art	Joost Raessens and Jeffrey Goldstein (eds), *Handbook of Computer Game Studies* (Cambridge, MA: The MIT Press), pp. 175–189.	I	7
2005	Jesper Juul	Games telling stories? A brief note on games and narratives	Joost Raessens and Jeffrey Goldstein (eds), *Handbook of Computer Game Studies* (Cambridge, MA: The MIT Press), pp. 219–226.	I	5
2005	David Myers	Bombs, barbarians, and backstories: meaning-making within *Sid Meier's Civilization*	Matteo Bittanti (ed), *Ludologica. Videogames d'Autore: Civilization and its Discontents. Virtual History: Real Fantasies* (Milan: Edizioni Unicopli, Costa and Nolan), original version available at http://www.loyno.edu/%7Edmyers/F99%20classes/Myers_BombsBarbarians_DRAFT.rft.	II	40
2005	Bernard Perron	Coming to play at frightening yourself: welcome to the world of horror video games	*Aesthetics of Play: A Conference on Computer Game Aesthetics* (Norway: University of Bergen), available at http://www.aestheticsofplay.org/perron.php.	III	55
2005	David Williamson Shaffer, Kurt R. Squire, Richard Halverson, and James P. Gee	Video games and the future of learning	*The Phi Delta Kappan*, 87(2), October, 104–111.	IV	76
2006	Thomas H. Apperley	Genre and game studies: toward a critical approach to video game genres	*Simulation Gaming*, 37(1), 6–23.	II	41
2006	Alexander R. Galloway	Allegories of control	*Gaming: Essays on Algorithmic Culture* (Minneapolis, MN: University of Minnesota Press), pp. 85–106.	III	58

Chronological table continued

Date	Author	Article/chapter	Source	Vol.	Chap.
2006	Alexander R. Galloway	Gamic action, four moments	*Gaming: Essays on Algorithmic Culture* (Minneapolis, MN: University of Minnesota Press), pp. 1–38.	II	32
2006	Celia Pearce	Productive play: game culture from the bottom up	*Games and Culture*, 1(1), January, 17–24.	IV	78
2006	Kurt Squire	From content to context: videogames as designed experience	*Educational Researcher*, 35(8), November, 19–29.	IV	74
2007	David H. Ahl	Mainframe games and simulations	Mark J. P. Wolf (ed.), *The Video Game Explosion: A History from PONG to PlayStation and Beyond* (Westport, CT: Greenwood Press), pp. 31–34.	I	20
2007	Espen Aarseth	I fought the law: transgressive play and the implied player	*Situated Play: Proceedings of DiGRA 2007 Conference*, Digital Games Research Association (DiGRA) (Japan: The University of Tokyo), pp. 130–133, available at http://www.digra.org/dl/db/07313.03489.pdf.	III	56
2007	Karen Collins	An introduction to the participatory and non-linear aspects of video games audio	Stan Hawkins and John Richardson (eds), *Essays on Sound and Vision* (Helsinki: Helsinki University Press), pp. 263–298.	II	27
2007	Karen Collins	In the loop: creativity and constraint in 8-bit video game audio	*Twentieth-Century Music*, 4(2), 209–227.	II	28
2007	Michele D. Dickey	Game design and learning: a conjectural analysis of how massively multiple online role-playing games (MMORPGs) foster intrinsic motivation	*Educational Technology Research and Development*, 55(3), June, 253–273.	IV	75
2007	Kevin Schut	Strategic simulations and our past: the bias of computer games in the presentation of history	*Games and Culture*, 2(3), 213–235.	I	19

Year	Author	Title	Source		
2007	F. Ted Tschang	Balancing the tensions between rationalization and creativity in the video games industry	Organization Science: Innovation at and across Multiple Levels of Analysis, 18(6), November–December, 989–1005.	IV	86
2008	Trevor Elkington	Too many cooks: media convergence and self-defeating adaptations	Bernard Perron and Mark J. P. Wolf (eds), The Video Game Theory Reader 2 (New York, NY: Routledge), pp. 213–235.	IV	89
2008	Anna Everett and S. Craig Watkins	The power of play: the portrayal and performance of race in video games	Katie Salen (ed.), The Ecology of Games: Connecting Youth, Games, and Learning (Cambridge, MA: The MIT Press), pp. 141–164.	III	52
2008	Andreas Gregersen and Torben Grodal	Embodiment and interface	Bernard Perron and Mark J. P. Wolf (eds), The Video Game Theory Reader 2 (New York, NY: Routledge), pp. 65–83.	III	46
2008	Jennifer Jenson and Suzanne de Castell	Theorizing gender and digital gameplay: oversights, accidents and surprises	Eludamos: Journal for Computer Game Culture, 2(1), 15–25.	III	50
2008	Jesper Juul	Fear of failing? The many meanings of difficulty in video games	Bernard Perron and Mark J. P. Wolf (eds), The Video Game Theory Reader 2 (New York: Routledge), pp. 237–252.	II	34
2008	Miguel Sicart	Defining game mechanics	Game Studies: The International Journal of Computer Game Research, 8(2), December, available at http://gamestudies.org/0802/articles/sicart.	I	2
2009	Will Brooker	Camera-eye, CG-eye: videogames and the "cinematic"	Cinema Journal, 48(3), Spring, 122–128.	II	42
2009	Mia Consalvo	Convergence and globalization in the Japanese videogame industry	Cinema Journal, 48(3), Spring, 135–141.	IV	87
2009	Mia Consalvo	Gaining advantage: how videogame players define and negotiate cheating	Cheating: Gaining Advantage in Videogames (Cambridge, MA: The MIT Press), pp. 83–105.	IV	83
2009	Mia Consalvo	There is no magic circle	Games and Culture, 4(4), 408–417.	III	60
2009	Henry Lowood	Videogames in Computer Space: the complex history of Pong	IEEE Annals in the History of Computing, July–September, 5–19.	I	21
2009	Nick Montfort and Ian Bogost	Racing the Beam: The Atari Video Computer System	(Cambridge, MA: The MIT Press), pp. 65–79.	II	29

Chronological table continued

Date	Author	Article/chapter	Source	Vol.	Chap.
2009	Andrew K. Przybylski, Richard M. Ryan, and C. Scott Rigby	The motivating role of violence in video games	*Personality and Social Psychology Bulletin*, 35(2), February, 243–259.	III	70
2009	T. L. Taylor	The assemblage of play	*Games and Culture*, 4(4), 331–339.	III	54
2010	Craig A. Anderson, Akiko Shibuya, Nobuko Ihori, Edward L. Swing, Brad J. Bushman, Akira Sakamoto, Hannah R. Rothstein, and Muniba Saleem	Violent video game effects on aggression, empathy, and prosocial behavior in Eastern and Western countries: a meta-analytic review	*Psychological Bulletin*, 136(2), 151–173.	III	68
2010	Ian Bogost	Procedural rhetoric	*Persuasive Games: The Expressive Power of Video Games* (Cambridge, MA: The MIT Press), pp. 1–64.	II	44
2010	David Myers	Social play	*Play Redux: The Form of Computer Games* (Ann Arbor, MI: University of Michigan Press), pp. 116–130.	IV	82
2010	Adrienne Shaw	What is video game culture? Cultural studies and game studies	*Games and Culture*, 5(4), 403–424. Originally published online May 7.	IV	77
2011	Laura Ermi and Frans Mäyrä	Fundamental components of the gameplay experience: analysing immersion	Stephan Günzel, Michael Liebe, and Dieter Mersch (eds), *DIGAREC Keynote-Lectures 2009/10* (Potsdam: Potsdam University Press), pp. 88–113, available at http://pub.ub.uni-potsdam.de/volltexte/2011/4983/ [urn:nbn:de:kobv:517-opus-49831].	III	62

Year	Author	Title	Source	Vol.	Page
2011	Mark J. P. Wolf	Theorizing navigable space in video games	Stephan Günzel, Michael Liebe, and Dieter Mersch (eds), *DIGAREC Keynote-Lectures 2009/10* (Potsdam: Potsdam University Press), pp. 18–48.	II	31
2012	Brett Camper	Color-cycled space fumes in the pixel particle shockwave: the technical aesthetics of *Defender* and the Williams arcade platform, 1980–82	Mark J. P. Wolf (ed.), *Before the Crash: Early Video Game History* (Detroit, MI: Wayne State University Press), pp. 168–188.	II	43
2012	James Newman	The centrality of play	*Best Before: Videogames, Supersession and Obsolescence* (excerpt) (New York and London: Routledge), pp. 149–160.	IV	90
2012	Carl Therrien	Video games caught up in history: accessibility, teleological distortion, and other methodological issues	Mark J. P. Wolf (ed.), *Before the Crash: Early Video Game History* (Detroit, MI: Wayne State University Press), pp. 9–29.	I	18
2012	Mark J. P. Wolf	*BattleZone* and the origins of first-person shooting games	Gerald Voorhees, Joshua Call, and Katie Whitlock (eds), *Guns, Grenades and Grunts: First Person Shooter Games* (New York, NY: Continuum), pp. 25–40.	I	22
2012	Eric Zimmerman	Jerked around by the magic circle – clearing the air ten years later	*Gamasutra.com*, available at http://www.gamasutra.com/view/feature/135063/jerked_around_by_the_magic_circle_.php.	III	61
2013	Eric Zimmerman	Manifesto for a Ludic century	*Kotaku.com*, available at http://kotaku.com/manifesto-the-21st-century-will-be-defined-by-games-1275355204, and republished in Steffen Walz and Sebastian Detering (eds), *The Gameful World: Approaches, Issues, Applications* (Cambridge, MA: The MIT Press, 2015), pp. 19–22.	I	8
2014	Roberto Dillon	Towards the definition of a framework and grammar for game analysis and design	*International Journal of Computer and Information Technology*, 3(2), March, 188–193.	II	39

Chronological table continued

Date	Author	Article/chapter	Source	Vol.	Chap.
2014	Anna Everett	Race	Mark J. P. Wolf and Bernard Perron (eds), *The Routledge Companion to Video Game Studies* (New York, NY: Routledge), pp. 396–406.	III	53
2014	Piotr Kubiński	Emersion as an element of gaming experience	Originally published as 'Immersion vs. Emersive Effects in Videogames' from Dawn Stobbart and Monica Evans (eds), *Engaging with Videogames: Play, Theory and Practice* (Oxford: Inter-Disciplinary Press), pp. 133-14 [e-book].	III	63
2014	Heikki Tyni and Olli Sotamaa	Material culture and Angry Birds	*Proceedings of Nordic DiGRA 2014 Conference*, Digital Games Research Association DiGRA.	IV	79
2015	Souvik Mukherjee	Introduction: videogames and storytelling	*Video Games and Storytelling: Reading Games and Playing Books* (New York, NY: Palgrave MacMillan), pp. 1–20.	I	6
2015	Mark J. P. Wolf	Introduction (excerpt) to *Video Games around the World*	Mark J. P. Wolf (ed.), *Video Games Around the World* (excerpt) (Cambridge, MA: The MIT Press), pp. 1–12.	IV	85

GENERAL INTRODUCTION

Mark J. P. Wolf

The field of video game studies is still new enough that none of its books or essays can really be said to have stood the test of time; as of 2015, the vast majority of them are still less than two decades old. Video game studies as a field arose in academia around the late 1990s and especially in the 2000s, when books, journals, and conferences devoted to the academic study of video games began to appear in greater numbers. Before that, there were individual books, by journalists, computer programmers, or psychologists, which looked at various aspects of games or the creation of games (like Chris Crawford's *The Art of Computer Game Design*, 1984), and video games were also studied as extensions of other topics (such as psychology—Patricia Marks Greenfield's *Mind and Media: The Effects of Television, Video Games, and Computers*, 1984; interactive fiction—Mary Ann Buckles's dissertation *Interactive Fiction: The Computer Storygame "Adventure"*, 1985; or children's media—Marsha Kinder's *Playing with Power in Movies, Television, and Video Games: From Muppet Babies to Teenage Mutant Ninja Turtles*, 1991). A number of journal articles, many of which were extensions of play studies, also appeared during this time. So what accounts for the meteoric rise in video game studies from the late 1990s onward?

Two factors seem to account for much of this expansion. One factor is that of timing; the generation that was the first to grow up with video games (of which I find myself a part, since I was born in 1967) was earning PhDs and starting careers in academia around this time and writing about what they knew and liked. The generation before had not grown up with video games and did not know them as intimately, nor would they look back on them as nostalgically. Like other entertainment arts, video games had to struggle for legitimacy in academia, and it was largely this group of new academics, writing in the late 1990s and 2000s, that would make the argument for them and produce the most in-depth work on them. The other factor was the contemporaneous rise of the World Wide Web, which made research easier and disseminated information, discussion, and new work much more quickly, allowing the phenomenon to spread faster than it would have in a wholly print-based culture. Together, these two factors helped video game research to expand quickly and become integrated firmly into media studies, changing it in the process as well and laying the groundwork for the exploration of other interactive media such as the Internet and mobile devices.

1

The sudden growth of the field, and the widespread nature of it due to the Internet, has made it harder for any particular works or theorists to stand out, or schools to form, the way they had in other academic areas that were slower to develop. The few positional groups that have been named, for example, the narratologists and ludologists (who supposedly had a debate going in the early 2000s), are rather broad in their outlook, and in this case not even truly exclusive of each other. While some national schools of video game research have appeared, the growing influence and spread of international work has kept individual movements from being isolated from the rest of the world, and thus we do not really have national movements or styles as distinct as those found in early cinema or other earlier media like painting.

Yet, as the decades advance, a universally-accepted canon of "great works" is gradually forming, which is slowly emerging as the field ages and reveals which works will stand the test of time. Another reason is that so much good work exists, from so many different approaches and angles and with ties to so many other disciplines, yet very few works can claim to be familiar to the vast majority of researchers. In a sense, the field was by nature always highly interdisciplinary, so perhaps its arrival is more like the meeting of various branches of study coming together to form a center, with video games the subject they have in common.

Deciding on which pieces should be in this collection, then, was difficult. I have relied upon the opinions of many of my colleagues in the field, whose suggestions have helped shape these volumes and have also broadened my own reading in the field. The four volumes reflect the major areas of video game studies. The first volume, "Foundations," defines and sets up some of the major themes and concerns of the field. It is divided into three sections, the first of which, "Defining video game studies," looks at what video games are, the terminology surrounding them, and some of the broad issues that divide the field or appear to divide it. The second section, "Game studies classics," contains older works in game studies, some of which preceded video games but which nonetheless provided ways to analyze games and play, which could be revised and adapted to the study of video games. The third section, "History and historiographical concerns," looks at the beginnings of video game history as well as some of the difficulties and pitfalls of doing video game history.

The second volume, "Design and Theory," is divided into two sections. The first, "Video game design and formal aspects," contains examples of formal analyses and discussions of video game design, some of which are influential pieces written by game designers from their personal experience, providing a very practical perspective on video game design. The second section, "Video game theory, methodology, and analysis," collects writings not only regarding video game theory itself but also the methodologies used in the analysis of games and related areas of game studies, such as genre, design grammar, technology, and other issues. Both sections consciously consider how video games, and their design and analysis, differ from other media, and they raise issues and questions for practitioner and theorist alike, which will likely affect the way games are designed in the future.

The third volume, "Play and Players," examines who plays games, how they play them, and the consequences of that play. The volume is divided into three sections, the first of which, "Embodiment and identity", looks at the act of playing video games and the connections between the physical and virtual worlds, including the relationships between players and their avatars through whom they vicariously inhabit the video game worlds in which they play. The second section, "Play, control, and the magic circle", contains writings on the operations of video games, their use and the issue of control, and the notion of the "magic circle," the arena in which game events occur and which is often thought to be separated by boundaries from the world outside of the game. The third section, "Threat, aggression, and violence", includes studies of video game violence and its effects, debates about the link between aggression and video game play, the role of violence in games, and the implications of violence for video game designers. Discussions of these topics have been occurring in the press and other media ever since the appearance of video games, and the interactivity found in video games adds a dimension to them that goes beyond discussions of violence in traditional media such as film and television.

Finally, the fourth volume, "Cultural Contexts", steps back to take a broad look at video games and their place within, as well as their effect on, the culture in which they are found. The first section, "Video games and education", looks at one of the fastest growing uses for video games and one of the longest running themes in the study of video games. The second section, "Video games and culture", collects writings which connect video games and their cultural contexts in a variety of ways, looking at game culture itself and trying to define what it is, exploring how video games fit into other areas of culture, including their social, material, technological, and industrial aspects, and global international culture as well. By far the broadest section in terms of theme, it also demonstrates the myriad ways in which video games have impacted, and continue to impact, contemporary popular culture.

The compilation of such a collection as this is still the product of careful consideration, discussions with colleagues, interdisciplinary balance, and, in the end, calculated guesswork regarding which pieces will likely stand the test of time and prove useful to future theorists and historians. Each considers some essential issue in video game studies from a fresh perspective, suggesting new ways of considering games while at the same time opening the way for debate and competing perspectives and together they provide a snapshot of the emerging discipline and its potential directions for growth. These particular essays, at the very least, have been useful for research and writings of the present time and cited repeatedly, and it is hoped that gathering them here together will provide a synergistic interaction between the ideas that they contain, providing a steady foundation upon which further study and research can expand and extend.

INTRODUCTION TO VOLUME I

Mark J. P. Wolf

Part 1: Defining video game studies

During the formation of any discipline or field of study, the early days will be spent justifying the field and demarcating its territory, in order to make it distinct from the other disciplines that previously covered (or attempted to cover) the same area. Video game studies was no exception and found itself trying to separate itself from film studies and other kind of media studies. And, in addition to this, considering that there is some debate defining such terms as "game", "video", and "computer", it is not surprising that there may be some question as what else video game studies should cover or constitute. These concerns also come at a time when video games themselves have expanded to a variety of technological venues, far beyond the video screens they were named after, and with a broad range of game mechanics and situations, some of which strain the traditional meaning of the word "game".

Thus, it seems fitting to begin this section, containing works in which video game studies attempts to define itself and its subject, with Katie Salen and Eric Zimmerman's "Defining Games" from their book *Rules of Play* (2003), which is an overview of various definitions of "game" that have appeared over the last hundred years or so, seeking to find how these definitions have evolved through time, including what appear to be the essential elements defining games and thus video games as well. The second essay, Miguel Sicart's "Defining Game Mechanics" (2008), seeks to find a way of defining and analyzing what exactly is meant by the term "game mechanics" and "open up for the possibility of connecting formal game analysis with research on controller designs and user experience." Such an attempt needs to cover not only all existing types of game mechanics but also all possible types of game mechanics that may be developed in future games. Like Salen and Zimmerman, Sicart begins with an overview of past definitions and then proceeds to give his own definition and an analysis of core, primary, and secondary mechanics as they occur in several games.

As the field of video game studies began to form and separate itself as a discipline, there were inevitable comparisons with other media and discussions as to what video games shared with them and what set them apart from other media. The importance of narrative loomed large in these discussions, to the point that some saw it as debate, framing it between the "narratologists" who described the relationship between video games and stories, and the "ludologists" who said that stories were not necessary to games, though they did not deny that many games did contain stories of a kind. In Markuu Eskelinen's polemic essay, "The Gaming Situation" (2001), he criticizes the application of outdated literary, drama, and narrative theory to games and even to twentieth-century avant-garde works. Following this, he looks at a series of ideas from narrative theory and then demonstrates how games differ from them in the way they operate, applying some existing game studies ideas and showing the need for new approaches. Also taking an adversarial stance, as evidenced by his use of "versus" in his title, Gonzalo Frasca's essay, "Simulation versus Narrative: Introduction to Ludology" (2003), states that a model based on storytelling is inaccurate and limits one's understanding of the new medium. He suggests simulation as a model for understanding games, mechanics, and rhetorical possibilities, with the dimension of interaction adding elements beyond what traditional narrative is able to do.

Changing his opinion from his earlier work, Jesper Juul, in his essay "Games Telling Stories? A Brief Note on Games and Narratives" (2005), takes a look at both sides of the issue of narrative, admitting that games and stories do share a number of similarities, while still showing that narratives are not a necessary part of games. He even examines some adaptations between movies and games, also noting the existence of avant-garde narrative works that expand the notion of narrative. Finally, Souvik Mukherjee's "Introduction: Videogames and Storytelling," from his book *Video Games and Storytelling: Reading Games and Playing Books* (2015), looks back with hindsight, summarizing and analyzing the whole supposed ludology-narratology debate and what it was really about, extending their ideas to cover more contemporary combinations of narratives and video games. His book shows how discussions regarding narrative have evolved over the years, but also that the topic continues to be a relevant one today.

The last two essays in the section, more celebratory though still polemic, demonstrate the cultural importance that video games have achieved and will likely continue to achieve into the twenty-first century. Henry Jenkins's essay, "Games, The New Lively Art" (2005), states its premise right in its title—that games can be considered an art, even if they have not yet realized their full potential—and takes Gilbert Seldes's position that popular culture can have aesthetic merits. He enthusiastically introduces ways that video games have impacted culture and proven their value and worth, all the while having to balance convention and innovation in order to bring new experiences to which audiences can relate. Eric Zimmerman's "Manifesto for a Ludic Century" (2013) completes the section with his succinct and spirited call for a fresh approach to games in the new century in which users' lives are more intertwined with complex systems of information, which provide a natural cultural fit for video games. He suggests not only that there is a need for gaming literacy but that we may find within answers to many of our present problems, which require the playful, innovative thinking that games can promote.

Part 2: Game studies classics

Long before video game studies began to develop, there was a tradition of game studies that considered such things as board games, sports, gambling, and, more broadly, the very notion of play itself. Many of these works were influential on the growing field of video game studies, and they continue to be today. Collected here in this section are some of the classic texts that are still often cited and whose ideas have shaped the way video games are considered and studied. The first two essays are the first and last chapters of Johan Huizinga's *Homo Ludens: A Study of the Play-Element in Culture* (1938), which attempt to define the notion of "play" and look at its appearance across a variety of cultural contexts. The first chapter, "Nature and the Significance of Play as a Cultural Phenomenon", attempts to find a definition of "play" while also showing the importance play has within culture, pointing out that play is older than culture itself. The last chapter, "The Play-Element in Contemporary Civilization", examines the ways in which play is present in modern life, in such areas as commerce, art, science, law, politics, and warfare. Huizinga's ideas have been the foundation for thinking about play and what it means to play, and for making the study of play into a serious subject.

Building on Huizinga's theories and definition of play, the next great theorist of play, Roger Caillois, wrote *Man, Play and Games* (1958), whose first two chapters, "The Definition of Play" and "The Classification of Games", are included here. In the first chapter, Caillois critiques Huizinga's definition of play and expands upon it, finally declaring that play must be free, separate (in its own space), uncertain, unproductive, governed by rules, and involve make-believe. With this definition in mind, in the second chapter, Caillois develops his classifications of games as *agôn* (competition), *alea* (chance), *mimicry* (simulation), and *ilinx* (vertigo, or a "voluptuous panic"), as well as his spectrum of game types from *paidia* (free play) to *ludus* (rule-based play), giving different examples of these among adults, children, and even animals. Animals also figure into Clifford Geertz's essay, "Deep Play: Notes on the Balinese Cockfight" (1972), which examines how cockfights in Balinese culture represent larger issues of status and domination in culture, with the cocks acting as stand-ins for their owners in contests—much as video game avatars do today.

The next essay, Brian Sutton-Smith's "Play and Ambiguity" from his book *The Ambiguity of Play* (1997), analyzes play theories of the past hundred years and the rhetorics that lay behind them, each advocating different ideas connected with the reasons for their use. Within the broad, diverse range of forms of play, he identifies seven different rhetorics in use, namely play as progress, play as fate, play as power, play as identity, play as the imaginary, play as frivolous, and the rhetoric of the self that applied to solitary play activities like hobbies or high-risk physical activities. By looking at these types, he shows the ambiguity of the concept of play, which is the subject of the rest of the book. Consideration of these rhetorics is useful to scholars of play, calling them to be more aware of their own assumptions and rhetorical positioning.

The last two essays in this section examine the ways players interact in multiplayer games and environments, which today have grown into massively multiplayer online role-playing games with millions of players around the world. "The Lessons of Lucasfilm's *Habitat*" (1990), by F. Randall Farmer and Chip Morningstar, examines *Habitat* (1986), one of the first graphical online multiuser environments. They describe the building of the world and how it was run and the design of player interaction within the world, summarizing what the designers learned from the experience, including how players made use of a flaw in the game to quintuple the money supply literally overnight. They end by proposing future directions for extending such work, along with warnings of mistakes to avoid. Next, Richard Bartle's famous essay, "Hearts, Clubs, Diamonds, Spades: Players Who Suit MUDs" (1996), looks at the players of MUDs and other online games and classifies their playing styles into four categories, along the dimensions of action versus interaction, a world-oriented outlook versus a player-oriented outlook, and how MUDs or online games themselves can be seen as either "social" or "gamelike".

Finally, Don Carson's essay, "Environmental Storytelling: Creating Immersive 3D Worlds Using Lessons Learned from the Theme Park Industry" (2000), considers the similarities between designing theme park rides and attractions and designing video games, which he sees as virtual forms or places through which an audience moves. He also suggests ways that stories and narrative material can be embedded within these environments, so that the audience's journey is a narrative one as well as a spatial one. He ends with a look at the advantages that games have over theme parks and encourages designers to reach their potential.

Part 3: History and historiographical concerns

Writings about video games appeared soon after the games themselves did, though the earliest works were typically highly technical and aimed at computer scientists. Games were only a side interest, and some early articles were ambiguously titled, like John D. Meng's essay "The Computer Game" (*American Scientist*, 1968), which referred to the rule-based usages of the computer, rather than actual games played on them. After less than a decade of games as a commercial product, the success and rapid growth of the industry caused some to already start to look back at the events comprising its rapid rise. Atari Vice President of Engineering Steven D. Bristow's essay, "The History of Video Games" (1977), published in the *IEEE Transactions on Consumer Electronics*, is probably the earliest historical essay on video games. He begins by noting how video games are the latest development in a long line of coin-operated amusements and electromechanical games and notes the advantages they have over older kinds of games. Although as an early work it omits details not widely known at the time (like the first coin-operated video game *Galaxy Game* (1971) which preceded Nolan Bushnell's *Computer Space* (1971) by only a month), the piece is interesting for its early point of view, intricate technical details (including a diagram of the electronics involved in coin detection), and its claim that video games already have a history. While the piece is predictably somewhat Atari-centric, it still provides an early glimpse of the industry explaining and assessing itself.

As the writing of video game history itself came of age, historiographical concerns specific to the medium became apparent and the object of discussion. Carl Therrien's essay, "Video Games Caught Up in History: Accessibility, Teleological Distortion, and Other Methodological Issues" (2012), examines various methodological issues of studying video game history, such as periodization, accessibility to older games and game systems, teleological distortion, and such things as emulation and the use of walkthroughs. It is included here as an example of what video game historians should be aware of when recording history. Next, Kevin Schut's essay, "Strategic Simulations and Our Past: The Bias of Computer Games in the Presentation of History" (2007), discusses the video game as a venue for the presentation of history and the various pitfalls and assumptions involved—for example, the way history simulation games are mechanical, spatially oriented, and stereotypically masculine—and some of the possible causes for these biases.

The last three essays in this section provide examples of historical writing in the field. In the first, David H. Ahl, the founder and editor-in-chief of *Creative Computing*, one of the earliest computer magazines for hobbyists, writes about the early days of computer gaming in his essay, "Mainframe Games and Simulations" (2007). Ahl's essay demonstrates that video games and computer games are not the same thing and that computer games have a slightly longer history, since mainframe computers were running games for some time before cathode ray tubes became the standard display devices. The misidentification of Atari's *PONG* (1972) as a computer game (it had no microprocessor and ran no program code) is discussed in Henry Lowood's essay, "Videogames in Computer Space: The Complex History of Pong" (2009), which examines the transition the games made from being experiments in university laboratories and research centers to commercial products available to consumers in arcades and stores, and the complicated relationship between arcades, computer technology, and video games themselves. Finally, my own essay, "*BattleZone* and the Origins of First-Person Shooting Games" (2012), examines the origins of first-person shooting games and the coalescence of the genre, from its early antecedents to the games that began to codify the genre's conventions and establish player expectations. It attempts to show how shooting games grew through the decades before video games appeared and how they made the transition from physical to digital.

Part 1

DEFINING VIDEO GAME STUDIES

1

DEFINING GAMES

Katie Salen and Eric Zimmerman

Source: *Rules of Play: Game Design Fundamentals* (Cambridge, MA: The MIT Press, 2003), pp. 71–83.

> The word [game] is used for so many different activities that it is not worth insisting on any proposed definition. All in all, it is a slippery lexicological customer, with many friends and relations in a wide variety of fields.
> —David Parlett, The Oxford History of Board Games

> What are games? Are they things in the sense of artifacts? Are they behavioral models, or simulations of social situations? Are they vestiges of ancient rituals, or magical rites? It is difficult and even curious when one tries to answer the question "what are games," since it is assumed that games are many things and at the same time specific games are different from one another—but are they?
> —E. M. Avedon, "The Structural Elements of Games"

Entering by way of meaningful play, following a path of embedded concepts connecting design to systems to interactivity, we have arrived at the heart of our study: games. It is therefore high time to define just what it is that makes a game a game. Should we even attempt such a definition? Perhaps, as game historian David Parlett warns in the quote that opens this chapter, any attempt to define the word "game" is a foolish endeavor. On the other hand, if one of our goals is to help formalize the field of game design, then it seems crucial to define the object that is so central to the discipline.

Historically, play and games have been studied in a myriad of ways, from economists using game-like simulations to literary theorists studying the "play" of meaning in language and literature. These investigations study games or play in the service of another field. Our intent, on the other hand, is to study play and games within the field of game design. A definition of "game" should help to not only distinguish game design from other design practices, but also bring us closer to an understanding of meaningful play.

11

Play and game

As a first step, let us see how *game* relates to the equally complex *play.* We begin with an obvious question: Is there a difference between the words "play" and "game"? Do they refer to the same thing? In English, there is a clear distinction between the two words. But as David Parlett points out in the *The Oxford History of Board Games,* not all languages separate the two concepts. The phrase "to play a game," in both German and French, for example, uses different versions of the same word for both "play" and "game." In French *"on joue á un jeu;* in German, *man spielt ein Spiel.*"[1] Although there are many ways to define play and games, we will take advantage of the difference that English affords to consider games and play as two separate ideas with related, but distinct meanings.

It turns out that play and games have a surprisingly complex relationship. Play is both a larger and a smaller term than "game," depending on the way it is framed. In one sense, "play" is a larger term that includes "game" as a subset. In another, the reverse is true: "game" is the bigger term, and includes "play" within it. Consider each of these relationships separately:

Relationship one: games are a subset of play

If we think about all of the activities we could call play, from two dogs playfully chasing each other in a grassy field, to a child singing a nursery rhyme, to a community of online role-players, it seems that only some of these forms of play would actually constitute what we might think of as a game. Playing Dodge Ball, for example, is playing a game: players obey a formalized set of rules and compete to win. The activities of playing on a seesaw, or horsing around on a jungle gym, however, are forms of play which do not constitute a game. Most forms of play are looser and less organized than games. However, some forms of play are formalized, and these forms of play can often be considered games. In this sense, it is clear that "game" is a subset of "play."This is a typological approach, one that defines the relationship between play and games according to the forms they take in the world.

Relationship two: play is a component of games

In a different sense, games can be thought of as containing play. This entire book is about games, and one component of games is play. The experience of play is but one of many ways of looking at and understanding games. Within the larger phenomenon of games, then, the play of the game represents one aspect of games. Although play is a crucial element of the larger concept of games, "play" is in fact a subset of "game." Rather than typological, this pairing of the terms represents a more conceptual approach that situates play and games within the field of game design.

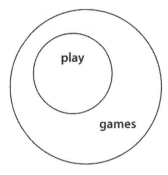

This double formulation of play and games may sound contradictory, but it is not simply a terminological sleight-of-hand. The point is that there are important differences between the words "game" and "play." English may be an anomaly in the way that it differentiates between these two terms, but it is an extremely useful distinction. A good definition of game should distinguish it clearly from play in both of the senses described here.

Comparing definitions

One challenge of understanding the term "game" is that it has so many uses. Consider, for example, many of the ways that the word is utilized in English:

- limp or crippled: a game leg
- a hunted animal: game hunting season is open
- being skilled, particularly in sports or in romance: having game; "he got game"
- to partake in gambling: to spend a night gaming in Vegas
- social and psychological manipulation: playing head games
- a procedure for gaining an end: playing the waiting game with a stubborn friend
- a field in which one earns a living: the writing game and, of course
- board games, card games, computer games, etc.

For our purposes, only a single subset of all of the possible meanings of "game" is relevant: the category of games proper, a category that includes board games, card games, sports, computer games, and similar activities. Put another way, games are what game designers create. Although this is an important qualification, it does not bring us any closer to a precise understanding of what is and what is not a game.

Luckily, we are not the first to attempt a definition of "game," so we will be taking a close and comparative look at eight definitions that come from a variety of fields. In and among the definitions a handful of thorny issues appear again and again. These issues not only include articulating the unique qualities that make a game a game, but also differentiating games from similar phenomena, such as other forms of play, conflict, and contestation. It is also clear that there is a difference between defining games themselves and defining the act of playing a game.

There is one final point to make regarding the difference between "play" and "game."The definitions of "game" to follow were written in many languages, and when translated to English there is some slippage between "play" and "game."As a result, we look at definitions of play as well as "game" in the course of our investigation. Bear in mind that we are not building a definition of play (that comes in a later chapter), but are using definitions of play to shed light on an understanding of games.

Definition 1: David Parlett

David Parlett is a game historian who has written extensively on card games and board games. Earlier we noted Parlett's skepticism regarding the ability to define the slippery term "game." Yet despite his assertion to the contrary, Parlett does provide a model for understanding games.

Parlett begins by distinguishing between formal and informal games. "An informal game is merely undirected play, or 'playing around,' as when children or puppies play at rough and tumble."He contrasts this kind of activity with a "formal game":

> A formal game has a twofold structure based on ends and means:
>
> *Ends.* It is a contest to achieve an objective. (The Greek for game is agôn, meaning contest.) Only one of the contenders, be they individuals or teams, can achieve it, since achieving it ends the game. To achieve that object is to win. Hence a formal game, by definition, has a winner; and winning is the "end" of the game in both senses of the word, as termination and as object.
>
> *Means.* It has an agreed set of equipment and of procedural "rules" by which the equipment is manipulated to produce a winning situation.[2]

Parlett's distinction between formal and informal games directly addresses a key challenge in arriving at a definition of "game:" how to distinguish games from other forms of play. What Parlett calls an "informal game" of two puppies romping about might more simply be called *play.* His definition of a "formal game" has two main components:

14

- *Ends:* The fact that a "formal game" is a contest with an endpoint as its goal.
- *Means:* The agreed-upon rules and materials by which one wins the contest.

Both components—the idea of winning and the idea of doing so by means of rules—are key ideas in defining games, and in distinguishing them from other, less "formal" kinds of play.

Definition 2: Clark C. Abt

In his book *Serious Games,* Clark C. Abt proposes the following definition of games:

> Reduced to its formal essence, a game is an *activity* among two or more independent *decision-makers* seeking to achieve their *objectives* in some *limiting context.* A more conventional definition would say that a game is a context with rules among adversaries trying to win objectives.[3]

Abt's definition offers an understanding of games that emphasizes the active role of players in a game. Here are the four key terms he highlights:

- *Activity:* a game is an activity, a process, an event;
- *Decision-makers:* games require players actively making decisions;
- *Objectives:* as with Parlett's definition, games have goals;
- *Limiting context:* there are rules that limit and structure the activity of the game.

Comparing Abt's definition to Parlett's, we have another instance where games are seen to have a goal or objective. Abt refines Parlett's idea of rules-based *means* by implying that rules are intrinsically limiting. But perhaps the most interesting component is Abt's acknowledgment that games are an activity in which players *make decisions.* We know from our discussion of meaningful play that the interactivity present in games is based on players making decisions that have meaningful outcomes.

Does the scope of Abt's definition feel appropriate? A definition of games can fail by being so narrow as to leave things out that are games or by being so broad that it includes things that are not games. Abt writes, in the same volume, that his definition fails on both accounts:

> The trouble with this definition is that not all games are contests among adversaries—in some games the players cooperate to achieve a common goal against an obstructing force or natural situation that is itself not really a player since it does not have objectives.[4]

Abt, of course is correct. With its requirement of two or more independent decision-makers and emphasis on adversarial contest, his definition is too narrow—it leaves out cooperative or solitaire games. And, as he goes on to add, the definition is also too broad:

> Of course, most real-life activities involve independent decision makers seeking to achieve objectives in some limiting context . . . . Political and social situations can often also be viewed as games. Every election is a game. International relations are a game. Every personal argument is a game. And almost all business activity is a game. Whether these contests of politics, war, economics, and interpersonal relations are played with resources of power, skill, knowledge, or luck, they always have the common characteristics of reciprocal decisions among independent actors with at least partly conflicting objectives."[5]

War? Elections? Arguments? Games do bear similarity to other forms of human conflict. Although there are some very useful concepts in Abt's definition, we still have a long way to go in demarcating exactly what does and does not constitute a game.

Definition 3: Johann Huizinga

In 1938, Dutch Anthropologist Johann Huizinga published a groundbreaking study of the play element in culture, *Homo Ludens* ("Man the Player"). Among other things, *Homo Ludens* provides a definition of what Huizinga calls "play":

> [Play is] a free activity standing quite consciously outside "ordinary" life as being "not serious," but at the same time absorbing the player intensely and utterly. It is an activity connected with no material interest, and no profit can be gained by it. It proceeds within its own proper boundaries of time and space according to fixed rules and in an orderly manner. It promotes the formation of social groupings, which tend to surround themselves with secrecy and to stress their difference from the common world by disguise or other means.[6]

In this definition, Huizinga asserts that play:

- is outside ordinary life;
- is "not serious";
- is utterly absorbing;
- is not to be associated with material interest or profit;
- takes place in its own boundaries of time and space;
- proceeds according to rules;
- creates social groups that separate themselves from the outside world.

One of strengths of this definition is that Huizinga manages to identify some of the more elusive and abstract qualities of play. The idea that play is both utterly absorbing but also not serious, for example, wonderfully describes the sense of being at play. On the other hand, it is not clear that these experiential qualities will help define a game: just because a poorly designed game fails to be absorbing doesn't mean that it is not a game. Other aspects of his definition, such as his emphasis on play's separation from ordinary life and the fact that play takes place within special boundaries of time and space, point to the intrinsic artificiality of games. Is this feature of artificiality a defining quality of games? We shall see.

Huizinga's definition includes many important ideas, but on the whole it has some problems. Several of the components, such as the fact that play creates social groups, address the effects of play and games rather than games themselves. Other elements, such as the disavowal of material gain from play, are too closely linked to the ideological agenda of *Homo Ludens.* In the end, the inclusive generality of Huizinga's definition is its greatest weakness. It does not, for example, ultimately differentiate between "play" and "game".

Definition 4: Roger Caillois

Expanding on the work of Huizinga during the 1960s, the French sociologist Roger Caillois published *Man, Play, and Games,* a book that is in many ways a direct response to *Homo Ludens.* Caillois also presents a definition of play, describing it as being:

- *Free:* in which playing is not obligatory; if it were, it would at once lose its attractive and joyous quality as diversion;
- *Separate:* circumscribed within limits of space and time, defined and fixed in advance;
- *Uncertain:* the course of which cannot be determined, nor the result attained beforehand, and some latitude for innovations being left to the player's initiative;
- *Unproductive:* creating neither goods, nor wealth, nor new elements of any kind; and, except for the exchange of property among the players, ending in a situation identical to that prevailing at the beginning of the game;
- *Governed by rules:* under conventions that suspend ordinary laws, and for the moment establish new legislation, which alone counts;
- *Make-believe:* accompanied by a special awareness of a second reality or of a free unreality, as against real life.[7]

Some of these ideas were part of the previous definitions; several are new. Every definition so far includes reference to the fact that play is governed by rules. The ideas that play exists in a separate space and does not create capital are borrowed from Huizinga. But Caillois extends an understanding of play by describing it as free or voluntary, by pointing out that the end of a game is uncertain, and by associating play with a sense of make-believe.

Do all of the elements Caillois lists really describe games? Although they seem to make intuitive sense, it is possible to think of situations where games are not voluntary, uncertain, or make-believe. If you are pressured by your friends into playing a game that you don't want to play, is it still a game? If a Chess master plays against a beginner, is the outcome of the game uncertain for the Chess master? Is there a make-believe element to Tic-Tac-Toe?

A central problem with Caillois' definition is that like Huizinga's definition, it is too broad for our purposes. In *Man, Play, and Games*, Caillois includes under the rubric of play activities such as theater and informal rough-housing. Although these activities might be considered play, we are looking for a definition that more narrowly addresses the particular instance of games.

Definition 5: Bernard Suits

Bernard Suits is a philosopher with a strong interest in games. His playful book *Grasshopper: Games, Life, and Utopia* is a retelling of the Grasshopper and the Ants fable; it is also a deep investigation into the nature of games. Suits offers this definition of games:

> To play a game is to engage in activity directed towards bringing about a specific state of affairs, using only means permitted by rules, where the rules prohibit more efficient in favour of less efficient means, and where such rules are accepted just because they make possible such activity.[8]
> —or more succinctly—

> I also offer the following simpler and, so to speak, more portable version of the above: playing a game is the voluntary effort to overcome unnecessary obstacles.[9]

Although Suit's definitions sound abstract, he is covering familiar territory. Here are the primary elements from both versions:

- *Activity*: as with Abt, Suits emphasizes the activity of playing a game;
- *Voluntary*: games are freely entered into;
- *A specific state of affairs*: games have a goal;
- *Rules*: as in the previous definitions, Suits identifies rules as a component of games;
- *Inefficiency*: the rules of games limit behavior, making it less efficient;
- *Rules are accepted*: playing a game means accepting the rules.

Other definitions have included many of these elements: the fact that a game is an activity, that it is voluntary, has a goal, and involves rules. However, Suits adds some new ideas to the mix. When he states that "the rules prohibit more efficient in favour of less efficient means . . . such rules are accepted just because they make possible such activity," he is referring to what he calls the *lusory attitude*, the peculiar state of mind of game players. Part of the lusory attitude is that the rules of a game make play inefficient: if a runner wanted to cross the finish line as efficiently as possible, she might leave the track and cut across the field—but the rules tell her to stay within the white lines. Another component of the lusory attitude is that players accept these rules, taking on the "unnecessary obstacles" of a game simply because they make play possible. Suits is actually pointing to the way that games create *meaning* as players accept these rules, goals, and obstacles in order to play.

As insightful as this definition is, it is important to note that Suits does not ultimately offer a definition of game, but a definition of the act of *playing a game.* In fact, the definitions of Huizinga and Caillois similarly focus on the activity of play rather than on games themselves. However, the next two definitions will bring us closer to the territory of games themselves.

Definition 6: Chris Crawford

Chris Crawford is a pioneering computer game designer who has written extensively about game design, narrative, and interactivity. In his influential book *The Art of Computer Game Design,* Crawford does not offer a succinct definition of games, but he does list four primary qualities that define the category of things we call games: representation, interaction, conflict, and safety. We have pulled together excerpts from the first chapter of his book, where he summarizes these four qualities:

> *Representation:* A game is a closed formal system that subjectively represents a subset of reality. By "closed" I mean that the game is complete and self-sufficient as a structure. The model world created by the game is internally complete; no reference need be made to agents outside of the game. By formal I mean only that the game has explicit rules. A game's a collection of parts which interact with each other, often in complex ways. It is a system. A game creates a subjective and deliberately simplified representation of emotional reality.[10]

> *Interaction:* The most fascinating thing about reality is not that it is, or even that it changes, but *how* it changes, the intricate webwork of cause and effect by which all things are tied together. The only way to properly represent this webwork is to allow the audience to explore its nooks and crannies, to let them generate causes and observe effects. Games provide this interactive element, and it is a crucial factor in their appeal.[11]

> *Conflict:* A third element appearing in all games is conflict. Conflict arises naturally from the interaction in a game. The player is actively pursuing some goal. Obstacles prevent him from easily achieving this goal. Conflict is an intrinsic element of all games. It can be direct or indirect, violent or nonviolent, but it is always present in every game.[12]

Safety: Conflict implies danger; danger means risk of harm; harm is undesirable. Therefore, a game is an artifice for providing the psychological experiences of conflict and danger while excluding their physical realizations. In short, a game is a safe way to experience reality. More accurately, the results of a game are always less harsh than the situations the game models.[13]

We can consider each of these four qualities separately. Crawford's notion of *representation* is reminiscent of the quality of make-believe listed by Caillois. But Crawford takes the concept one step further, linking the game's capacity for representation directly to its rules, and to its status as a *system* of interlocking parts. In fact, Crawford's definition is the first to explicitly call games a system, perhaps because he is the first of these authors writing from a digital game point of view. Tied closely to the systemic nature of games is Crawford's element of *interaction.* His scheme of interactive "cause and effect" parallels the ideas of action and outcome outlined in the previous chapter.

Crawford's definition names *conflict* for the first time. Although Parlett's "contest to achieve an objective" and Abt's "contest among adversaries" imply conflict, Crawford names conflict explicitly, linking it directly to the fact that games have goals. His final characteristic of games, *safety,* echoes the emphasis made in other definitions on the artificiality of games, that they take place in a space and time separate from ordinary life. Although these four characteristics describe games, they are not, strictly speaking, definitional.

Definition 7: Greg Costikyan

Greg Costikyan, a game designer and writer who has authored many articles on games, proposes a definition for the term in his essay, "I Have No Words and I Must Design:"[14]

A game is a form of art in which participants, termed players, make decisions in order to manage resources through game tokens in the pursuit of a goal.

The key terms in this definition are:

- *Art:* games are identified as a form of culture;
- *Decision-making players:* games require active participation as choices are made;
- *Resource management:* player decisions hinge on manipulating resources;
- *Game tokens:* the means by which players enact their decisions;
- *Goal:* a game has an objective.

Like Crawford, Costikyan is influenced by digital game design and shares an emphasis on the decision-making, interactive quality of game playing. Although his acknowledgement of the goal of a game is something mentioned in other definitions, Costikyan's formulation has a number of unique elements. For example, his is the only definition to leave out the special quality of rules in defining a game. Also notable is a detailed explication of the systemic quality of a game: the way that players manage game resources through game tokens. Costikyan is also the only writer to link games to art, or to any other cultural practice, for that matter. While we also emphasize the fact that games are cultural, Costikyan's decision to associate games with "art" is less useful for our purposes. Labeling games as art embroils them in contemporary debates about games and art, high culture and low culture, and the social status of games. Undoubtedly, this is Costikyan's provocative intention.

Definition 8: Elliot Avedon and Brian Sutton-Smith

Brian Sutton-Smith is perhaps the most prolific and important scholar of play and games in the twentieth century. In *The Study of Games,* which Sutton-Smith co-edited with Elliot Avedon, the authors present an extremely concise and powerful definition of games:

> Games are an exercise of voluntary control systems, in which there is a contest between powers, confined by rules in order to produce a disequilibrial outcome.[15]

The key elements of this definition are:

- *Exercise of control systems:* games involve some form of physical or intellectual activity:
- *Voluntary:* games are freely entered into;
- *Contest between powers:* games embody a conflict between players;
- *Confined by rules:* the limiting nature of rules is emphasized;
- *Disequilibrial outcome:* the outcome of a game is a goal state which is different than the starting state of the game.

Although none of these elements are wholly original to this definition, the strength of Avedon and Sutton-Smith's formulation is that it is compact, clear, and addresses games themselves, rather than the activity of playing them. Elegantly narrow in scope, their definition clearly demarcates games from less formal play activities. On the other hand, it doesn't contain all of the elements found in other definitions. Perhaps it is time to step back and take stock.

A comparison

The chart below summarizes the elements of a game, as described in each of the definitions.

Elements of a game definition	Parlett	Abt	Huizinga	Caillois	Suits	Crawford	Costikyan	Avedon|Sutton-Smith
Proceeds according to rules that limit players	✓	✓	✓	✓	✓	✓		✓
Conflict or contest	✓					✓		✓
Goal-oriented/outcome-oriented	✓	✓		✓	✓			✓
Activity, process, or event		✓				✓	✓	
Involves decision-making		✓					✓	
Not serious and Absorbing			✓					
Never associated with material gain			✓	✓				
Artificial/Safe/Outside ordinary life			✓	✓		✓		
Creates special social groups			✓					✓
Voluntary				✓				
Uncertain				✓	✓			
Make-believe/Representational				✓		✓		
Inefficient					✓	✓		
System of parts/Resources and Tokens						✓	✓	
A form of art							✓	

In simplifying complex ideas to a grid of common elements, much of the context and subtlety of the authors' ideas is clearly lost. Each author defines games for particular reasons within specific contexts; for example, with the exception of Chris Crawford and Greg Costikyan, none of the authors are operating from within the field of game design. On the other hand, this cannibalistic dissection of their approaches to defining games yields some interesting comparative results. All of the authors except Costikyan include rules as a key component. Beyond this there is no clear consensus. Although 10 of the 15 elements are shared by more than one author, apart from rules and goals, there is no majority agreement on any one of them.

It is clear that not all of the elements need to be included in a definition of game. Some elements, such as games being voluntary or inefficient, do not seem to apply to all games. Others, such as the fact that games create social groups, describe the effects of games rather than games themselves. Still other elements, such as the representational or make-believe quality of games, appear in many other media and do not help differentiate games from other kinds of designed experiences.

Our definition

Cobbling together elements from the previous definitions and whittling away the unnecessary bits leaves us with the following definition:

> A *game* is a system in which players engage in an artificial conflict, defined by rules, that results in a quantifiable outcome.

This definition structurally resembles that of Avedon and Sutton-Smith, but contains concepts from many of the other authors as well. Here are the definition's primary ideas:

> *System*: We introduced the concept of a system in chapter 5. Systems are fundamental to our approach to games.

> *Players*: A game is something that one or more participants actively play. Players interact with the system of a game in order to experience the play of the game.

> *Artificial*: Games maintain a boundary from so-called "real life" in both time and space. Although games obviously occur within the real world, artificiality is one of their defining features.

> *Conflict*: All games embody a contest of powers. The contest can take many forms, from cooperation to competition, from solo conflict with a game system to multiplayer social conflict. Conflict is central to games.

> *Rules*: We concur with the authors that rules are a crucial part of games. Rules provide the structure out of which play emerges, by delimiting what the player can and cannot do.

23

Quantifiable outcome: Games have a quantifiable goal or outcome. At the conclusion of a game, a player has either won or lost or received some kind of numerical score. A quantifiable outcome is what usually distinguishes a game from less formal play activities.

For the rest of this book, this definition is what we mean when we say "game."It applies to all kinds of games, from computer and video games to parlor games and sports. We can also use this definition to define the field of study at the center of this book:

> Game design is the process by which a game designer creates a game, to be encountered by a player, from which meaningful play emerges.

Aren't you happy to finally know what it is this book is about?

The puzzle of puzzles

This definition of games is intentionally quite narrow. It is not our intent to understand the broad phenomena of play, but instead to clearly demarcate the realm of games and game design. But is the definition *too* narrow? Are there things that are clearly are games but that don't fit this definition? This chapter on defining games concludes by looking at two kinds of game-activities that may or may not fit into the category of games this definition delineates. These "limit cases" will help clarify how this definition can help us investigate game-like phenomena.

First, puzzles. According to puzzle and game designer Scott Kim, puzzles are different from games because puzzles have a correct answer or outcome. Think of a crossword puzzle: the puzzle designer creates the correct answer, and the player's activity consists of trying to reconstruct that answer. This is a very different situation than a game of Poker, for example, in which there is no fixed "right answer" posed by the creator of the game. Instead, in Poker, players make complex decisions at every moment, taking into account the evolving dynamics of the game.

But this does not mean that a puzzle is not a game. Recall our definition:

> A *game* is a system in which players engage in an artificial conflict, defined by rules, that results in a quantifiable outcome.

A crossword puzzle contains all of the elements of this definition. It is a system of squares, letters, and clues, in which a player follows rules in order to arrive at an appropriate outcome. Although the conflict is between the player and the system rather than between a set of players, a crossword puzzle is most certainly a game. In fact, all kinds of puzzles are games. They might be considered a special subset of games, but they clearly meet the requirements of the definition.

Sometimes, it is difficult to determine whether or not a game is a puzzle. In his article, "What is a Puzzle?"[16] Kim references game designer Kevin Maroney, who points to Solitaire as a borderline case. If we think about Solitaire as an open-ended activity that can play out in many ways, it is not a puzzle. On the other hand, as Kim states, "in fact it is a kind of puzzle, since any given deck has a definite solution (or sometimes no solution). Shuffling the cards is a way to randomly generate a new puzzle."[17]

We are not going to split hairs. In our opinion, all puzzles are games, although they constitute a special kind of game. Thinking about a game as a puzzle, a game with a correct answer or set of answers, can be a useful way to frame a game. For example, is your 3D adventure game lacking a sense of play? Perhaps it is too puzzle-like, with all of the outcomes predetermined, and you need to ease the overall design away from puzzle territory. Alternately, if your adventure game feels too open-ended, perhaps you can inject some puzzle-like game play into it and better shape the player's sense of accomplishment. The idea of the "puzzle" can be a helpful way to frame game design problems.

Role-playing games

The second game "limit case" is role-playing games. Off the computer, these are games such as Dungeons & Dragons, in which players are cast as characters in an imaginary world. Digital role-playing games can be single-player adventures like the classic Ultima games, or multiplayer community worlds like Ever Quest. In both cases, the player controls and evolves a character over time within a narrative setting.

Role-playing games (or RPGs) certainly have the trappings of games. A paper-based, tabletop RPG usually involves dice, rulebooks, statistics, and a fair amount of strategic play. Role playing games clearly embody every component of our definition of game, except one: a quantifiable outcome. As an RPG player, you move through game-stories, following the rules, overcoming obstacles, accomplishing tasks, and generally increasing the abilities of your character. What is usually lacking, however, is a single endpoint to the game. Role-playing games are structured like serial narratives that grow and evolve from session to session. Sometimes they end; sometimes they do not. Even if a character dies, a player can rejoin as a different character. In other words, there is no single goal toward which all players strive during a role-playing game. If a game does end, it does not do so quantifiably, with players winning or losing or receiving a score. Gary Gygax, co-designer of Dungeons & Dragons, would concur: "Advanced Dungeons and Dragons is, as are most role-playing games, open-ended. There is no 'winner,' no final objective, and the campaign grows and changes as it matures."[18] This is true of both digital and non-digital multiplayer RPGs. (Note that single-player digital RPGs are structured differently—usually with an adventure game-style winning outcome.)

From this description, it would appear that multiplayer role playing games are not, in fact, games. But this seems like a ridiculous conclusion, because RPGs are so closely bound up in the development of games and gaming culture. Our position is this: RPGs can be framed either way—as having or not having a quantifiable outcome. If you look at the game as whole, there may not be a single, overriding quantifiable goal. But if you consider the session-to-session missions that players complete, the personal goals players set for themselves, the levels of power that players attain, then yes, RPGs do have quantifiable outcomes. In this sense, an RPG is a larger system that facilitates game play within it, giving rise to a series of outcomes that build on each other over time. Game designer Greg Costikyan puts it this way: "No victory conditions, true. But certainly [RPGs] have goals; lots of them, you get to pick. Rack up the old experience points. Or fulfill the quest your friendly GM has just inflicted on you. Or rebuild the imperium and stave off civilization's final collapse. Or strive towards spiritual perfection. Whatever."[19]

It is possible, of course, for RPGs to become more game-like. At game conventions, there are often "tournament-style" games, in which players or teams earn points for completing certain actions and accomplishing goals, and a single winner can in fact be declared. Conversely, there are RPGs that de-emphasize power, statistics, and advancement and instead focus on storytelling and narrative. This form of RPG seems very unlike games as we have defined them.

Role-playing games are not the only kind of play activity that exists on the border of our definition. A computer program like Sim City does not have explicit goals, and in that way is more like a toy than a game. However, as its designer Will Wright has often stated, players can turn it into a game by constructing their own goals. Does this make Sim City an informal play activity or a formalized game? It all depends on how it is framed.

Sometimes the answer to the question of whether or not a game is a game rests in the eye of the beholder. Any definition of a phenomena as complex as games is going to encounter instances where the application of the definition is somewhat fuzzy. Rather than seeing these moments as a breakdown of the definition, we view them as valuable opportunities to understand games as a whole. The terrain along the borders of more rigid definitions offers fertile ground for insight and investigation. In these playful and liminal spaces, assumptions are challenged, ideas evolve, and definitions change. It is this kind of transformative play that is at the heart of our model of game design.

Further reading

Man, Play, and Games, by Roger Caillois

A book that builds directly from the work of Johann Huizinga's *Homo Ludens, Man, Play, and Games* by philosopher Roger Caillois has a similar agenda: to identify and analyze the general phenomenon of play and locate its larger significance within culture. For our purposes, his early chapters on defining and classifying games are the most useful, providing insightful typologies and definitions for understanding play in and out of games.

Recommended:

I. The Definition of Play
II. The Classification of Games

Summary

* The words play and games have a unique relationship in the English language. There are two ways to frame their relationship, both of which are useful:

    1 *Games are a subset of play*: The category of play represents many kinds of playful activities. Some of these activities are games, but many of them are not. In this sense, games are contained within play.
    2 *Play is a subset of games*: Games are complex phenomena and there are many ways to frame them and understand them. RULES, PLAY, and CULTURE are three aspects of the phenomena of games. In this sense, play is contained within games.

* *A game is a system in which players engage in an artificial conflict, defined by rules, that results in a quantifiable outcome.* The key elements of this definition are the fact that a game is a system, players interact with the system, a game is an instance of conflict, the conflict in games is artificial, rules limit player behavior and define the game, and every game has a quantifiable outcome or goal.
* *A puzzle* is a special kind of game in which there is a single correct answer or set of correct answers. All puzzles are games.
* Multiplayer *Role-playing games* (RPGs) do not clearly possess a quantifiable outcome. Whether or not they fit the definition of a game depends on how they are framed. As with other open-ended game-like experiences such as Sim City, RPGs have emergent quantifiable goals but usually no single over-riding outcome.

Notes

1 David Parlett, *The Oxford History of Board Games* (New York: Oxford University Press, 1999), p. 1.
2 Ibid. p. 3.
3 Clark C. Abt, *Serious Games* (New York: Viking Press, 1970), p. 6.
4 Ibid. p. 7.
5 Ibid. pp. 7–9.
6 Johann Huizinga, *Homo Ludens: A Study of the Play Element in Culture* (Boston: Beacon Press, 1955), p. 13.
7 Roger Caillois, *Man, Play, and Games,* Translated from the French by Meyer Barash (Champaign: University of Illinois Press, 2001), pp. 9–10.
8 Bernard Suits, *Grasshopper: Games, Life, and Utopia* (Boston: David R. Godine, 1990), p. 34.
9 Ibid. p. 41.

10 Chris Crawford, *The Art of Computer Game Design.* <http://www.vancouver.wsu.edu/ fac/peabody/game-book/Coverpage.html>.

11 Ibid.

12 Ibid.

13 Ibid.

14 Greg Costikyan, "I Have No Words and I Must Design." *Interactive Fantasy #2,* 1994. <www.geocities.com/SiliconValley/Bay/2535/nowords.html>.

15 Elliott Avedon and Brian Sutton-Smith, eds. *The Study of Games* (New York: John Wiley & Sons, 1971), p. 405.

16 Scott Kim, "What is a Puzzle?" <www.scottkim.com/articles.html>.

17 Ibid.

18 Gary Gygax, *Advanced Dungeons and Dragons Players Handbook* (Lake Geneva: TRS Hobbies, 1978), p. 7.

19 Costikyan, "I Have No Words and I Must Design." <http://www.geocities.com/ SiliconValley/Bay/2535/nowords.html>.

Bibliography

Abt, Clark C. *Serious Games.* New York: Viking Press, 1970.

Avedon, E. M. "The Structural Elements of Games." In *The Study of Games,* ed. E. M. Avedon and Brian Sutton-Smith. New York: John Wiley, 1971, pp. 419–426.

Avedon, E. M., and Brian Sutton-Smith, eds. *The Study of Games.* New York: John Wiley, 1971.

Caillois, Roger. *Man, Play, and Games.* London: Thames and Hudson, 1962.

Costikyan, Greg. "I Have No Words and I Must Design." In *Interactive Fantasy #2* <www. geocities.com/SiliconValley/Bay/2535/nowords.html>.

Crawford, Chris. *The Art of Computer Game Design.* <www.vancouver.wsu.edu/fac/ peabody/game-book/Coverpage.html>.

Gygax, Gary. *Advanced Dungeons and Dragons Players Handbook.* Lake Geneva: TRS Hobbies, 1978.

Huizinga, Johann. *Homo Ludens: A Study of the Play Element in Culture.* Boston: Beacon Press, 1955.

Kim, Scott. "What is a Puzzle?" <www.scottkim.com/articles.html>.

Parlett, David. *The Oxford History of Board Games.* Oxford: Oxford University Press, 1999.

Suits, Bernard. *Grasshopper: Games, Life, and Utopia.* Boston: David R. Godine, 1990.

2

DEFINING GAME MECHANICS

Miguel Sicart

Source: *Game Studies: The International Journal of Computer Game Research*, 8(2), December 2008, available at http://gamestudies.org/0802/articles/sicart.

Abstract

This article defines game mechanics in relation to rules and challenges. Game mechanics are methods invoked by agents for interacting with the game world. I apply this definition to a comparative analysis of the games *Rez*, *Every Extend Extra* and *Shadow of the Colossus* that will show the relevance of a formal definition of game mechanics.

Introduction

Gears of War (Epic Games, 2006) showcased the impressive graphical capacities of the then-called "Next Generation" consoles. Making good use of the XBox 360 hardware, *Gears of War* models, textures and general aesthetics excelled. Yet, it is likely that this game will be remembered not as an exhibition of what archaic technology could do, but as the title that popularized the cover mechanics in third-person action games. Inspired by the cover system of *kill.switch* (Namco, 2003), *Gears of War* combined a linear level structure with action sequences where the dominant strategy is to take cover and patiently create an effective combat tactic. The influence of this design choice is such that even titles like *Grand Theft Auto IV* (RockStar North, 2008) have implemented a cover mechanic. Taking cover has arguably become one the features that all triple-A third-person action games ought to have nowadays.

The question is: what does "mechanic" mean in this context? Seasoned players would probably not hesitate to call the cover system a "mechanic", something that connects players' actions with the purpose of the game and its main challenges. But the meaning of the term is not always clear.

During the summer of 2006, Nintendo released *Bit Generations*, a collection of seven games focused on minimalist game design. In *Orbital* (Nintendo, 2006), the player controls a small unit, flying between planets and meteorites. The goal is to collect items so that the initial particle grows until it has its own gravitational field, which can be used to attract a star and thus finish a level. The challenge is provided by the different gravitational fields of the other space bodies, and the fact that a crash with any stellar element will lead to the destruction of the player's unit. The player can only attract or repel her unit from these gravitational fields, and so use them as slingshots, safe havens, or u-turns.

Given this description, what are the mechanics of *Orbital*? A common answer could be the attraction/repulsion actions that the player can use, but also the gravitational fields of the planets or even the use of gravity for sling-shot flying. In this sense, then, game mechanics also describes the mechanisms of the game simulation. This lack of conceptual precision points to a definitional problem: it is unclear what game mechanics are, and how the term can be used in game analysis.

Game researchers and designers have provided a number of definitions of game mechanics that have been used in different contexts, from analysis (Järvinen, 2008) to game design (Hunicke, LeBlanc, Zubek, 2004). In this article, I propose a definition of game mechanics useful for the analysis of games and their formal constituents. This definition will allow for formalized analysis of game structures, and it will also open up for the possibility of connecting formal game analysis with research on controller designs and user experience.

I define game mechanics, using concepts from object-oriented programming, as methods invoked by agents, designed for interaction with the game state. With this formalized definition, I intend to:

- Provide a tool to discover, describe, and interrelate game mechanics in any given game.
- Define mechanics also in relation to elements of the game system, game hardware and player experience, mapping mechanics to input procedures and player emotions.

Even though I will be mentioning concepts like game rules, challenges, emotions and user experience, it is not my intention to enter the debate on those topics. Here, I use those concepts in a relational way: defining game mechanics requires mentioning and acknowledging rules, challenges and emotions. I do so in an instrumental way and leave for further research the implications of this definition for understanding other systemic components of games.

Since both game researchers and game designers have covered the topic of game mechanics, I begin this article with an analytical summary of the major works on this topic, providing a general overview of these previous definitions of game mechanics and place my work within this tradition.

The second part of this article presents the definition of game mechanics, detailing the elements that compose it. I then present a brief reflection on primary and secondary mechanics and how they can be derived from this definition.

These concepts are put into practice in the third part, where I perform a comparative analysis of *Shadow of the Colossus* (Team Ico, 2005), *Rez* (United Game Artists, 2002), and *Every Extend Extra* (Q Entertainment, 2006), highlighting the use of this concept of mechanics in the research on game structure and user experience. The article concludes with a summary of the results, and a reflection on the shortcomings of this definition.

With this article I intend to provide a practical analytical tool for describing game systems as formal structures that create gameplay. I also intend to focus on how variations in game design can innovate and deeply engage players in aesthetic experiences created by means of gameplay design.

Previous definitions of game mechanics

There is a relatively long and multidisciplinary tradition of studying the ontology of games (Juul, 2005). The ontological question has often implied describing the elements of games, how players relate to these elements, and the contextualized act of play (*ibid*, p. 28). This study of games lead to analysis disregarding the overarching definitions of what games are and focused on each of the elements that constitute a game: the system, the player or the player-and-system in context. Eventually, this area of research was defined as game studies (Aarseth, 2001).

The research on games as systems lead to formal analysis of the game components and how they interrelate. Formal analysis is understood as descriptions of game components that can be discerned from others by means of their unique characteristics and properties. "Formal" should be understood in relation to aesthetic formalism, which contrasts "the artifact itself with its relations to entities outside itself" (Audi, 1999, p. 11).

Some formalist approaches makes a difference between the rules of the game and the actions afforded to players by those rules. This conceptual perspective can be tracked back to Avedon (1971) who suggests a formal structure of games in which there are "specific operations, required courses of action, method of play," which he defines as the "procedure for action", as opposed to the "rules governing action", which are "fixed principles that determine conduct and standards for behavior" (p. 422).

However, this formal distinction between rules and mechanics is not always applied in game mechanics research. Lundgren and Björk (2003) define game mechanics as "any part of the rule system of a game that covers one, and only one, possible kind of interaction that takes place during the game, be it general or specific (. . .) mechanics are regarded as a way to summarize game rules". In this view, mechanics is a term that encompasses those rules that are applied when the player interacts with the game, and there is no need for a definitional distinction between rules and mechanics. Game mechanics would be low-level descriptions of game rules or clusters of game rules.

Game designer Richard Rouse (2005) offers a more pragmatic approach to defining game mechanics, with the goal of teaching the basics of game documentation of game design. For Rouse, game mechanics are "the guts of a design document", since they describe "what the players are able to do in the game-world, how they do it, and how that leads to a compelling game experience" (p. 310).

31

A similar pedagogical approach is taken by Fullerton, Hoffman and Swain (2004), who define "game procedures" (a similar concept to mechanics), as "the actions or methods of play allowed by the rules (. . .) they guide player behaviour, creating interactions" (p. 25). In teaching game design, then, there is a need to apply Avedon's conceptual distinction between rules and mechanics. The design process is understood as the creation of a system, and the interaction possibilities that a player has with that system. However, these approaches lack a deep explanation of the connections between rules and mechanics. These connections are fundamental for the formal analysis of games, as Björk and Holopainen (2005) stated in their argumentation for the development of Game Design Patterns.

Other definitions, like Cook's (2005): "game mechanics are rule based system/simulations that facilitate and encourage a user to explore and learn the properties of their possibility space through the use of feedback mechanisms", while acknowledging the relations between players, rules and mechanics, fail to provide a sufficiently clear set of properties that allows the concept to be applied in a formal analysis of games. This definition is valuable since it incorporates the notion of feedback to the understanding of mechanics, but it falls short in explaining how we can identify a mechanic, or a set of mechanics, and how it is based in the rule system.

The MDA Framework (Hunicke, Zubek, LeBlanc, 2004) provides some more detail on the formal nature of game mechanics: "mechanics describes the particular components of the game, at the level of data representations and algorithms (. . .) mechanics are the various actions, behaviours, and control mechanisms afforded to the player within a game context". The latter part of the definition provides a set of elements that will allow us to identify a mechanic. However, this definition would require more precision in its formulation: for instance, behaviours afforded to the player can be both strategies suggested by the game design (the level layout in *Gears of War* suggests the behaviour or covering, yet it does not directly afford that action); and the operations that the game system does in the background to calculate the success of player actions (as the effect of gravitational fields in *Orbital*—external to player agency, yet related with the player's actions).

The MDA framework provides insights into the relations between the formal, algorithmic elements of games and how they are presented to and manipulated by players. Nevertheless, it is a model that does not allow for the description and analysis of a mechanic due to a relative inconsistency in the formulation of the definition.

A much more precise approach is taken by Järvinen (2008), who not only distinguishes rules from mechanics but also relates the latter with player agency, both in terms of psychological and game play experiences. Järvinen defines mechanics as "means to guide the player into particular behaviour by constraining the space of possible plans to attain goals" (p. 254). In this sense, "game mechanics are best described with verbs" (p. 263), and so "take cover" would be a key mechanic in *Gears of War*, while the two dominant mechanics in *Orbital* would be "attract" and "repel".

In relation to rules, Järvinen perceives mechanics as making "a particular set of rules available to the player in the form of prescribed causal relations between game elements and their consequence to particular game states" (p. 254), which leads to the creation of player strategies derived from the intersection of rules and mechanics (p. 258).

Järvinen's approach is thorough, describing how players appropriate mechanics and how systems should be designed to afford strategy-generating mechanics. However, Järvinen's approach is rather deterministic: mechanics seem to exist so that goals can be achieved, and thus there would be no mechanics if the game, or a specific set of actions, has no goals. Cases like *Sim City* (Maxis, 1989) or some of the sandbox play in *Crackdown* (RealTime Worlds, 2007) encourage player action without the requirement of goals. Destroying a city by invoking Godzilla or exploring a sprawling postmodern metropolis using superhuman abilities are pleasurable interactions with(in) a game that are not determined by any in-game goal.

Within the general research tradition on game mechanics, the concept is used to analyze elements of the game system. Game mechanics are used to describe how players interact with rules, and as more formal properties of a game such as game goals, player actions and strategies, and game states. However, these definitions do not provide a single, dominant approach that encompasses all these aspects. All the previous definitions have attempted to provide pragmatic approaches to allow for a flexible understanding of game mechanics in games and how they relate to player agency and game rules. In the following section I present a formal definition of game mechanics, together with the arguments that make it a more precise and inclusive approach than those reviewed in this section.

Defining game mechanics

Let's start with a definition: game mechanics are methods invoked by agents, designed for interaction with the game state.

The different components of this definition require further explanation:

"Methods invoked by agents" defines this approach to game mechanics, as it formalizes the use of terminology taken from the object oriented programming paradigm (Weisfeld, 2000). In this appropriation of the terminology, object orientation provides a set of metaphors that describe the elements of systems and their interrelations. I do not want to imply that the analysis of the source code of a game will reveal that all game mechanics have been implemented as methods of classes or that object-oriented programming should be considered a default methodology for the actual production of computer games. Nor am I implying that the Object Oriented Framework should be extended to a formal analysis of all elements of the game. Object Orientation provides a clear, formal framework for the description of games and as such is a useful analytical tool. It is useful because it provides a formalistic approach to actions taken within information systems like games, which may lead to the application of modeling languages like UML to the description of game systems. The Object Oriented framework is also appropriate because

it facilitates an analysis that does not require human players to understand in-game agency. In other words, by using an Object-Oriented approach, we can analyze game mechanics as available both to human and artificial agents.[1]

Following object oriented programming terminology, a method is understood as the actions or behaviors available to a class (Weisfeld, 2000, p. 13). Methods are the mechanisms an object has for accessing data within another object. A game mechanic, then, is the action invoked by an agent to interact with the game world, as constrained by the game rules. In *Gears of War*, if the player wants to take cover, she has to press the A button in the controller. This will make the avatar seek cover in the closest environment object that can provide that cover. In that sense, a mechanic is limited by the rules that apply to the gameworld (the general physics simulations, for instance, whose objects are suitable for providing some kind of cover), and, on occasion, to rules that apply exclusively to that particular mechanic for example, some mechanics can only be invoked in certain environments or gameplay contexts.

Following Järvinen (2008), the best way of understanding mechanics as methods is to formalize them as verbs, with other syntactical/structural elements, such as rules, having influence on how those verbs act in the game. For example, in *Shadow of the Colossus* we find the following mechanics: to climb, ride (the horse), stab, jump, shoot (arrows), whistle, grab, run (and variations like swim or dive). In *Gears of War*, a non-comprehensive list would be: cover, shoot, reload, throw (grenade), look (at a point of interest), use, give orders, switch weapons.[2] All of these are methods for agency within the game world, actions the player can take within the space of possibility created by the rules.

This definition departs from the implicit anthropocentrism of previous approaches. Game mechanics can be invoked by any agent, be that human or part of the computer system. For instance, AI agents also have a number of methods available to interact with the gameworld. On occasion, those methods will be other than the ones made available to the human player, which can have consequences worth of analysis. This approach can be particularly interesting when trying to understand the effect of bots in MMORPGs, since bots are agents that optimize their interaction by focusing on a core set of mechanics. This design choice may lead to an imbalance in the game system, in terms of its dynamics or its economy. Another extension of this approach would draw a distinction between agents in a game with mechanics and agents without access to mechanics. For example, some bots do have access to mechanics while other game agents do not have access to mechanics and hence cannot interact with the game state. This line of research, however, is outside the scope of this article.

The second advantage is that it eases the mapping of mechanics to input devices, allowing for a great degree of granularity in the analysis of games. Applying the conceptual framework of Object Oriented programming determines that an agent invokes a mechanic in order to interact with the game.[3] When it comes to players, input devices—from mouse and keyboard to the Wii Fit Board—mediate this process. In *Gears of War*, the cover mechanic is invoked by pressing the

A button in the controller. In *Orbital*, the two mechanics are mapped to the two buttons of the GameBoy Advance device. Thanks to the formal precision of Object oriented terminology, it would be possible to use an abstract modeling language, like UML, to describe the interaction possibilities afforded to players, and how those are mapped to specific input device triggers.

For game analysis, this suggests the possibility of closely studying the relations between input device design, and player actions. It would allow, for instance, the study of how in some fighting games, one mechanic is not triggered by one button, but by a combination of input processes. Thus, it could be argued from a formal perspective that mastery in fighting games comes from the mapping (Norman, 2002, pp. 17, 75–77), of one mechanic with a set of input procedures, which leads to both psychological and physiological mappings—how the "body" of a player learns to forget about the remembering the illogical sequence of inputs, and maps one mechanic to one set of coordinated, not necessarily conscious moves.

Another interesting approach from this formal perspective is the possibility of describing mechanics that are triggered depending on the context of the player presence in the game world, what I define as "context mechanics". In *Gears of War*, the cover mechanic depends not only on the specific input from the player, but also on the proximity of suitable objects to the player avatar. Contextual mechanics have also been used in *Assassins' Creed* (Ubisoft Montreal, 2007) to expand the possible interactions of the player with the gameworld, without overtly complicating the layout of the controller device.

Contextual mechanics are analytical concepts that can be used to understand how players decode the information in a level—how a player perceives certain structures and how those structures are used to communicate intended uses or behaviors. Furthermore, contextual mechanics can also be used to analyze a game like *Wario Ware, Inc., Mega Microgames!* (Nintendo R&D1, 2003) that builds its design by mapping multiple mechanics (Järvinen, 2008, pp. 266–269) to one button, easing the players' learning process and focusing on stress coping challenges (Rollings and Adams, 2007, pp. 287–288).

Implicit in this definition is an ontological difference between rules and mechanics. Game mechanics are concerned with the actual interaction with the game state, while rules provide the possibility space where that interaction is possible, regulating as well the transition between states. In this sense, rules are modeled after agency, while mechanics are modeled for agency.

In this object oriented framework, rules could be considered general or particular properties of the game system and its agents. All objects in games have properties. These properties are often either rules or determined by rules. These rules are evaluated by a game loop, an algorithm that relates the current state of the game and the properties of the objects with a number of conditions that consequently can modify the game state. For example, the winning condition, the losing condition and the effects of action in the player's avatar health are calculated when running the game loop. This algorithm relates rules with mechanics, exemplifying the applicability of an ontological distinction between rules and mechanics.

For example, in *Shadow of the Colossus* players have a game mechanic called "climb", but they are also determined by a property called "stamina", which is the algorithmic translation of a rule: "players have x stamina units". The climbing mechanic states that when invoked, stamina is lost at a certain ratio. A property/rule states that if stamina is below a certain threshold, climbing is not possible anymore. The game loop checks the game state; if the player invokes the climb mechanic, those functions that determine the consequences and boundaries of the players' interaction are called, and the resulting changes in the game state are evaluated against the rules of the game. Then, the player will succeed or not in "climbing", depending on their "stamina".

The second part of the definition claims that game mechanics are methods "designed for interaction with the game state". This implies that the task of game designers is to create mechanics that agents can use to interact with the game. These interactions modify the game state (Juul, 2005, 59–64). Game mechanics are often, but not necessarily, designed to overcome challenges, looking for specific transitions of the game state. Designers create the basic mechanics for the player correlating the central challenges of the game with the set of mechanics useful for overcoming them.

Challenges, like rules, are one of the contested areas in game research. Much has been written about what challenges are and how can they be analyzed, and it is not my intention to suggest a new interpretation of the term. In this article, I use challenge to refer to a situation in which the outcome desired by the player requires an effort to accomplish. For instance, every colossus in *Shadow of the Colossus* is a challenge, each of which is composed of a subset of challenges: the fifth colossus is a flying creature with weak spots in each wing and the tail. The challenge is to run from one weak spot to another without falling, since player movement is affected by the wind and the speed of the moving colossus. All these challenges are matched with a mechanic: by shooting arrows, the player calls the attention of the creature; by jumping and then grabbing to the hair of the creature, the player accesses a more or less stable surface where she can then run to the weak spots and stab them. All challenges in this example are mapped to particular game mechanics.

Even though this formal definition determines that games are structured as systems with mechanics, rules and challenges, understood as the essential grammar of computer games (and probably of all games), there is more to the act of playing a game than just interacting with mechanics constrained by rules. In the act of playing, players will appropriate agency within the game world and behave in unpredicted ways. One thing is what a designer previews, and another, very different one, is how players actually interact with the game world. The formal, analytical understanding of mechanics only allows us to design and predict courses of interaction, but not to determine how the game will always be played, or what the outcome of that experience will be.

Furthermore, it can happen that what was designed as a game mechanic is used in a non-gameplay related behavior: players of *Shadow of the Colossus* used the climbing mechanic to reach some of the farthest areas of the game world, which had no influence, or interest, for the central gameplay sequence and narrative of the game. Game mechanics are designed for gameplay, but they can be used for toy-play (Bateman and Boon, 2006). The only variation would be the level of abstraction: for a player who is playing the game, a mechanic serves a specific set of purposes, while a player that is playing with or within the game, a game mechanic loses its formal game design origin and becomes an instrument for agency.

For designers and theorists, game mechanics are discrete units that can be created, analyzed and put in relation to others. But for any agent in a game, the mechanics is everything that affords agency in the game world. Mechanics is thus tied to agency in the game system.

With this definition of game mechanics, I have intended to contribute to game studies by:

- Formalizing an ontological difference between rules and mechanics that can potentially lead to detailed game analysis, and
- Suggesting a mapping between game mechanics, input procedures, and player experience.

This very formal definition still leaves some questions unanswered, especially with regards to well-known terminology such as core mechanics. In the next section, I present some further implications of this definition for the analysis of games.

Interlude: core, primary and secondary mechanics

Game design literature uses the "game mechanics" concept extensively, incorporating certain qualifiers to it. It is not rare to find in the literature notions like "core mechanics" (Järvinen, 2998, p. 255; Rollings and Adams, 2007, pp. 316–357), and in more casual settings, an implicit categorization like primary mechanics and secondary mechanics (Järvinen, 2008, p. 268). These qualifiers do not describe what concept of game mechanics the authors are adopting—if a rule based one, in which mechanics is a subset of rules, or one that advocates for an ontological differentiation of both. In this section, I briefly discuss how core mechanics, primary mechanics and secondary mechanics can be used as functional terms within the context of the definition I have introduced. These concepts are, as said, widely used in game design literature, thus it is important to define them according to this article's definition of game mechanics.

Core mechanics, in the traditional sense, have been defined as "the essential play activity players perform again and again in a game (. . .) however, in many games, the core mechanic is a compound activity composed of a suite of actions" (Salen and Zimmerman, 2004, p. 316). Järvinen defined core mechanics as "the possible or preferred or encouraged means with which the player can interact with game elements as she is trying to influence the game state at hand towards the attainment of a goal" (255). Understanding core mechanics as those that describe the actions a player repeatedly performs is a useful formalism, but it falls short in precision. Players often perform play activities again and again in a game without using so called core mechanics. Jumping, for instance, is extensively used in multi-player First Person Shooters, where almost all players spend some time "hopping" around—as a humorous display or for entertainment. Salen and Zimmerman and Järvinen are right in pointing out that the core mechanics have to do with repeated performance in the play context, but the actions performed ought to be defined from a systemic perspective, if the formal framework should be upheld.

From that systemic perspective, I define core mechanics as the game mechanics (repeatedly) used by agents to achieve a systemically rewarded end-game state. For instance, stabbing is a core mechanic of *Shadow of the Colossus*, since the player will perform it repeatedly to achieve the end state of the game, rewarded with the completion of the fictional framework of the game. In *Orbital*, the core mechanics are the only mechanics. Both games are examples of focused game design, in which player actions are limited, yet tuned to create emergent game play (Juul, 2005, pp. 67–83; Sweetster, 2008).

Games like *Sim City* or *Ever Quest* (Sony Online Entertainment, 1999) do not have an end state as such. However, there are desired states towards which players focus their efforts, be those reaching the cap character level or keeping the city budget in the black. These games have a specific set of game mechanics oriented to reaching those states, and as such it is possible to speak of core mechanics even in the case of games with no systemically determined end state. In the case of simulations like *Sim City*, core mechanics are those that focus on reaching an equilibrium state; in games like *Ever Quest*, core mechanics are those that allow players to reach a level cap, and further expand their agency by fine tuning their characters' abilities.

At this stage, readers will most likely object that complex games like *Grand Theft Auto IV* have such a vast number of mechanics, and so many are used to make the game progress, that the very use of the core mechanics concept may be useless. It is a valid point complexity requires a precise terminology. Thus, I will use the concepts of primary (core) mechanics and secondary (core) mechanics to solve some of these issues.

The concept of primary mechanics has been defined by Järvinen (2008, p. 268) as "what the player does in relation to a game state during a standard turn or sequence", differentiating then between submechanics, or actions available to the player "as a consequence of the primary mechanic" (*ibid*), and modifier mechanics, or actions the player does "in a specific game state which occurs on some condition (. . .) specified in the rules" (*ibid*). Again, Järvinen's comprehensive approach is highly relevant, but its formal ties to games understood as goal-oriented systems with which (human) agents interact determine this classification of mechanics. In the following I will suggest an approach to the concepts closer to the approach taken in this article.

Primary mechanics can be understood as core mechanics that can be directly applied to solving challenges that lead to the desired end state. Primary mechanics are readily available, explained in the early stages of the game, and consistent throughout the game experience. In *Grand Theft Auto IV*, primary mechanics are shooting, melee fighting, and driving: they are readily available to the player, mapped to the most obvious and tradition-conforming controller inputs and remain consistent throughout the game experience: shooting is always performed using the same button combination, and when players have control, they always have access to that mechanic, provided they have a firearm. Interestingly, this use of the primary mechanics concept explains the design experiment of *Orbital*: players only have primary mechanics available to interact with the gameworld.

Secondary mechanics, on the other hand, are core mechanics that ease the player's interaction with the game towards reaching the end state. Secondary mechanics are either available occasionally or require their combination with a primary mechanic in order to be functional. The cover mechanic in *Grand Theft Auto IV* is an example: it cannot be used exclusively to solve the main challenges of the game, but once mastered, it can prove of help to achieve the end state of the game. In comparison, the cover mechanic of *Gears of War* is primary, since not using it implies the almost immediate death of any game agent.

Again, readers may claim that there are mechanics in a game beyond those tied to the goal/reward structure. And they are right – in many modern, complex computer games there are many mechanics available for player agency, and several of them play a role in achieving the goals. I would prefer not to categorize those, though: the importance of the terms of primary and secondary is their explanation of the game system as it was intended to be played by an ideal player.[4] Any formalist approach, such as the one proposed in this article, falls short of trying to explain all possible player interactions. As such, I would like to leave all mechanics that cannot be consistently defined as primary or secondary without any type of classification. It is still relevant to understand them and to describe how their importance is perceived in actual gameplay. However, those goals are beyond the scope of this article.

The distinction between primary and secondary, then, allows for a granular understanding of the agency methods available for players in the game experience, and their importance in terms of design and analysis. However, these terms should not be used as rigid categories: on occasions, secondary mechanics can turn into primary mechanics during the designed gameplay progression, and some primary mechanics may even disappear in the length of a game. These concepts should be used as analytical aids, as a first step into a formal categorization of mechanics depending on their impact on gameplay.

One last question remains: within this formal, object oriented framework, it is not possible to describe systems like the driving mechanic in *Grand Theft Auto IV*: more precisely, driving would consist of braking, accelerating, steering and handbreaking. All of these are, effectively, the methods invoked by agents in order to interact with the game. However, using this very detailed description is not always a useful approach. Thus, the concept of compound game mechanics can be of use: a compound game mechanic is a set of related game mechanics that function together within one delimited agent interaction mode. These modes are defined by the interaction of these different modalities: as such, the driving compound mechanic is composed by a set of mechanics interrelated to provide a relatively accurate model of driving. When playing, and, on occasion, when analyzing, it is useful to think about these compound mechanics as a whole and not as a collection of formally differentiated mechanics. This concept provides an appropriate shelter for those complex interaction processes that, while composed by a number of smaller formally determined mechanics, we as players, analysts and designers, think of as unified.

So far, this article has been a rather dry presentation and argumentation for a terminological, analytical position. In the next section I will apply this definition, with attention to input-interface configuration and plausible player experience, to the analysis of the common mechanics and effects of *Rez*, *Shadow of the Colossus* and *Every Extend Extra*.

Applying the definition: theory and design

To prove the analytical use of my definition of game mechanics, I apply it to three different games. This application will show that game mechanics can be used not only to formally describe a game but also to thread connections between different games and intended player experiences. In the following examples, I trace such a connection between *Shadow of the Colossus*, *Rez* and *Every Extend Extra* by analyzing dominant game mechanics and their implementation, and interpreting how the design choices could be meant to affect the player experience.

The basic mechanic in *Shadow of the Colossus* can be called "stabbing", which requires players to select a specific weapon when placed in a specific spot of a colossus, then press once the x button to "charge" her attack, then press once again to release and effectively stab the colossus. The intensity of the attack depends on the time lapse between the two inputs: the longer the player waits to unleash the attack, the more damaging it will be.

From a purely analytical perspective, this mechanic introduces an interesting observation: as opposed to the more classical "aggression" mechanics, in *SoTC* players do not obtain direct output from their initial input, nor do they have to push down the button for "charging" the attack. This is arguably a design choice, and it could be tied to the aesthetic goals of the game: the player is in a weak position between inputs, which reinforces the sense of awe these colossi suggest. In many computer games, players are supposed to feel empowered, yet challenged by their enemies. *SoTC* is designed to present players with what appears like an insurmountable enemy and equips them with just the bare abilities to epically undergo the slaying of these creatures.

By slightly modifying a well-known game mechanic, it could be argued that the design of *Shadow of the Colossus* is intended to create an experience of powerlessness and epic achievement. The player is not only faced with the colossi as challenges, but also their repertoire (Juul: 2005) is challenged by the control configuration of the attack mechanic. This challenge has likely been designed to have a significant emotional impact on the player, which I will analyze at a later stage in this section.

Even though this analysis could itself justify the use of this formal definition of game mechanic, it also allows for extending the study of mechanics to comparative approaches. In the rhythm shooter *Rez*, players have a general mechanic "shoot" that is invoked as follows: while holding the x button, players can select enemies with their crosshair, up to a limit of 8. When releasing the x button, players destroy the enemies. For each enemy destroyed, a rule states that a beat is played, hence the rhythm-based gameplay of the game.

From this brief description, we can argue that there are similarities between the two mechanics, as they both modify the conventional input/output mechanic: instead of pushing a button to produce an output, players have to release it to produce the output. The analysis can be extended: there is a principle of tension and release at work both in the stab mechanic of *Shadow of the Colossus* and in the shoot mechanic of *Rez*, and both can be interpreted as design choices that create a specific player experience.

Music can sometimes be structured as harmonic periods of tension and release: a composition builds up to a moment where the chord progression, for example, is culminated in a tonal change or a different tempo (A more detailed explanation of the structure of music and how it can be interpreted in the context of technological experience can be found in McCarthy and Wright, 2006). The same principle dominates *Rez*: players build up tension by targeting multiple enemies, then releasing and creating music beats. And in *Shadow of the Colossus,* players experience tension while their stabbing "strength" is being loaded and release when the player hits the button to stab the colossus. By examining the formal properties of these two mechanics, we can argue for a connection to an intended player experience, which means that it is possible to recognize patterns or typologies in the design of mechanics.

This tension and release effect through mechanics can also be found in the game *Every Extend Extra*,[5] where the main mechanic "to explode" is executed by pressing the x button. This input makes the avatar explode and start a chain reaction rewarded with points. Tension is created by avoiding collision with the incoming enemies, which would destroy the player avatar without causing a chain reaction, while waiting for the perfect combination of enemies onscreen that would allow for a large chain-reaction effect. Gameplay is built around the exploding mechanic, another tension-release mechanic type: tension is built while avoiding enemies without providing any input, and release comes when the player finds the right timing and place to trigger the explosion.

These three reasonably different games are connected by a similar interpretation of a game mechanic. All these games play with player expectations (action on release) with the intention of creating a specific emotional experience in players. In the case of *Shadow of the Colossus* the experience is associated with the excitement of attacking the colossi with maximum power without falling. In *Rez* and *Every Extend Extra*, it could be argued that the synaesthetic goal of these games is communicated also by means of the mechanic: players experience the musical tension and release structure while actually playing the game.

From a formal analytical perspective, there is a connection between *Shadow of the Colossus*, *Rez* and *Every Extend Extra*, since all this games have manipulated a well-known core mechanic into a process based one of tension and release. This connection also leads to a plausible relation between the design of these mechanics and its possible impact on the player experience. By modifying the player expectations, and meaningfully changing the input procedures, these games are intended to create emotional experiences based on the agency of players with the game state and how it reacts to their input.

By tracing relationships between game mechanics, and arguing for their intended effects on players, game designers may innovate their approach to agency through the design of the game system. It could be argued that the developers of the three aforementioned games did so by formally isolating the basic processes of those mechanics, partially altering them, consequently modifying player expectations and experience.

As I have already hinted at, game mechanics are not only formally recognizable by designers; they are also a big part of the players' repertoire (Juul, 2005, p. 97–102). By modifying the basic interaction patterns of a mechanic, designers can arguably expect to break player expectations. A possible use of this definition, then, is as a formal tool for describing and modifying mechanics in a coherent and comprehensive way, by understanding the relations between the different methods, its properties, and how those are mapped onto the control interface.

Another potential contribution to game design is related to its documentation and communication. When writing a design document, game designers often have to translate into words their ideas about player interaction with the game world how that interaction is constrained by rules and how those mechanics can help overcoming the challenges in interesting ways. The literature on game documentation is vast (Rollings and Adams, 2007, pp. 63–65; Rouse, 2005, pp. 355–381; Fullerton, 2008, pp. 394–412; Schuytema, 2007, pp. 83–116), and most of it is based on tradition or a set of common practices more than on a research-based approach to the formal elements of games. With this definition of game mechanics, designers could more easily translate their ideas into a formal set of methods (mechanics), properties (rules that define the scope of those mechanics) and challenges.

Finally, for design and development purposes, this definition's focus on an object-oriented approach can facilitate the communication between programmers and designers with limited technical background. By thinking about rules and mechanics as designed methods and properties, game designers could perhaps document and explain their concepts with more precision, enhancing productivity while creating more comprehensive documentation for game development.

Conclusion

This article was born out of necessity: having an analytical vocabulary for defining game structures and systems that allowed a formal, precise, and scalable description of games as systems and how they interrelate with player practices. The result of this necessity is a formal definition of game mechanics that owes to object-oriented programming its formal phrasing, while inheriting from game studies the figure of players, or agents, as fundamental to understand how games are designed and played.

This article has defined game mechanics as methods invoked by agents for interacting with the game world. This definition allows the study of the systemic structure of games in terms of actions afforded to agents to overcome challenges, but also the analysis of how actions are mapped onto input devices and how mechanics can be used to create specific emotional experiences in players.

There are, however, many grey areas I do not have the space to focus on here. Perhaps the most significant is the ontological distinction between rules and mechanics. Game researchers have argued convincingly that mechanics could be understood as subsets of rules. However, rules are normative, while mechanics are performative, and I have argued that this ontological distinction can be extremely beneficial for the analysis of computer games.

Game studies history shows that there is no dominant definition of key concepts like rules or mechanics, and that those that attempted have yet to succeed. This article should not be read as the ultimate definition of game mechanics. This definition is flawed, yet less so than some previous ones. My goal will be achieved if I have succeeded in communicating to the reader one simple notion: that it is possible and useful to understand game mechanics as different from game rules, and in that understanding, we can more clearly describe how games can be designed to affect players in unprecedented ways.

Acknowledgements

The author would like to express his gratitude to the anonymous Game Studies reviewers who offered constructive and illuminating feedback, and to Aki Järvinen, Jesper Juul and Olli Leino, who helped shape earlier versions of this article with their comments.

Notes

1 It is possible to find other applications of Object Oriented modeling to the study of computer games. For instance, the concept of Inheritance, or how some classes are derived from preexisting classes, can be used to explain different mechanics available to different agents in a gameworld. Other uses of the Object Oriented framework in the analysis of information systems can be found in Floridi and Sanders (2004).
2 Järvinen (2008) has a detailed list of all the mechanics, understood as verbs, present in the micro-game collection *Wario Ware*. My approach is deeply inspired by that listing.
3 In the case of analyzing mechanics as available to artificial agents (i.e. A.I. controlled bots), it is possible to disregard the mapping between mechanics and input controllers.
4 Even though the use of the "ideal player" here can invoke literary theory approaches to the ideal reader (Iser, 1980, pp. 27–30), I will be using "ideal player" in a more design-oriented perspective, as the abstraction of a user that will use the object designed as predicted by the design team (see Dillon, 1995).
5 *Every Extend Extra* is the PSP version of an earlier game built with the same mechanics, *Every Extend* (2004).

References

Aarseth, E. (2001). "Game Studies: Year One". *Game Studies*. Volume One, Issue One. Retrieved September 22nd, 2008.

Abelson, H. & Gerald Jay Sussman with Julie Susman (1985). *Structure and Interpretation of Computer Programs*. Cambridge, Massachusetts: The MIT Press.

Adams, E. & Andrew Rollings (2007). *Fundamentals of Game Design*. New Jersey: Pearson-Prentice Hall.

Audi, Robert (ed.) (1999). *The Cambridge Dictionary of Philosophy*. Cambridge: Cambridge University Press.

Avedon, E. M. (1971). "The Structural Elements of Games". In Avedon, E. M. & Brian Sutton-Smith (eds.), *The Study of Games*. New York: John Wiley and Sons.

Bateman, C. & Richard Boon (2006). *XXI Century Game Design*. Hingham, Massachusetts: Charles River Media.

Björk, S. & Jussi Holopainen (2005). *Patterns in Game Design*, Hingham, Massachusetts: Charles River Media.

Cook, D. (2006). "What are game mechanics?" Lostgarden.com. Available at http://lostgarden.com/2006/10/what-are-gamemechanics.html (accessed: 26/3/2008).

Dillon, A. (1995). "Artifacts as theories: Convergence through user-centered design". In Kinney, T. (ed.), *Proceedings American Society for Information Science*, 32, pp. 208–210.

Floridi, L. & Jeff Sanders (2004), "Levellism and the Method of Abstraction". Information Ethics Group Research Report. Available at http://web2.comlab.ox.ac.uk/oucl/research/areas/ieg/research_reports/ieg_rr221104.pdf (accessed: 26/3/2008).

Fullerton, T. & Christopher Swain & Steven Hoffman (2004). *Game Design Workshop: Designing, Prototyping, and Playtesting Games*. San Francisco: CMP Books.

Fullerton, Tracy (2008). *Game Design Workshop. Second Edition: A Playcentric Approach to Creating Innovative Games*. New York: Morgan Kaufmann.

Hunicke, R. & Marc LeBlanc & Robert Zubek (2004). "MDA: A Formal Approach to Game Design and Game Research". Available at http://www.cs.northwestern.edu/~hunicke/MDA.pdf (accessed: 26/3/2008).

Iser, W. (1980). *The Act of Reading. A Theory of Aesthetic Response*. Baltimore: The Johns Hopkins University Press.

Järvinen, A. (2008). *Games without Frontiers: Theories and Methods for Game Studies and Design*. Tampere: Tampere University Press. Available at http://acta.uta.fi/english/teos.phtml?11046 (accessed: 26/3/2008)

Juul, J. (2005). *Half Real. Videogames between Real Rules and Fictional Worlds*. Cambridge, Massachusetts: The MIT Press.

Lundgren, S. & Staffan Björk (2003). "Game Mechanics: Describing Computer-Augmented Games in Terms of Interaction". In *Terms of Interaction. Proceedings of TIDSE 2003*, pp. 45–56. Available at http://citeseerx.ist.psu.edu/viewdoc/summary?doi=10.1.1.13.5147 (accessed 1/9/2008).

McCarthy, J. & Peter Wright (2006). *Technology as Experience*. Cambridge, Massachusetts: The MIT Press.

Norman, D. (2002). *The Design of Everyday Things*. New York: Basic Books.

Rollings, A. & Dave Morris (2004). *Game Architecture and Design: A New Edition*. Indianapolis, Indiana: New Riders Press.

Rollings, A. & Ernst Adams (2007). *Fundamentals of Game Design*. New Jersey: Pearson Prentice Hall.

Rouse III, R (2005). *Game Design Theory and Practice*. Plano, Texas: Wordware Publishing Inc.

Salen, K. & Eric Zimmerman (2004). *Rules of Play: Game Design Fundamentals*. Cambridge, Massachusetts: The MIT Press.

Schuytema, P. (2008). *Game Design: A Practical Approach*. Boston: Charles River Media.

Sweetster, P. (2008). *Emergence in Games*. Boston: Charles River Media.

Weisfeld, Matt (2000). *The Object Oriented Thought Process*. Indianapolis, Indiana: Sams Publishing.

Ludography

Epic Games (2006), *Gears of War* (Xbox 360)

Matsuhisa, Kanta (2004), *Every Extend* (Windows)

Maxis (1989), *Sim City* (Windows)

Namco (2003), *kill.switch* (PlayStation 2)

Nintendo (2006), *New Super Mario Bros.* (Nintendo DS)

Nintendo (2006), *Orbital* (GameBoy Advanced)

Nintendo R&D1 (2003), *Wario Ware, Inc.: Mega Microgames!* (GameBoy Advanced)

Q Entertainment (2006), *Every Extend Extra* (PSP)

RealTime Worlds (2007), *Crackdown* (Xbox 360)

RockStar North (2008), *Grand Theft Auto IV* (Xbox 360)

Sony Online Entertainment (1999), *EverQuest* (Windows)

Team Ico (2005), *Shadow of the Colossus* (PlayStation 2)

Ubisoft Montreal (2008), *Assassins' Creed* (Xbox 360)

United Game Artists (2002), *Rez* (PlayStation 2)

3

THE GAMING SITUATION

Markku Eskelinen

Source: *Game Studies: The International Journal of Computer Game Research*, 1(1), July 2001, available at http://www.gamestudies.org/0101/eskelinen.

Introduction

The first point of departure for this article is a kind of paradox or contradiction. Outside academic theory people are usually excellent at making distinctions between narrative, drama and games. If I throw a ball at you I don't expect you to drop it and wait until it starts telling stories. On the other hand, if and when games and especially computer games are studied and theorized they are almost without exception colonised from the fields of literary, theatre, drama and film studies. Games are seen as interactive narratives, procedural stories or remediated cinema.[1] On top of everything else, such definitions, despite being successful in terms of influence or funding, are conceptually weak and ill-grounded, as they are usually derived from a very limited knowledge of mere mainstream drama or outdated literary theory, or both. Consequently, the seriously and hilariously obsolete presuppositions of Aristotelian drama, commedia dell'arte, Victorian novels, and Proppian folklore continue to dominate the scene. To put it less nicely, it's an attempt to skip the 20th century altogether and avoid any intellectual contact with it, a consumerist double assassination of both the avant-garde and advanced theory. The final irony is of course that in the long run such a practice may turn out to be even commercially incorrect.

In any case, in what follows I'll try to make some sense of what I call the gaming situation by trying to pinpoint or at least locate the most crucial and elementary qualities that set it apart from dramatic and narrative situations, both of the latter being rather well-studied constellations by now, and existing slightly beyond the necessary formalistic phase that computer game studies have to enter in order to gain independence, or at least relative independence. Historically speaking this is a bit like the 1910s in film studies; there were attractions, practices and very little understanding of what was actually going on, not to mention lots of money to be made and lost.

As we study computer games, we need to have some idea of digital media as well as of games. For that purpose we'll use the theories of Espen Aarseth, Roger

Caillois, Warren Motte and David Parlett in particular. They form a filter through which the possibly heuristic findings and borrowings from various neighbouring disciplines and predatory theory formations are viewed, tested, modified and transformed. While discussing articulation, materiality, functionality, typology and orientation, among other things, we are confronting the bare essentials of the gaming situation: the manipulation or the configuration of temporal, spatial, causal and functional relations and properties in different registers.

Gaming as configurative practice

Regarding the so-called remediation or cross-media influence the simplest possible statement would be that computer games are remediated games (and not presentations or narratives). So what are games then? According to David Parlett formal games are systems of ends and means (Parlett 1999, 3). The latter part consists of specific procedural rules of how to manipulate the equipment (pieces or tokens or whatever).

Gaming is seen here as configurative practice, and the gaming situation as a combination of ends, means, rules, equipment, and manipulative action. There are one or two parallels to draw. First, the equipment (the "what" of gaming) and manipulation (the "how") of this ludology-in-progress resemble the story and discourse of narratology. Still, according to the famous statement of Christian Metz "one of the functions of narrative is to invent one time scheme in terms of another time scheme" (Metz 1974, 18). Contrary to this, in games there's only one necessary time scheme: the movement from the beginning to the winning or some other situation. In cases where another time scheme is invented, it is not as important as the first one.

In discussing computer games we should take into account the unique dual materiality of cybernetic sign production (see Aarseth 1997, 40), and the resulting difference between strings of signs as they exist in the game (textonic game elements)

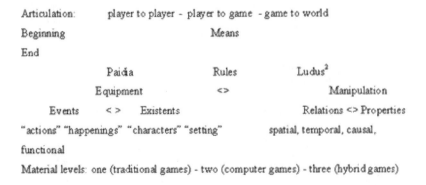

Figure 1 The gaming situation

47

and strings of signs as they are presented to the player (scriptonic game elements). It may well be that events in computer games should be described in three interplaying registers. In addition to textonic events, there are two kinds of scriptonic events: prefabricated and completed. The former are events presented to the player, and the latter the combination of the former and the player's actions.

Another quick look at Espen Aarseth's typology of cybertexts (Aarseth 1997, 62–65) should make us see that the dominant user function in literature, theatre and film is interpretative, but in games it is the configurative one. To generalize: in art we might have to configure in order to be able to interpret whereas in games we have to interpret in order to be able to configure, and proceed from the beginning to the winning or some other situation.[3]

In literature, theatre and film everything matters or is conventionally supposed to matter equally—if you've seen 90% of the presentation that's not enough, you have to see or read it all (or everything you can). This is characteristic of dominantly interpretative practices in general. In contrast, in computer games you either can't or don't have to encounter every possible combinatory event and existent the game contains, as these differ in their ergodic importance. Some actions and reactions in relation to certain events will bring the player quicker to a solution or help her reach the winning situation sooner or more effectively than others. There are events and existents the player has to manipulate or configure in order to progress in the game or just to be able to continue it. Events, existents and the relations between them can be described at least in spatial, temporal, causal and functional terms. It's equally self-evident that the importance of these dimensions varies from game to game and sometimes also within the phases and levels of an individual game.

The equipment: situations, events and existents

Situations. In order to understand the equipment side better, it's useful to explore traditional, but sophisticated accounts of narratives, stories and their basic components. According to Gerald Prince's well-known definition a narrative is "the recounting (as product and process, object and act, structure and structuration) of one or more real or fictitious events communicated by one, two or several (more or less overt) narrators to one, two or several (more or less overt) narratees." Before going into the details of this definition it is important to note one of its most obvious consequences: "a dramatic performance representing (many fascinating) events does not constitute a narrative either, since these events, rather than being recounted, occur directly on stage." (Prince 1987, 58) This is perhaps the most efficient way of distinguishing narrative situations from dramatic and performative situations. We can show the main differences among four major situations in the following chart (Figure 2).

So a mere story is not sufficient to make something a narrative, as there must also be a narrative situation implying the presence of narrators and narratees. To continue this digression, the story "always involves temporal sequence (it consists of at least one modification of a state of affairs obtaining at time t0 into

Elements	Activity	Situation/frame
Story (events and existents)	recounted	narrative
Story (events and existents)	enacted	dramatic (matrixed[*])
Events and existents	taking place	performative (non-matrixed)
Equipment goals)	manipulated	gaming (with rules and

Figure 2 Elements, activities and situations

another state of affairs obtaining at time tN), and this is its most distinctive feature" (Prince 1987, 59). This definition leaves the degree of causality between the situations and events making up the story open to a wide variety of tastes to the greater or lesser annoyance of plot-lovers. The latter often conceive stories as mere plots or closed sequences of events, in which case they should come to grips with games containing open series of events, and that probably can't be achieved without major revisions in their favourite narrative theories, which are not my concern here at all.

The fundamental constituents of the story are usually divided into events and existents. It should already be obvious that it is possible to combine existents and events in ways that do not form or become stories. In abstract games like *Tetris* there are settings, objects and events but definitely no characters. In addition there are events in games that change situations but do not convey or carry or communicate stories. A goal in a soccer game is an event that changes the situation, but there's no story in it; a goal is a goal is a goal. The same can be said for most actions and happenings in performance or circus art. The main thing is of course that any element can be turned into a game element, and only one element is enough to constitute a game if it allows manipulation, and this fact alone allows combinations not witnessed in narratives or drama. Consequently, both the number of game elements and the relations between them can be different in specific ways that are typical of (computer) games and only of them, and don't have to respect any conventions and traditional boundaries inherited from oral or written narratives, drama, theatre or films.

Events

In narratology, events are divided into actions and happenings based on their agency, and into kernels and satellites based on their relative importance. There's also a difference between punctual acts and more durational actions, and that's about it (Chatman 1978, 32–56). As games require configurative approaches from the players, satellites are of no importance to them, and in principle they could and should be skipped (something that's not advisable to do in interpretative practices). Instead of actions and happenings, we have user events and system events (or intransient and transient events) in computer games, and events are either independent or dependent of the player.[5] Those latter could be divided into successful and unsuccessful ones that are a bit like happy and unhappy performatives in speech act theory,[6] in contrast to true or false and more or less important narrative constatives describing (what exists and happens in) the fictive world(s).

Existents

Traditionally, existents are divided into characters and settings based on their significance for the plot, and they are also divided according to different degrees of permanence into identities, traits and moods (Chatman 1978, 267). Regarding the significance for a game, it is entirely a matter of usability or functionality, affecting equally well settings (or event spaces), objects, tools, NPCs and player representations. Consequently, in computer games the distinction between static settings and dynamic characters transforms into a more complex continuum of combinations, alterations, and middle terms, because the distribution of static and dynamic game elements doesn't have to mimic any practices in other modes of expression and communication.

Manipulation and articulation

In discussing Jacques Ehrmann's close reading of Huizinga and Caillois Warren Motte introduces three basic articulations suggested by Ehrmann's article: the relations of player to player, player to game and game to world (Motte 1995, 26–27). They can be combined with the most important types of potentially manipulatable relations in games: the temporal, causal, spatial and functional ones. The resulting preliminary taxonomical grid can be seen below (Figure 3).

Let's take the player-to-player dimension first, as it helps to describe the player's position and positioning in the game. In this register static relations are those guaranteed to be and remain equal (or unchanging) between players in and during the game. Static temporal relations indicate turn-based arrangements whereas

Relations:	Temporal	Causal	Spatial
Functional			
Type:	static/dynamic	static/dynamic	static/dynamic
static/dynamic			
Articulation:			
Player to player			
Player to game			
Game to world			

Figure 3 Manipulation and articulation

dynamic temporal relations refer to action taken in real time without fixed turns—here time is a resource not shared or distributed equally among players. Static and dynamic causalities are somewhat similar to intratextonic and textonic dynamics in cybertext theory (Aarseth 1997, 62), dynamic causality referring to the player's possibilities to add new elements triggering novel chains of causality into the game (e.g. by building characters, objects and rooms in a MUD). Spatial relations are static if the players can't change the spatiality of the game world in which case it's only a ready-made playground however complex it might be in other respects. In contrast, spatial relations among players are dynamic if the game space can be built or expanded by the players as in *Civilization*.[7] The static and dynamic functional relations among players refer to the functional capabilities of their representations (characters) in and during the game: they can either acquire new qualities and capabilities in the course of the game, or not. One should also make a distinction between functional similarity and dissimilarity of available roles in a game, as whenever there's a team there is usually also a division of labour.

When discussing the third articulation, the relation of game to world, it should be remembered this is not an interpretative or referential question (or if it is then it focuses on the relation between the simulation and the simulated whatever the latter is interpreted to be). Instead of that I take it to be operational and pragmatic. Here the category of static relations implies readymade relations not to be tampered with. This means that the game is every way closed or separated from the rest of the world. There are alternatives to this: causal, spatial, temporal and functional connections could well exceed the confines of a game.[8] The dynamic dimension could then be understood as containing various violations of this default separateness of games.

The second articulation between the player and the game concerns first and foremost the aspect of manipulation or configuring: what relations can be affected, how deeply, for how long, under what conditions and so on. Basically, static relations can only be interpreted but dynamic relations allow manipulation. To continue any further with this, we must study our four types of relation (spatial, temporal, causal, functional) more closely and find suitable subcategories in each of them. That will be the focus of the latter half of this essay.

The static/dynamic opposition could be made more detailed by introducing the cybertextual concept of user function (Aarseth 1997, 64) that could easily be applied to our four major types of temporal, causal, spatial and functional relations. Each one of the latter may potentially be interpreted, explored, configured, or changed permanently with the constraint that at least one of these relations must always be configurable. For example: in *Tetris* the player can only interpret the space or arena,[9] in adventure games the space exists to be explored; in *Civilization* the space can be configured; and in many MUDs you can build permanent new spaces and objects to be shared with other players. Obviously, there are totally irrelevant things too, but they may be important to learn too, as the concealed dividing line between relevance and irrelevance can be an essential part of the game structure.

Relations and properties

Causal relations

Let's say your character is an average U.S. president in a relatively complex environmental world simulation with climate changes. Your task is to represent the complexities of this world in a simple model the presidential puppet can comprehend and act upon, in a word to reduce them to suit his worldview. To prevent the game turning into an orgy of continuous annihilation, there's an extra mechanism for determining what the puppet can and can't do in the game: the central artificial intelligence responsible for running the president is responsive to a stock exchange and the second-by-second fluctuations in the market value of certain lobbying industrial complexes. The point being that in this pompous age of the Internet we could easily design computer games in which real-life or real-world parameters further limit the player's freedom of action.

The underlying question is where to limit or expand the system of causalities and dependencies; they can be networked to the user space too, that is, to a complex of home or office or mobile appliances communicating with each other via Bluetooth. The pokemons on the screen and in your living room will pretty soon be able to team up and steal your credit card numbers to order reinforcements. In a little less nightmarish setting, there's potential for connecting games and toys in a player's PAN (personal area network).

Spatial relations

The spatial dimension could be studied from the perspective of abstract animation as a combination of spatial co-ordinates and durational values of pixels, but that would not be a very useful way to approach movement within the projected spaces. In any case, and in addition to on- and off-screen spaces (all six types of the latter, see Burch 1973, 17), it's also important to pay attention to the uses of both the sonic space (in anticipating visual events, building suspense and surprise, or preparing the player for the next encounter etc.) and the user space.

In some games the player may have to decide or try to decide exactly where some event should take place. In others, that's not possible or even important: the killing can happen everywhere in the arena, and only the rate of occurrence counts. There are at least four important factors affecting the possibilities and constraints of space: positioning, movement (including its freedom, speed and direction), the so-called point of view and the access to information. The latter dimension may have to be divided into interplaying channels, at least one each for audio, visual and textual information. Spatiality is also a matter of perception; one can only wonder why the military paradigm of complete clarity and visibility of targets is so prevalent in computer games. There are countless possibilities for conditioning the player's perceptions by playing with the sharpness of focus, lightning, visibility, distance, angle, transition and various continuity matches common to cinematic and pre-cinematic conventions of visual representation, in the spirit of Noel Burch's parametric cinema (see Burch 1973 and Bordwell 1985, 278–279). But for some reason, I can't blacken my opponent's screen.

Conventions

There are a few curiously infrequently discussed conventions of spatial representation in computer games. They concern reliability, subjectivity and normality. Ask yourself why 2D maps should always be reliable, or first-and third-person POV's compatible, why everything should be represented objectively to a player who is always assumed to be in a normal and not altered perceptual state—and why the space or spatiality in a game is seldom or never self-contradictory. Or why the player can move a virtual camera but doesn't have to deconstruct or reconstruct or peel its multi-layered images. Maybe the reason for these peculiarities is that we are still stuck with defining moving images in terms of pre-digital cinema and its reality-capturing mythology, and with the idea of the playground that can't be manipulated on the fly as all the players are supposed to share it as a neutral field all the time.

Unreliability

In narratives and many other kinds of fiction it is acceptable and sometimes even preferable that users are misled by being given wrong instructions. But in games the deliberate frustration of action seems clearly to be an intolerable option. One might think of unreliable maps giving false and incorrect information about the location of the player or of the objects he's seeking—that's something almost every writer would like to do, and almost every player and game designer to avoid—the explanation for this difference in taste lies perhaps in the ergodic (pseudo) physicality of the game. Or in the difference between two kinds of obstacles or modes: lies and riddles.

Interface

There is also an important connection or at least a functional similarity between computer games and so-called lower forms of cinema, especially the genres that cause or arouse physical reactions in the viewer-spectator, including melodrama (tears), comedy (laughing), horror (fear) and pornography (sexual excitement). Certain simulations, especially those loaded with action to be handled with quick reactions and excellent hand-eye-coordination, often cause physical or physiological reactions, the control of which is in the best interest of the player. In this respect computer games are situated in between physical and non-physical games.

This is also a question of interface as there's no reason why the playing of a game could not also be physically demanding or even exhausting—obviously to achieve the latter goal, we'd need paraphernalia very different from keyboards and joysticks, or the pressure mat of *Dance Dance Revolution*. The relation between the player's psychophysical presence and his or her virtual presence in a game is usually designed to be both control- and consciousness-oriented (another military paradigm). However, there are alternatives to this, like *Brainscore* by Slovenian media artists Darij Kreuh and Davide Grass, where the users' eye movements and brain waves direct audiovisual objects and processes. Fully conscious control is thereby denied, and the performers must stay in a relaxed state of body and mind in order to direct the presentation successfully. *Brainscore* is not a game, but its partly parasympathetic control mechanisms could be (and perhaps already are) transported into the realm of computer games.

Example of temporal relations: the phenomenology of *Tetris*

Temporality can be studied using the same abstract categories as those used for narratives in narratology, since the categories are neither narrative nor gamelike in themselves: order, speed, frequency, duration, simultaneity, and time of the action. These are specifications of both the actions of the player and the events the player encounters and is perhaps able to modify in the course of a game.[10]

Janet Murray's approach to *Tetris* (Murray 1997, 143–144) is an ultimate counter example to this. She's quite content to interpret this Soviet game as "a perfect enactment of the over tasked lives of Americans in the 1990s—of the constant bombardment of tasks that demand our attention and that we must somehow fit into our overcrowded schedules and clear off our desks in order to make room for the next onslaught." It would be equally far beside the point if someone interpreted chess as a perfect American game because there's a constant struggle between hierarchically organized white and black communities, genders are not equal, and there's no health care for the stricken pieces. Of course, there's one crucial difference: after this kind of analysis you'd have no intellectual future in the chess-playing community.

Instead of studying the actual game Murray tries to interpret its supposed content, or better yet, project her favourite content on it; consequently we don't learn anything of the features that make *Tetris* a game. The explanation for this interpretative violence seems to be equally horrid: the determination to find or forge a story at any cost, as games can't be games because if they were, they apparently couldn't be studied at all. In contrast, here's a provisional attempt to apply some key temporal concepts to *Tetris*, probably the most successful abstract computer game ever (Figure 4).

The dominant temporal relation in (computer) games is the one between user time (the actions of the player) and event time (the happenings of the game),[12] whereas in narratives it's between story time (the time of the events told) and discourse time (the time of the telling). Despite possible hybrids the underlying restrictions of temporality remain the same: there's no narrative without story and discourse times and no game without user and event times—everything else is optional.

54

	story time < narratives > discourse time/event time < games > user time	
Order	....	X (random)
Speed	....	X (accelerating)
Frequency (repetition)	....	0
Duration	....	0
Simultaneity	....	X (no simultaneity)
Time of narration/action	....	X (during and after)

Figure 4 Temporal relations in Tetris[11]

The goals and progression of the game

Goals and sub-goals could also be divided into spatial, temporal, causal and functional ones. At least it's usually easy to choose the dominant one of these, whether it's the task of traversing the space, completing something in time, plotting out an enemy, gaining more power and wealth in the game world, or something completely different. In order to understand the progression of a game it is important to study the deictic orientation of the player. Keir Elam's dramatological model divides this into spatial, temporal, object, person[13] and action deixis with the further specification between present and absent entities and processes (Elam 1980, 185–191). It might help us to see the difference between two game dynamics: the one between present and absent elements, and the other between present components.

Roger Caillois argued there are four broad types of games, those of agon (competition), alea (chance), mimicry, and ilynx (vertigo). In all these categories there's also an inherent division into paidia and ludus, similar to the distinction between play and game. It's only reasonable to suspect we can find different combinations of these eight possibilities distributed among and inscribed into the manipulatable relations of game components. It's also clear these broad types create different expectations and orientations in terms of goals, sub-goals and rules, and in the dynamics of ends and means; for example in ilynx and alea the player is a passive intrigant[14] whereas in agon and mimicry she has to be more active.

Not all of these components go or combine easily with the other elements, which is also the reason to use the concept of the dominant once more. This goes slightly against Caillois' study that excludes certain combinations like agonilynx and mimicry-alea—on the other hand I'm just arguing this is only or mainly a question of level and hierarchy. It should be easy to imagine a scene dominated by competitive orientation containing embedded elements of chance, role-play and vertigo, especially if the latter is taken to mean shocking or perceptually challenging action.

Conclusion

The old and new game components, their dynamic combination and distribution, the registers, the necessary manipulation of temporal, causal, spatial and functional relations and properties not to mention the rules and the goals and the lack of audience should suffice to set games and the gaming situation apart from narrative and drama, and to annihilate for good the discussion of games as stories, narratives or cinema. In this scenario stories are just uninteresting ornaments or gift-wrappings to games, and laying any emphasis on studying these kinds of marketing tools is just a waste of time and energy. It's no wonder gaming mechanisms are suffering from slow or even lethargic states of development, as they are constantly and intentionally confused with narrative or dramatic or cinematic mechanisms.

Finally, one could argue that computer games, literature and drama/theatre are all equally distant from the traditional or non-computer games where there's something at stake like death or some other irrevocable loss. I'm thinking about such all time classics as Russian roulette, certain events, actions and happenings that took place in the Roman arena and Mesoamerican ball courts, and extreme cases and consequences of serious gambling. If these are the roots of computer games too, then we may want to think what to think of possible hybrids of non-computer and computer games (to come via mobile phones and technologies like Bluetooth or X-10). And with thinking I actually mean thinking and not various kinds of moral panic witnessed before with comic books, videos, movies, rap, rock, jazz and other forms of popular culture.

Acknowledgements

I'd like to thank Gonzalo Frasca for getting me interested in ludology or game studies, Espen Aarseth for providing heuristic theory to be exploited and abused, Ragnhild Tronstad for valuable comments and suggestions during the writing process, and Julianne Chatelain for saving my English from myself. Needless to say, mistakes are all mine.

Notes

1 "Curiously", there are no attempts to define games as narratives in Elliott M. Avedon's and Brian Sutton-Smith's classic *The Study of Games* (1971) that contains and compresses a century of Western game studies. The words and contested concepts like narrative, story, drama, or theatre do not come up even in its subject index. So should we believe that suddenly, by the advent of computer games, games turned into narratives? Maybe something happened in the marketing department instead.

2 Gonzalo Frasca divides rules into paidia rules defining how the simulation functions and ludus rules defining the winner or the outcome of a game (Frasca 2001, 9). The concepts of paidia and ludus were coined by Roger Caillois in his classic study of games *Les jeux et les hommes* (see Caillois 1979).

3 Despite occasional references I'll exclude MUDs from consideration in what follows. MUDs and MUD adventure games may very well turn out to contain situations, events and functions too complex to be fully or adequately conceptualised by the scheme presented here, or perhaps within any one traditional scheme, be it narrative, performance, or games. See Tronstad 2001.

4 The distinction between matrixed and non-matrixed performances is based on Michael Kirby's "The New Theatre". For example: "The actor functions within subjective or objective person-place matrices. The musician (♦) is non-matrixed. He attempts to be no one other than himself, nor does he function in a place other than that which physically contains him and the audience." (Kirby 1982, 326) It should also be clear that I'm not reducing theatre here to the most boring theatre of words, as there is a huge continuum and variety of theatre and performance art, and matrixed and non-matrixed performances, between the two extreme positions presented in Figure 2. In other words, the "dramatic" is just an extremely story-oriented form or genre of matrixed performances. Alternatively, we might perhaps construct another continuum from interpretative (theatre) to non-interpretative (performance art) and configurative (games) performances.

5 For more detailed description of events one could apply four cybertextual categories, those of dynamics, determinability, transience and perspective. This would give us 24 basic types of events.

6 On theatrical and real performatives, and performatives turning into constatives in MUD adventures and quests see Tronstad 2001.

7 Alternatively, one could state computer games are usually spatially static in contrast to physical games like soccer and mobile games, where the players constantly change their (physical and spatial) positions to each other.

8 These transgressions could be modelled after gambling, hybrid games, Noah Wardrip-Fruin's *The Impermanence Agent*, or the presidential example coming up later in this article.

9 We should make a distinction between the arena or spatial setting and the operational space it gives to the player. The former is only interpretable in Tetris while the latter changes throughout the game.

10 For more detailed specifications see Eskelinen 2001. There might very well exist other temporal categories worth examining than the six mentioned here. See for example Eskelinen and Koskimaa 2001.

11 Explanation: dotted line = non-existent relation, X = non-manipulatable relation, 0 = manipulatable relation. Discourse time in narratology is similar to event time in ludology. The former could be seen as a series or a combination of individual event times, either fixed or semi-fixed as in print or hypertext narratives or variable as in games. Still, because the time needed to complete a game usually varies considerably from player to player I prefer to call it event time instead of discourse time.

12 See Aarseth 1998b, 31–41.

13 Person (and object) deixis could be combined with Elliott M. Avedon's interaction patterns. See Avedon 1971, 424–425.

14 On intrigants, intrigees and intrigues in adventure games see Aarseth 1997, 97–128.

References

Aarseth, Espen (1997) *Cybertext: Perspectives on Ergodic Literature*. Baltimore: The Johns Hopkins University Press.

Aarseth, Espen (1998a [1995]) "Dataspillets diskurs" in Espen Aarseth (ed.) *Digitalkultur og nettverkskommunikasjon*, 75–98. Bergen: Espen Aarseth.

Aarseth, Espen (1998b) "Aporia and Epiphany in Doom and The Speaking Clock: Temporality in Ergodic Art" in Marie-Laure Ryan (ed.) *Cyberspace Textuality*, 1–14. Bloomington and Indianapolis: University of Indiana Press.

Aarseth, Espen (2001) "Allegories of Space. The Question of Spatiality in Computer Games" in Markku Eskelinen and Raine Koskimaa (eds.) *Cybertext Yearbook 2000*,

152–171. Saarij�rvi: Publications of the Research Centre for Contemporary Culture, University of Jyv�skyl�.

Avedon, Elliott M. (1971) "The Structural Elements of Games" in Elliott M. Avedon and Brian Sutton-Smith (eds.) *The Study of Games*, 419–426. New York: Wiley.

Avedon, Elliott M. and Brian Sutton-Smith (1971) *The Study of Games*. New York: Wiley.

Bolter, Jay David and Richard Grusin (1999) *Remediation. Understanding New Media*. Cambridge, MA: The MIT Press.

Bordwell, David (1984) *Narration in the Fiction Film*. Madison: University of Wisconsin Press.

Burch, Noel (1973 [1969]) *Theory of Film Practice*. Translated by Helen R. Lane. Princeton, NJ: Praeger.

Caillois, Roger (1979 [1958]) *Man, Play, Games*. Translated by Meyer Barash. New York: Schocken Books.

Chatman, Seymour (1978) *Story and Discourse*. Ithaca: Cornell University Press.

Ehrmann, Jacques (1968) "Homo Ludens Revisited" in *Yale French Studies* 41: 38–57.

Elam, Keir (1980) *The Semiotics of Theatre and Drama*. London: Routledge.

Eskelinen, Markku (2001) "Towards Computer Game Studies". Forthcoming in the proceedings of *SIGGRAPH 2001*.

Eskelinen, Markku and Koskimaa, Raine (2001) "Discourse Timer–Towards Temporally Dynamic Texts" in *Dichtung Digital*, June 2001. Available online at http://www.dichtung-digital.de

Frasca, Gonzalo (1998) "Ludology meets Narratology". Available online at http://www.jacaranda.org/frasca/ludology.html

Frasca, Gonzalo (2001) *Videogames of the Oppressed: Videogames as a means for critical thinking and debate*. MA thesis, School of Literature, Communication and Culture, Georgia Institute of Technology. Available online at http://www.jacaranda.org/frasca/thesis

Genette, Gerard (1980 [1972]) *Narrative Discourse*. Translated by Janet E Lewin. Ithaca: Cornell University Press.

Genette, Gerard (1988 [1984]) *Narrative Discourse Revisited*. Translated by Janet E Lewin. Ithaca: Cornell University Press.

Kirby, Michael (1982) "The New Theatre" in Richard Kostelanetz (ed.) *The Avant-Garde Tradition in Literature*, 324–340. Buffalo: Prometheus Books.

Metz, Christian (1974) *Film Language. A Semiotics of Cinema*. New York: Oxford University Press.

Motte, Warren (1995) *Playtexts*. Lincoln & London: University of Nebraska Press.

Murray, Janet (1997) *Hamlet on the Holodeck*. New York: The Free Press.

Parlett, David (1999) *The Oxford History of Board Games*. Oxford and New York: Oxford University Press.

Prince, Gerald (1982) *Narratology*. The Hague: Mouton.

Prince, Gerald (1987) *The Dictionary of Narratology*. Lincoln and London: University of Nebraska Press.

Tronstad, Ragnhild (2001) "Performing the MUD Adventure" in G. Liestoel, A. Morrison, and T. Rasmussen (eds.) *INNOVATIONS -Media, Methods and Theories*. The MIT Press (forthcoming).

Wardrip-Fruin, Noah (1999) *The Impermanence Agent*. Available online at http://www.impermanenceagent.com/agent

4

SIMULATION VERSUS NARRATIVE

Introduction to ludology

Gonzalo Frasca

Source: Mark J. P. Wolf and Bernard Perron (eds), *The Video Game Theory Reader* (New York, NY: Routledge, 2003), pp. 221–235.

Academic video game studies have known an incredible development during the last couple of years. Slowly, academic interest has shifted from the early do-games-induce-violent-behaviors studies toward analyses that acknowledge the relevance of this new medium. Several international conferences on game studies took place in 2001, plus the publication of *Game Studies*, the first peer-reviewed online journal on the field.[1] In 2002 and 2003, the number of conferences and workshops kept growing steadily. After an early start as a subset of digital text studies, video game studies is finding its own academic space. Probably the most promising change comes from a new generation of researchers who grew up with computer games and now are bringing to this new field both their passion and expertise on this form of entertainment.

So far, the traditional—and most popular—research approach from both the industry and the academy has been to consider video games as extensions of drama[2] and narrative.[3] While this notion has been contested (especially by Espen Aarseth[4]) and generated a sometimes passionate debate, the narrative paradigm still prevails. My goal in this essay is to contribute to this discussion by offering more reasons as to why the storytelling model is not only an inaccurate one but also how it limits our understanding of the medium and our ability to create even more compelling games. The central argument I will explore is that, unlike traditional media, video games are not just based on representation but on an alternative semiotical structure known as simulation. Even if simulations and narratives do share some common elements (characters, settings, and events) their mechanics are essentially different. More important, they also offer distinct rhetorical possibilities. Therefore, my strategy will be to explore a particular topic and show how games and narratives provide authors with essentially different tools for conveying their opinions and feelings. In addition to this, I will explore how the concept of authorship fits within two different genres of simulation, *paidia* and *ludus*. In order to accomplish this, it will be necessary to introduce some concepts of ludology, the still-nascent formal discipline of game studies.

What is ludology?

Ludology can be defined as a discipline that studies games in general, and video games in particular. The term is not new and it has been previously used in relation with non-electronic games, particularly among the board gaming community. In 1999, I pointed out the lack of a coherent, formal discipline that dealt with games as one of the reasons why researchers were looking for theoretical tools in literary and film theory and narratology.[5] Since then, the term "ludologist" grew in popularity among the game academic community to describe someone[6] who is against the common assumption that video games should be viewed as extensions of narrative. Personally, I think this is quite a simplification. Of course, we need a better understanding of the elements that games do share with stories, such as characters, settings, and events. Ludology does not disdain this dimension of video games but claims that they are not held together by a narrative structure. Nevertheless, it is important to keep in mind that ludology's ultimate goal is not a capricious attempt to unveil the technical inaccuracy of the narrative paradigm. As a formalist discipline, it should focus on the understanding of its structure and elements—particularly its rules—as well as creating typologies and models for explaining the mechanics of games. However, formalism is not the flavor of the month in these post everything times. Certainly, formal approaches are limited—and ludologists should always keep that in mind—but they are probably the easiest way to uncover the structural differences between stories and games. I personally see this structural approach as a first, necessary step in video game studies, which we will definitively outgrow once it helps us to better grasp the basic characteristics of video games.

Simulation versus representation

Representation is such a powerful and ubiquitous formal mode that it has become transparent to our civilization. For millennia, we have relied on it for both understanding and explaining our realities. This is especially true with a particular form of structuring representation: narrative. Some authors, such as Mark Turner,[7] even state that narrative mechanisms are cognitive structures deeply hard-wired into the human mind. It is because of its omnipresence that it is usually difficult to accept that there is an alternative to representation and narrative: simulation.

Simulation is not a new tool. It has always been present through such common things as toys and games but also through scientific models or cybertexts like the *I-Ching*. However, the potential of simulation has been somehow limited because of a technological problem: it is extremely difficult to model complex systems through cogwheels. Naturally, the invention of the computer changed this situation.

In the late 1990s, Espen Aarseth revolutionized electronic text studies with the following observation: electronic texts can be better understood if they are analyzed as cybernetic systems. He created a typology of texts and showed that hypertext is just one possible dimension of these systemic texts, which he called "cybertexts." Traditional literary theory and semiotics simply could not deal with these texts, adventure games, and textual-based multiuser environments because these works are not just made of sequences of signs but, rather, behave like machines or sign-generators. The reign of representation was academically contested, opening the path for simulation and game studies.

Scientists have traditionally used simulation for explanatory purposes and particularly for predicting the behavior of complex systems. Treatises abound on simulation theory but generally they provide an approach that is too technical and goal-oriented for our task of understanding it as an alternative to representation. What follows is a working definition that I distilled from combining elements of semiotics with several computer simulation theory essays.[8] I removed any references to the computer, since simulation can exist in nonelectronic devices such as traditional toys. This definition is provisory; it does not aim to be exhaustive and it will certainly change as we increase our understanding of simulation semiotics or "simitiocs." Therefore: "to simulate is to model a (source) system through a different system which maintains (for somebody) some of the behaviors of the original system." The key term here is "behavior." Simulation does not simply retain the—generally audiovisual—characteristics of the object but it also includes a model of its behaviors. This model reacts to certain stimuli (input data, pushing buttons, joystick movements), according to a set of conditions.

Traditional media are representational, not simulational. They excel at producing both descriptions of traits and sequences of events (narrative). A photograph of a plane will tell us information about its shape and color, but it will not fly or crash when manipulated. A flight simulator or a simple toy plane are not only signs, but machines that generate signs according to rules that model some of the behaviors of a real plane. A film about a plane landing is a narrative: an observer could interpret it in different ways (i.e., "it's a normal landing" or "it's an emergency landing"), but she cannot manipulate it and influence how the plane will land since film sequences are fixed and unalterable. By contrast, the flight simulator allows the player to perform actions that will modify the behavior of the system in a way that is similar to the behavior of the actual plane.[9] If the player increases the power variable on the simulator, the simulated plane will move faster through the virtual sky on the computer screen. As we will later see, video games are just a particular way of structuring simulation, just like narrative is a form of structuring representation.

To an external observer, the sequence of signs produced by both the film and the simulation could look exactly the same. This is what many supporters of the narrative paradigm fail to understand: their semiotic sequences might be identical, but simulation cannot be understood just through its output.[10] This is absolutely evident to anybody who played a game: the feeling of playing soccer cannot be compared to the one of watching a match. Apparently, this phenomenological explanation is not as evident as it may seem. As Markku Eskelinen argues, "Outside academic theory people are usually excellent at making distinctions between narrative, drama, and games. If I throw a ball at you I don't expect you to drop it and wait until it starts telling stories."[11] This problem might be because we are so used to see the world through narrative lenses that it is hard for us to imagine an alternative. But it may also be true that it is easier to try to apply narratology, which most researchers are already familiar with, than starting from scratch from a whole new approach. Also, because both the public and the media production industry are already extremely proficient in consuming and creating narratives, the temptation to constrain games to this existing channel may be too high. Video games imply an enormous paradigm shift for our culture because they represent the first complex simulational media for the masses.[12] It will probably take several generations for us to fully understand the cultural potential of simulation, but it is currently encouraged from different fields, such as the constructionist school of education and Boalian drama. One of the most interesting cognitive consequences of simulation is its encouragement for decentralized thinking,[13] which may in the long-term contest Mark Turner's claim of a "literary mind" by introducing the possibility of an alternative "simulational" way of thinking.

For several years, I have tried, with mixed success, to expose my nonnarrative theory of games to both researchers and designers by isolating the structural formal differences between the two. In this essay, I will propose a complementary approach based on their rhetoric characteristics. For my argument, I will assume that video games are capable of conveying the ideas and feelings of an author. My claim is that simulations can express messages in ways that narrative simply cannot, and vice versa. Sadly, our current knowledge of simulation rhetoric is extremely limited but I am confident that it will develop in the near future. Interestingly, it may not be through the game industry—that has been quite conservative since the marketing people took over the show, encouraging cloning over originality—but, rather, through *advergames*. *Advergaming* is one of the new buzzwords that are popular among e-marketers. According to *Wired*'s Jargon Watch,[14] an *advergame* is: "A downloadable or Web-based game created solely to enable product placements." I am not fully satisfied with this definition, since it clearly denotes the problems of shifting from a representational paradigm to a representational one. In my opinion, "product placement" is probably the most straightforward and obvious form of *advergaming*. Instead, this genre's key lays in modeling—not simply representing—the product or a related experience in the form of a toy or game. Many *advergames* are still satisfied to show an image of the product or its brand logo within the game instead of trying to convey experiences that are related to what is being sold. While I am a big supporter of the concept of the video game designer as an auteur, and it is true that many of them do use the medium to express their thoughts, their main goal remains to entertain. Advertisers, by contrast, use entertainment as a means but not as an end. What they want is to promote their brands and products and, because of this, they see in games a tool for persuasion. This puts them in an extremely privileged position for realizing that the potential of games is not to tell a story but to simulate: to create an environment for experimentation. An agency can place an ad in a magazine to enumerate the set of gizmos in a new car, but images, sound and text are not enough if they want their audience to be able to play around with them. In such a case, a simulated environment provides an experience that traditional advertising cannot deliver. As *advergaming* grows in popularity, it will hopefully also spread the idea that games may not just be a form of entertainment. Gaming literacy will some day make players aware that games are not free of ideological content and certainly *advergames* will play a role in this education because they have a clear agenda.

Game rhetoric: freedom of speech, freedom of play?

On Friday, April 19, 2002, senior U.S. District Judge Stephen Limbaugh rejected a request against a St. Louis ordinance passed in 2000 that limited the access of minors to video game arcades.[15] According to the Associated Press, Limbaugh reviewed four games and found "no conveyance of ideas, expression, or anything else that could possibly amount to speech. The court finds that video games have more in common with board games and sports than they do with motion pictures." One week later, CBS reported that former wrestler and Minnesota governor Jesse Ventura was considering the use of video games for political propaganda.[16] Obviously, Ventura's campaign committee did regard games as a form of speech. Political video games are not new—a great example is the popularity of amateur anti-Osama online games[17] that were posted after September 11—but until now they have almost always relied on parody. If Ventura had gone through with his proposal,[18] he would have broken into new rhetorical ground, because electoral propaganda is one of the most visible examples of ideological speech.[19] Because of Ventura's status as a pop icon, his games would have probably been related to the action genre (he is supposed to be a tough guy, after all). However, political video games would probably shine with more dynamic, exploratory genres such as real-time strategy or simulators. Simulation has been used, with different degrees of complexity, to showcase urban dynamics (*SimCity*) or South-American dictatorships (*Trópico*).[20] It would not be surprising if in the near future politicians tried to explain their plans on tax or health reform through simulation. As Ted Friedman has pointed out,[21] Marx's *Capital* would make a much better simulator than a film.

Even if *advergames* are likely to be the Petri dish for simulation rhetoric, the example that I will propose is closer to art than to marketing. This is because most advocates of the narrativity of games always compare them to novels, films, or drama. So, I will suggest a topic that has both known success in traditional narrative and is as distant as possible from today's commercial video games: a worker's strike. In the late nineteenth century, Emile Zola wrote *Germinal*,[22] a novel about a strike held by mine workers in the north of France. At the end, the workers are defeated. All their efforts were in vain; their fight was not able to change their miserable work conditions. In the late twentieth century, Ken Loach described in his film *Bread and Roses*[23] a similar story about janitors in Los Angeles. The story ends differently: the janitors are victorious, even if their leader, an illegal immigrant, is deported back to Mexico.

Traditional storytelling normally deals with endings in a binary way. When Zola wrote *Germinal* he faced two options: the strikers could win or lose.[24] He opted for the second one, probably for conveying the idea that the social revolution was going to be a hard task. By contrast, Loach seems more optimistic. He depicts these oppressed janitors who stood up for their rights and were able to obtain better working conditions, even if their leader failed on a personal level. Narrative rhetoric is a well-lubricated tool. As we can see in these two examples, it allows authors to state that even a defeat could mean hope and even victories cannot be attained without losing something. Both storytellers are arguing that change is possible. However, neither of them is telling us to what degree that change is possible. We learn that workers may fail or win, but diegetic media is not able to break its inherent binary structure. Narrative authors or "narrauthors" only have one shot in their gun—a fixed sequence of events.[25] At most, they could write five or six different stories describing strikes, so the reader could make an average and decide the probabilities that workers have to succeed. But traditional narrative media lacks the "feature" of allowing modifications to the stories, even if exceptions happen in oral storytelling and dramatic performances. In such media, it is always possible for an audience to go through several iterations of a story. In a game, going through several sessions is not only a possibility but a requirement of the medium. Games are not isolated experiences: we recognize them as games because we know we can always start over. Certainly, you could play a game only once, but the knowledge and interpretation of simulations requires repetition.

Unlike narrative, simulations are not just made of sequences of events, they also incorporate behavioral rules. Imagine that we designed *Strikeman*, a real-time strategy game in the tradition of Ensemble Studio's *Age of Empires* in which you could play the role of a labor organizer. Your goal would be to have the most workers join your strike and then deal with its organization and implementation. Unlike what would happen in storytelling, the sequence of events in a simulation is never fixed. You can play it dozens of times and things would be different. In one session, the boss could call the police and repress your workers. In another game, you may have to deal with spies infiltrated into your organization or another worker may contest your leadership and try to sabotage your actions. Games always carry a certain degree of indeterminacy that prevents players from knowing the final outcome beforehand. To paraphrase Heraclitus, you never step in the same video game twice.

Let's focus on two characteristics of such a game. First, the result of the strike is in part a consequence of your performance as a labor leader. This may seem obvious—we like to believe that we are responsible of the consequences of our actions—but it is not a feature available in storytelling. After all, as we learned from classical Greek drama, stories and fate go together. No matter how badly literary theorists remind us of the active role of the reader, that train will hit Anna Karenina and Oedipus will kill his father and sleep with his mother. Similarly, the strike in *Germinal* is going to be a failure because the narrauthor decided beforehand that it should be that way. Nevertheless, simulation authors or "simauthors" can also incorporate different degrees of fate (through hard-coded events, cut-scenes, or by manipulating pseudorandom events) into their games. Victory is partly because of the player's performance but other things are beyond her control. The software could randomly slip in constraints (like an infiltrated saboteur), making your goal more difficult to reach. The simauthor always has the final word: she will be able to decide the frequency and degree of events that are beyond the player's control.

Second, imagine that we had a library of different simulations dealing with strikes, designed by different simauthors from different cultures and ideologies. Even assuming that all simulations would incorporate a winning scenario, some would be much difficult than others, depending on how they we reprogrammed. Some might depend more on chance while others would define their outcome based solely on the player's performance. Whoever designs a strike simulator that is extremely hard to play is describing his beliefs regarding social mechanics through the game's rules rather than through events. Simulations provide simauthors with a technique that narrauthors lack. They are not only able to state if social change is possible or not, but they have the chance of expressing how likely they think it may be. This is not just by stating info (for example, "the probability of winning is 93 percent") but, rather, by modeling difficulty. This technique is also transparent: it is well hidden inside the model not as a piece of information but as a rule. Narrative may excel at taking snapshots at particular events but simulation provides us with a rhetorical tool for understanding the big picture.

Aristotle on the holodeck

I previously described stories as being heavily associated with the concept of fate. This idea is the backbone behind the Marxist drama school, developed by Bertolt Brecht and more recently expanded by Augusto Boal. Marxists argue that Aristotelian drama and storytelling neutralize social change because they present reality as an inexorable progression of incidents without room for alterations. Boal's answer to this problem can be found in his corpus of drama techniques, the Theater of the Oppressed,[26] which combines theater with games in order to encourage critical debate over social, political, and personal issues. The forum theater, one of his most popular techniques, reenacts the same play several times by allowing different audience members to get into the stage and take the protagonist's role. This short play always depicts an oppressive situation and the audience is encouraged to participate by improvising possible solutions to the problem that is being staged. Boal's ultimate goal is not to find an actual solution to the crisis— even if sometimes the technique actually accomplishes this—but, rather, to create an environment for debating not just through verbal communication but also through performance. Forum theater perfectly fits the definition of simulation:[27] it models a system (the oppressive situation) through another system (the play).[28]

Video game designers have searched for decades for a way of bringing together the pleasures of stories and "interactivity." As Lev Manovich states, "Interactive narrative remains a holy grail for new media."[29] Brenda Laurel, a long-time advocate of interactive stories' feasibility has recently defined them as "a hypothetical beast in the mythology of computing, an elusive unicorn we can imagine but have yet to capture."[30] Nevertheless, Boal was able to create a non-computer-based environment that combines a high degree of freedom for participants while creating a compelling experience. However, Boal's success is probably due to the fact that he took a different path than the one suggested by Laurel in her now classic *Computers as Theater*. Laurel, as well as most "interactive narrative" supporters, focuses on Aristotelian closure as the source of the user's pleasure. The biggest fallacy of "interactive narrative" is that it pretends to give freedom to the player while maintaining narrative coherence. The pleasure in Boalian drama is given not by its seamless three-act structure but by the opposite: the ability to interrupt and modify it. Simulations are laboratories for experimentation where user action is not only allowed but also required. Coherence from session to session is simply not a requirement in the game world. The gratification for Boalian actors is not the one of the professional actor but rather the one of the child who plays make-believe. The child is constantly adapting his fantasy to different changes, without the grown-up's obsession with closure. Certainly, simulation challenges narrauthors because it takes away their source of power: the ability to make statements through sequences of causes and effects. To use a metaphor, narrauthors "train" their stories so they will always perform in an almost predictable way.[31] By contrast, simauthors "educate" their simulations: they teach them some rules and may have an idea of how they might behave in the future, but they can never be sure of the exact final sequence of events and result. The key trait of simulational media is that it relies on rules: rules that can be manipulated, accepted, rejected, and even contested. Narrauthors have executive power: they deal with particular issues. On the other hand, simauthors behavore more like legislators: they are the ones who craft laws. They do take more authorial risks than narrauthors because they give away part of their control over their work.

Chances are that Aristotle's famous lost book of Poetics was not about video games, but the fact is that Aristotelianism is also present in the world of games. There are different typologies of games, which can generally be useful even if they usually do not comply with the formal rules of scientific taxonomy. Roger Caillois's game categorization of *alea, agôn, ilinx,* and *mimicry* is one of the best known.[32] However, I do not find this classification extremely useful as its groups constantly overlap. Instead, I prefer Caillois's distinction between *paidia* and *ludus*, which describes the difference between "play" and "game."[33] *Paidia* refers to the form of play present in early children (construction kits, games of make-believe, kinetic play) while *ludus* represents games with social rules (chess, soccer, poker). Although Caillois describes these categories through examples, he does not provide a strict definition. It is common to think that *paidia* has no rules, but this is not the case: a child who pretends to be a soldier is following the rule of behaving like a soldier and not as a doctor. In a previous essay, I have suggested[34] that the difference between *paidia* and *ludus* is that the latter incorporates rules that define a winner and a loser, whereas the former does not.

Structurally, *ludus* follows the same three-act rule behind Aristotelian stories. *Ludus* sessions go through a first act in which the rules are acknowledged, a second act in which players perform, and, finally, a third act that concludes the game and draws the line between victors and losers. Accordingly, the same terms that the Marxist drama school uses in its critique of Aristotelian theater could be applied to *ludus*. *Ludus* games provide an "organic whole," a closed product that can only be explored within a secluded set of rules defined by the author. Certainly, just as it happens in narrative, the reader/player is free to participate within those limits and this is where the pleasure of reading/playing resides. Even so, *ludus* remains ideologically too attached to the idea of a centralized author. By contrast, *paidia* games are more "open-ended" than their *ludus* counterparts.

In both drama and games, the Aristotelian/*ludus* approaches are definitively the most widely popular and perfected. We are all familiar with "Hollywood endings" and the generally manicheist philosophy behind industrialized narratives. In a similar way, *ludus* provides us with two possible endings: winning and losing. The popularity of this formula is almost surely because of the simplicity of its binary structure. However, this is also its most important limitation. Certainly, *ludus* works great within worlds built around dichotomies. This explains, in part, why current computer games have so much trouble in trying to escape from the fantasy and science-fiction realms. In other words, the binary logic found in *ludus* stands out when delivering games set in fairy-tale-like environments, where things are generally black or white. When you move onto other topics such as human relationships, suddenly distinctions are not so clear-cut. Only *paidia*, with its fuzzier logic and its scope beyond winners and losers, can provide an environment for games to grow in their scope and artistry.

The choice between *paidia* and *ludus* structures is ideologically essential for a simauthor because both carry different agendas. The simulated world in *ludus* games seems more coherent because the player's goals are clear: you must do X in order to reach Y and therefore become a winner. This implies that Y is a desired objective and therefore it is morally charged. Saving the world, rescuing a princess or destroying the alien menace are all classic examples of *ludus* goals. By stating a rule that defines a winning scenario, the simauthor is claiming that these goals are preferable to their opposite (letting the world crumble apart, leaving the princess behind, and sharing our living space with the aliens). *Ludus* is the simulational structure of choice for modernist simauthors: these designers have moral certitudes (Mario is good, the monsters are bad). Clearly defined goals do not generally leave much room neither for doubts nor for contesting that particular objective. Not surprisingly, all military games are *ludus* because

67

they do not admit options that break its binary logic (friend or foe, dead or alive, with us or against us). Based on this, it would seem that *paidia* is a less modernist technique aimed at designers who have more doubts than certitudes. Well, this is only partly true. Any *paidia* game, such as *Sim City*, leaves its main goal up to the player who can build any kind of city she wants (the biggest, the most ecological, the prettiest, etc.). In other words, *SimCity* is not necessarily forcing players to model their cities to resemble New York, Tokyo, or Paris. However, even if the designer left out a winning scenario (or a desirable urban structure) ideology is not just conveyed through goal rules. A more subtle—and therefore more persuasive—way to accomplish this is through what I will call "manipulation rules." These rules are opposed to goal rules in that they do not imply a winning scenario. The following is a list of manipulation rules from different games: "you cannot touch the ball with your hands unless you are the goalkeeper" (soccer); "pawns can only move forward" (chess); "fruits will give you extra score" (*Ms. Pac-Man*). As all simulations are constrained, limited approaches to (real or fictional) systems, designers have a limited amount of manipulation rules. In the *SimCity* example, the designer could convey his ideology by adding or leaving out manipulation rules that deal with, say, public transportation, racial issues, or ecology. In other media, such as cinema, we have learned that it is essential to discern between what is shown on the screen and what is being left out. In the realm of simulation, things are more complex: it is about which rules are included in the model and how they are implemented. For example, films can be analyzed on how they portray certain minority groups. A game like *The Sims* does showcase characters from different races, genders, and ages (you can even get a tool to design your own character, selecting from different body structures and skin colors). However, the way that *The Sims*'s designers dealt with gay couples was not just through representation (for example, by allowing players to put gay banners on their yards), they also decided to build a rule about it. In this game, same-gender relationships are possible. In other words, homosexuality is really an option for the players and it is included in the simulation's model. However, we could perfectly imagine a conservative game where the designers would have ruled out same-gender relationships. Homosexuality is not the goal of *The Sims*, just a possibility. By incorporating this rule, the designers are showing tolerance towards this sexual option but we could hardly say that they are encouraging it (in order to proselytize, for example, a rewarding *ludus* rule could be implemented where players could be rewarded by their homosexual behavior).

So far, we can distinguish three different ideological levels in simulations that can be manipulated in order to convey ideology. The first level is the one that simulation shares with narrative and deals with representation and events. This includes the characteristics of objects and characters, backgrounds, settings, and cut scenes. For example, a simple switch of character skins could turn *Quake* into a deathmatch between Israelis and Palestinians. (Actually, there is a pro-Palestinian first-person shooter, *Under Ash*, available at <http://www.underash.net/emessage.htm>). Here the rules of the game remain unchanged: only the characters and settings are modified. However, on an ideological level, this game completely differs from the original.

The second level is the one of manipulation rules: what the player is able to do within the model. In same cases, certain manipulation rules state a possibility. In others, they are necessary to attain a level three goal. For example, in *Grand Theft Auto III* (*GTA III*) it is possible to shoot prostitutes in order to get money after having sex with them. Even if many people were disgusted by this possibility, it is essential to point out that this is not the goal of the game. Rhetorically, a game where you may kill sexworkers is very different from a game where you must kill them in order to win. Most *paidia* games work within this level.

The third level is the one of goal rules: what the player must do in order to win. It deals with what the author states as mandatory within the simulation. While it is possible to have fun in *Super Mario* without rescuing the princess, the player cannot win unless he accomplishes this goal. Games with goal rules provide both a personal and social reward: whoever reaches the end of a game will be recognized as a good player. On this third level, simauthors funnel through all the available actions and encourage some that will lead to the winning scenario.

At first, it would seem that these three levels are enough for a basic description of how ideology works within simulation. However, there is at least one extra one. The fourth ideological level is the one that deals with meta-rules. Certain simauthors do allow players to contest the model's built in assumption by giving different degrees of freedom to partially modify the three levels that I have just described. A meta-rule is a rule that states how rules can be changed. Many games include editors that allow players to build "mods" or modified versions of the original games. Other games are open-source and can be changed on their source code level. Some only allow you to do cosmetic changes while others permit more drastic modifications. Still, it is important to keep in mind that meta-rules do not imply neither the death of the author nor the player's freedom. Indeed, meta-rules are rules and as such they are present in the game because the author wanted them to be there. In other words, it is the author's decision to make the source code or editing tools available to the player. Certainly, a simauthor who allows her public to alter her work is quite different from the traditional idea that we have of the role of the narrauthor. Nevertheless, with or without meta-rules, the simauthor always has the final word and remains in charge because total player freedom is impossible since it would imply that no rules are unchangeable and therefore the game could literally become anything.

I have just suggested a typology of simulation rules (manipulation rules, goal rules, and meta-rules) that can help us to better understand how the designer's agenda can slip into the game's inner laws. However, this typology is not exhaustive and could certainly be expanded (for example, by analyzing the ideological role of the interface rules or by examining the nuances between games which have both winning and losing scenarios and those where you can only lose). I am convinced that it will take us a long time to grasp the potential of simulation as opposed to narrative, mainly because we are so familiar and proficient with the latter. Simulation contests our notions of authorship and also the boundaries that we are used to apply to works of art.

In the rules of the rose is the rose

In his poem "The Golem,"[35] Borges tells the story of the rabbi of Prague who, after long permutations, is able to find the key word that holds the secret of life. A monster, the Golem, is created, but the process involves more than magic words. Borges describes how the rabbi modeled his puppet and then trained him, like an ancient virtual pet, into the mysteries "of the Letters, Time, and Space." The Golem learned very much like an expert system. But in this pessimistic view (similar to them myth of Frankenstein) this "simulacrum," as Borges calls it, fails to reproduce the human soul. Certainly, simulation has its limitations, just like representation. Simulation is only an approximation and even if narrauthors may feel threatened by it, it does not announce the end of representation: it is an alternative, not a replacement.[36]

For the first time in history, humanity has found in the computer the natural medium for modeling reality and fiction. Simulation, in both its *paidia* and *ludus* flavors, provides a different—not necessarily better—environment for expressing the way we see the world. It is common to contrast narrative and drama because the former is the form of the past, of what cannot be changed, while the latter unfolds in present time. To take the analogy further, simulation is the form of the future. It does not deal with what happened or is happening, but with what may happen. Unlike narrative and drama, its essence lays on a basic assumption: change is possible. It is up to both game designers and game players to keep simulation as a form of entertainment or to turn it into a subversive way of contesting the inalterability of our lives.

Representation and narrative may still hold a lot of tricks in their bags, but the promise of the yet unexplored field of simulation and games is so vast and appealing that some of us can hardly wait to start experimenting with it. Whoever slowly walked back home after buying a long-awaited video game knows exactly the kind of excitement that I am talking about.

Notes

1 See <www.gamestudies.org>.
2 Brenda Laurel, *Computers as Theater* (London: Addison Wesley, 1993).
3 Janet H. Murray, *Hamlet on the Holodeck: The Future of Narrative in Cyberspace* (New York: Free Press, 1997).
4 Espen Aarseth, *Cybertext. Perspectives on Ergodic Literature* (Baltimore: Johns Hopkins, 1997).
5 Gonzalo Frasca, "Ludologia kohtaa narratologian," *Parnasso* 3 (1999), 365–371. Also published as "Ludology Meets Narratology: Similitudes and Differences between (Video) Games and Narrative." Available online at <http://www.ludology.org>.
6 Particularly part of the *Game Studies* journal crew, including Espen Aarseth, Markku Eskelinen, Jesper Juul, Aki Järvinen, and myself, among others.

7 Mark Turner, *The Literary Mind* (Oxford: Oxford University Press, 1998).

8 Gonzalo Frasca, *Videogames of the Oppressed: Videogames as a Means for Critical Thinking and Debate* (Master's thesis, Georgia Institute of Technology, 2001). Available online at <http://www.ludology.org>.

9 The accuracy of the simulated model, just as it happens in traditional representation, depends on the observer. A simple flight simulator could be very sophisticated for an amateur but dismissed as simplistic by an expert pilot.

10 Espen Aarseth, *Cybertext. Perspectives on Ergodic Literature.*

11 Markku Eskelinen, "The Gaming Situation," *Game Studies* 1, No. 1 (July 2001). Available online at <http://www.gamestudies.org/0101/eskelinen/>.

12 Toys and games (particularly board games) are indeed previous examples of simulational media. However, their models cannot match the complexity of the ones generated with computers.

13 Mitchell Resnick, *Turtles, Termites, and Traffic Jams* (Cambridge, MA: MIT Press, 2001).

14 See <http://www.wired.com/wired/archive/9.10/mustread_pr.html>.

15 "St. Louis County's regulations on video games upheld," *The Nando Times* (April 25, 2002). Available online at <http://www.nando.com/technology/story/379154p-3030283c.html>.

16 Ashley H. Grant, "Jesse "Video Game" Ventura," *CBS News.com*, April 26, 2002. Available online at <http://www.cbsnews.com/stories/2002/04/26/politics/ main507378.shtml>.

17 For a collection of Osama games, see <http://www.newgrounds.com/collections.osama. html>. While political games have not yet caught massive attention, games based on news and political events are also a great field for experimenting with game rhetoric. Personally, I especially enjoy the challenges created by this new genre-which I propose to call *newsgaming* that combines the characteristics of political cartoons with video games.

18 Ventura later decided he would not run for reelection, so we may never see his political video games.

19 The closest antecedent would be Augusto Boal's use of his game/theatrical techniques—which are nothing but computer-less simulations—for his political campaign as a legislator in Rio de Janeiro. For more information on this unique and fascinating project, see Augusto Boal, *Legislative Theater* (London: Routledge, 1999).

20 While this simulation is definitively a parody, its extreme use of cliches and simplification are a clear example of a colonialist attitude in video game design. Having grown up myself during a dictatorship in Uruguay, I find the game insulting. I would not object to a simulation that dealt with issues such as torture or political imprisonment if it aimed at understanding politics and sociology. In this case, however, it is simply used for entertainment, which is nothing short of disgusting. Alas, I guess South American oppressed are not yet a powerful lobby in the land of political-correctness.

21 Ted Friedman, "The Semiotics of Sim City," *First Monday* 4 (1999). Available online at <http://www.firstmonday.dk/issues/issue4_4/friedman/>.

22 Émile Zola, *Germinal* (Paris: Hatier, 2001).

23 Ken Loach, *Bread and Roses* (Studio Home Entertainment, 2001).

24 It would be possible for the author to create an "open" ending that would rely on the reader's imagination to decide what happened to the strikers. But again, it is the author and not the reader who ultimately decides the use of this form of ending.

25 The fixed sequence that I am referring to is the one of the actual events. The events as told can be rearranged in nonlinear ways through techniques such as flash-forwards and flashbacks. This is the difference between story and discourse, a distinction widely accepted in narratology.

26 Augusto Boal, *The Theater of the Oppressed* (New York: TCG, 1998).

27 Boal even describes the original forum theater play as a "model" or "antimodel."

28 For a more extensive analysis among Boal's drama, games, and video games, see Frasca, 2001.

29 See <http://www.pause-effect.com/reviews.html>.
30 Brenda Laurel, *Utopian Entrepreneur* (Cambridge, MA: MIT Press, 2001), 72.
31 Again, while the reader's interpretation is not predictable, the mechanics of the narration remain inalterable.
32 Roger Caillois, *Les jeux et les hommes: Le masque et le vertige* (Paris: Gallimard, 1967).
33 Unlike English, French and Spanish only have one term for referring to both "play" and "game." Nevertheless, I still use Caillois's terms, because of the different meanings that English attributes to "play," which can both be a noun or a verb.
34 Gonzalo Frasca, "Ludologia kohtaa narratologian."
35 Jorge Luis Borges, *Ficciones* (Buenos Aires: Emecé, 1971).
36 Actually, I have suggested in my work *Videogames of the Oppressed* (following Aarseth's ideas) that simulation and representation only differ in a matter of degree. But for the sake of clarity during these early days of ludology, it may be safer to consider them as different.

Bibliography

Aarseth, Espen. *Cybertext. Perspectives on Ergodic Literature.* Baltimore and London: The Johns Hopkins University Press, 1997.

Boal, Augusto. *Legislative Theater.* London: Routledge, 1999.

——. *The Theater of the Oppressed.* New York: TCG, 1998.

Borges, Jorge Luis. *Ficciones.* Buenos Aires: Emecé, 1971.

Bread and Roses. Directed by Ken Loach, Studio Home Entertainment, 2001.

Caillois, Roger. *Les jeux et les hommes. Le masque et le vertige.* Paris: Nrf Gallimard, 1958. Other editions: Paris: Gallimard, 1967; *Man, Play, and Games.* Translated by Meyer Barash. New York: Schocken Books, 1979. Polish edition: *Gry i ludzie.* Translated by Anna Tatarkiewicz and Maria Zurowska. Warszawa: Volumen, 1997.

Eskelinen, Markku. "The Gaming Situation," *Game Studies* 1, No. 1 (July 2001). Available online at <http://www.gamestudies.org/0101/eskelinen.html>.

Frasca, Gonzalo. "Ludologia kohtaa narratologian." *Parnasso* 3 (1999), 365–371. Also published as "Ludology Meets Narratology: Similitudes and Differences between (Video)Games and Narrative." Available online at <http://www.ludology.org>.

——. *Videogames of the Oppressed: Videogames as a Means for Critical Thinking and Debate.* Master's thesis, Georgia Institute of Technology, 2001.

Friedman, Ted. "The Semiotics of Sim City." *First Monday* 4 (1999). Available online at <http://www. firstmonday.dk/issues/issue4_4/friedman/>.

Grant, Ashley H. "Jesse 'Video Game' Ventura." *CBS News.com*, April 26, 2002. Available online at <http://www.cbsnews.com/stories/2002/04/26/politics/main507378.shtml>.

Laurel, Brenda. *Utopian Entrepreneur.* Cambridge, MA: MIT Press, 2001.

——. *Computers as Theater.* London: Addison Wesley, 1993.

Murray, Janet H. *Hamlet on the Holodeck: The Future of Narrative in Cyberspace.* Cambridge, MA: MIT Press, 1997. [Other editions: New York: Free Press, 1997; and Cambridge, MA: MIT Press, 1998.]

Nakamura, Lisa. *Cybertypes: Race, Ethnicity and Identity on the Internet.* New York: Routledge, 2002.

Resnick, Mitchell. *Turtles, Termites, and Traffic Jams.* Cambridge, MA: MIT Press, 2001.

"St. Louis County's regulations on video games upheld." *The Nando Times*, April 25, 2002. Available online at <http://www.nando.com/technology/story/379154p-3030283c.html>.

Turner, Mark. *The Literary Mind.* Oxford: Oxford University Press, 1998.

Zola, Émile. *Germinal.* Paris: Hatier, 2001.

5

GAMES TELLING STORIES?

A brief note on games and narratives[1]

Jesper Juul

Source: Joost Raessens and Jeffrey Goldstein (eds), *Handbook of Computer Game Studies* (Cambridge, MA: The MIT Press, 2005), pp. 219–226.

Introduction

As questions go, this is not a bad one: Do games tell stories? Answering this should tell us both *how* to study games and *who* should study them. The affirmative answer suggests that games are easily studied from within existing paradigms. The negative implies that we must start afresh.

But the answer depends, of course, on how you define any of the words involved. In this article, I will be examining some of the different ways to discuss this. Lest this turns into a battle of words (i.e. who has the right to define "narrative"), my agenda is not to save or protect any specific term, the basic point of this article is rather that we should allow ourselves to make distinctions.

The operation of framing something as something else works by taking some notions of the source domain (narratives) and applying them to the target domain (games). This is not neutral; it emphasises some traits and suppresses others. Unlike this, the act of *comparing* furthers the understanding of differences and similarities, and may bare hidden assumptions.

The article begins by examining some standard arguments *for* games being narrative. There are at least three common arguments: 1) We use narratives for everything. 2) Most games feature narrative introductions and back-stories. 3) Games share some traits with narratives.

The article then explores three important reasons for describing games as being non-narrative: 1) Games are not part of the narrative media ecology formed by movies, novels, and theatre. 2) Time in games works differently than in narratives. 3) The relation between the reader/viewer and the story world is different than the relation between the player and the game world.

The article works with fairly traditional definitions of stories and narratives, so as a final point I will consider whether various experimental narratives of the 20th century can in some reconcile games and narratives.

Telling stories

Everything is narrative/everything can be presented as narratives

The first argument is a compelling one, as it promises a kind of holistic view of the world: Since we use narratives to make sense of our lives, to process information, and since we can tell stories about a game we have played, no genre or form can be *outside* the narrative.

The problem is that this really is an *a priori* argument. Narratives may be fundamental to human thought, but this does not mean that everything *should* be described in narrative terms. And that something can be presented in narrative form does not mean that it *is* narrative.

Ideal stories/back-stories

A more interesting argument centres on the fact that most games have a story written on the package, in the manual, or in intro-sequences, placing the player's playing in the context of a larger story (back-story), and/or creating an ideal story that the player has to realise:

Space Invaders (Taito 1977)

If we play *Space Invaders* (Taito 1977), we are presented with an ideal story that we have to realise using skill. A prehistory is suggested in *Invaders*: An invasion presupposes a situation before the invasion. It is clear from the science fiction we know that these aliens are evil and should be chased away. So the title suggests a simple structure with a positive state broken by an external evil force. It is the role of the player to recreate this original positive state. This is, of course, a sequence often found in folk tales: An initial state, an overturning of this state, and a restoration of the state.

But it works in a different way: If we *play* Space Invaders, we find that we cannot actually restore the initial state; we cannot win since every wave of aliens is followed by another. As players we are fighting to *realise* an ideal sequence of events, but the actual playing is not this sequence.

74

Most modern, single player non-arcade games such as *Half-Life* (Valve software 1998) actually lets you complete the game: through countless saves and reloads it is possible to realise the ideal sequence that Half-life defines. Obviously, only a microscopic fraction of the play sessions actually follow the ideal path, but Half-Life does succeed in presenting a fixed sequence of events that the player can then afterwards retell.[2] This means that some games *use* narratives for some purposes.

Similarities

The above Space Invaders example also means that games share some traits with narratives: Many games feature reversals such as movements from a lack to the lack being resolved. Jens F. Jensen has used this trait of Space Invaders to argue that computer games, while being deviant, are narratives (1988).

Additionally, many games have quest structures, and most computer games have protagonists (though this is less common in non-electronic games). As Janet Murray suggests in *Hamlet on the Holodeck*, such similarities would indicate that there is a promising future for digital storytelling and interactive narratives, that games and narratives are not very far apart.

It is also an oft-repeated but problematic point that game sessions are experienced linearly, just like narratives. (See Aarseth 1997, p.2.) I will return to this but briefly note that this idea ignores the player's experience of being an active participant—this experience is so strong that most people will involuntarily change bodily position when encountering interactivity, from the lean backward position of narratives to the lean forward position of games. And playing a game includes the awareness that the game session is just one out of many possible to be had from *this game*.

Is this it?

It is thus possible, in different ways, to view games as being in some way connected to narratives, but does this really answer the opening question? The above points would indicate that games and narratives do not live in different worlds, but can in some ways work together: A narrative may be used for telling the player what to do or as rewards for playing. Games may spawn narratives that a player can use to tell others of what went on in a game session. Games and narratives can on some points be said to have similar traits. This does mean that the strong position of claiming games and narratives to be *completely* unrelated (my own text, Juul 1999 is a good example) is untenable.

But we also have to look at differences.

The problem of translation

I will now use some narrative theory in an operation for which it was not intended. The basic problem of *the narrative* is the fact that a narrative can never be viewed independently, *an sich*. We can never see the story itself; we can only see it through another medium like oral storytelling, novels, and movies. The classical argument for the existence of narratives is then the fact that a story can be translated from one medium to another:

> This transposability of the story is the strongest reason for arguing that narratives are indeed structures independent of any medium. (Chatman 1978, p.20)

Correspondingly, Peter Brooks says:

> Narrative may be a special ability or competence that [. . .] when mastered, allows us to summarise and retransmit narratives in other words and other languages, to transfer them into other media, while remaining recognisably faithful to the original narrative structure and message. (Brooks 1984, pp.3–4)

And this may seem somewhat unproblematic; we can never get everything between media, but at least something seems to get transported from medium to medium. A recounting of Pride and Prejudice the movie will be recognisable to somebody who has read the book.

Translating what?

This brings us to the problem of what we actually mean by saying that something can be translated from one medium to another. In a probably slightly limited view of narratives, narratives can be split into a level of discourse (the telling of the story) and the story (the story told). The story-part can then be split into two parts, *existents* (actors and settings) and *events* (actions and happenings). (Chatman, p.19) A story can then be recognised by having the same existents (with the same names) and the same events; this is what we usually mean by talking of "the same story".

This can be used the other way, as a test of whether the computer game is a narrative medium: If the computer game is a narrative medium, stories from other media must be retellable in computer games, and computer games must be retellable in other media. On a superficial level, this seems straightforward since many commercial movies are repackaged as games, Star Wars is an obvious example. The other way around, games transferred into movies are less common, but examples include Mario Brothers, Mortal Kombat, and Tomb Raider. Upon further examination, we will find the situation to be much more complex:

From movie to game: Star Wars

The arcade game *Star Wars* (Atari 1983) is based on the George Lucas movie of the same name (1977). In *the movie* Star Wars, an army of rebels fight a heroic battle against the evil galactic empire. The dramatic peak of the movie is when the rebel army and the protagonist *Luke Skywalker* must attack the evil empire's new weapon *the death star*. The Star Wars game is in three phases, in all of which the player controls a spaceship from the inside, presumably as Luke Skywalker. The first phase takes place in space, where we fight hostile spacecraft. The second phase is on the death star, fighting different objects on the death star surface. In the third phase we fly through a tunnel in the death star to attack an exhaust port. This makes the death star explode. First phase corresponds to an in-movie battle before Luke flies to the death star—except that the rebel fleet is absent. Second phase has no clear correlate in the movie. The third phase corresponds to a scene in the movie—again with the rebel fleet being absent. If you complete the mission, the death star explodes. So the game copies a small part of the movie.

Star Wars (Atari 1983)

The primary thing that encourages the player to connect game and movie is the title "Star Wars" on the machine and on the screen. If we imagine the title removed from the game, the connection would not be at all obvious. It would be a game where one should hit an "exhaust port" (or simply a square), and the player could note a similarity with a scene in Star Wars, but you would not be able to reconstruct the events in the movie from the game. The prehistory is missing, the rest of the movie, all personal relations. Possibly we are even missing the understanding that we are fighting a death star (whatever that is). Finally the most obvious: If you do not complete the mission, this is unlike the movie; if you complete the mission, another death star appears—which is also unlike the movie.

Thus, Star Wars the game can not be said to contain a narrative that can be recognised from Star Wars the movie: Most characters from the movie are missing, and the few events that are included in the game have become simulations where the player can either win or fail. The same thing goes for the second batch of Star Wars games. *Star Wars: Racer* (Lucasarts 1999) features the race sequence of *Star Wars: Episode I* (Lucas 1999), but only that.[3]

From game to story

I will only briefly be covering game-story translations, since they are fairly uncommon. If we look at the Mortal Kombat (Midway games 1993) game, it is a fighting game (beat'em'up) where different opponents (humans or computer players) battle in an arena. It is thus a dynamic system that allows many different people to interact with many different outcomes. The Mortal Kombat movie (Anderson 1995) is not a dynamic system, but a story with a specific set of characters entering a Mortal Kombat game and playing through with specific outcomes. The fairly non-descript game characters and open player positions become more detailed movie characters; the simulation is converted into specific events.

Correspondingly, if we recount a game of chess, our playing of the entire Half-Life game or a multi player game of Starcraft, the existents and events will be transferred, but not the dynamic systems.[4] Our retelling will not be a game, and in fact much of the vast journey that it takes to complete Half-life would be excruciatingly dull if retold in any detail.

The concept of existents is best suited for physical games, where the number of manipulable elements is, at least in principle, finite. Problem is that programs are basically existent-creating machines: Computer games allow for the easy production of infinite numbers of existents, many action games in fact come with a infinite number of existents in the form of opponents. The other problem with the concept of existents is that it in itself does not specify what attributes of the existent are important, whereas game rules feature a strict hierarchy of important and non-important features—Erving Goffman calls this the "rules of irrelevance". (Goffman, p.19)

We should also note that most modern games feature cut-scenes, i.e. passages where the player cannot do anything but most simply watch events unfolding. Cut-scenes typically come in the form of introductions and scenes when the player has completed part of the game.

It is then possible to describe in a more general way how games get translated into narratives, and how narratives get translated in to games:

A table of narrative–game translations

Movies/Novels etc.	Game
Existent	Existent
	or
	Continuous production of existents (i.e. hordes of opponents)
Event	Event (cut-scene)
	or
	Simulation with multiple outcomes
Sequence of events	Selected events as events or simulations
	or
	Ideal sequence of events that the player has to actualise by mastering the simulations[5]
Character	Character (cut-scene)
	or
	Player position (game)

Note that both directions of the translation leave plenty of room for improvisation and carry many optional operations. In short, games based on movies tend to pick a few select action sequences, which are then simulated in game sequences—as we saw with Star Wars. Character description and development is either ignored or done in cut-scenes (since this is too hard to implement in game form). Working from game to movie, the game is no longer a game, but is rather presented as specific game sessions, played by specific characters, with specific outcomes. The characters also tend to become more developed: Tomb Raider's heroine Lara Croft acquires much more of a past and personality in the Tomb Raider movie.

Time, game, and narrative

> Narrative is a . . . double temporal sequence . . . : There is the time of the thing told and the time of the narrative (the time of the signified and the time of the signifier). This duality not only renders possible all the temporal distortions that are commonplace in narratives (three years of the hero's life summed up in two sentences of a novel or in a few shots of a "frequentative" montage in film, etc.). More basically, it invites us to consider that one of the functions of narrative is to invent one time scheme in terms of another time scheme. (Christian Metz, quoted from Genette 1980, p.33)

In the classical narratological framework, a narrative has two distinct kinds of time, the *story time*, denoting the time of the events told, in their chronological order, and the *discourse time*, denoting the time of the telling of events (in the order in which they are told). To read a novel or watch a movie is to a large extent about reconstructing a story on the basis of the discourse presented.

In a verbal narrative, the grammatical tense will necessarily present a temporal relation between the time of the narration (narrative time) and the events told (story time). Additionally, it is possible to talk of a third time, the reading or viewing time (Genette, p.34). While movies and theatre do not have a grammatical tense to indicate the temporal relations, they still carry a basic sense that even though the viewer is watching a movie, now, or even though the players are on stage performing, the events told are *not* happening *now*.

> In Eisenstein's account there is the sense that the text before us, the play or the film, is the performance of a "prior" story. (Bordwell, p.15)

We cannot necessarily describe this as a specific temporal relation (hence "prior") but there is a fundamental distance between the story time and discourse time. As Christian Metz notes in the above quote, narratives rely heavily on this distance or non-identity between the events and the presentation of these events.

Time in the computer game

Doom II, level 2

If we then play an action-based computer game like *Doom II* (ID Software 1994), it is hard to find a distance between story time, narrative time, and reading/viewing time. We may find a representation, and as a player you try to reconstruct some events from this representation: The blocky graphics can be interpreted so far as the player controls a character, whose facial expression is represented in the bottom centre. On the illustration this person has been cornered by a large pink monster, whose hostile intents are clearly identifiable. Players are attacked by monsters; puzzles must be solved to get to the next level.

It is clear that the events represented cannot be *past* or *prior*, since we as players can influence them. By pressing the CTRL key, we fire the current weapon, which influences the game world. In this way, the game constructs the story time as *synchronous* with narrative time and reading/viewing time: the story time is *now*. Now, not just in the sense that the viewer witnesses events now, but in the sense that the events are *happening* now, and that what comes next is not yet determined.

In an "interactive story" game where the user watches video clips and occasionally makes choices, story time, narrative time, and reading/viewing time will move apart, but when the user can act, they must necessarily implode: it is impossible to influence something that has already happened. This means that *you cannot have interactivity and narration at the same time*. And this means in practice that games almost never perform basic narrative operations like flashback and flash forward.[6] Games are almost always chronological.

This article is not about all the intricacies of time in games (see Juul, forthcoming). Let us simply note that games may also have a speed that is not equal to the playing time—a day & night in the online multi player game EverQuest takes 72 actual minutes to complete, and a game played in 2001 may be labelled as taking place in 1941. But playing a game requires at least points or periods of temporal convergence where the time of the game world and the time of the playing merge—and the player can actually *do* something.

The player and the game

The next major question is less structural and more oriented towards the reader: How does the player and the game interact?

Movies and other stories are largely about humans (or anthropomorphic things) that the viewer/reader identifies with cognitively. It is basically boring to view/read fictions without anthropomorphic actors. This is not true for games. Games with no actors represented on screen have appeared throughout the history of the computer game.[7] Many of these have been extremely popular. An early example is *Missile Command* (Atari 1980), where a number of cities are attacked by missiles that you then have to destroy using rockets from three missile batteries. The player is the not represented on screen as an entity or actor, but only sees the results of his/her actions. It would be possible to create a "job description" for the player—a soldier controlling missiles: a typical hero. It is harder to understand *Tetris* (Pazhitnov 1985), where you must combine a series of falling bricks.

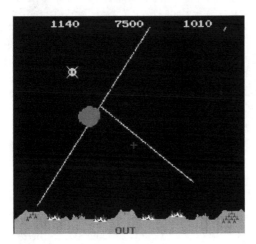

Missile Command (Atari 1980)   *Tetris* (Atari's 1986 version)

Tetris does not have a visible actor either, and it does not seem possible to construct any actor controlling the falling bricks. "Tetris—the movie" does not seem like a viable concept. But Tetris is incredibly popular, and nobody is disputing its status as a computer game.

But how can computer games be abstract and without points of identification, and yet be interesting?—No matter how variable or even absent the protagonist in computer games, the player is always constant. The reader/viewer need an emotional motivation for investing energy in the movie or book; we need a human actant to identify with. This is probably also true for the computer game, only this actant is always present—it is the player. The player is motivated to invest energy in the game because the game evaluates the player's performance. And this is why a game can be much more abstract than a movie or a novel, because games involve the player in a direct way.

This discrepancy raises many issues. In a game, the player works to reach a goal. The thing is then that this goal has to mimic the player's situation. It seems, for example, that a game cannot have the goal that the player should work hard to throw the protagonist under a train.[8] As a player, the goal has to be one that you would conceivably want to work for.[9]

A final argument: the avant-garde fallacy

There is a final counter-argument to the points set forth here: The problem with my description of story as having existents and events, my description of time, my description of the player/game relation as unique could be this: That I am ignoring the experimental narratives of the 20th century, works that do not simply subscribe to the story/discourse duality, activate the reader much more, and do not have a sense of being past or prior. We can explore this with a few select examples.

Jean-Luc Godard's *Pierrot le fou* would serve as an example of a movie where it is hard to construct a coherent story due to numerous temporal skips and distanciations such as the actor's addressing the camera. This foregrounding of the discourse has a sense of immediacy that would make it ripe for a game adaptation—if only we could figure what the game should be about.

And during the creation of *Naked Lunch*, William Burroughs writes the follow explanation to Allen Ginsberg:

> [. . .] the usual novel *has happened.* This novel *is happening.* (Burroughs 1993, p.375)

It may be obvious that the more open a narrative is to interpretation, the more emphasis will be on the reader/viewer's efforts *now*. The difference between the now in narratives and the now in games is that first now concerns the situation where the reader's effort in interpreting obscures the story—the text becomes *all* discourse, and consequently the temporal tensions ease. The now of the game means that story time converge with playing time, *without the story/game world disappearing.*

Games rely on having goals that can be deciphered by the player and something obstructing the player's possibility of reaching the goals. Narratives are basically interpretative, whereas games are formal. Or, in cybertextual terms, stories have an interpretative dominant, whereas games have a configurative dominant. (Eskelinen 2001.) While readers and viewers are clearly more active than some theories have previously assumed, they are active in a different way.

The idea of using experimental narratives to answer the opening question suffers from the problem that the very emphasis on interpretation and ontological instability that would make the narrative more immediate and thus closer to the game, in itself would make a game unplayable.[10]

Conclusion

I would like to repeat that I believe that: 1) The player can tell stories of a game session. 2) Many computer games contain narrative elements, and in many cases the player may play to see a cut-scene or realise a narrative sequence. 3) Games and narratives share some structural traits. Nevertheless, my point is that: 1) Games and stories actually do not translate to each other in the way that novels and movies do. 2) There is an inherent conflict between the *now* of the interaction and the *past* or "*prior*" of the narrative. You can't have narration and interactivity at the same time; there is no such thing as a continuously interactive story. 3) The relations between reader/story and player/game are completely different—the player inhabits a twilight zone where he/she is both an empirical subject outside the game *and* undertakes a role inside the game.

Even if this article has been somewhat structural in its orientation, I would like to state that I think we need to consider games as fairly formal structures that in complex ways spawn and feed player experiences. This means that we cannot afford to ignore the effect of interactivity: The non-determined state of the story/ game world and the active state of the player when playing a game has huge implications for how we perceive games. Even if we were to *play* only a single game session of a hypothetical game and end up performing exactly the same sequence of events that constitute *Hamlet*,[11] we would not have had the same experience as had we *watched* Hamlet performed. We would also not consider the game to be the same object as the play since we would think of the game as an explorable dynamic system that allowed for a multitude of sequences.

The narrative turn of the last 20 years has seen the concept of narrative emerge as a privileged master concept in the description of all aspects of human society and sign-production. Expanding a concept can in many cases be useful, but the expansion process is also one that blurs boundaries and muddles concepts, be this is desirable or not. With any sufficiently broad definition of *x*, everything will be *x*. This rapidly expands the possible uses of a theory but also brings the danger of exhaustion, the kind of exhaustion that eventually closes departments and feeds indifference: Having established that everything is *x*, there is nothing else to do than to repeat the statement.

Using other media as starting points, we may learn many things about the construction of fictive worlds, characters . . . but relying too heavily on existing theories will make us forget what makes games games: Such as rules, goals, player activity, the projection of the player's actions into the game world, the way the game defines the possible actions of the player. It is the unique parts that we need to study now.

These are both descriptive and normative issues. It does not make much sense to describe *everything* in the same terms. It also is quite limiting to suppose that all cultural forms *should* work in the same way. The discussion of games and narratives is a relevant one and I can not hope to close it here. This article has argued for telling the difference.

Notes

1 Parts of this article have previously appeared in a different form in Kritik #135. Copenhagen: Gyldendal 1998.

2 Note that multi player games rarely contain ideal sequences but rather allow the players to replay the same setting with new results—think of Chess or Starcraft. As such they are very far from narratives. On the other hand, the retelling of a game session in a single player game ("and then I . . . and then I . . . and then I . . . ") is less interesting than the retelling of a multi player game since the latter can include intrigues, lies, and deceit between people ("we had agreed to combine forces on the eastern front, but only in the end did I realise that she was actually conspiring with Joe").

3 This also relates to the maturation of the game industry: The first Star Wars movie resulted in one computer game, the latest movie has spawned somewhere around ten different games on different platforms featuring different pieces of the movie or of the Star Wars universe.

4 The other major problem is that games are formalised and rule-bound; and as such much more fit for physics & firearms than existential problems, since the latter are not easily formalised. (See Juul 2000) This means that some events are very, very hard to create as dynamic systems.

5 The ideal sequence is much harder to actualise than the numerous non-ideal sequences—this is what makes it a game.

6 Flash forward is more of a problem than flash back, since describing events in the future means that the player cannot do anything.

7 Traditional board and card games tend to be much more abstract than computer games.

8 The Anna Karenina example was presented by Marie-Laure Ryan (2001).

9 This does not rule out ironies, but all examples I know of work by putting the player in an active position doing things normally considered negative: Destroying houses and killing people in Rampage (Bally Midway 1986), killing pedestrians in Death Race (Exidy 1976) and Carmageddon (Sales Curve Interactive 1997). I know of no games where the goal of the player is to die or be destroyed.

10 This still leaves open numerous unexplored possibilities such as multiple contradictory goals, games of Tetris that cause the destruction of famous artworks in another window on the screen etc. The point is that we should not expect (or demand) that game experiments mimic narrative experiments.

11 Hamlet is actually a poor choice for game adaptation since it (like many narratives) has several scenes where the protagonist is absent, and thus gives the audience more information than is available to the characters. Such common devices of knowledge and suspense are not in any obvious way implementable in a game format where audience and protagonist are the same person.

References

Literature

Aarseth, Espen J.: *Cybertext: Perspectives on Ergodic Literature*. Baltimore & London: Johns Hopkins University Press, 1997.

——: "Aporia and Epiphany in *Doom* and *The Speaking Clock*: The temporality of Ergodic Art" In: Marie-Laure Ryan (ed.): *Cyberspace Textuality: Computer Technology and Literary Theory*. Bloomington: Indiana Press, 1999.

Bordwell, David: *Narration in the Fiction Film*. Wisconsin: The University of Wisconsin Press, 1985.

Brooks, Peter: *Reading for the Plot*. Cambridge, Massachusetts: Harvard University Paperback Edition, 1992 (New York: Knopf, 1984).

Burroughs, William S.: *The letters of William Burroughs 1945–1959*. Ed. by Oliver Harris. London: Penguin Books, 1993.

Chatman, Seymour: *Story and Discourse: Narrative Structure in Fiction and Film*. Ithaca: Cornell University Press, 1978.

Eskelinen, Markku: *The Gaming Situation*. Paper presented at the Digital Arts and Culture conference, Providence April 2001.

Genette, Gerard: *Narrative Discourse*. Ithaca: Cornell University Press, 1980.

Goffman, Erving: *Encounters: Two studies in the Sociology of Interaction*. London: The Penguin Press, 1972 (The Bobbs-Merril Company, Inc. 1961).

Jensen, Jens F.: "Adventures in Computerville: Games, Inter-Action & High Tech Paranoia in Arkadia". In Kultur & Klasse 63. Copenhagen: Medusa 1988.

Juul, Jesper: *A clash between game and narrative*. M.A. Thesis. 1999. http://www.jesperjuul. dk/thesis

——. *What computer games can and can't do*. Paper presented at the Digital Arts and Culture conference, Bergen August 2000. http://www.jesperjuul.dk/text/WCGCACD.html

——. *Game Time* (Forthcoming).

Murray, Janet H.: *Hamlet on the Holodeck: The Future of Narrative in Cyberspace*. New York: The Free Press, 1997.

Ryan, Marie-Laure: *Beyond Myth and Metaphor: The Case of Narrative in Digital Media*. Keynote speech at the Computer Games & Digital Textualities conference, Copenhagen March 2001.

Movies

Paul Anderson: *Mortal Kombat*. 1995.

Jean-Luc Godard: *Pierrot le Fou*. 1965.

Lucas, George: *Star Wars*. 1977

—— *Star Wars: Episode 1*. 1999.

West, Simon: *Tomb Raider*. 2001.

Games

Atari: *Missile Command*. 1980.

—— *Star Wars*. 1983.

—— *Tetris*. 1986.

Bally Midway: *Rampage*. 1986.

Blizzard Entertainment: *Starcraft*. 1998.

Core Design Ltd.: *Tomb Raider*. Eidos Interactive 1996.

Exidy: *Death Race*. 1976.

Lucascarts: *Star Wars: Episode 1: Racer*. Lucascarts 1999.

Midway Games: *Mortal Kombat*. Acclaim 1993.

Pazhitnov, Alexey: *Tetris*. Spectrum Holobyte 1985.

Sales Curve Interactive: *Carmageddon*. PC Game, Interplay 1997.

Taito: *Space Invaders*. 1977.

Valve Software: *Half-life*. Sierra 1998.

Verant Interactive: *EverQuest*. Sony Online Entertainment 1999.

6

INTRODUCTION: VIDEOGAMES AND STORYTELLING

Souvik Mukherjee

Source: *Video Games and Storytelling: Reading Games and Playing Books* (New York, NY: Palgrave MacMillan, 2015), pp. 1–20.

Videogames telling stories: a debate revisited

Imagine being told to 'start this mission by entering the red marker at the Johnson House' (GTA Net, 2015) and then as you, Carl Johnson or CJ, meet your brother Sweet, a rival gang performs an unexpected drive-by shooting and you are to 'hop on a bicycle and follow Sweet, repeatedly tapping X to build up momentum' (GTA Net, 2015). Is this a story, is it another violent episode in a soap opera, or is the reader being mistaken for a member of a real-life criminal gang? The uninitiated reader will probably be having serious doubts about what is happening in the above quote. At first sight, this extract seems to be the story of a certain gangster, Carl Johnson; if it is, then, the story strangely seems to be waiting for the reader to create all the events that follow. You, the player (or reader, one could say), are suddenly thrown into someone else's story and are expected to continue the tale. The part about 'repeatedly tapping "X" to build up momentum' makes it seem even stranger: it is as if, besides all the possibilities described above, there is also some kind of interaction with a machine. Given this hybrid scenario, the reader must be excused if she does not guess that this is an extract from a 'walkthrough', or a set of possible strategies for playing the videogame called *Grand Theft Auto: San Andreas* (Rockstar North, 2004).

Paradoxical as this may sound, this book is about playing stories and reading games. As the extract from the *GTA: San Andreas* walkthrough shows, videogames have started raising questions about their own ludicity (or 'gamelike-ness'; *ludus* is the Latin word for 'game') and about whether this intrinsically involves storytelling. In simple words, this is an analysis of whether videogames tell stories and if so, of how they do this. The relevance of such discussions has increased manifold in recent years: the Entertainment and Software Association (ESA) declares that 'no other sector has experienced the same explosive growth as the computer and videogame industry' (Interactive Games & Entertainment Association, 2013) and almost as if to prove them right, *Grand Theft Auto V* (Rockstar North, 2013) sales reached a billion US dollars in just three days—a global record. With the soaring profits and the burgeoning user-base of the videogame industry, games have now attracted the attention of the researchers from various disciplines the world over and issues relating to gaming culture and the gamer's experience have gained more relevance. Despite the increased research focus, one crucial issue—that of storytelling in videogames, retains its complexity and still remains hotly debated.

The popularity and currency of the issue is clear from the fact that critics from other media have entered the discussion: a good example is the late Roger Ebert's famous (or notorious) assertion that videogames are not art. Other celebrities from the film industry, the directors Steven Spielberg and George Lucas, have commented directly on the storytelling potential of videogames. Lucas claims that the game industry is now beginning to discover how to build characters but that 'by its very nature there cannot be a plot in a game. You can't plot out a football game. You can't plot out feeding Christians to lions. It's not a plot' (Empire Online, 2015). For him, the story is author-driven: 'you are leading the audience along [. . .] if you just let everybody go in and do whatever they want then it's not a story anymore [but] it's simply a game' (Empire Online, 2015). Spielberg, who himself has a past with gaming, feels that the bottleneck is simple: once the game-controller itself is gone, the storytelling experience will improve. He states that the game has 'got to put the player inside the experience, where no matter where you look you're surrounded by a three-dimensional world. And that's the future.' Will Wright, the designer of *The Sims* (Maxis, 2000) games declared in a CNN interview that 'games are not the right medium to tell stories' (Millan, 2011) but conceded that they are about 'story possibilities'.

However, gamers from all over the world think differently. In his recent book on videogames, *A Mind Forever Voyaging*, Dylan Holmes comments: 'Games are bringing something new to the table. As the first widely adopted form of interactive media, video games have served as the testing ground for interactive storytelling techniques' (Holmes, 2012, p. 10). Celebrity game designer and the creator of the *Metal Gear* series, Hideo Kojima, has no illusions about the storytelling potential of games. He believes that 'games are able to achieve something neither movies nor novels can do, it's a unique form of story telling' (Metal Gear Informer, 2012). Intriguingly, Wright states that he does not like playing the *Metal Gear* games that Kojima is famous for (Millan, 2011). Other game designers, however, agree that storytelling is important. When asked about stories in videogames, Tim Schafer, the creator of legendary games such as *Monkey Island* and *Grim Fandango*, states that 'I put story in my games just because I like making up stories. I think it makes the world real and makes the experience more immersive and engaging for the player. Also, the desire to see the story unfold provides a motivation for the player' (Kasavin, 2005). Ragnar Tornquist, designer of *Dreamfall*, adds that although 'all games don't need stories [. . .] the fact is, once you're dealing with quests, characters, worlds, role-playing—and more complex human (or, hey, alien) emotions—then you need to tie everything together with some sort of narrative' (Kasavin, 2005). Adding his influential voice to the argument of the literariness of videogames, is the author Salman Rushdie. Rushdie famously announced that he played videogames during the trauma of his fatwa years. In his recent novel, *Luka and the Fire of Life* (Rushdie, 2010), videogames feature importantly and in an interview about the novel, Rushdie declares: 'There is all kinds of excursions and digressions that you can choose to go on and find many stories to participate in instead of the big story, the macro story. I think that really interests me as a storyteller because I've always thought that one of the things that the Internet and the gaming world permits as a narrative technique is to not tell the story from beginning to end—to tell stories sideways, to give alternative possibilities that the reader can, in a way, choose between' (Rushdie, 2010).

Given the contentiousness of the issue, it is hardly surprising that the academic discussions around gaming as a cultural phenomenon, should have started off by framing themselves around storytelling and that storytelling in videogames continues to provoke critical debates. Writing on his blog 'The Ludologist', eminent game studies academic and one of the pioneering researchers in the area, Jesper Juul gently dismisses Rushdie's comments on storytelling in videogames as being 'a bit on the short side' although he concedes that Rushdie 'understands Rockstar's typical mostly-linear + sandbox game structure' (Juul, 2011). Juul's earlier work clearly delineates a 'clash' between games and narratives and his reservations to Rushdie's claim for storytelling in videogames are understandable if one delves into the history of game studies.

The establishment of Game studies as an academic discipline is a very recent phenomenon and the initial academic responses to seeing videogames as an emergent storytelling medium were markedly polarised into the theoretical camps of the so-called Ludologists and the Narratologists. The Ludologists, mainly academics such as Juul, Espen Aarseth and Markku Eskelinen, argued that although some videogames may have 'artistic ambitions', they are 'fundamentally games' (Aarseth, 2006, p. 45). The so-named Narratologists, such as Janet Murray and Marie-Laure Ryan, argue that videogames are a storytelling medium because they 'promise to reshape the spectrum of narrative expression, not by replacing the novel or the movie but by continuing their timeless bardic work within another framework' (Murray, 1997, p. 10). In 1997, Murray and Aarseth were writing separate pioneering studies on videogames. Both recognised the capacity of videogames to form multicursal structures and also their potential to be recognised as texts (although Aarseth later altered his position somewhat), but their respective approaches were very divergent.

In *Hamlet on the Holodeck*, Murray argued for an approach wherein the 'interactor in digital environments can be the recipient of an externally authored world' (Murray, p. 275) For her, 'To play *Mario Brothers* or *King's Quest* is to open ourselves to the vision of the shaping author in the same way we open ourselves to the author's voice in the novel'. The externally-authored world of the videogame is described by her as a proto-Holodeck. The ambitiousness of Murray's agenda for videogames emerges more clearly in the following assertion:

As the most powerful representational medium yet invented, it should be put to the highest tasks of society. Whether or not we will one day be rewarded with the arrival of the cyberbard, we should hasten to place this new compositional tool as firmly as possible in the hands of the storytellers. (Murray, p. 284)

As the title of her book suggests, she sees the videogame as a step towards achieving literature of the calibre of *Hamlet* in a Holodeck-like electronic media. The Holodeck metaphor itself has major shortcomings when applied to videogames but a deeper exploration of this is reserved for later. This section focuses instead on Murray's intention to place the videogame 'firmly in the hands of storytellers'. Aarseth, for one, poses a strong objection to such a claim.

In his early study of videogames in *Cybertext: Perspectives on Ergodic Literature*, Aarseth describes his attempt to define a 'a *perspective* on all forms of textuality, a way to expand the scope of literary studies to include phenomena that today are perceived as outside of, or marginalised by, the field of literature—or even in opposition to it' (Aarseth, 1997, p. 18). It is understandable that for such an enterprise he needed to develop a different notion of textuality. As he states: 'Instead of defining *text* as a chain of signifiers, as linguists and semioticians do, I use the word for a whole range of phenomena, from short poems to complex computer programs and databases' (Aarseth, 1997, p. 20). Aarseth maintains that the videogame is an 'ergodic' medium, which means that it requires the reader/player to experience the text actively and using skills which go beyond using 'eye movement and the periodic or arbitrary turning of pages' (Aarseth, 1997, p. 2). Surprisingly, however, in a later essay he asserts that 'games are not textual or at least not primarily textual' (Aarseth, 2006, p. 47). Ergodicity, therefore, gets a different connotation and as ergodic media, videogames are not seen as texts *per se* and even less so as stories. Following Aarseth, commentators like Markku Eskelinen, Gonzalo Frasca, Juul and Greg Costikyan came up with a sustained (and often harsh) criticism of attempts to see videogames as storytelling media, which they variously termed 'Narrativist' or 'Narratological'.[1] Their own position came to be known as 'Ludology', a neologism coined by Frasca meaning the 'study of games'. The 'Ludologists' found their most vocal representative in Eskelinen who declaims:

If I throw a ball at you I don't expect you to drop it and wait until it starts telling stories. On the other hand, if and when games and especially videogames are studied and theorised they are almost without exception colonised from the fields of literary, theatre, drama and film studies. (Eskelinen, 2001)

For the firmer adherents of Ludology such as Eskelinen, the videogame needs to be studied in isolation as a game and as nothing else.

Eskelinen attributes a kind of extraneousness to the story—he believes that the story in the computer game is like a prosthesis that simply enhances the marketability and is not essential to the gameplay. Aarseth, predictably, supports this idea: 'the artistic elements are merely supports for what the Finnish avant-garde writer and game theorist Markku Eskelinen (2001) calls "the gaming situation", the gameplay' (Aarseth, 2006, p. 47). In a rather hyperbolic attack on stories in videogames, he states: 'Even the most entertaining of these games, like Warren Spector's *Deus Ex* (1999), contains a clichéd storyline that would make a B-movie writer blush, and characters so wooden that they make *The Flintstones* look like Strindberg' (Aarseth, 2004, p. 51). This statement is, needless to say, rather extreme in its assertiveness and would probably upset many *Deus Ex* fans who enjoy the storyline of *Deus Ex*. In a recent lecture, Aarseth has spoken of the possibility of a 'broken' fictionality in videogames; he still does not agree that videogames tell stories. For the Ludologists, the story is still shown as an extraneous element: for the Ludologists, it is a prosthesis. Lending more weight to the Ludologist position, popular videogame commentator Steven Poole (2000, p. 170), in his book *Trigger Happy*, refers to the back-story of a computer game as the 'meat' of the game, the actual storyline of which is nothing more than a record of steps and jumps. This idea of the prosthesis, however, is itself one that has come under scrutiny. A subsequent section shall explore it in detail.

Game-designers have also started losing patience with the Ludology-Narratology debate because of the polarisation of opinions. As designer Ernest Adams complains:

> There's a lack of a common vocabulary; a lack of a common approach. And there are turf wars. Literary theorists of narrative—'narratologists' believe that narrative is rightly their turf, so it's up to them to decide what *interactive* narrative will be. Theorists of gameplay—'ludologists'— believe that interactive entertainment is *their* turf, and only they can properly decide what interactive narrative will be. (Adams, 2005)

Adams is right in pointing out that the sparring between rival academic camps does not help at all and that such extreme positions, whether they are Murray's holistic claims for narratives in electronic media or the Ludologist argument against it, had game studies critics locked in a decade-long impasse regarding the nature of videogames. Recently, however, Ludologists such as Juul, and those on the narratologist (or rather 'narrativist') camp, such as Marie-Laure Ryan and Celia Pearce, make much more moderate claims than those being made in the late nineties. In *Avatars of Story*, Ryan claims that storytelling in videogames 'must resist the temptation to try to rival the great classics of literature—a temptation that finds its expression in the title of Janet Murray's well-known book *Hamlet on the Holodeck*—and it must learn instead how to customize narrative patterns to the properties of the medium' (Ryan, 2006, p. xviii). She prefers what she calls 'the middle ground' in engaging with the problem. She defines narrative as a cognitive construct that can take a variety of shapes or what she calls 'avatars of story'. Pearce also recognises the importance of the ludic element in games and that '[n]arrative, again, operates at a fundamentally different level in games than it does in other media' (Pearce, 2004). Such a response perhaps complements and extends Henry Jenkins's concept of transmedial storytelling that he defines as being 'based not on individual characters or specific plots but rather complex fictional worlds which can sustain multiple interrelated characters and their stories' (Jenkins, 2007). Jenkins's description fits the complex worlds of the story-based (and especially sandbox-type) videogames well. Pearce's recognition of the importance of the ludic element develops the transmedial angle that Jenkins introduced earlier on.

In a similar more-moderate Ludologist response perspective, Gonzalo Frasca advocates Ludology as another important method besides Narratology in analysing games where the intention is to 'not to replace the narratologic approach, but to complement it' (Frasca, 1999). In a later work, Juul contends that videogames are 'half real' (Juul, 2005, p. 166). He agrees that most videogames 'project a fictional world' and that the fiction is contingent on the game's rules. Juul's shift in the Ludologist position is important—fiction is not defined as a prosthesis as it was in the earlier writings of the Ludologists, including Juul himself. Neither is the game and fiction seen as being mutually exclusive (as in his Masters' thesis, titled 'A Clash between Game and Narrative' claims). Rather surprisingly, Juul does not agree that videogames tell stories; he argues that fiction is different from storytelling. Unlike the 'middle ground' advocated by Ryan, for Juul the story simply does not exist in multiple kinds: he believes that fiction is any kind of imagined world but 'story' is necessarily a fixed sequence of events.

Such a restrictive definition inevitably opens more avenues for more debate and storytelling in videogames remains as contested as ever despite many attempts to resolve the problem. In his recent book, Steven E. Jones echoes other theorists, such as Ian Bogost and Rune Klevjer, in describing the Ludology-Narratology debate as being an exaggeration on both sides and Ludology as a reductive formalism. However, he expresses his sympathy with the Ludologists in recognising the uniqueness of games as a form although he does not wish to 'cut them off from the larger culture' (Jones, 2008, p. 6). In trying to locate the 'meaning' of videogames, Jones concludes that these games are complex social networks and that meaning flows *through* these games and link up to other forms of media such as texts, institutions and groups. One could argue that there is a similarity here with Rushdie's idea of videogames allowing a 'sideways' reading of the text and its multiple alternatives.

As mentioned earlier, though, eminent critics (such as Juul) still do not agree with such a description, often making the claim that videogames are about the experience of playing ('fiction', according to some commentators) than about storytelling. Tom Bissell has a useful rejoinder to such claims:

Too many games insist on telling stories in a manner in which some facility with plot and character is fundamental to—and often even determinative of—successful storytelling. The counterargument to all this is that

91

games such as *Fallout 3* are more about the world in which the game takes place than the story concocted to govern one's progress through it. It is a fair point, especially given how beautifully devastated and hypnotically lonely the world of *Fallout 3* is. But if the world is paramount, why bother with a story at all? Why not simply cut the ribbon on the invented world and let gamers explore it? The answer is that such a game would probably not be very involving. Traps, after all, need bait. In a narrative game, story and world combine to create an experience. (Bissell, 2011, p. 11)

Judging from the many responses, it is hardly surprising that the complexity of videogames makes them difficult to understand, resulting in much controversy and confusion. This is because videogames show up some important characteristics of textuality that are not comprehensible under traditional methods of textual analysis. There are two assumptions related to this, in the main, which need to be noted. The first is that there is a tendency to club all videogames, despite their disparities, as 'the videogame'. The second is, as stated earlier, to consider one aspect of gameplay as a prosthesis of another: this is usually either the storytelling experience as the prosthesis of the pure play experience or the technical (the machine and the code) as a prosthesis of pure play. Bissell, importantly, clarifies that he is discussing a particular type of game (games such as *Fallout 3*) as opposed to a general concept of 'the videogame' and he also believes that stories and the game-world cannot be seen separately when one thinks of gameplay. This book will argue for more: it will aim to analyse the story, the game rules and the experience of the game world as intrinsically linked.

Videogames, supplementarity and assemblages

Before commenting further on textuality in videogames, it will be useful to note the significant growth of interest that the last few decades have seen in redefining textuality itself. Writing in 1971, Roland Barthes was already pointing to the plurality of the text in his essay 'From Work to Text' and even linking the process of play to the text and the reception of the text.[2] In the decades immediately afterwards, the authorship of the text was being contested by thinkers like Barthes, Michel Foucault and the reader-response theorists. Poststructuralist thought, such as that of Jacques Derrida or Gilles Deleuze and Felix Guattari, also carries the notion of the text as being informed by the process of play and as being characterised by multiplicity. By now, of course, all of this is firmly established in Humanities curricula, especially in Literary Studies, Cultural Studies and Film Studies. Recent critical theory is increasingly concerned with technicity, with the need to understand the text as a machinic entity and with how this relates to the reader's own identity.

'Machinic', as used here, has a Deleuzoguattarian connotation. It indicates the relationship between the heterogenous elements in an assemblage and this does not imply that machines are necessarily mechanical. Guattari states that even thought is machinic: the relationship between the machine and the body is fluid and by implication both are intrinsically linked to each other. This also applies to any understanding of the text as being machinic—irrespective of whether the entity in question is the computer-mediated storytelling in videogames or its non-digital counterpart.

Videogames, which embody much more complex levels of all of these aspects within them, can significantly contribute to the analysis of the playful, the multiple and the machinic aspects of texts by taking them beyond their present limitations. Game studies, although growing rapidly as a discipline in its own right as well as part of the burgeoning Digital Humanities programme all over the world, is still relatively a newcomer to the mainstream Humanities debates and there is a need to establish how games 'plug in' into aspects of Humanities studies in ways that are vital.

One of the possible reasons for this is that videogames simultaneously connect to many aspects of cultural and social life, as mentioned above; their multiplicity itself can be a problem for commentators who have hitherto been used to the older linear conceptions of textuality. Secondly, so far, Game studies itself has remained confined to parts of Europe and the US and as such, has not addressed other gaming cultures and their notions of textuality.[3] Games also connect constantly to other narrative media, for example, *S.T.A.L.K.E.R: Shadow of Chernobyl* (GSC Gameworld, 2007) can be seen as an adaptation of the Strugatsky brothers' novel *Roadside Picnic* (Strugatsky and Strugatsky, 1978) and Andrey Tarkovsky's film *Stalker* (Tarkovsky, 1980), as well as to other games (the *Assassin's Creed* series, for example).

The first thing to observe is that if videogames are rapidly gaining importance then this is so because of the multiplicity of networks (socio-cultural, political or economic) to which they connect. In themselves, too, they are characterised by multiplicity: they have a multiplicity of endings and game events take place in multiple points in time. Only by studying the multiple nature of videogames is it possible to gain a fuller understanding of the growing influence of videogames and to envisage their role in the future. To do so, however, the methodology of analysing games in terms of opposing binaries, out of which emerges the assumption that videogames as one core essence, needs to be challenged. Instead of binaries, perhaps a model that considers games as a multiplicity of assemblages would be more appropriate.

The basic problem with exclusive positions such as that of Eskelinen and Poole is that one or other aspect of the videogame is treated as prosthetic. To his and the Ludologists' argument about how storytelling in videogames is prosthetic to the playing experience, Poole also applies the idea of prosthesis to the technological aspect of videogames. Arguing that videogames prostheticise play, Poole maintains that while football can be played with a 'scrunched up newspaper' (p. 281), one needs a computer to play videogames. He states that:

Writing in English, for instance, cannot take place without an alphabet, which is itself a technology [. . .] But in the modern sense of technology

93

as a physical device or gadget, videogames clearly belong in the lineage that was started only by photography, in which the execution of the artwork (or form of entertainment) is impossible without certain complex apparatus. (Poole, p. 174)

Such a statement involves the assumption of a 'pure' form of play/game to which technology can only exist as prosthesis. This is again similar to the Ludologist argument, where narrative is the prosthesis of a 'pure play'.

The fact that many commentators tend to think through the situation in this manner begs further questions. Obviously, what is being assumed here is the watertight categorisation of the various aspects of videogames and the resulting binarisms. Such a conception of the 'pure' has been contested in the playful (non)philosophy of Derrida where the categories themselves are seen 'in play' and the process of play subverts rigid categorisations and displaces centrality. Poole's comment on prosthesis makes a differentiation between the 'modern sense of technology' and the alphabet as a writing technology. Such a differentiation is an oversimplification that has long been refuted by poststructuralist theory. Derrida's own position on writing is outlined in his seminal text, *Of Grammatology* as follows:

We say 'writing' for all that gives rise to an inscription in general, whether it is literal or not and even if what it distributes in space is alien to the order of the voice: cinematography, choreography, of course, but also pictorial, musical, sculptural 'writing' [. . .] And finally, whether it has essential limits or not, the entire field covered by the cybernetic *program* will be the field of writing. (Derrida, 1976, p. 9)

The alphabet and indeed writing, itself, therefore, should not be differentiated from any 'modern sense of technology' simply because all modern technology can be seen as types of inscription or 'writing'. In fact the suffix '-graphy' comes from the Greek *graphein* meaning 'to write'. The computer program (from the Latin *pro gramme*, 'of writing') could then also be deemed a type of writing as, for Derrida, are photography and cinematography. Following Derrida's argument, all technology, being forms of writing, are not prostheses. Instead of being prosthetic, they also inform the (non)centres of each other; at the same time, these elements are separate objects in themselves.

Poole's example of football as not being technology-specific (and therefore, perhaps, embodying 'pure' play) while videogames are entirely dependent on computers, therefore, rests on a questionable notion of technicity. Just as football can be played using 'scrunched up paper' (as well as in a *FIFA* videogame or boardgame), videogames are not limited to the computer. It can be played on the various consoles, mobile phones, handheld devices or even in books which, as some examples in the later chapters will show, sometimes exhibit clear signs of being protovideogames. Whatever be the technology that is being referred to, it must be noted that the relation of the game to the technology is neither extrinsic nor prosthetic.

Derrida offers a nuanced perspective in what he addresses as the 'the *techno-logical condition*'. According to him:

> There is no natural originary body: technology has not simply added itself, from the outside or after the fact, as a foreign body. Or at least this foreign or dangerous supplement is 'originarily' at work and in place in the supposedly ideal interiority of the 'body and soul'. It is indeed at the heart of the heart. (Derrida, 1995, p. 244–5)

Technology has not merely been added after the fact or as a foreign body but is rather, to be found 'at the heart of the heart' of other cultural phenomena; in this case, the game. As described above, this addition is viewed as a threat or as 'foreign or dangerous', described by Derrida as 'that dangerous supplement' (Derrida, 1976, p. 281). For him, this is not restricted to modern technology; even writing is such a 'supplement', as is evident in the following comment:

> If supplementarity is a necessarily indefinite process, writing is the supplement par excellence since it marks the point where the supplement proposes itself as a supplement of the supplement, sign of sign, *taking the place* of a speech already significant: it displaces the *proper* place of a sentence. (Derrida, 1976, p. 281)

As Derrida defines it, the supplement is neither presence nor absence and when one wishes to go from the supplement to the source, one must recognise that there is a supplement at the source itself. In these terms, when narrative, technicity and play are analysed in videogames, 'pure' play cannot exist: the machinic and narrative aspects illustrate the problem of conceiving of any centrality that privileges any of these aspects.

Such a conception clearly challenges the Ludologists' and Poole's positions. If the 'dangerous supplement' is a threat then this is not because of its externality to a 'pure' conception of play; rather the danger applies to traditional conceptions of prosthesis because it is evident now that the story, machine and the game need to be seen as supplements to each other and not prostheses. Throughout this book, supplementarity will be used to describe Derrida's concept of originary presence and interiority, and will provide the framework for rethinking the binaries of game/story, game/machine and story/machine. Revisited in terms of this framework, the debates around the storytelling capabilities of videogames will be seen as being problematic and in some respects, lacking credibility.

To continue with Poole's comparison between his assumed prostheticity of videogames vis-a-vis writing, if writing is the key example of the supplement, then the 'writing' in modern technologies like computer software (such as videogames) clearly also functions in terms of supplementarity. The object-oriented programming approach, developed in the 1980s, is an important example. In traditional approaches to programming there was a clear distinction made between data (the information-base) and program (the process that would operate on the data). This probably created the impression of a prosthetic relationship between the data and the program or between the non-technical element and the technical code. The object-oriented approach dispenses with this division. An object is composed of both the data that describes it and the code that will operate on it. Every object has within itself all that it needs to go about its business: if an object is to be drawn, it will draw itself. It will contain its own code for doing so and will not need to refer to or be acted upon by an external program. The data and the code in the Object-Oriented Program (OOP) therefore are supplementary and are constantly modifying each other. The data gets modified by the code and the new data that is created, in turn, makes the code modify itself. (Biggs, 2004, p. 181)

The OOP approach describes a supplementary relationship between the technical and the non-technical in an area was previously understood solely in terms of the data-program binarism. Surely, then, even in videogame software this binarism is no more the relevant explanation. The code constantly adjusts to the events taking place at the game-level. The analogy, especially the example of the working of the object-oriented program can also be extended to an analysis of the game and the story elements in the computer game. Simply put, the story in the computer game is usually modified by the gameplay and the gameplay has to change constantly to keep pace with the story. So videogames, it can be argued work as a functional whole involving the player (game element), the story engine (story element) and the game engine (technology element). None of these is completely central in the manner the Ludologists tend to imply, although they are characterisable by a certain degree of centrality. The nature of supplementarity, here, is similar to that in object-oriented programs.

Gregory Bateson's answer to the question 'Can machines think?' is a similarly useful entry-point to the analysis of the role of game elements. Although Bateson, of course, is not thinking of videogames per se, his response is important for understanding all artificially intelligent media. According to him: 'what "thinks" and engages in "trial and error" is the man *plus* the computer *plus* the environment. And the lines between man, computer and environment are purely artificial, fictitious lines' (Bateson, 1972, p. 191). In a similar comparison, it can be seen how videogames work as a combination of the player *plus* story *plus* game technology. Bateson's description, here, seems quite close to Derridean supplementarity. Noting the Derridean parallel, Timothy Clark states that, 'Bateson effectively deconstructs at one stroke the distinction between the natural and the technical. [. . .] Deconstruction then upsets received concepts of the human and the technological by affirming their mutually constitutive relation or, paradoxically, their constitutive disjunction' (Clark, 2000, p. 247). This comment applies importantly to videogames, where the human-computer relationship is mutually constitutive and yet also complicated by a disjunction.[4]

Clark's analysis moves on to point toward a videogame-like machine as an embodiment of the relation between technicity and non–technicity. In this context, he discusses Derrida's own textual innovations, such as *Glas*, which make multi-interaction and cross-reading possible, as genuine harbingers of some future Turing Test that will resemble some 'peculiar form of book or hypertext' (Clark, p. 253). Describing the effect of the hypothetical machine, Clark comments:

> Our hypothetical machine will reinforce the status of the human as a particular but not inherently unique moment of a partial formalisation, already crudely anticipated in the case of computer chess programs. To cope with the mechanical opponent, a human player, incapable of tracing the complex algorithms that generate the other's moves, cannot treat the program as an automatic formal system, i.e. as a computer. Conscious anthropomorphism is required—the machine must be played like any other opponent. (p. 253)

What Clark describes as 'crudely anticipated in the case of computer chess programs' is now much more technologically sophisticated: videogames are many times more complex and artificially intelligent than chess-playing programs. The level of conscious (and unconscious) anthropomorphism that accompanies gameplay is increasingly greater. In any playing session, the machine and the player participate in the ludic action in an intrinsic relationship, which is at the same time that of a unit and a multiplicity. Further, the 'machine' itself is the coded algorithm as well as the game rules and the two cannot really be seen as separate. A similar originary relationship also exists between the game and the story.

The natural conclusion would then be that the narrative element acts as the supplement for the game-centred view of videogames and the reverse is also true in that the traditional notion of reading and experiencing stories is constantly being threatened by the inherent ludicity of narratives, as phenomena like videogames keep pointing out. In either case, to privilege one element over the other would be to miss the point. Similarly, given the originary nature of this relationship, it must be noted that even older media show similar characteristics as videogames, albeit in different media-specific forms.

Instead of the earlier watertight categorisation that ends up missing the complexity of how videogames function as texts, a more flexible framework is necessary. There is also another reason behind why commentators struggle to explore the ways in which videogames relate to older media: videogames take the multiplicity inherent in narrative media to an extremely complex level of perception. Hence it is not surprising that, as Adams comments, there is a lack of common vocabulary about them and some critics even see them as an entirely new phenomenon that is quite separate from earlier narrative and ludic media. The story of videogames, now, is somewhat like that of the blind men trying to know what an elephant looks like: critics focus on single aspects and err in considering them to be the primary approach for understanding videogames.

Instead, the fact that videogames exist as an assemblage of aspects needs to be kept in mind. Assemblage, as used here, is a concept borrowed from Deleuze and Guattari (the original French word used by them is *agencement*) and as John

Phillips describes it, it carries 'the senses of either "arrangement", "fitting" or "fixing" [. . . and] one would speak of the arrangement of parts of a body or machine; one might talk of fixing (fitting or affixing) two or more parts together; and one might use the term for both the act of fixing and the arrangement itself' (Phillips, 2006, p. 108–9).

Arriving at a precise definition of assemblage is difficult because of its multiple characteristics; John MacGregor Wise, in his essay on assemblage, does well to define the concept by stating what it is not:

> An assemblage is not a set of predetermined parts (such as pieces of a plastic model aeroplane) that are then put together in order to or into an already-conceived structure (the model aeroplane). Nor is an assemblage a random collection of things, since there is a sense that an assemblage is a whole of some sort that possesses some identity. (McGregor-Wise, 2005, p. 77)

Both of these factors are relevant to videogames, which do not have a preconceived structure, and yet are not random. Wise provides an example of an assemblage that compares with videogames in many ways: the mobile phone. Like videogames, when mobile phones first came into circulation, their role was restricted: their potential to perform tasks other than telephony was not yet realised and any extra features were looked on as add-ons or extrinsic appendages. Further—similar to notions of technology, such as computers and consoles, as being prosthetic to 'pure' play—the mobile phone was seen as prosthetic to the function of verbal communication.

Such notions have changed in the two decades in which mobile technology developed from 1G to 4G (in terms of chronology, too, there is a striking parallel with the development of videogames). The iPhone 5 clearly 'plugs-in' to a range of aspects besides telephony: television, radio, internet, office applications, photography and even videogames (Apple iPhone website, 2014). 'Plugging in', in the Deleuzoguattarian sense, means a multidirectional process wherein any entity may form flexible and variable attachments with others. True to the original sense of *agencement*, according to Manuel DeLanda, 'a component part of an assemblage may be detached from it and plugged into a different assemblage in which its interactions are different. [. . .] Assemblages may be taken apart while at the same time [. . .] the interaction between parts may result in a true synthesis' (DeLanda, 2006, pp. 10–11). Deleuze and Guattari identify this flexible relationship in symbiosis, such as that between the wasp and the orchid: characterised by exteriority and yet, simultaneously, by an intrinsic inclusiveness. Describing the nature of the assemblage, Couze Venn states that 'whilst Deleuze and Guattari suggest desiring machines as exemplar, one could instead refer to weather formation and the genome, or, for that matter, to the formation of identity' (Venn, 2006, p. 177).

Viewed in terms of their flexible relationship with multiple facets of life; it is problematic to call mobile phones prostheses because of the originary nature of the plugging-in. Speaking of the *oyayubikosu* (or 'thumb tribe') as the texting teenagers in Japan are now being called, Wise describes the phenomenon of the phone-becoming-hand and hand-becoming-phone in the act of texting. The hand has already originarily been a communication tool even in the earliest conceptions of communication technology. The plugging-in that occurs for the mobile phone is, therefore, already a sharing in originary terms. Videogames also show similar characteristics. As assemblages, they are games, stories, political and economic platforms, simulations and fitness trainers among other things; moreover, they also plug into all these aspects as well as to the human player and to the machine (literally) in an intrinsic relationship. The *Grand Theft Auto* walkthrough, with which this chapter began, can be said to plug into the *GTA* assemblage, which includes the entire series of games, the individual game-plays of the players, the cheat-codes, the geography of the American cities in which the games take place, the design elements and much more. It would be difficult to leave any of these separate elements out of any critique or appreciation of *GTA V* or *GTA: San Andreas* because of the multiplicity of narratives and related play-experiences they bring together. In fact, attempts to describe the *GTA* world inevitably result in resources such as the *GTA Wiki*, the ever-growing database of information related to the games that advertises having '99,100 pages and 9,560 articles since July 2006' (GTA Wiki, 2015). This is not just true of the *Grand Theft Auto* games but videogames in general, with their multiple play and narrative experiences form not *a text* but a text as an assemblage.

Anyone who has played videogames will know that there are some aspects of 'gameplay' (as the playing experience is called) that are unmappable and that are perceivable but not describable. The colloquial description for this is that the player is 'in the game'. The story, the game rules and the machine code constantly intersect and transform each other as well as the emotions, the muscular movements and the spontaneous reactions of the player. A traditional Humanities framework cannot grasp these less perceivable elements of the being 'in the game' experience. This is why, despite their popularity, the Humanities are hesitant to admit videogames into the folds of serious study: within the discourse of traditional and 'major' concepts of literature, videogames are 'minor'. In the Deleuzoguattarian sense, minoritarian literature leads to many significant developments in understanding the nature of the literary. The rising importance of videogames as a storytelling device can, therefore, no longer be deemed accidental.

The concept of the assemblage provides an important entry-point into analysing videogames as a minoritarian literature assemblage: the following chapters will explore this in fuller terms. The videogame-assemblage necessarily includes the changes in movements relative to the gameplay and to other people who might be around and the words spoken during gameplay. According to Deleuze and Guattari, they might 'group themselves into vast constellations constituting "cultures" or even "ages"' (Deleuze and Guattari, 1987, p. 448). The assemblage contains various 'flows', which, according to Claire Colebrook, 'produce diverging and multiple relations' (Colebrook, 2002, p. xv) and are even constitutive of the entities themselves.

Here, it must be clarified that there is a difference between the Deleuzoguattarian idea of 'flow' and the same term as already popular in game studies, particularly following the theory of psychologist Mihaly Csikszentmihalyi. The latter concept also relates to the experience of gameplay when the player is absorbed in the game and in Csikszentmihalyi's work this is a general concept that he believes is applicable to many aspects of life and especially to sports (Csikszentmihalyi, 1990, pp. 53–4). For him, the 'flow' experience is described as being goal-oriented or based on a merging of action and awareness as well as a sense of personal control. While there may be similarities on some levels with the Deleuzoguattarian 'flow', Csikszentmihalyi's concept is limited to a single kind of experience whereas in Deleuze and Guattari 'flow' occurs across multiplicities and occurs across various levels of the assemblage. It is both the breakdown of boundaries between entities as well as an interruption—flows can interrupt other flows.

In the assemblage, it is possible for the 'flows' to shift from certain levels of connection to other very unrelated levels: in Deleuzoguattarian terms this is called 'lines of flight'. Colebrook describes the lines of flight using various examples from human experience:

> Any connection also enables a line of flight; there can always be genetic mutation. The definition of the human as rational can also allow for a dispute over just what constitutes the human: is it rational to stockpile nuclear weapons? So any definition, territory or body can open up to a line of flight that would transform it into something else. (Colebrook, p. xv)

An analysis of the sandbox style of storytelling in *GTA: San Andreas*, as shown in the opening quotation, can also include or shift to a discussion of the question of violence in such videogames as what would constitute a line of flight. In terms of this introduction, it must be clarified that this does not mean the shift to an issue different from its immediate concerns, but rather the awareness of such issues as linked elements in the multiplicity that videogames constitute.

The vast range of issues raised in connection with videogames exhibit such a structure in the videogame-assemblage. The concept of assemblage, therefore, needs to be invoked to be able to describe the multiplicity that videogames constitute, simply because even an analysis of the narrative, ludic and machinic elements, which is the chief concern of this book, cannot be carried out without consideration of the various other aspects and conceptions into which videogames plug-in. In the following chapters, the concept of the assemblage will be a key framework for describing the multiplicity of videogames; the conception of 'flow', where relevant, will inform subsequent discussions of assemblages.

For this book, the supplementarity of the narrative, ludic and machinic aspects of videogames, as well as the multiplicity of their associations need to be considered for understanding how gameplay functions; hence theoretical frameworks that view single aspects as isolated units or parts of binaries do not suffice. It must be remembered that earlier conclusions about videogames were a result of problems that theorists faced in trying to analyse videogames in terms of the peculiar properties that they exhibit. Instead of claiming that they are 'new' properties of a new medium, it will be instructive to examine them within the framework of supplementarity and multiplicity that has been adumbrated above. This framework will consist of three sections, broadly classified, as the machine, game and the story. The names of each section are merely indicative of the key focus: in consonance with the argument of this book, often all the elements emerge as equally important, because of their originary relationship.

Section One, comprising chapters two and three, will further explore the originary link between the machinic and the narrative aspects of videogames. Chapter two will focus on how even earlier textual forms, such as the printed text, are characterised by machinicity, showing, therefore, that the manifestation of a similar relation in videogames has its roots in the very origins of narrative media. This chapter also compares the multiplicity of both printed and videogame narratives and for this purpose, it elaborates on the account of the assemblage, outlined above, to compare the book-assemblage with the videogame-assemblage. Chapter three shows parallels between the technologies employed for reading a printed text and those for experiencing videogames. Using the popular neologism *(w)reading*,[5] it illustrates, within a Derridean framework, the supplementarity of the processes of reading and writing thus pointing to the fact that the simultaneous active and passive experience in playing a videogame is a characteristic shared by all narrative media and not videogames alone. The same argument also strengthens the case for considering videogames as a narrative medium.

Following the deconstruction of the story/machine binary in the first section, Section Two combines an analysis of the nature of gameplay by revisiting and challenging the game/play (*ludus/paidia*) and the story/game binaries. Chapter four returns to the Ludology-Narratology debate examining some of its new avatars and going on to close-read and compare videogames that are overtly narrative in their gameplay and those that are less so, thereby revisiting issues related to the validity of the various positions on storytelling in games. In Chapter five, two of the less focused-on aspects of game studies are discussed. The ephemeral story-experience of videogames is understood through a critical analysis of its played instances, for example through descriptions of gameplay such as walkthroughs and after-action reports. Because of the multiplicity that applies to the medium, videogame narratives are analysed here as a story-assemblage.

In Section Three, chapters six, seven and eight analyse three major issues of contention about videogame narratives: their multitelic characteristics, the issue of agency, and, finally, the various positions regarding immersiveness in videogames. Chapter six examines the complex temporality of videogame-stories, especially as one considers the mesh of saves, reloads, incomplete and completed iterations of gameplay that go into the story experience of the games. The next chapter addresses the freedom and choice in the narrative construction that is often attributed to videogames in order to highlight the complexity of the action in videogames. Instead of granting full agency to the player, it is argued here, that the gameplay takes place in a 'Zone' where, in each decision, one event out of many possibilities is actualised. This is the 'Zone of Becoming', which, in chapter eight, also works as a metaphor with which the deep involvement, which videogame stories often create, is understood. These chapters argue that only by exploring the above characteristics as part of a multiplicity is it possible to approach an understanding of gameplay.

In a rethinking of games studies perspectives, then, the framework of viewing videogame narratives in terms of the Derridean 'originary technicity' moves the discussion away from the theories of prosthesis. Similarly, to better understand the multiplicity that videogame narratives form, Deleuze and Guattari's notion of the assemblage proves useful. Taken together, these two main concepts form part of a growing recent discourse that takes a nuanced approach towards the nature of videogames. The aim, therefore, is not to privilege any univocal model—be it the game rules, the story or the code. These theories as well as key concepts from game studies, which they re-inform, together form the base for more substantive readings of videogames and the stories they create, whether as direct gameplay experiences or as player diaries and walkthroughs.

While it is possible to say that the 'walkthrough' of *GTA: San Andreas* in the opening section of this chapter is a reading of a game, it is also the playing of a story. Videogames like *GTA* make the multiplicity of the text even more obvious than ever and, from the analysis of the experience of 'reading' such games, there comes the realisation that in the encounter with any form of text, there is also an implicit playing with stories.

Notes

1 It must be noted that the term 'Narratological' is a rather loose application by the Ludologists and the implications of this are pointed out later in this chapter.

2 Roland Barthes states that the '*infinity* of the signifier refers not to some idea of the ineffable (the unnameable signified) but to that of a playing [. . .] the Text is plural'. Source: Barthes, R., 1977. Image, Music, Text, in: Heath, S. (Tran.), *Fontana Communications Series*. Fontana, London. pp. 158–159.

3 In *Gaming Globally: Production, Play, and Place* (Huntemann and Aslinger, 2012), the editors acknowledge that 'while gaming may be global, gaming cultures and practices very widely depending on the power and voice of various stakeholders' (p. 27). The paucity of games, such as South Korea, China and India, to name a few, is markedly noticeable. The lack of representation of non-Western conceptions of play culture and storytelling traditions is similarly problematic.

4 Chapter 8 will engage with this issue in more detail.

5 '(W)reading' is preferred over the more commonly used neologism 'wreading' to emphasise the supplementarity of the reading and writing processes and also to differentiate it from earlier usage that might claim that the two processes are the *same thing*.

Bibliography

Aarseth, E., 2006. Genre Trouble, in: Wardrip-Fruin, N., Harrigan, P. (Eds.), First Person— New Media as Story, Performance and Game. MIT Press, Cambridge, Mass., p. 45.

Aarseth, E.J., 1997. Cybertext: Perspectives on Ergodic Literature. Johns Hopkins University Press, Baltimore, Md.; London.

Aarseth, E.J., 2004. Quest Games as Post-Narrative Discourse, in: Ryan, M.-L. (Ed.), Narrative across Media: The Languages of Storytelling. University of Nebraska Press, Lincoln, Neb; London.

Adams, E.W., 2005. Interactive Narratives Revisited [WWW Document]. Interactive Narratives Revisited: Ten Years of Research. URL http://www.designersnotebook. com/Lectures/Interactive_Narratives_Revisit/body_interactive_narratives_revisit.htm (accessed 1.29.15).

Apple iPhone website, 2014. Apple—iPhone 5s—Features [WWW Document]. Apple iPhone website. URL https://www.apple.com/iphone-5s/specs/ (accessed 7.1.14).

Barthes, R., 1977. Image, Music, Text, in: Heath, S. (Tran.), Fontana Communications Series. Fontana, London].

Bateson, G., 1972. Steps to an Ecology of Mind: Collected Essays in Anthropology, Psychiatry, Evolution, and Epistemology, in: Chandler Publications for Health Sciences. Chandler Pub. Co., San Francisco.

Biggs, S., 2004. On Navigation and Interactivity, in: Block, F.W. (Ed.), p0es1s: The Aesthetics of Digital Poetry. Hatje Cantz, Germany.

Bissell, T., 2011. Extra Lives: Why Video Games Matter, Reprint edition. ed. Vintage, New York.

Clark, T., 2000. Deconstruction and Technology, in: Royle, N. (Ed.), Deconstructions: A User's Guide. Palgrave Macmillan, Basingstoke.

Colebrook, C., 2002. Understanding Deleuze. Allen & Unwin; London: Orion [distributor], Crows Nest, N.S.W.

Csikszentmihalyi, M., 1990. Flow: The Psychology of Optimal Experience, 1st ed. ed. Harper & Row, New York.

DeLanda, M., 2006. A New Philosophy of Society: Assemblage Theory and Social Complexity, annotated edition. ed. Bloomsbury Academic, London; New York.

Deleuze, G., Guattari, F., 1987. A Thousand Plateaus: Capitalism and Schizophrenia. Continuum, London.

Derrida, J., 1976. Of Grammatology, 1st American ed. ed. Johns Hopkins University Press, Baltimore.

Derrida, J., 1995. Points . . . : Interviews, 1974–1994, Meridian: Crossing Aesthetics. Stanford University Press, Stanford, Calif.

Empire Online, 2015. Steven Spielberg and George Lucas on Hollywood's Future | Interviews [WWW Document]. Empireonline.com. URL http://www.empireonline. com/interviews/interview.asp?IID=1714 (accessed 1.28.15).

Eskelinen, M., 2001. Game Studies 0101: Eskelinen: The Gaming Situation. Game Studies 1.

Frasca, G., 1999. Ludology Meets Narratology: Similtude and Differences between (Video) games and Narrative. [WWW Document]. Ludology.org. URL http://www.ludology. org/articles/ludology.htm (accessed 1.29.15).

GSC Gameworld, 2007. S.T.A.L.K.E.R.: Shadow of Chernobyl [DISC]. THQ, California.

GTA Wiki, 2015. GTA Wiki [WWW Document]. GTA WIKI. URL http://gta.wikia.com/ Main_Page (accessed 1.30.15).

Holmes, D., 2012. A Mind Forever Voyaging: A History of Storytelling in Video Games. CreateSpace Independent Publishing Platform, S.l.

Huntemann, N.B., Aslinger, B. (Eds.), 2012. Gaming Globally: Production, Play, and Place. Palgrave Macmillan.

Interactive Games & Entertainment Association, 2013. 2013 Essential Facts about the Computer and Video Game Industry from the ESA [WWW Document]. iGEA. URL http://

www.igea.net/2013/06/2013-essential-facts-about-the-computer-and-video-game-indus-try-from-the-esa/ (accessed 1.28.15).

Jenkins, H., 2007. Transmedia Storytelling 101. Confessions of an Aca-Fan: The Official Weblog of Henry Jenkins.

jiiiiim, 2008. The Rise and Fall of The House of Jimius. The Rise and Fall of the House of Jimius.

Jones, S.E., 2008. The Meaning of Video Games: Gaming and Textual Strategies. Routledge, New York.

Juul, J., 2005. Half-real: Video Games between Real Rules and Fictional Worlds. MIT Press, Cambridge, Mass.

Juul, J., 2011. Salman Rushdie on Video Games & Storytelling. The Ludologist.

Kasavin, G., 2005. "Everything is Possible": Inside the Minds of Gaming's Master Storytellers [WWW Document]. GameSpot. URL http://www.gamespot.com/articles/everything-is-possible-inside-the-minds-of-gamings-master-storytellers/1100-6120427/ (accessed 1.28.15).

Maxis, 2000. The Sims [DISC]. Electronic Arts, Redwood City, CA.

McGregor-Wise, J., 2005. On Assemblage, in: Stivale, C.J. (Ed.), Gilles Deleuze: Key: Concepts. Acumen, Chesham.

Metal Gear Informer, 2012. Hideo Kojima BAFTA Interview—Storytelling, characters, and game design | Metal Gear Informer [WWW Document]. Metal Gear Informer. URL http://www.metalgearinformer.com/?p=2775 (accessed 1.28.15).

Millan, M., 2011. "Sims" creator: "Games are not the right medium to tell stories" [WWW Document]. CNN. URL http://edition.cnn.com/2011/TECH/gaming.gadgets/02/18/will.wright/ (accessed 1.28.15).

Molyneux, P., 2003. Lionhead Studios' Black and White, in: Grossman, A. (Ed.), Postmortems from Game Developer. CMP Books, San Francisco, CA.

Murray, J., 1997. Hamlet on the Holodeck: the Future of Narrative in Cyberspace. Free Press, New York; London.

Pearce, C., 2004. Towards a Game Theory of Game | Electronic Book Review [WWW Document]. Electronic Book Review. URL http://www.electronicbookreview.com/thread/firstperson/tamagotchi (accessed 1.29.15).

Phillips, J., 2006. Agencement/Assemblage. Theory, Culture & Society 23, 108–109. doi: 10.1177/026327640602300219

Poole, S., 2000. Trigger Happy: Videogames and the Entertainment Revolution, 1 edition. ed. Arcade Publishing, New York.

Rockstar North, 2004. Grand Theft Auto: San Andreas [DISC]. Rockstar Games, New York.

Rockstar North, 2013. Grand Theft Auto V [DISC]. Rockstar Games, New York.

Rushdie, S., 2010. Luka and the Fire of Life: A Novel, 1 edition. ed. Random House, New York.

Ryan, M.-L., 2006. Avatars of Story, 1 edition. ed. Univ Of Minnesota Press, Minneapolis.

Spector, W., 2006. Gamasutra—Postmortem: Ion Storm's Deus Ex [WWW Document]. GamaSutra.com. URL http://www.gamasutra.com/view/feature/3114/postmortem_ion_storms_deus_ex.php (accessed 2.10.15).

Strugatsky, A., Strugatsky, B., 1978. Roadside Picnic, Tale of the Troika. Pocket Books, New York, N.Y.

Tarkovsky, A., 1980. Stalker.

The GTA Network, 2015. GTA San Andreas: Walkthrough/Guide [WWW Document]. GTASanAn.com. URL http://www.gtasanandreas.net/walkthrough/beginning.php (accessed 1.28.15).

Venn, C., 2006. The Postcolonial Challenge: Towards Alternative Worlds. SAGE Publications Ltd, London; Thousand Oaks, CA.

7

GAMES, THE NEW LIVELY ART

Henry Jenkins

Source: Joost Raessens and Jeffrey Goldstein (eds), *Handbook of Computer Game Studies* (Cambridge, MA: The MIT Press, 2005), pp. 175–189.

"Another important element is a belief that creators are artists. At the same time, however, it's necessary for us creators to be engineers, because of the skill required for the creations."[1]

—Shigeru Miyamoto, Nintendo

"Why can't these game wizards be satisfied with their ingenuity, their $7 billion (and rising) in sales, their capture of a huge chunk of youth around the world? Why must they claim that what they are doing is 'art'? . . . Games can be fun and rewarding in many ways, but they can't transmit the emotional complexity that is the root of art."[2]

—Jack Kroll, *Newsweek*

"Let's imagine games as an art form. I know, I know—for many of us inn contact with the so-called real arts, the notion sounds pretentious. It also makes developers who are former computer science majors edgy, because it challenges assumptions that games are founded upon technology. Still, it's a useful concept. It's especially useful when we start to think about the mediocre state of our profession, and about ways to elevate our aims, aspirations, and attitudes."[3]

—Hal Barwood, LucasArts

Over the past three decades, computer and video games have progressed from the primitive two-paddles-and-a-ball *Pong* to the sophistication of *Final Fantasy*, a participatory story with cinema-quality graphics that unfolds over nearly 100 hours of game play, or *Black and White*, an ambitious moral tale where the player's god-like choices between good and evil leave tangible marks on the landscape.[4] The computer game has been a killer app for the home PC, increasing consumer demand for vivid graphics, rapid processing, greater memory and better sound. One could make the case that games have been to the PC what NASA was to the mainframe—the thing that pushes forward innovation and experimentation.

The release of the Sony Playstation 2, the Microsoft X-Box, and the Nintendo Game Cube signals a dramatic increase in the resources available to game designers.

In anticipation of these new technological breakthroughs, people within and beyond the game industry began to focus attention on the creative potentials of this emerging medium. Mapping the aesthetics of game design, they argued, would not only enable them to consolidate decades of experimentation and innovation but would also push them forward towards greater artistic accomplishment. Game designers were being urged to think of themselves not simply as technicians producing corporate commodities but rather as artists mapping the dimensions and potentials of an emerging medium; this reorientation, it was hoped, would force them to ask harder questions in their design meetings and to aspire towards more depth and substance in the product they shipped. At the same time, the games industry confronted increased public and government scrutiny. If you parsed the rhetoric of the moral reformers, it was clear that their analogies to pollution or carcinogens revealed their base-level assumption that games were utterly without redeeming value, lacking any claim to meaningful content or artistic form. Seeing games as art, however, shifted the terms of the debate. Most of these discussions started from the premise that games were an emerging art form, one which had not yet realized its full potentials. Game designer Warren Specter, for example, told a *Joystick 101* interviewer, "We're just emerging from infancy. We're still making (and remaking!) *The Great Train Robbery* or *Birth of a Nation* or, to be really generous, maybe we're at the beginning of what might be called our talkies period. But as Al Jolson said in *The Jazz Singer*, "You ain't heard nothing yet!"[5] In this context, critical discussions sought to promote experimentation and diversification of game form, content, and audience, not to develop prescriptive norms.

These debates were staged at trade shows and academic conferences, in the pages of national magazines (such as *Newsweek* and *Technology Review*) and newspapers (such as the *New York Times*), and in online zines aimed at the gaming community (such as *Joystick101* and *Gamasutra*). Game designers, policy makers, art critics, fans, and academics all took a position on the question of whether computer games could be considered an art form and what kinds of aesthetic categories made sense for discussing them.

Games increasingly influence contemporary cinema, helping to define the frantic pace and model the multi-directional plotting of *Run Lola Run*, providing the role-playing metaphor for *Being John Malkovich*, encouraging a fascination with the slippery line between reality and digital illusions in *The Matrix*, inspiring the fascination with decipherment and puzzle solving at the heart of *Memento*, and even providing a new way of thinking about Shakespearean tragedy in *Titus*. Game interfaces and genres have increasingly surfaced as metaphors or design elements in *avant-garde* installations. Matthew Barney, currently the darling of the New York art museum, transformed the Guggenheim into a giant video game for one of his *Cremaster* films, having his protagonist battle their way up the ramps, boss by boss.[6] If critics, like Kroll, were reluctant to ascribe artistic merit to games, artists in other media seemed ready to absorb aspects of game aesthetics into their work. At high schools and colleges across the country, students discussed games with the same passions with which earlier generations debated the merits of the New American Cinema or the French New Wave. Media studies programs reported that a growing number of their students want to be game designers rather than filmmakers.

At the same time, academics were finally embracing games as a topic worthy of serious examination—not simply as a social problem, a technological challenge, a cultural phenomenon, or an economic force within the entertainment industry, but also as an art form which demanded serious aesthetic evaluation.[7] Conferences on the art and culture of games were hosted at MIT, the University of Southern California, The University of Chicago, and the University of West England. As academics have confronted games, they have often found it easier to discuss them in social, economic, and cultural terms than through aesthetic categories. The thrust of Media Studies writing in recent years has been focused around the category of popular culture and been framed through ideological categories, rather than in terms of popular art, a concept which carried far greater resonance in the first half of the 20th century.

My goal here is not to argue against the values of applying concepts and categories from cultural studies to the analysis of games, but rather to make the case that something was lost when we abandoned a focus on popular aesthetics. The category of aesthetics has considerable power in our culture, helping to define not only cultural hierarchies but also social, economic, and political ones as well. The ability to dismiss certain forms of art as inherently without value paves the way for regulatory policies; the ability to characterize certain media forms as "cultural pollution" also impacts how the general public perceives those people who consume such material; and the ability to foreclose certain works from artistic consideration narrows the ambitions and devalues the accomplishments of people who work in those media. I will admit that discussing the art of video games conjures up comic images: tuxedo-clad and jewel-bedecked patrons admiring the latest *Streetfighter*, middle-aged academics pontificating on the impact of Cubism on *Tetris*, bleeps and zaps disrupting our silent contemplation at the Guggenheim. Such images tell us more about our contemporary notion of art—as arid and stuffy, as the property of an educated and economic elite, as cut off from everyday experience—than they tell us about games.

The lively criticism of Gilbert Seldes

What I want to do in the following pages is revisit one important effort to spark a debate about the aesthetic merits of popular culture—Gilbert Seldes' *Seven Lively Arts* (1924)—and suggest how reclaiming Seldes might contribute to our current debates about the artistic status of computer and video games. Adopting what was then a controversial position, Seldes argued that America's primary contributions to artistic expression had come through emerging forms of popular culture such

107

as jazz, the Broadway musical, Vaudeville, Hollywood cinema, the comic strip, and the vernacular humor column.[8] While some of these arts have gained cultural respectability over the past 75 years (and others have died out entirely), each was disreputable when Seldes staked out his position. Seldes wanted his book to serve two purposes: first, he wanted to give readers fresh ways of thinking about and engaging with the contents of popular art; second, he wanted to use the vitality and innovation of these emerging forms to challenge the "monotonous stupidity," "the ridiculous postures," and "stained glass attitudes" of what we might now call Middle Brow culture.[9]

Readers then were skeptical of Seldes' claims about cinema for many of the same reasons that contemporary critics dismiss games—they were suspicious of cinema's commercial motivations and technological origins, concerned about Hollywood's appeals to violence and eroticism, and insistent that cinema had not yet produced works of lasting value. Seldes, on the other hand, argued that cinema's popularity demanded that we reassess its aesthetic qualities. Cinema and other popular arts were to be celebrated, Seldes insisted, because they were so deeply imbedded in everyday life, because they were democratic arts embraced by average citizens. Through streamlined styling and syncopated rhythms, they captured the vitality of contemporary urban experience. They took the very machinery of the industrial age, which many felt dehumanizing, and found within it the resources for expressing individual visions, for reasserting basic human needs, desires, and fantasies. And these new forms were still open to experimentation and discovery. They were, in Seldes' words, "lively arts."

My thinking about Seldes' value for reflecting on game aesthetics first took shape when I was sitting in the audience at the USC Interactive Frictions conference and heard two panels back to back, one composed on digital artists, the other of game designers. The first discussion was sluggish and pretentious; the artists were trying—without much success—to describe what the computer brought to their art, but they kept falling back on high modernist and early postmodernist categories. I knew exactly what they were going to say before they opened their mouths. On the other hand, the game designers were struggling to find words and concepts to express fresh discoveries about their media; they were working on the very edge of the technology, stretching it to its limits, and having to produce work which would fascinate an increasingly jaded marketplace. They were keeping on the top of their toes trying to learn not only from their own production practices but from each other. I scribbled on my notepad, "If art enlivens and commerce deadens, then how do we explain the immediacy of this panel and the dullness of the previous one." I suddenly flashed on Seldes' characterization of the attitude that dominated the art institutions and criticism of the early 20th century: "What is worthwhile must be dull. We suffer fools gladly if we can pretend they are mystics."[10]

Games represent a new lively art, one as appropriate for the digital age as those earlier media were for the machine age. They open up new aesthetic experiences and transform the computer screen into a realm of experimentation and innovation that is broadly accessible. And games have been embraced by a public that has otherwise been unimpressed by much of what passes for digital art. Much as the salon arts of the 1920s seemed sterile alongside the vitality and inventiveness of popular culture, contemporary efforts to create interactive narrative through modernist hypertext or avant-garde installation art seem lifeless and pretentious alongside the creativity and exploration, the sense of fun and wonder, that game designers bring to their craft. As Hal Barwood explained to readers of *Game Developer* magazine in February 2002, "Art is what people accomplish when they don't quite know what to do, when the lines on the road map are faint, when the formula is vague, when the product of their labors is new and unique."[11] Art exists, in other words, on the cutting edge and that was where games had remained for most of their history. The game designers were creating works that sparked the imagination and made our hearts race. And they were doing so without the safety net that inherited modernist rhetoric provides for installation and hypertext artists. They can offer no simple, straightforward justification for what they are doing or why they doing it except by way of talking about "the fun factor," that is, the quality of the emotional experience they offer players.

Although his writing was impressionistic and evocative, rather than developing a systematic argument or framework, one can read *The Seven Lively Arts* as mapping an aesthetic of popular culture, one which is broadly enough defined to be useful for discussing a wide range of specific media and cultural practices including many that did not exist at the time he wrote the book. Seldes drew a distinction between the "great arts," which seek to express universal and timeless values, and the "lively arts," which seek to give shape and form to immediate experiences and impressions. "Great" and "lively" arts differed "not in the degree of their intensity but in the degree of their intellect."[12] Seldes, in fact, often showed signs of admiring the broad strokes of the popular arts—where the needs for clarity and immediate recognition from a broadly defined audience allowed "no fuzzy edges, no blurred contours"—over the nuance and complexity of Great Art.[13] Seldes consistently values affect over intellect, immediate impact over long term consequences, the spontaneous impulse over the calculated effect.

Seldes defined art through its affective force, its ability to provoke strong and immediate reactions. As popular artists master the basic building block of their media, they developed techniques enabling them to shape and intensify affective experience. Creativity, Seldes argued, was all bound up with our sense of play and with our demands to refresh our sensual apparatus and add new energy to our mental life, which was apt to become dulled through the routine cognition and perception of everyday life. He wrote, "we require, for nourishment, something fresh and transient."[14]

From the start, games were able to create strong emotional impressions—this accounts for the enormous staying power with consumers. An early game of *Pacman* or *Asteroids* could provoke strong feelings of tension or paranoia. The works of Shigeru Miyagawa represented imaginative landscapes, as idiosyncratic and witty in their way as the *Krazy Kat* comic strips or Mack Sennett comedies Seldes admired. Seldes wrote at a moment when cinema was starting to consolidate what it had learned over its first three decades of experimentation and produce works that mixed and matched affective elements to create new kinds of experiences. One could argue that recent games, such as *Deus X, Grand Theft Auto 3*, or *Shenmue*, represent a similar consolidation of earlier game genres, whereas games like *The Sims, Majestic, Rez* or *Black & White* are expanding the repertoire of game mechanics and by doing so, expanding the medium's potential audience.

The great arts and the lively arts shared a common enemy, the "bogus arts," the middle brow arts, which sought to substitute "refinement of taste" for "refinement of technique," and in the process, cut themselves off from the culture around them.[15] The popular arts, he warned, often promised more than they could deliver; their commercial imperative required that they leave us somewhat unsatisfied and thus eager to consume more, but in their straightforward appeal to emotion, they do not "corrupt." Middlebrow culture, however, often seduces us with fantasies of social and cultural betterment at the expense of novelty and innovation. Seldes wanted to deploy the shock value of contemporary popular culture to shake up the settled thinking of the art world, to force it to reconsider the relationship between art and everyday life.

At a time when the United States was emerging as a world leader, Seldes wanted to identify what he felt was a distinctively American voice. He protested, "Our life is energetic, varied, constantly changing; our art is imitative, anemic."[16] Contemporary intellectuals, he felt, had accepted too narrow a conception of what counted as art, seeing America as a new country which had not yet won the approval of its old world counterparts. Their search for refinement constituted a "genteel corruption," a "thinning out of the blood," which cut them off from what was vital in the surrounding culture. European artists, he suggested, had often revitalized their work by returning to folk art traditions, but operating in a new country with few folk roots, American artists would need to find their vitality through a constant engagement with what was fresh and novel in popular culture. As Seldes explained, "For America, the classic and the folk arts are both imported goods . . . . But the circumstance that our popular arts are homegrown, without the prestige of Europe and of the past, had thrown upon them a shadow of vulgarity, as if they were the products of ignorance and intellectual bad manners."[17]

Seldes wrote at a time when American dominance over popular culture and European dominance over high culture were taken for granted. The aesthetics of contemporary game design, however, operates in a global context. One would have to concede, for example, that our current game genres took shape as a conversation between Japanese and American industries (with plenty of input from consumers and creators elsewhere). Increasingly, American popular culture is responding to Asian influences with the rise in violence in mass market entertainment a property of heightened competition between Japan, India, Hong Kong, and Hollywood for access to international markets. Action elements surface, not only in games but also in film, television, and comics, because such elements are more readily translated across linguistic and national boundaries.

The need to appeal to a mass consumer, Seldes insisted, meant that popular artists could not give themselves over to morbid self-absorption. Creating works in media that were still taking shape, popular artists were not burdened with a heritage but had to constantly explore new directions and form new relationships with their publics. The lively arts look toward the future rather than toward the past. Similarly, game designers work in a commercially competitive environment and within an emerging medium. Thus, they must continually push and stretch formal boundaries in order to create novelty, while they also have to insure that their experimentation remains widely accessible to their desired audience. The context is dramatically different when one turns their attention to middlebrow art, which often wants to build on well-established traditions rather than rely on formal experimentation, or high art, which can engage in avant garde experimentation accessible only to an educated elite.

Seldes wrote during an era of media in transition. The cinema was maturing as an expressive medium—making a move from mere spectacle towards character and consequence, from a "cinema of attractions" to a classical storytelling system.[18] A decade earlier, many intellectuals might have freely dismissed cinema as a parlor entertainment, whose primary content consisted of little more than chase scenes and pratfalls. A decade later, few would have doubted that cinema had earned its status as one of the most important contemporary arts. Seldes' respect for cinema's popular roots set him at odds with many contemporary critics who saw the refinement of narrative techniques as essential for the maturation of the medium. Cinema, Seldes argued, "was a toy and should have remained a toy—something for our delight."[19] For Seldes, cinema was not an art despite slapstick; it was an art because slapstick had helped us to realize that the fullest potentials of motion pictures lay in their ability to capture motion and express emotion. "Everything in slapstick was cinematographic," Seldes proclaimed, remaining deeply suspicious of filmmakers like Thomas Ince or D.W. Griffith, who he feared had sought to impose literary and theatrical standards alien to cinema's core aesthetic impulses.[20] He explained, "the rightness of the spectacle film is implicit in its name: the screen is a place on which things can be seen and so long as a film depends on the eye it is right for the screen."[21]

The maturing of the cinematic medium may well have been what enabled Seldes to recognize its artistic accomplishments. However, in aspiring towards cultural respectability, cinema ran a high risk of losing touch with its own primitive roots. Seldes sounded a warning which would seem familiar to many contemporary observers of video and computer games, suggesting that the cinema was confusing technological enhancement with aesthetic advancement, confusing the desire to reproduce reality for the desire to create an emotionally engaging experience. What had given filmgoers the "highest degree of pleasure," he argued, was "escaping actuality and entering into a created world, built on its own inherent logic, keeping time to its own rhythm—where we feel ourselves at once strangers and at home."[22]

Newsweek's Jack Kroll sparked heated debates in the gamer community when he argued that audiences will probably never be able to care as deeply about pixels on the computer screen as they care about characters in films: "Moviemakers don't have to simulate human beings; they are right there, to be recorded and orchestrated . . . . The top-heavy titillation of *Tomb Raider's* Lara Croft falls flat next to the face of Sharon Stone . . . Any player who's moved to tumescence by digibimbo Lara is in big trouble."[23] Yet countless viewers cry when Bambi's mother dies, and World War II veterans can tell you they felt real lust for *Esquire's* Vargas girls. We have learned to care as much about creatures of pigment as we care about images of real people. Why should pixels be different? If we haven't yet cared this deeply about game characters (a debatable proposition as the response to Kroll's article indicated), it is because the game design community has not yet found the right techniques for evoking such emotions, and not because there is an intrinsic problem in achieving emotional complexity in the medium itself. Kroll, like the respectable critics of early cinema whom Seldes battled, assumes that realism is necessary in order to achieve a high degree of emotional engagement. The art of games may not come from reproducing the world of the senses. As Steve Poole has written:

> "Whereas film—at least naturalistic, 'live-action' film—is tied down to real spaces, the special virtue of videogames is precisely their limit-less plasticity. And only when that virtue is exploited more fully will videogames become a truly unprecedented art—when their level of world-building competence is matched with a comparable level of pure invention. We want to be shocked by novelty. We want to lose ourselves in a space that is utterly different. We want environments that have never been seen, never been imagined before."[24]

As I visit game companies, I see some of the industry's best minds struggling with this challenge. As they search for answers, they will need to avoid the temp-tation to port solutions over wholesale from cinema and other more established arts. Independent game designers, such as Eric Zimmerman, have argued that games need to return to a garage aesthetic, stripping aside fancy graphics and elaborate cinematics, to reclaim the core elements that make games distinctive from other expressive media. Protesting that games are more than simply "mutant cinema," Zimmerman warns that "mistaken attempts to apply the skills and methods of Hollywood to the world of electronic gaming resulted in CD-ROMs bloated with full-motion video sequences and lacking meaningful gameplay."[25] Similarly, Seldes warned that long intertitles substituted literary for cinematic values, seeking to "explain everything except the lack of action," and resulting in scenes devoid of visual interest.[26] The result were movies that no longer moved. Zimmerman and others warn that extended cinematics, often the favored mean of adding narrative and character to games, cuts the player off from the action and thus sacrifice those elements of interactivity which make games games. One could argue that a similar tension is at the heart of the ongoing debates among game scholars between the so-called narratologists and the ludologists. The ludologists fear that the narratologist want to impose an alien aesthetic sensibility onto games and thus cut the medium off from its basic building blocks in gameplay. Games should not achieve aesthetic recognition by giving themselves over to "cinema envy," they warn, but should remain true to their roots. Seldes's concept of the lively arts may, in fact, offer us a way out of this binary, since he focuses primarily on the kinetic aspects of popular culture, aspects that can operate inside or outside a narrative frame. Poole arrives at a similar conclusion:

> "A beautifully designed videogame invokes wonder as the fine arts do, only in a uniquely kinetic way. Because the videogame *must* move, it cannot offer the lapidary balance of composition that we value in painting; on the other hand, because it *can* move, it is a way to experience architecture, and more than that to create it, in a way which photographs or drawings can never compete. If architecture is frozen music, then a videogame is liquid architecture."[27]

Memorable moments

What Seldes offers us might be described as a theory of "memorable moments," a concept which surfaces often in discussions with game designers but only rarely in academic writing about the emerging medium. Writing about the German Expressionist film, *The Cabinet of Dr. Caligari*, Seldes praises not its plot but its lingering aftertaste: "I cannot think of half a dozen movies which have left so many clear images in my mind."[28] Or later in the book, he writes about the pleasures of finding peak experiences within otherwise banal works: "A moment comes when everything is exactly right, and you have an occurrence—it may be something exquisite or something unnameably gross; there is in it an ecstasy which sets it apart from everything else."[29] Such peak experiences seem fully within reach of contemporary game designers in a way that the development of complex causally-integrated yet open-ended narratives or psychological rounded yet fully interactive characters are not. If games are going to become an art, right now, rather than in some distant future, when all of our technical challenges have been resolved, it may come from game designers who are struggling with the mechanics of motion and emotion, rather than those of story and character.

As game designers evaluate games on the basis of their emotional appeal, their criteria often emphasize moments of emotional intensity or visual spectacle—the big skies that can suddenly open before you when you ride your snow board in *SSX*, the huge shots in a hockey game when the puck goes much further than it could possibly do in real life, the pleasure of sending your car soaring off a cliff or smashing through pedestrians in *Grand Theft Auto 3*. Increasingly, games enable us to grab snapshots of such moments, to replay them and watch them unfold from multiple angles, and to share them with our friends, pushing them to see if they can match our exploits and duplicate accomplishments. Game companies encourage their staffs to think of their designs in terms of the images on boxes or in previews, the way that the demo is going to look on the trade show floor. Yet, this may be to reduce the concept of memorable moments down to "eye candy" or spectacle, something which can be readily extracted from the play experience, something which can be communicated effectively in a still image. Other game designers would contest this understanding of the concept, arguing that memorable moments emerge when all of the elements of the medium come together to create a distinctive and compelling experience.

Often, in games, those memorable moments don't simply depend on spectacle. After all, spectacle refers to something that stops you dead in your tracks, forces you to stand and look. Game play becomes memorable when it creates the opposite effect—when it makes you want to move, when it convinces you that you really are in charge of what's happening in the game, when the computer seems to be totally responsive. Frequently, the memorable moment comes when the computer does something that follows logically from your actions, yet doesn't feel like it was prescribed and preprogrammed. As *Deus X* designer Warren Spector explains: "Great gameplay comes, I think, from our ability to drop players into compelling situations, provide clear goals for them, give them a variety of tools with which they can impact their environment and then get out of their way . . . That has to be so much more compelling for players—thrilling even— than simply guessing the canned solution to a puzzle or pressing a mouse button faster than a computer opponent can react."[30]

Seldes was one of a number of early 20th century writers who sought to better understand the "mechanics of emotion" which shaped popular entertainment. The Italian futurist Flippo Marinetti saw within the variety theater "the crucible in which the elements of an emergent new sensibility are seething," describing it as an art which had "only one reason for existing and triumphing: incessantly to invent new elements of astonishment."[31] The Soviet film theorist Sergei Eisenstein developed a theory of "attractions," a term which he saw as broad enough to encompass any device—whether formal, narrative, or thematic—which could solicit powerful emotions from a spectator, arguing that film and theater should seek their inspiration from the circus and the music hall.[32] Inspired in part by Pavlovian refloxology, they tried to document and master basic "surefire" stimuli which could provoke a predictable emotional response from the spectator and then to streamline their works, cutting out anything that would obscure or retard that affective impact. Eddie Cantor warned, "A comedian in vaudeville . . . is like a salesman who has only fifteen minutes in which to make a sale. You go on stage knowing every moment counts. You've got to get your audience the instant you appear."[33] Theater critic Vadim Uraneff explained in 1923, "the [vaudeville] actor works with the idea of an immediate response from the audience: and with regard to its demands. By cutting out everything—every line, gesture, movement—to which the audience does not react and by improvising new things, he establishes unusual unity between the audience and himself."[34]

Game designers engage in a similar process as they seek to identify "what's not in the game," that is, to determine what elements would get in the way of the game mechanic or confuse the player. Game designers speak of "hooks" which will grab the consumers attention and keep them playing, a concept which would have been familiar to vaudeville showman and circus barkers. Longtime game designers cite back to the challenges of developing games which played well in the arcades, which offered a compelling experience that could be staged in under two minutes and ramped up to an emotional high that would leave the player reaching for another quarter. Early console games also demanded economy, given the limited memory capacity of the early systems.[35] However, as consoles have developed greater capacity and thus enabled lengthier and more complex game experiences, some fear that game designers are adding too many features which get in the way of the core mechanics. The lengthy cut scenes of narrative exposition and character back story, which academics praise for their aesthetic advancements, are often received with hostility by serious gamers because they slow down the play and result in a relatively passive experience. A great deal of effort goes into the first few minutes of game play, in particular, to insure that they offer a solid emotional payoff for the player rather than ending in frustration: an early moment of mastery or movement is to spark their appetite for bigger and better things to come.[36]

Play as performance

Seldes and the other early 20th century critics saw the emotional intensity of popular culture as emerging from the central performer, whose mastery over his or her craft enabled them to "command" the spectator's attention. Seldes writes about the "daemonic" authority of Al Jolson: "he never saves up—for the next scene, or the next week, or the next show . . . . He flings into a comic song or three-minute impersonation so much energy, violence, so much of the totality of one human being, that you feel it would suffice for a hundred others."[37] His contemporary, Robert Lytell, described the characteristics of the best revue performers:

> "Human horsepower, size, electricity, energy, zingo . . . . These people have a fire in their belly which makes you sit up and listen whether you want to or not, which silences criticism until their act is over, and you can start thinking again . . . . They seize you and do pretty nearly anything they want with you and while it is going on, you sit with your mouth open and laugh and laugh again."[38]

Such comments reflected the performer-centered aesthetic of vaudeville and the Broadway revue. One might well understand the pleasures of game play according to performance criteria but as we do so, we need to understand it as a pas de deux between the designer and the player. As game designer David Perry explains, "A good game designer always knows what the players are thinking and is looking over their shoulders every step of the way."[39] The game designer's craft makes it possible for the player to feel as if they are in control of the situation at all time, even though their game play and emotional experience is significantly sculpted by the designer. It is a tricky balancing act, making the player aware of the challenges they confront, and at the same time, insuring they have the resources necessary to overcome those challenges. If the game play becomes transparently easy or impossibly hard, the players lose interest. The players need to feel they can run faster, shoot more accurately, jump further, and think smarter than in their everyday life and it is this expansion of the player's capacity which accounts for the emotional intensity of most games. I still recall the first time I grabbed the controls of *Sonic the Hedgehog*, got a good burst of speed, and started running as fast I could around the loop-to-loops, collecting gold coins, and sending all obstacles scattering. I am not an especially good game player, yet I felt at that moment totally invincible, and everything in the game's design—the layout of the space, the properties of the character, the selection of the soundtrack—contributed to giving me that sense of effortless control, that release from normal constraints.

As many observers have noted, we don't speak of controlling a cursor on the screen when we describe the experience of playing a game; we act as if we had unmediated access to the fictional space. We refer to our game characters in the first person and act as if their experiences were our own. James Newman has argued that we might understand the immediacy of game play not in terms of how convincing the representation of the character and the fictional world is but rather in terms of the character's "capacity" to respond to our impulses and desires. A relatively iconic, simplified character may produce an immediate emotional response; a relatively stylized world can nevertheless be immersive. Once we engage with the game, the character may become simply a vehicle we use to navigate the game world. As Newman explains:

> "Lara Croft is defined less by appearance than by the fact that 'she' allows the player to jump distance x, while the ravine in front of us is larger than that, so we better start thinking of a new way round . . . . Characters are defined around game play affecting characteristics. It doesn't matter that it's a burly guy—or even a guy—or perhaps even a human. That the hang glider can turn faster is a big deal; this affects the way the game plays. This affects my chances of getting a good score. "[40]

A number of game designers have reminded me that Shigeru Miyamoto, whom many regard as the medium's first real master, designs his games around verbs, that is, around the actions which the game enables players to perform. He wants each game to introduce a new kind of mission, making it possible for the consumer to do something that no other game has allowed before. A close examination of Miyamoto's games suggests, at the same time, that he designs a playing space which at once facilitates and thwarts our ability to carry out that action and thus creates a dramatic context in which these actions take aesthetic shape and narrative significance.

Many contemporary games seek to expand that sense of player mastery beyond the game space, encouraging players to dance to the rhythm, to shake maracas, twist turntables, beat drums, as the domestic space or the arcade space become performance spaces. The spectacular and performative dimensions of these games are summarized by this player's account of his experience of being a *Dance Dance Revolution* devotee:

"The first song starts and finishes, and I did well. I hear a man ask me "How in the hell do you do that?" I just laugh and pick the next song, a harder one. I can hear people milling around behind me and I can see their reflection on screen. I hear whispers of "wow", and "damn!" The song ends. I hear a woman shout "Wooooo!" I turn and smile. Her and her friend blush and turn away . . . . Of course, Friday and Saturday nights are the big days to show off. Big crowds, loud crowds, and occasionally rowdy, mean crowds. These are the days for the big dogs, and competition is tough. Very hard songs are done, and feet fly like hummingbird wings . . . . But you take the good with the bad, and it's still fun when you get a good, loud reaction, and there's more than "hoots" to it. There's that feeling when you finally beat that tough song, or when you help a buddy learn to play. It still boils down to just having fun, whether the crowd cheers or not."[41]

Here, the player gets to enjoy the same kind of experience that fueled Jolson or Cantor's performances—the pleasure of intense and immediate feedback from an engaged audience. At the same time, the game instructs the performance, giving the kinds of structured feedback that enables players to quickly master the necessary skills to impress friends and strangers alike.

The designers of *Frequency* and *Rez*, two recent music-making games, have sought to expand the sensory experience available to players. Both games start with the sensation of traveling at high speeds down winding tunnels of light and color. As we move through these stylized but representational spaces, our interactions help to shape the sound and rhythm of their technobased soundtracks. As we get into the spirit of the game, we stop thinking simply in terms of our physical movements and become more in tune with the pulse of the music. Such games start to blur the line between play and performance, creating a context where even novice musicians can start to jam and advanced players can create complex and original musical compositions. *Frequency* designer Alex Rigopulos describes the trajectory of a player through his game:

"When a gamer starts to play *Frequency*, he plays it using the gaming skills he already has: the ability to react to symbolic visual information with a precisely timed manual response . . . . What we noticed again and again in playtesting was that there is a certain point at which novice players stop playing entirely with their eyes and start playing with their ears (or, rather, their "internal ears"): they start to feel the musical beat; then, as a stream of gems approaches, they look at the oncoming stream, "imagine" in their ears what that phrase will feel like or sound like rhythmically, and begin to "play the notes" (rather than "shoot the gems"). As soon as players cross this threshold, they begin excelling much more rapidly in the game."[42]

Rez's designers have suggested that they based their designs on the theories of abstract artist Wassily Kandinsky: "*Rez* is an experience, a fusion of light, vibration and sound completely immersed in synaesthesia."[43] Here, the game controller vibrates and even develops the rhythm of a heart beat in response to the player's actions, creating yet another dimension to what is a complex multimedia experience.

These games build on the excess kinetic energy that has always surrounded gameplay. Watch children play games and they sway with the movement of the figures on the screen, bouncing with the action, totally engaged with the moment. One could argue that such responses reflect the degree of control they feel over what happens on the screen. We speak not just of controlling the characters but of "owning" the space of the game. It is even more interesting to observe the responses of people watching them play, since they also mimic the actions which are occurring on the screen, even though their actions have no consequences on the game play. Cinema has never achieved this same visceral impact, unless we are talking about the kind of fairground attractions which are designed to give us the sensation of driving down a racetrack or riding a rollercoaster. People do sometimes feel like they are about to fall out of their seats when watching an IMAX image, for example. Games routinely create the same degree of immersion without having to totally surround us. Sometimes they achieve it by the use of first person perspective, but one can have the same sensation watching an early Mario Brothers game that relies totally on third person point of view and a relatively iconographic landscape. One could argue that it is our knowledge of the interactive potential of games which produces these kinetic effects, yet I have observed similar kinds of behavior from people watching prerecorded clips from games, suggesting that the response has as much to do with the visual presentation of the action as any real-time engagement with the controller.

Expressive amplification

David Bordwell makes a similar argument about the Hong Kong action film:

"We need no special training to grasp vigorous, well structured movement. More exactly, it's not so much that we grasp it as that it grabs us; we respond kinesthetically, as when we tap our toes to music, or hammer the air at a basketball game. These films literally grip us; we can watch ourselves tense and relax, twitch or flinch. By arousing us through highly legible motion and staccato rhythms, and by intensifying their arousal through composition and editing and sound, the films seem to ask our bodies to recall elemental and universal events like striking, swinging, twisting, leaping, rolling."[44]

By now, the aesthetics of the action movie and the video game are hopelessly intertwined: game aesthetics have clearly and directly shaped the emergence of the genres Bordwell discusses and at the same time, game designers have consciously internalized lessons from filmmakers like Akira Kurosowa, James Cameron, and John Woo. As game criticism emerges as a field, it will need to address not only the stories that games tell, or the kinds of play that they facilitate, but also the formal principles that shape our emotional responses to them. Bordwell's account of the Hong Kong martial arts movie, here, suggests two intertwined factors—first, the ways that commonly staged actions appeal to bodily memories, and second, the ways that various aesthetic devices can intensify and exaggerate the impact of the actions, making them both more legible and more intense than their real world counterpoints.

Bordwell describes this second process as "expressive amplification."[45] Action film directors combine circus acrobatics and special effects with rapid-fire editing and stylized sound effects to amp up the intensity of a fight sequence. Similarly, game designers use movement, camera angle, sound effects, and other devices to exaggerate the impact of punches or to expand the flight of a skateboarder. The protagonists in *Jet Grind Radio* run riot through the streets of a futuristic Tokyo, sliding up and down ramps or along rails at high speeds, their in-line skates sending out a shower of sparks, the sounds of the cops' boots pounding right on their heels and the crackle of the police radio breathing down their necks. Here, we see "expressive amplification" at work. We take pleasure not simply in the outcome of the player's actions but the style with which they/we execute them.

Games and silent cinema

And this brings us back to what Seldes had to say about the cinema. The police in *Jet Grind Radio* display the exaggerated dignity and one-track thinking we associate with the Keystone Cops, as they hurl themselves onto the protagonist and end up in a heap, face down on the asphalt. Silent Cinema, Seldes argued, was an art of expressive movement. He valued the speed and dynamism of Griffith's last minute races to the rescue, the physical grace of Chaplin's pratfalls and the ingenuity of Buster Keaton's engineering feats. He argued that each silent performer developed their own characteristic way of moving, their own posture, their own rhythm, which defined them for the spectator the moment they appeared on the screen.

Chaplin "created his own trajectory across the screen which was absolutely his own line of movement."[46] This distinctive way of moving occurred through stylization, reducing screen action to simple units of action, which could recur across a broad range of narrative situations. Moviegoers came to love the slight bounce in Chaplin's walk, the daintiness of his hands, his slightly bow-legged stance. James Agee would make a similar claim in his essay, "Comedy's Greatest

Era," describing the unique personalities on screen as emerging from a rhetoric of comic clichés:

> "The man who could handle them properly combined several of the more difficult accomplishments of the acrobat, the dancer, the clown, and the mime. Some very gifted comedians, unforgettably Ben Turpin, had an immense vocabulary of these clichés and were in part so lovable because they were deeply conservative classicists and never tried to break away from them. The still more gifted men, of course, simplified and invented, finding out new and much deeper uses for the idiom. They learned to show emotion through it, and comic psychology, more eloquently than most language has ever managed to, and they discovered beauties of comic motion which are hopelessly beyond the reach of words."[47]

Games also depend upon an art of expressive movement, with characters defined through their distinctive ways of propelling themselves through space. Game designers have had to reduce character down to a limited range of preprogrammed expressions, movements, and gestures, but as they have done so, they have produced characters, like Mario and Luigi or Sonic, who are enormously evocative, who provoke strong emotional reactions.

The art of silent cinema was also an art of atmospheric design. To watch a silent masterpiece like Fritz Lang's *Metropolis* is to be drawn into a world where meaning is carried by the placement of shadows, the movement of machinery and the organization of space. If anything, game designers have pushed beyond cinema in terms of developing expressive and fantastic environments that convey a powerful sense of mood, provoke our curiosity and amusement, and motivate us to explore. The German expressionists had to construct the world's largest sound stage so that they could insure that every element in their shot was fully under their control. Game designers start with a blank screen: every element is there because they chose to put it there and so there is no excuse for elements which do not capture the imagination, shape our emotions, or convey meanings. Game designers are seeking inspiration from stage design, amusement park "imagineering," and postmodern architecture as they develop a better understanding of spatial design. Across a range of essays, I have made the case that games might best be discussed through a spatial aesthetic, one which sees the art of game design as a kind of narrative and affective architecture, as linked in important ways to the art of designing amusement park attractions.[48] I have argued that games compensate their players for their loss of mobility across real world spaces, at a time when children enjoy diminished access to real world play spaces.[49] With Kurt Squire, I have expanded that analysis to look more closely at the ways that a range of games create spaces which encourage our exploration and which are well-designed as staging grounds for conflicts.[50]

Many of the most memorable moments in the silent films Seldes discussed centered around the struggles of characters against spatial features. Consider, for example, the extended sequence in *Safety Last* where Harold Lloyd must climb the side of a building, floor by floor, confronting a series of obstacles, and ends up hanging from the hands of a clock face. To be sure, some of the sequence's fascination has to do with the photographic basis of cinema—the fact that Lloyd is actually hanging several stories off the ground (a stunt rendered all the more remarkable by the fact that Lloyd is missing several fingers from one of his hands). Yet, the scene also depends on a challenge-mastery-complication structure remarkably similar to that found in contemporary games: the higher Lloyd climbs the more intense the risk and the more likely he is to fall. Will future generations look back on *Tomb Raider's* Lara Croft doing battle with a pack of snarling wolves as the 21st century equivalent of Lillian Gish making her way across the ice floes in *Way Down East*?

In making these analogies, I am not necessarily advocating that games should become more cinematic, any more than Seldes felt cinema should become more theatrical or literary. Game designers should study a wide range of different arts, searching not only for what they have done best but also for what they have failed to achieve, for those "roads not taken" which might be more fully realized within a game aesthetic. Game designers will need to experiment with the broadest possible range of approaches and styles, breaking with the still somewhat limited conventions of the existing game genres in some cases and deepening our appreciation of their potentials in others. In the end, games may not take the same path as cinema. Game designers will almost certainly develop their own aesthetic principles as they confront the challenge of balancing our competing desires for storytelling and interactivity. As Spector explains:

> "The art in gaming lies in the tension between the elements we put in our game worlds and what players choose to do with those elements. The developers who get that—the ones who aren't just making expensive, sophisticated pick-a-path books or movies where you get to determine what the next shot is—are the ones who will expand the boundaries of this new art form."[51]

It remains to be seen whether games can provide players the freedom they want and still provide an emotionally satisfying and thematically meaningful shape to the experience. Some of the best games—*Snood* and *Tetris* come to mind—have nothing to do with storytelling. For all we know, the future art of games may look more like architecture or dance than cinema.

Mode of production

If we are to see games accepted as a contemporary art form, game designers are going to have to stop using "market pressures" as an excuse for their lack of experimentation. True, game designers need to ship product and that can place serious limitations on how much innovation can occur within a single game.

Yet, it is worth remembering that all art occurs within an economic context. The Hollywood filmmakers of the 1920s and 1930s often produced five to seven feature films per year, yet somewhere in that rush to the marketplace, they nevertheless came to more fully realize the potentials of their medium and developed that has withstood the test of time. Seldes describes popular art in terms of a careful balance between convention and invention: convention insures accessibility, invention novelty. What keeps the lively arts lively is that they are the site of consistent experimentation and innovation. No sooner are genre conventions mapped than popular artists start to twist and turn them to yield new effects. The constant push for emotional immediacy demands a constant refinement of the art itself, keeping creators on their toes and forcing them to acknowledge audience response into their creative decision-making.

Seldes worried whether the conditions that had led to an enormous flowering of popular arts in the early twentieth century could be sustained in the face of increasingly industrialized modes of production. He blamed the studio system for much of what was wrong with contemporary cinema, yet he ended the book with a prediction that the costs of film production are likely to decrease steadily as the core technology of film production becomes standardized, thus returning filmmaking to its artisan roots. He predicts: "the first cheap film will startle you; but the film will grow less and less expensive. Presently it will be within the reach of artists ... The artists will give back to the screen the thing you have debauched—imagination."[52] Several decades later, in his book, *The Great Public*, Seldes would be even more emphatic that the rise of corporate media had strangled the aesthetic experimentation and personal expression which had enabled these "lively arts" to exist in the first place.[53] With the coming of sound, the costs of film production had increased rather than decreased, further consolidating the major studios' control over the filmmaking process, and thus delaying by several decades the rise of independent cinema he had predicted.

What does this suggest about the future of innovation in game design? For starters, the basic apparatus of the camera and the projector were standardized by the turn of the century, enabling early filmmakers to focus on the expressive potential of the medium rather than continuing to have to relearn the basic technology. Game designers, on the other hand, have confronted dramatic shifts in their basic tools and resources on average every 18 months since the emergence of their medium. This constant need to respond to a shifting technological infrastructure has shifted attention onto mastering tools which could otherwise have been devoted to exploring the properties and potentials of the medium. Secondly, despite a pretty rigorous patents war, the early history of filmmaking was marked by relatively low barriers of entry into the marketplace. Although many film histories still focus on a small number of key innovators, we now know that the basic language of cinema emerged through widespread experimentation amongst filmmakers scattered across the country and around the world. The early history of computer games, by contrast, was dominated by a relatively small number of game platforms, with all games having to pass through this corporate oversight before they could reach the market. The proliferation of authoring tools and open-source game engines have helped to lower barriers of entry into the game market-place, paving the way for more independent and smaller game companies. In such a context, those emerging companies have often been forced to innovate in order to differentiate their product from what was already on the market. The rise of the girls game movement, for example, can be explained in terms of female-run start-ups seeking to expand the game market in order to create a niche for their product in the face of competition with larger corporations.

At the same time as these new delivery technologies have loosened the hold of the platform manufacturers over game content, the cost of game development for those platforms has dramatically increased. We have seen rising technical standards which make it difficult for garage game designers to compete. Some have worried that the result will be an increased focus on blockbuster games with surefire market potential and the constant upgrading of popular franchises. What would contemporary cinema look like if it supported a succession of summer popcorn movies but could not support lower-budget and independent films. The situation is not totally hopeless. The sheer size of some of the major game publish-ers has encouraged them to diversify game design and content. A company like Electronic Arts, for example, draws on profits from its cash cow sports games to sustain a variety of smaller boutique companies, such as Maxis or Bullfrog, which are producing some of the most original and genre-breaking content.

The value of criticism

How can we insure the continued creative evolution of games? What will games look like as a mature artform, given the extraordinary shifts it has undergone over the past few decades? What modes of production or forms of authorship will insure the diversification necessary to expand the core gaming market to reach a broader public? Seldes was quite clear that sustained and rigorous criticism of the "lively arts" was the key to their long-term development. Such criticism must start from a sympathetic position, one which takes the popular arts on their own terms, one which respects the defining properties of specific media and genres. This criticism offers a measure of success quite independent from, but every bit as important as, the results of the box office. As he explains, "the box office is gross; it detects no errors, nor does it sufficiently encourage improvement."[54] Criticism encourages experimentation and innovation; commercial pressures insure acces-sibility. The lively arts grow through a careful balancing between the two.

The nature and value of these aesthetic experiments warrant close and passion-ate engagement not only within the games industry or academia, but also by the press and around the dinner table. Even Kroll's grumpy dismissal of games has sparked heated discussion and forced designers to refine their own grasp of the medium's distinctive features. Imagine what a more robust form of criticism could contribute. We need critics who know and care about games the way Pauline Kael knew movies. We need critics who write about them with that same degree of wit, wisdom, and passion. Early film critics played vital functions in documenting innovations and speculating about their potential. As a new media, computer games demand this same kind of close critical engagement. We have not had time to codify what experienced game designers know, and we have certainly not yet established a canon of great works that might serve as exemplars. There have been real creative accomplishments across the first three decades of game design, but we haven't really sorted out what they are and why they matter.

The problem with many contemporary games isn't that they are violent but that so many of them are banal, formulaic, and predictable. Thoughtful criticism can marshal support for innovation and experimentation in the industry, much as good film criticism helps focus attention on neglected independent films. At the present time, game critics represent a conservative force on aesthetic innovation, with most reviews organized around pre-existing genre preferences. They are also mostly organized around technical elements as opposed to the game's emotional impact or its aesthetic statement. It is hard, in many cases, for truly innovative games to get the attention of consumers, though the success of products like *The Sims* suggest it is certainly not impossible.

Thoughtful criticism could even contribute to our debates about violence. Rather than bemoaning "meaningless violence," we should explore ways that games could not simply stage or simulate violence but offer us new ways to understand the place of violence within our culture. Moreover, game criticism may provide a means of holding the game industry more accountable for its choices. In the wake of the Columbine shootings, game designers are struggling with their ethical responsibilities as never before, searching for ways of appealing to empowerment fantasies that don't require exploding heads and gushing organs. A serious public discussion of this medium might constructively influence these debates, helping identify and evaluate alternatives as they emerge.

As Seldes grew older, his initial enthusiasm for the "daemonic" force of popular art gave rise to growing concerns that it could be used to negatively shape public opinion and he became a key supporter of Frederic Wertham's campaign to regulate comic books.[55] Seldes' career trajectory—from defender of *Krazy Kat* to persecutor of E.C. horror comics—suggests the ambivalence at the heart of his celebration of the "lively arts." We should recognize that ambivalence within our own response to games as an emerging medium and use our criticism to debate the merits of different approaches to representing violence in games.[56] The goal should be the creation of a context which supports more thoughtful game content rather than the promotion of censorship.

As the art of games matures, progress will be driven by the most creative and forward thinking minds in the industry, those who know that games can be more than they have been, those who recognize the potential of reaching a broader public, of having a greater cultural impact, of generating more diverse and ethically responsible content and of creating richer and more emotionally engaging content. But without the support of an informed public and the perspective of thoughtful critics, game developers may never realize that potential.

Notes

1 Shigeru Miyamoto as quoted in Marc Saltzman (ed.), *Game Design Secrets of the Sages*, Second Edition (Indianapolis: MacMillan, 2000), p. 10.

2 Jack Kroll, "Emotional Engines? I Don't Think So," *Newsweek*, February 27 2000.

3 Hal Barwood, "The Envelope Please?" *Game Developer*, February 2002.

4 The core argument in this essay initially took shape as remarks presented at the Video and Computer Games Come of Age conference, jointly sponsored by the MIT Comparative Media Studies Program and the Interactive Digital Software Association. It was presented as a talk at various venues, including the Game Developers Conference, The Electronic Entertainment Exposition, Queensland Institute of Technology, and the University of Western England-Bristol. It was expanded and published as "Artform for the Digital Age," *Technology Review*, September–October 2000, and subsequently reprinted in an abbreviated form in the *New York Times* Arts and Entertainment Section. I am grateful for the feedback it has received in these various venues. I am especially thankful to advice on this current revision from Kurt Squire, Alex Chisholm, Philip Tan Boon, Eric Zimmerman, and Kevin Johnson, as well as the insights of the larger Games to Teach team and the great variety of people in the games industry who have volunteered their time to help us with our efforts.

5 Kurt Squire, "Educating Game Designers: An Interview with Warren Spector," http://www.joystick101.org/?op=displaystory&sid=2001/5/23/155255/302

6 For more on Matthew Barney and his relationship to the aesthetics of popular culture, see Henry Jenkins, "Monstrous Beauty and the Mutant Aesthetic: Rethinking Matthew Barney's Relationship to the Horror Genre," http://web.mit.edu/21fms/www/faculty/henry3/horror.html.

7 For example, see Noah Wardrip-Fruin and Pat Harrigan (ed.), *First Person* (Cambridge: MIT Press, forthcoming); Lucian King and Conrad Bain (eds.), *Game On* (London: Barbican, 2002); Game Studies, http://www.gamestudies.org/; or the current volume as examples of the new scholarship emerging around games.

8 For a useful overview of Seldes's contributions to American arts and letters, see Michael G. Kammen, *The Lively Arts: Gilbert Seldes and the Transformation of Cultural Criticism in the United States* (Oxford: Oxford University Press, 1996). It should be noted that while he borrowed the concept of the Seven Arts from the classical tradition, the book remains ambiguous about how to breakdown the topics he discusses into seven distinct traditions. What one takes from Seldes is less a taxonomy of popular arts than a way of understanding the relationship of popular, middlebrow, and high art.

9 Gilbert Seldes, *The Seven Lively Arts* (New York: Sagmore Press, 1957), p. 193.

10 Seldes, p. 264.

11 Barwood.

12 Seldes, p. 272.

13 Seldes, p. 228.

14 Seldes, p. 293. Seldes's arguments about sensory restoration need to be understood in the context of larger discourses about sensation and expression at the turn of the century. For an overview of those discussions, see Ben Singer, *Melodrama and Modernity: Early Sensational Cinema and Its Contexts* (New York: Columbia University Press, 2001) and Henry Jenkins, *What Made Pistachio Nuts? Early Sound Comedy and the Vaudeville Aesthetic* (New York: Columbia University Press, 1992).

15 Seldes, p. 223.

16 Seldes, p. 300.

17 Seldes, p. 299.

18 These shifts have attracted considerable scholarly attention within film studies circles. For a useful overview of these historical transitions, see Thomas Elsaesser and Adam Barker (eds.), *Early Cinema: Space-Frame Narrative* (London: BFI, 1990).

19 Seldes, p. 288.

20 Seldes, p. 16.
21 Seldes, p. 18.
22 Seldes, p. 288.
23 Kroll, ibid.
24 Steven Poole, *Trigger Happy: Videogames and the Entertainment Revolution* (New York: Arcade Publishing, 2000), pp. 218–220.
25 Frank Lantz and Eric Zimmerman, "Checkmate: Rules, Play and Culture," Merge, 1999, http://www.ericzimmerman.com/acastuff/checkmate.html. See also Eric Zimmerman, "Do Independent Games Exist?" in," in Lucian King and Conrad Bain (eds.), *Game On* (London: Barbican, 2002: "**Games suffer from cinema envy.** What passes for "realism" in games is an awkward and unimaginative use of 3D computer graphics. It's time for game developers to stop trying to replicate the pleasures of film. Games need to find their own forms of expression, capitalizing on their unique properties as dynamic, participatory systems.")
26 Seldes, p. 286.
27 Poole, p. 226.
28 Seldes, p. 19.
29 Seldes, p. 186.
30 Squire, ibid.
31 Flippo Tommaso Marintetti, "The Variety Theatre," in Michael Kirby (ed.), *Futurist Performance* (New York: Dutton, 1971), pp. 179–186.
32 Sergei Eisenstein, "Montage of Attractions," *Drama Review*, March 1974, pp. 77–85.
33 Eddie Cantor as qouted in Mary B. Mullet, "We All Like the Medicine 'Doctor' Eddie Cantor Gives," *American Magazine*, July 1924, pp. 34ff.
34 Vadim Uraneff, "Commedia Dell'Arte and American Vaudeville," *Theatre Arts*, October 1923, p. 326.
35 For a useful discussion of the aesthetics of early video games, see Van Burnham and Ralph H. Baer, *Supercade* (Cambridge: MIT Press, 2001).
36 I am indebted to the participants of the Comparative Media Studies-Electronic Arts Creative Leaders workshop series for these insights into the game design process.
37 Seldes, p. 175.
38 Robert Lytell, "Vaudeville Old and Young," *New Republic*, July 1 1925, p. 156
39 David Perry as qouted in Saltzman, p. 18.
40 James Newman, "On Being a Tetraminoe: Mapping the Contours of the Videogame Character," paper delivered at the International Game Cultures Conference, Bristol, England, June–July 2001.
41 Dikarika, "Tales from a DDR Adict," Joystick 101, http://www.joystick101.org/?op=d isplaystory&sid=2002/1/12/133339/317
42 Alex Rigopulos, E-mail Correspondence with the author, March 1 2002.
43 "Gamers Set for Sensory Overload," *BBC News*, March 1 2002, http://news.bbc.co.uk/ hi/english/sci/tech/newsid_1846000/1846561.stm
44 David Bordwell, *Planet Hong Kong: Popular Cinema and the Art of Entertainment* (Cambridge: Harvard University Press, 2000), p. 244.
45 Bordwell, p. 232
46 Seldes, p. 37.
47 James Agee, "Comedy's Greatest Era," in Gerald Mast and Marshall Cohen (eds.), *Film Theory and Criticism* (New York: Oxford University Press, 1974), p. 439. For a fuller discussion of Agee's theory of comic performance, see Henry Jenkins and Kristine Brunovska Karnick, "Acting Funny," in Kristine Brunovska Karnick and Henry Jenkins (eds.), *Classical Hollywood Comedy* (New York: Routledge/AFI, 1995).
48 Henry Jenkins, "Game Design as Narrative Architecture," in Noah Wardrip-Fruin and Pat Harrigan (ed.), *First Person* (Cambridge: MIT Press, forthcoming).

49 Henry Jenkins, "Complete Freedom of Movement': Video Games as Gendered Play Spaces" in Justine Cassell and Henry Jenkins (eds.), *From Barbie to Mortal Kombat: Gender and Computer Games* (Cambridge: MIT Press, 1998).

50 Kurt Squire and Henry Jenkins, "The Art of Contested Spaces," in Lucian King and Conrad Bain (eds.), *Game On* (London: Barbican, 2002).

51 Squire, ibid.

52 Seldes, p. 289.

53 Gilbert Seldes, *The Great Audience* (New York: Viking, 1950).

54 Seldes, *The Seven Lively Arts*, p. 303.

55 Seldes, *Great Audience*, pp. 271–278, offer the fullest summary of his views on the comic book industry.

56 See James Cain and Henry Jenkins, "'I'm Gonna Git Medieval on Your Ass: A Conversation about Violence and Culture," in Helaine Postner (ed.), *Culture of Violence* (Amherst: University of Massachusetts Press, 2002).

8

MANIFESTO FOR A LUDIC CENTURY

Eric Zimmerman

Source: *Kotaku.com*, 2013, available at http://kotaku.com/manifesto-the-21st-century-will-be-defined-by-games-1275355204, and republished in Steffen Walz and Sebastian Detering (eds), *The Gameful World: Approaches, Issues, Applications* (Cambridge, MA: The MIT Press, 2015), pp. 19–22.

Games are ancient

Like making music, telling stories, and creating images, playing games is part of what it means to be human. Games are perhaps the first designed interactive systems our species invented.

Digital technology has given games a new relevance

The rise of computers has paralleled the resurgence of games in our culture. This is no accident. Games like Chess, Go, and Parcheesi are much like digital computers, machines for creating and storing numerical states. In this sense, computers didn't create games; games created computers.

The 20th century was the century of information

Systems theory, communications theory, cybernetics, artificial intelligence, computer science—these fields, many of them emerging well before electronic computers, helped create the "information revolution."

The abstraction of information has made possible massively complex bureaucracies and technologies, from telegraph and telephone networks to NASDAQ and Facebook.

In our Ludic century, information has been put at play

Our information networks no longer take the form of vast card catalogs or webs of pneumatic tubes. Digital networks are flexible and organic.

In the last few decades, information has taken a playful turn. To take a prime example, Wikipedia is not about users accessing a storehouse of expert knowledge. It is a messy, chaotic community in which the users are also the experts, who together create the information while also evolving the system as a whole.

In the 20th century, the moving image was the dominant cultural form

While music, architecture, the written word, and many other forms of expression flourished in the last century, the moving image came to dominate. Personal storytelling, news reporting, epic cultural narratives, political propaganda—all were expressed most powerfully through film and video.

The rise of the moving image is tightly bound to the rise of information; film and video as media represent linear, non-interactive information that is accessed by a viewer.

The Ludic century is an era of games

When information is put at play, game-like experiences replace linear media. Media and culture in the Ludic Century is increasingly systemic, modular, customizable, and participatory. Games embody all of these characteristics in a very direct sense.

Increasingly, the ways that people spend their leisure time and consume art, design, and entertainment will be games—or experiences very much like games.

We live in a world of systems

The ways that we work and communicate, research and learn, socialize and romance, conduct our finances and communicate with our governments, are all intimately intertwined with complex systems of information—in a way that could not have existed a few decades ago.

For such a systemic society, games make a natural fit. While every poem or every song is certainly a system, games are dynamic systems in a much more literal sense. From Poker to Pac-Man to Warcraft, games are machines of inputs and outputs that are inhabited, manipulated, and explored.

There is a need to be playful

It is not enough to merely be a systems-literate person; to understand systems in an analytic sense. We also must learn to be playful in them. A playful system is a human system, a social system rife with contradictions and with possibility.

Being playful is the engine of innovation and creativity: as we play, we think about thinking and we learn to act in new ways. As a cultural form, games have a particularly direct connection with play.

We should think like designers

In the Ludic Century, we cannot have a passive relationship to the systems that we inhabit. We must learn to be designers, to recognize how and why systems are constructed, and to try to make them better.

It took several decades for automobiles to shift from being a hobbyist technology requiring expert knowledge to being a locked-in consumer product. The constant change of digital technology means that our hardware and software systems may never stabilize in this way. To fully engage with our world of systems, we must all think like designers.

Games are a literacy

Systems, play, design: these are not just aspects of the Ludic Century, they are also elements of *gaming literacy*. Literacy is about creating and understanding meaning, which allows people to write (create) and read (understand).

New literacies, such as visual and technological literacy, have also been identified in recent decades. However, to be truly literate in the Ludic Century also requires gaming literacy. The rise of games in our culture is both cause and effect of gaming literacy in the Ludic Century.

Gaming literacy can address our problems

The problems the world faces today requires the kinds of thinking that gaming literacy engenders. How does the price of gas in California affect the politics of the Middle East affect the Amazon ecosystem? These problems force us to understand how the parts of a system fit together to create a complex whole with emergent effects. They require playful, innovative, trans-disciplinary thinking in which systems can be analyzed, redesigned, and transformed into something new.

In the Ludic century, everyone will be a game designer

Games alter the very nature of cultural consumption. Music is *played* by musicians, but most people are not musicians—they listen to music that someone else has made. Games, on the other hand, require active participation.

Game design involves systems logic, social psychology, and culture hacking. To play a game deeply is to think more and more like a game designer—to tinker, retro-engineer, and modify a game in order to find new ways to play. As more people play more deeply in the Ludic Century, the lines will become increasingly blurred between game players and game designers.

Games are beautiful. They do not need to be justified

This above all: games are not valuable because they can teach someone a skill or make the world a better place. Like other forms of cultural expression, games and play are important because they are beautiful.

Appreciating the aesthetics of games—how dynamic interactive systems create beauty and meaning—is one of the delightful and daunting challenges we face in this dawning Ludic Century.

The ideas in this essay first grew out of my interaction with literacy scholars Jim Gee, Rich Halverson, Betty Hayes, David Shaffer, Kurt Squire, and Constance Steinkuehler. Very special thanks to the brilliant Heather Chaplin for developing the ideas with me over many conversations and arguments. Thanks to Nathalie Pozzi and John Sharp for insightful editing and to Kirk Hamilton and Stephen Totilo for publishing it on Kotaku.com.

Part 2

GAME STUDIES CLASSICS

9

NATURE AND SIGNIFICANCE OF PLAY AS A CULTURAL PHENOMENON

Johan Huizinga

Source: *Homo Ludens: A Study of the Play-Element in Culture* (New York: Routledge, 1949), pp. 1–27. Originally published in Dutch, 1938.

Play is older than culture, for culture, however inadequately defined, always pre-supposes human society, and animals have not waited for man to teach them their playing. We can safely assert, even, that human civilization has added no essential feature to the general idea of play. Animals play just like men. We have only to watch young dogs to see that all the essentials of human play are present in their merry gambols. They invite one another to play by a certain ceremoniousness of attitude and gesture. They keep to the rule that you shall not bite, or not bite hard, your brother's ear. They pretend to get terribly angry. And—what is most important—in all these doings they plainly experience tremendous fun and enjoyment. Such rompings of young dogs are only one of the simpler forms of animal play. There are other, much more highly developed forms: regular contests and beautiful performances before an admiring public.

Here we have at once a very important point: even in its simplest forms on the animal level, play is more than a mere physiological phenomenon or a psychological reflex. It goes beyond the confines of purely physical or purely biological activity. It is a *significant* function—that is to say, there is some sense to it. In play there is something "at play" which transcends the immediate needs of life and imparts meaning to the action. All play means something. If we call the active principle that makes up the essence of play, "instinct", we explain nothing; if we call it "mind" or "will" we say too much. However we may regard it, the very fact that play has a meaning implies a non-materialistic quality in the nature of the thing itself.

Psychology and physiology deal with the observation, description and explanation of the play of animals, children, and grown-ups. They try to determine the nature and significance of play and to assign it its place in the scheme of life. The high importance of this place and the necessity, or at least the utility, of play as a function are generally taken for granted and form the starting-point of all such scientific researches. The numerous attempts to define the biological function of

135

play show a striking variation. By some the origin and fundamentals of play have been described as a discharge of superabundant vital energy, by others as the satisfaction of some "imitative instinct", or again as simply a "need" for relaxation. According to one theory play constitutes a training of the young creature for the serious work that life will demand later on. According to another it serves as an exercise in restraint needful to the individual. Some find the principle of play in an innate urge to exercise a certain faculty, or in the desire to dominate or compete. Yet others regard it as an "abreaction"—an outlet for harmful impulses, as the necessary restorer of energy wasted by one-sided activity, as "wish-fulfilment", as a fiction designed to keep up the feeling of personal value, etc.[1]

All these hypotheses have one thing in common: they all start from the assumption that play must serve something which is *not* play, that it must have some kind of biological purpose. They all enquire into the why and the wherefore of play. The various answers they give tend rather to overlap than to exclude one another. It would be perfectly possible to accept nearly all the explanations without getting into any real confusion of thought—and without coming much nearer to a real understanding of the play-concept. They are all only partial solutions of the problem. If any of them were really decisive it ought either to exclude all the others or comprehend them in a higher unity. Most of them only deal incidentally with the question of what play is *in itself* and what it means for the player. They attack play direct with the quantitative methods of experimental science without first paying attention to its profoundly aesthetic quality. As a rule they leave the primary quality of play as such, virtually untouched. To each and every one of the above "explanations" it might well be objected: "So far so good, but what actually is the *fun* of playing? Why does the baby crow with pleasure? Why does the gambler lose himself in his passion? Why is a huge crowd roused to frenzy by a football match?" This intensity of, and absorption in, play finds no explanation in biological analysis. Yet in this intensity, this absorption, this power of maddening, lies the very essence, the primordial quality of play. Nature, so our reasoning mind tells us, could just as easily have given her children all those useful functions of discharging superabundant energy, of relaxing after exertion, of training for the demands of life, of compensating for unfulfilled longings, etc., in the form of purely mechanical exercises and reactions. But no, she gave us play, with its tension, its mirth, and its fun.

Now this last-named element, the *fun* of playing, resists all analysis, all logical interpretation. As a concept, it cannot be reduced to any other mental category. No other modern language known to me has the exact equivalent of the English "fun". The Dutch "aardigkeit" perhaps comes nearest to it (derived from "aard" which means the same as "Art" and "Wesen"[2] in German, and thus evidence, perhaps, that the matter cannot be reduced further). We may note in passing that "fun" in its current usage is of rather recent origin. French, oddly enough, has no corresponding term at all; German half makes up for it by "Spass" and "Witz" together. Nevertheless it is precisely this fun-element that characterizes the essence of play. Here we have to do with an absolutely primary category of life, familiar

136

to everybody at a glance right down to the animal level. We may well call play a "totality" in the modern sense of the word, and it is as a totality that we must try to understand and evaluate it.

Since the reality of play extends beyond the sphere of human life it cannot have its foundations in any rational nexus, because this would limit it to mankind. The incidence of play is not associated with any particular stage of civilization or view of the universe. Any thinking person can see at a glance that play is a thing on its own, even if his language possesses no general concept to express it. Play cannot be denied. You can deny, if you like, nearly all abstractions: justice, beauty, truth, goodness, mind, God. You can deny seriousness, but not play.

But in acknowledging play you acknowledge mind, for whatever else play is, it is not matter. Even in the animal world it bursts the bounds of the physically existent. From the point of view of a world wholly determined by the operation of blind forces, play would be altogether superfluous. Play only becomes possible, thinkable and understandable when an influx of *mind* breaks down the absolute determinism of the cosmos. The very existence of play continually confirms the supra-logical nature of the human situation. Animals play, so they must be more than merely mechanical things. We play and know that we play, so we must be more than merely rational beings, for play is irrational.

In tackling the problem of play as a function of culture proper and not as it appears in the life of the animal or the child, we begin where biology and psychology leave off. In culture we find play as a given magnitude existing before culture itself existed, accompanying it and pervading it from the earliest beginnings right up to the phase of civilization we are now living in. We find play present everywhere as a well-defined quality of action which is different from "ordinary" life. We can disregard the question of how far science has succeeded in reducing this quality to quantitative factors. In our opinion it has not. At all events it is precisely this quality, itself so characteristic of the form of life we call "play", which matters. Play as a special form of activity, as a "significant form", as a social function—that is our subject. We shall not look for the natural impulses and habits conditioning play in general, but shall consider play in its manifold concrete forms as itself a social construction. We shall try to take play as the player himself takes it: in its primary significance. If we find that play is based on the manipulation of certain images, on a certain "imagination" of reality (i.e. its conversion into images), then our main concern will be to grasp the value and significance of these images and their "imagination". We shall observe their action in play itself and thus try to understand play as a cultural factor in life.

The great archetypal activities of human society are all permeated with play from the start. Take language, for instance—that first and supreme instrument which man shapes in order to communicate, to teach, to command. Language allows him to distinguish, to establish, to state things; in short, to name them and by naming them to raise them into the domain of the spirit. In the making of speech and language the spirit is continually "sparking" between matter and mind, as it were, playing with this wondrous nominative faculty. Behind every abstract expression there lie the boldest of metaphors, and every metaphor is a play upon words. Thus in giving expression to life man creates a second, poetic world alongside the world of nature.

Or take myth. This, too, is a transformation or an "imagination" of the outer world, only here the process is more elaborate and ornate than is the case with individual words. In myth, primitive man seeks to account for the world of phenomena by grounding it in the Divine. In all the wild imaginings of mythology a fanciful spirit is playing on the border-line between jest and earnest. Or finally, let us take ritual. Primitive society performs its sacred rites, its sacrifices, consecrations and mysteries, all of which serve to guarantee the well-being of the world, in a spirit of pure play truly understood.

Now in myth and ritual the great instinctive forces of civilized life have their origin: law and order, commerce and profit, craft and art, poetry, wisdom and science. All are rooted in the primaeval soil of play.

The object of the present essay is to demonstrate that it is more than a rhetorical comparison to view culture *sub specie ludi*. The thought is not at all new. There was a time when it was generally accepted, though in a limited sense quite different from the one intended here: in the 17th century, the age of world theatre. Drama, in a glittering succession of figures ranging from Shakespeare and Calderon to Racine, then dominated the literature of the West. It was the fashion to liken the world to a stage on which every man plays his part. Does this mean that the play-element in civilization was openly acknowledged? Not at all. On closer examination this fashionable comparison of life to a stage proves to be little more than an echo of the Neo-platonism that was then in vogue, with a markedly moralistic accent. It was a variation on the ancient theme of the vanity of all things. The fact that play and culture are actually interwoven with one another was neither observed nor expressed, whereas for us the whole point is to show that genuine, pure play is one of the main bases of civilisation.

To our way of thinking, play is the direct opposite of seriousness. At first sight this opposition seems as irreducible to other categories as the play-concept itself. Examined more closely, however, the contrast between play and seriousness proves to be neither conclusive nor fixed. We can say: play is non-seriousness. But apart from the fact that this proposition tells us nothing about the positive qualities of play, it is extraordinarily easy to refute. As soon as we proceed from "play is non-seriousness" to "play is not serious", the contrast leaves us in the lurch—for some play can be very serious indeed. Moreover we can immediately name several other fundamental categories that likewise come under the heading "non-seriousness" yet have no correspondence whatever with "play". Laughter, for instance, is in a sense the opposite of seriousness without being absolutely bound up with play. Children's games, football, and chess are played in profound seriousness; the players have not the slightest inclination to laugh. It is worth noting that the purely physiological act of laughing is exclusive to man, whilst the significant function of play is common to both men and animals. The Aristotelian *animal ridens* characterizes man as distinct from the animal almost more absolutely than *homo sapiens*.

What is true of laughter is true also of the comic. The comic comes under the category of non-seriousness and has certain affinities with laughter—it provokes to laughter. But its relation to play is subsidiary. In itself play is not comical either for player or public. The play of young animals or small children may sometimes be ludicrous, but the sight of grown dogs chasing one another hardly moves us to laughter. When we call a farce or a comedy "comic", it is not so much on account of the play-acting as such as on account of the situation or the thoughts expressed. The mimic and laughter-provoking art of the clown is comic as well as ludicrous, but it can scarcely be termed genuine play.

The category of the comic is closely connected with *folly* in the highest and lowest sense of that word. Play, however, is not foolish. It lies outside the antithesis of wisdom and folly. The later Middle Ages tended to express the two cardinal moods of life play and seriousness—somewhat imperfectly by opposing *folie* to *sense*, until Erasmus in his *Laus Stultitiae* showed the inadequacy of the contrast.

All the terms in this loosely connected group of ideas—play, laughter, folly, wit, jest, joke, the comic, etc.—share the characteristic which we had to attribute to play, namely, that of resisting any attempt to reduce it to other terms. Their rationale and their mutual relationships must lie in a very deep layer of our mental being.

The more we try to mark off the form we call "play" from other forms apparently related to it, the more the absolute independence of the play-concept stands out. And the segregation of play from the domain of the great categorical antitheses does not stop there. Play lies outside the antithesis of wisdom and folly, and equally outside those of truth and falsehood, good and evil. Although it is a non-material activity it has no moral function. The valuations of vice and virtue do not apply here.

If, therefore, play cannot be directly referred to the categories of truth or goodness, can it be included perhaps in the realm of the aesthetic? Here our judgement wavers. For although the attribute of beauty does not attach to play as such, play nevertheless tends to assume marked elements of beauty. Mirth and grace adhere at the outset to the more primitive forms of play. In play the beauty of the human body in motion reaches its zenith. In its more developed forms it is saturated with rhythm and harmony, the noblest gifts of aesthetic perception known to man. Many and close are the links that connect play with beauty. All the same, we cannot say that beauty is inherent in play as such; so we must leave it at that: play is a function of the living, but is not susceptible of exact definition either logically, biologically, or aesthetically. The play-concept must always remain distinct from all the other forms of thought in which we express the structure of mental and social life. Hence we shall have to confine ourselves to describing the main characteristics of play.

Since our theme is the relation of play to culture we need not enter into all the possible forms of play but can restrict ourselves to its social manifestations. These we might call the higher forms of play. They are generally much easier to describe than the more primitive play of infants and young animals, because they are more distinct and articulate in form and their features more various and conspicuous, whereas in interpreting primitive play we immediately come up against that irreducible quality of pure playfulness which is not, in our opinion, amenable to further analysis. We shall have to speak of contests and races, of performances and exhibitions, of dancing and music, pageants, masquerades and tournaments. Some of the characteristics we shall enumerate are proper to play in general, others to social play in particular.

First and foremost, then, all play is a voluntary activity. Play to order is no longer play: it could at best be but a forcible imitation of it. By this quality of freedom alone, play marks itself off from the course of the natural process. It is something added thereto and spread out over it like a flowering, an ornament, a garment. Obviously, freedom must be understood here in the wider sense that leaves untouched the philosophical problem of determinism. It may be objected that this freedom does not exist for the animal and the child; they *must* play because their instinct drives them to it and because it serves to develop their bodily faculties and their powers of selection. The term "instinct", however, introduces an unknown quantity, and to presuppose the utility of play from the start is to be guilty of a *petitio principii*. Child and animal play because they enjoy playing, and therein precisely lies their freedom.

Be that as it may, for the adult and responsible human being play is a function which he could equally well leave alone. Play is superfluous. The need for it is only urgent to the extent that the enjoyment of it makes it a need. Play can be deferred or suspended at any time. It is never imposed by physical necessity or moral duty. It is never a task. It is done at leisure, during "free time". Only when play is a recognized cultural function—a rite, a ceremony—is it bound up with notions of obligation and duty.

Here, then, we have the first main characteristic of play: that it is free, is in fact freedom. A second characteristic is closely connected with this, namely, that play is not "ordinary" or "real" life. It is rather a stepping out of "real" life into a temporary sphere of activity with a disposition all of its own. Every child knows perfectly well that he is "only pretending", or that it was "only for fun". How deep-seated this awareness is in the child's soul is strikingly illustrated by the following story, told to me by the father of the boy in question. He found his four-year-old son sitting at the front of a row of chairs, playing "trains". As he hugged him the boy said: "Don't kiss the engine, Daddy, or the carriages won't think it's real". This "only pretending" quality of play betrays a consciousness of the inferiority of play compared with "seriousness", a feeling that seems to be something as primary as play itself. Nevertheless, as we have already pointed out, the consciousness of play being "only a pretend" does not by any means prevent it from proceeding with the utmost seriousness, with an absorption, a devotion that passes into rapture and, temporarily at least, completely abolishes that troublesome "only" feeling. Any game can at any time wholly run away with the players. The contrast between play and seriousness is always fluid. The inferiority of play is continually being offset by the corresponding superiority of its seriousness. Play turns to seriousness and seriousness to play. Play may rise to heights of beauty and sublimity that leave seriousness far beneath. Tricky questions such as these will come up for discussion when we start examining the relationship between play and ritual.

As regards its formal characteristics all students lay stress on the *disinterestedness* of play. Not being "ordinary" life it stands outside the immediate satisfaction of wants and appetites, indeed it interrupts the appetitive process. It interpolates itself as a temporary activity satisfying in itself and ending there. Such at least is the way in which play presents itself to us in the first instance: as an intermezzo, an *interlude* in our daily lives. As a regularly recurring relaxation, however, it becomes the accompaniment, the complement, in fact an integral part of life in general. It adorns life, amplifies it and is to that extent a necessity both for the individual—as a life function—and for society by reason of the meaning it contains, its significance, its expressive value, its spiritual and social associations, in short, as a culture function. The expression of it satisfies all kinds of communal ideals. It thus has its place in a sphere superior to the strictly biological processes of nutrition, reproduction and self-preservation. This assertion is apparently contradicted by the fact that play, or rather sexual display, is predominant in animal life precisely at the mating-season. But would it be too absurd to assign a place *outside* the purely physiological, to the singing, cooing and strutting of birds just as we do to human play? In all its higher forms the latter at any rate always belongs to the sphere of festival and ritual—the sacred sphere.

Now, does the fact that play is a necessity, that it subserves culture, or indeed that it actually becomes culture, detract from its disinterested character? No, for the purposes it serves are external to immediate material interests or the individual satisfaction of biological needs. As a sacred activity play naturally contributes to the well-being of the group, but in quite another way and by other means than the acquisition of the necessities of life.

Play is distinct from "ordinary" life both as to locality and duration. This is the third main characteristic of play: its secludedness, its limitedness. It is "played out" within certain limits of time and place. It contains its own course and meaning.

Play begins, and then at a certain moment it is "over". It plays itself to an end. While it is in progress all is movement, change, alternation, succession, association, separation. But immediately connected with its limitation as to time there is a further curious feature of play: it at once assumes fixed form as a cultural phenomenon. Once played, it endures as a new-found creation of the mind, a treasure to be retained by the memory. It is transmitted, it becomes tradition. It can be repeated at any time, whether it be "child's play" or a game of chess, or at fixed intervals like a mystery. In this faculty of repetition lies one of the most essential qualities of play. It holds good not only of play as a whole but also of its inner structure. In nearly all the higher forms of play the elements of repetition and alternation (as in the *refrain*), are like the warp and woof of a fabric.

More striking even than the limitation as to time is the limitation as to space. All play moves and has its being within a play-ground marked off beforehand either materially or ideally, deliberately or as a matter of course. Just as there is no formal difference between play and ritual, so the "consecrated spot" cannot be formally distinguished from the play-ground. The arena, the card-table, the magic circle, the temple, the stage, the screen, the tennis court, the court of justice, etc., are all in form and function play-grounds, i.e. forbidden spots, isolated, hedged round, hallowed, within which special rules obtain. All are temporary worlds within the ordinary world, dedicated to the performance of an act apart.

Inside the play-ground an absolute and peculiar order reigns. Here we come across another, very positive feature of play: it creates order, *is* order. Into an imperfect world and into the confusion of life it brings a temporary, a limited perfection. Play demands order absolute and supreme. The least deviation from it "spoils the game", robs it of its character and makes it worthless. The profound affinity between play and order is perhaps the reason why play, as we noted in passing, seems to lie to such a large extent in the field of aesthetics. Play has a tendency to be beautiful. It may be that this aesthetic factor is identical with the impulse to create orderly form, which animates play in all its aspects. The words we use to denote the elements of play belong for the most part to aesthetics, terms with which we try to describe the effects of beauty: tension, poise, balance, contrast, variation, solution, resolution, etc. Play casts a spell over us; it is "enchanting", "captivating". It is invested with the noblest qualities we are capable of perceiving in things: rhythm and harmony.

The element of tension in play to which we have just referred plays a particularly important part. Tension means uncertainty, chanciness; a striving to decide the issue and so end it. The player wants something to "go", to "come off"; he wants to "succeed" by his own exertions. Baby reaching for a toy, pussy patting a bobbin, a little girl playing ball—all want to achieve something difficult, to succeed, to end a tension. Play is "tense", as we say. It is this element of tension and solution that governs all solitary games of skill and application such as puzzles, jig-saws, mosaic-making, patience, target-shooting, and the more play bears the character of competition the more fervent it will be. In gambling and athletics it is at its height. Though play as such is outside the range of good and bad, the element of tension imparts to it a certain ethical value in so far as it means a testing of the player's prowess: his courage, tenacity, resources and, last but not least, his spiritual powers-his "fairness"; because, despite his ardent desire to win, he must still stick to the rules of the game.

These rules in their turn are a very important factor in the play-concept. All play has its rules. They determine what "holds" in the temporary world circumscribed by play. The rules of a game are absolutely binding and allow no doubt. Paul Valery once in passing gave expression to a very cogent thought when he said: "No scepticism is possible where the rules of a game are concerned, for the principle underlying them is an unshakable truth. . . . " Indeed, as soon as the rules are transgressed the whole play-world collapses. The game is over. The umpire's whistle breaks the spell and sets "real" life going again.

The player who trespasses against the rules or ignores them is a "spoil-sport". The spoil-sport is not the same as the false player, the cheat; for the latter pretends to be playing the game and, on the face of it, still acknowledges the magic circle.

It is curious to note how much more lenient society is to the cheat than to the spoil-sport. This is because the spoil-sport shatters the play-world itself. By withdrawing from the game he reveals the relativity and fragility of the play-world in which he had temporarily shut himself with others. He robs play of its *illusion*—a pregnant word which means literally "in-play" (from *inlusio, illudere* or *inludere*). Therefore he must be cast out, for he threatens the existence of the play-community. The figure of the spoil-sport is most apparent in boys' games. The little community does not enquire whether the spoil-sport is guilty of defection because he dares not enter into the game or because he is not allowed to. Rather, it does not recognize "not being allowed" and calls it "not daring". For it, the problem of obedience and conscience is no more than fear of punishment. The spoil-sport breaks the magic world, therefore he is a coward and must be ejected. In the world of high seriousness, too, the cheat and the hypocrite have always had an easier time of it than the spoil-sports, here called apostates, heretics, innovators, prophets, conscientious objectors, etc. It sometimes happens, however, that the spoil-sports in their turn make a new community with rules of its own. The outlaw, the revolutionary, the cabbalist or member of a secret society, indeed heretics of all kinds are of a highly associative if not sociable disposition, and a certain element of play is prominent in all their doings.

A play-community generally tends to become permanent even after the game is over. Of course, not every game of marbles or every bridge-party leads to the founding of a club. But the feeling of being "apart together" in an exceptional situation, of sharing something important, of mutually withdrawing from the rest of the world and rejecting the usual norms, retains its magic beyond the duration of the individual game. The club pertains to play as the hat to the head. It would be rash to explain all the associations which the anthropologist calls "phratria"— e.g. clans, brotherhoods, etc.-simply as play-communities; nevertheless it has been shown again and again how difficult it is to draw the line between, on the one hand, permanent social grouping particularly in archaic cultures with their extremely important, solemn, indeed sacred customs—and the sphere of play on the other.

The exceptional and special position of play is most tellingly illustrated by the fact that it loves to surround itself with an air of secrecy. Even in early childhood the charm of play is enhanced by making a "secret" out of it. This is for *us*, not for the "others". What the "others" do "outside" is no concern of ours at the moment. Inside the circle of the game the laws and customs of ordinary life no longer count. We are different and do things differently. This temporary abolition of the ordinary world is fully acknowledged in child-life, but it is no less evident in the great ceremonial games of savage societies. During the great feast of initiation when the youths are accepted into the male community, it is not the neophytes only that are exempt from the ordinary laws and regulations: there is a truce to all feuds in the tribe. All retaliatory acts and vendettas are suspended. This temporary suspension of normal social life on account of the sacred play-season has numerous traces in the more advanced civilizations as well. Everything that pertains to saturnalia and carnival customs belongs to it. Even with us a bygone age of robuster private habits than ours, more marked class-privileges and a more complaisant police recognized the orgies of young men of rank under the name of a "rag". The saturnalian licence of young men still survives, in fact, in the ragging at English universities, which the *Oxford English Dictionary* defines as "an extensive display of noisy and disorderly conduct carried out in defiance of authority and discipline".

The "differentness" and secrecy of play are most vividly expressed in "dressing up". Here the "extraordinary" nature of play reaches perfection. The disguised or masked individual "plays" another part, another being. He *is* another being. The terrors of childhood, open-hearted gaiety, mystic fantasy and sacred awe are all inextricably entangled in this strange business of masks and disguises.

Summing up the formal characteristics of play we might call it a free activity standing quite consciously outside "ordinary" life as being "not serious", but at the same time absorbing the player intensely and utterly It is an activity connected with no material interest, and no profit can be gained by it. It proceeds within its own proper boundaries of time and space according to fixed rules and in an orderly manner. It promotes the formation of social groupings which tend to surround themselves with secrecy and to stress their difference from the common world by disguise or other means.

The function of play in the higher forms which concern us here can largely be derived from the two basic aspects under which we meet it: as a contest *for* something or a representation *of* something. These two functions can unite in such a way that the game "represents" a contest, or else becomes a contest for the best representation of something.

Representation means display, and this may simply consist in the exhibition of something naturally given, before an audience. The peacock and the turkey merely display their gorgeous plumage to the females, but the essential feature of it lies in the parading of something out of the ordinary and calculated to arouse admiration. If the bird accompanies this exhibition with dance-steps we have a performance, a *stepping out of* common reality into a higher order. We are ignorant of the bird's sensations while so engaged. We know, however, that in child-life performances of this kind are full of imagination. The child is *making an image* of something different, something more beautiful, or more sublime, or more dangerous than what he usually is. One is a Prince, or one is Daddy or a wicked witch or a tiger. The child is quite literally "beside himself" with delight, transported beyond himself to such an extent that he almost believes he actually is such and such a thing, without, however, wholly losing consciousness of "ordinary reality". His representation is not so much a sham-reality as a realization in appearance: "imagination" in the original sense of the word.

Passing now from children's games to the sacred performances in archaic culture we find that there is more of a mental element "at play" in the latter, though it is excessively difficult to define. The sacred performance is more than an actualization in appearance only, a sham reality; it is also more than a symbolical actualization—it is a mystical one. In it, something invisible and inactual takes beautiful, actual, holy form. The participants in the rite are convinced that the action actualizes and effects a definite beatification, brings about an order of things higher than that in which they customarily live. All the same this "actualization by representation" still retains the formal characteristics of play in every respect. It is played or performed within a playground that is literally "staked out", and played moreover as a feast, i.e. in mirth and freedom. A sacred space, a temporarily real world of its own, has been expressly hedged off for it. But with the end of the play its effect is not lost; rather it continues to shed its radiance on the ordinary world outside, a wholesome influence working security, order and prosperity for the whole community until the sacred play-season comes round again.

Examples can be taken from all over the world. According to ancient Chinese lore the purpose of music and the dance is to keep the world in its right course and to force Nature into benevolence towards man. The year's prosperity will depend on the right performance of sacred contests at the seasonal feasts. If these gatherings do not take place the crops will not ripen.[3]

The rite is a *dromenon*, which means "something acted", an act, action. That which is enacted, or the stuff of the action, is a *drama*, which again means act, action represented on a stage. Such action may occur as a performance or a contest. The rite, or "ritual act" represents a cosmic happening, an event in the natural process. The word "represents", however, does not cover the exact meaning of the act, at least not in its looser, modern connotation; for here "representation" is really *identification*, the mystic repetition or *re-presentation* of the event. The rite produces the effect which is then not so much *shown figuratively* as *actually reproduced* in the action. The function of the rite, therefore, is far from being merely imitative; it causes the worshippers to participate in the sacred happening itself. As the Greeks would say, "it is *methectic* rather than *mimetic*".[4] It is "a helping-out of the action".[5]

Anthropology is not primarily interested in how psychology will assess the mental attitude displayed in these phenomena. The psychologist may seek to settle the matter by calling such performances an *identification compensatrice*, a kind of substitute, "a representative act undertaken in view of the impossibility of staging real, purposive action".[6] Are the performers mocking, or are they mocked? The business of the anthropologist is to understand the significance of these "imaginations" in the mind of the peoples who practise and believe in them.

We touch here on the very core of comparative religion: the nature and essence of ritual and mystery. The whole of the ancient Vedic sacrificial rites rests on the idea that the ceremony—be it sacrifice, contest or performance—by representing a certain desired cosmic event, compels the gods to effect that event in reality. We could well say, by "playing" it. Leaving the religious issues aside we shall only concern ourselves here with the play-element in archaic ritual.

Ritual is thus in the main a matter of shows, representations, dramatic performances, imaginative actualizations of a vicarious nature. At the great seasonal festivals the community celebrates the grand happenings in the life of nature by staging sacred performances, which represent the change of seasons, the rising and

145

setting of the constellations, the growth and ripening of crops, birth, life and death in man and beast. As Leo Frobenius puts it, archaic man *plays* the order of nature as imprinted on his consciousness.[7] In the remote past, so Frobenius thinks, man first assimilated the phenomena of vegetation and animal life and then conceived an idea of time and space, of months and seasons, of the course of the sun and moon. And now he plays this great processional order of existence in a sacred play, in and through which he actualizes anew, or "recreates", the events represented and thus helps to maintain the cosmic order. Frobenius draws even more far-reaching conclusions from this "playing at nature". He deems it the starting-point of all social order and social institutions, too. Through this ritual play, savage society acquires its rude forms of government. The king is the sun, his kingship the image of the sun's course. All his life the king plays "sun" and in the end he suffers the fate of the sun: he must be killed in ritual forms by his own people.

We can leave aside the question of how far this explanation of ritual regicide and the whole underlying conception can be taken as "proved". The question that interests us here is: what are we to think of this concrete projection of primitive nature-consciousness? What are we to make of a mental process that begins with an unexpressed experience of cosmic phenomena and ends in an imaginative rendering of them in play?

Frobenius is right to discard the facile hypothesis which contents itself with hypothecating an innate "play instinct". The term "instinct", he says, is "a makeshift, an admission of helplessness before the problem of reality".[8] Equally explicitly and for even better reasons he rejects as a vestige of obsolete thinking the tendency to explain every advance in culture in terms of a "special purpose", a "why" and a "wherefore" thrust down the throat of the culture-creating community. "Tyranny of causality at its worst," "antiquated utilitarianism" he calls such a point of view.[9]

The conception Frobenius has of the mental process in question is roughly as follows. In archaic man the experience of life and nature, still unexpressed, takes the form of a "seizure"—being seized on, thrilled, enraptured. "The creative faculty in a people as in the child or every creative person, springs from this state of being seized." "Man is seized by the revelation of fate." "The reality of the natural rhythm of genesis and extinction has seized hold of his consciousness, and this, inevitably and by reflex action, leads him to represent his emotion in an act." So that according to him we are dealing with a necessary mental process of transformation. The thrill, the "being seized" by the phenomena of life and nature is condensed by reflex action, as it were, to poetic expression and art. It is difficult to describe the process of creative imagination in words that are more to the point, though they can hardly be called a true "explanation". The mental road from aesthetic or mystical, or at any rate meta-logical, perception of cosmic order to ritual play remains as dark as before.

While repeatedly using the term "play" for these performances the great anthropologist omits, however, to state what exactly he understands by it. He would even seem to have surreptitiously re-admitted the very thing he so strongly deprecates and which does not altogether fit in with the essential quality of play: the concept of purpose. For, in Frobenius' description of it, play quite explicitly *serves* to represent a cosmic event and thus bring it about. A quasi-rationalistic element irresistibly creeps in. For Frobenius, play and representation have their *raison d' etre* after all, in the expression of something else, namely, the "being seized" by a cosmic event. But the very fact that the dramatization is *played* is, apparently, of secondary importance for him. Theoretically at least, the emotion could have been communicated in some other way. In our view, on the contrary, the whole point is the *playing*. Such ritual play is essentially no different from one of the higher forms of common child-play or indeed animal-play. Now in the case of these two latter forms one could hardly suppose their origin to lie in some cosmic emotion struggling for expression. Child-play possesses the play-form in its veriest essence, and most purely.

We might, perhaps, describe the process leading from "seizure" by nature to ritual performance, in terms that would avoid the above-mentioned inadequacy without, however, claiming to lay bare the inscrutable. Archaic society, we would say, plays as the child or animal plays. Such playing contains at the outset all the elements proper to play: order, tension, movement, change, solemnity, rhythm, rapture. Only in a later phase of society is play associated with the idea of something to be expressed in and by it, namely, what we would call "life" or "nature". Then, what was wordless play assumes poetic form. In the form and function of play, itself an independent entity which is senseless and irrational, man's consciousness that he is embedded in a sacred order of things finds its first, highest, and holiest expression. Gradually the significance of a sacred act permeates the playing. Ritual grafts itself upon it; but the primary thing is and remains play.

We are hovering over spheres of thought barely accessible either to psychology or to philosophy. Such questions as these plumb the depths of our consciousness. Ritual is seriousness at its highest and holiest. Can it nevertheless be play? We began by saying that all play, both of children and of grown-ups, can be performed in the most perfect seriousness. Does this go so far as to imply that play is still bound up with the sacred emotion of the sacramental act? Our conclusions are to some extent impeded by the rigidity of our accepted ideas. We are accustomed to think of play and seriousness as an absolute antithesis. It would seem, however, that this does not go to the heart of the matter.

Let us consider for a moment the following argument. The child plays in complete—we can well say, in sacred—earnest. But it plays and knows that it plays. The sportsman, too, plays with all the fervour of a man enraptured, but he still knows that he is playing. The actor on the stage is wholly absorbed in his playing, but is all the time conscious of "the play". The same holds good of the violinist, though he may soar to realms beyond this world. The play-character, therefore, may attach to the sublimest forms of action. Can we now extend the line to ritual and say that the priest performing the rites of sacrifice is only playing? At first sight it seems preposterous, for if you grant it for one religion you must grant it for all. Hence our ideas of ritual, magic, liturgy, sacrament and mystery would all fall within the play-concept. In dealing with abstractions we must always guard against overstraining their significance. We would merely be playing with words were we to stretch the play-concept unduly. But, all things considered, I do not think we are falling into that error when we characterize ritual as play. The ritual act has all the formal and essential characteristics of play which we enumerated above, particularly in so far as it transports the participants to another world. This identity of ritual and play was unreservedly recognized by Plato as a given fact. He had no hesitation in comprising the *sacra* in the category of play. "I say that a man must be serious with the serious," he says (*Laws, vii, 803)*. "God alone is worthy of supreme seriousness, but man is made God's plaything, and that is the best part of him. Therefore every man and woman should live life accordingly, and play the noblest games and be of another mind from what they are at present. . . . For they deem war a serious thing, though in war there is neither play nor culture worthy the name (οὔτ' οὖν παιδιά . . . οὔτ' αὖ παιδεία), which are the things *we* deem most serious. Hence all must live in peace as well as 'they possibly can. What, then, is the right way of living? Life must be lived as play, playing certain games, making sacrifices, singing and dancing, and then a man will be able to propitiate the gods, and defend himself against his enemies, and win in the contest."[10]

The close connections between mystery and play have been touched on most tellingly by Romano Guardini in his book The *Spirit of the Liturgy* (Ecclesia Orans I, Freiburg, 1922), particularly the chapter entitled "Die Liturgie als Spiel". He does not actually cite Plato, but comes as near the above quotation as may be. He ascribes to liturgy more than one of the features we held to be characteristic of play, amongst others the fact that, in its highest examples, liturgy is "zwecklos aber doch sinnvoll" —"pointless but significant".

The Platonic identification of play and holiness does not defile the latter by calling it play, rather it exalts the concept of play to the highest regions of the spirit. We said at the beginning that play was anterior to culture; in a certain sense it is also superior to it or at least detached from it. In play we may move below the level of the serious, as the child does; but we can also move above it—in the realm of the beautiful and the sacred.

From this point of view we can now define the relationship between ritual and play more closely. We are no longer astonished at the substantial similarity of the two forms, and the question as to how far every ritual act falls within the category of play continues to hold our attention.

We found that one of the most important characteristics of play was its spatial separation from ordinary life. A closed space is marked out for it, either materially or ideally, hedged off from the everyday surroundings. Inside this space the play proceeds, inside it the rules obtain. Now, the marking out of some sacred spot is also the primary characteristic of every sacred act. This requirement of isolation for ritual, including magic and law, is much more than merely spatial and temporal. Nearly all rites of consecration and initiation entail a certain artificial seclusion for the performers and those to be initiated. Whenever it is a question of taking a vow or being received into an Order or confraternity, or of oaths and secret societies, in one way or another there is always such a delimitation of room for play. The magician, the augur, the sacrificer begins his work by circumscribing his sacred space. Sacrament and mystery presuppose a hallowed spot.

Formally speaking, there is no distinction whatever between marking out a space for a sacred purpose and marking it out for purposes of sheer play. The turf, the tennis-court, the chessboard and pavement-hopscotch cannot formally be distinguished from the temple or the magic circle. The striking similarity between sacrificial rites all over the earth shows that such customs must be rooted in a very fundamental, an aboriginal layer of the human mind. As a rule people reduce this over-all congruity of cultural forms to some "reasonable", "logical" cause by explaining the need for isolation and seclusion as an anxiety to protect the conse-crated individual from noxious influences—because, in his consecrated state, he is particularly exposed to the malign workings of ghosts, besides being himself a danger to his surroundings. Such an explanation puts intellection and utilitarian purpose at the beginning of the cultural process: the very thing Frobenius warned against. Even if we do not fall back here on the antiquated notion of a priestcraft inventing religion, we are still introducing a rationalistic element better avoided. If, on the other hand, we accept the essential and original identity of play and ritual we simply recognize the hallowed spot as a play-ground, and the misleading question of the "why and the wherefore" does not arise at all.

If ritual proves to be formally indistinguishable from play the question remains whether this resemblance goes further than the purely formal. It is surprising that anthropology and comparative religion have paid so little attention to the problem of how far such sacred activities as proceed within the forms of play also proceed in the attitude and mood of play. Even Frobenius has not, to my knowledge, asked this question.

Needless to say, the mental attitude in which a community performs and expe-riences its sacred rites is one of high and holy earnest. But let it be emphasized again that genuine and spontaneous play can also be profoundly serious. The player can abandon himself body and soul to the game, and the consciousness of its being "merely" a game can be thrust into the background. The joy inextricably bound up with playing can turn not only into tension, but into elation. Frivolity and ecstasy are the twin poles between which play moves.

The play-mood is *labile* in its very nature. At any moment "ordinary life" may reassert its rights either by an impact from without, which interrupts the game, or by an offence against the rules, or else from within, by a collapse of the play spirit, a sobering, a disenchantment.

What, then, is the attitude and mood prevailing at holy festivals? The sacred act is "celebrated" on a "holiday"—i.e. it forms part of a general feast on the occasion of a holy day. When the people foregather at the sanctuary they gather together for collective rejoicing. Consecrations, sacrifices, sacred dances and con-tests, performances, mysteries—all are comprehended within the act of celebrat-ing a festival. The rites may be bloody, the probations of the young men awaiting initiation may be cruel, the masks may be terrifying, but the whole thing has a festal nature. Ordinary life is at a standstill. Banquets, junketings and all kinds of wanton revels are going on all the time the feast lasts. Whether we think of the Ancient Greek festivities or of the African religions to-day we can hardly draw any sharp line between the festival mood in general and the holy frenzy surrounding the central mystery.

Almost simultaneously with the appearance of the Dutch edition of this book the Hungarian scholar Karl Kerényi published a treatise on the nature of the festival which has the closest ties with our theme.[11] According to Kerényi, the festival too has that character of primacy and absolute independence which we predicated of play. "Among the psychic realities," he says, "the feast is a thing in itself, not to be confused with anything else in the world." Just as we thought the play-concept somewhat negligently treated by the anthropologist, so in his view is the feast. "The phenomenon of the feast appears to have been completely passed over by the ethnologist." "For all science is concerned it might not exist at all." Neither might play, we would like to add.

In the very nature of things the relationship between feast and play is very close. Both proclaim a standstill to ordinary life. In both mirth and joy dominate, though not necessarily—for the feast too can be serious; both are limited as to time and place; both combine strict rules with genuine freedom. In short, feast and play have their main characteristics in common. The two seem most intimately related in dancing. According to Kerényi, the Cora Indians inhabiting the Pacific coast of Mexico call their sacred feast of the young corn-cobs and the corn-roasting the "play" of their highest god.

Kerényi's ideas about the feast as an autonomous culture-concept amplify and corroborate those on which this book is built. For all that, however, the establishment of a close connection between the spirit of play and ritual does not explain everything. Genuine play possesses besides its formal characteristics and its joyful mood, at least one further very essential feature, namely, the consciousness, however latent, of "only pretending". The question remains how far such a consciousness is compatible with the ritual act performed in devotion.

If we confine ourselves to the sacred rites in archaic culture it is not impossible to adumbrate the degree of seriousness with which they are performed. As far as I know, ethnologists and anthropologists concur in the opinion that the mental attitude in which the great religious feasts of savages are celebrated and witnessed is not one of complete illusion. There is an underlying consciousness of things "not being real". A vivid picture of this attitude is given by Ad. E. Jensen in his book on the circumcision and puberty ceremonies in savage society.[12] The men seem to have no fear of the ghosts that are hovering about everywhere during the feast and appear to everyone at its height. This is small wonder, seeing that these same men have had the staging of the whole ceremony: they have carved and decorated the masks, wear them themselves and after use conceal them from the women. They make the noises heralding the appearance of the ghosts, they trace their footprints in the sand, they blow the flutes that represent the voices of the ancestors, and brandish the bull-roarers. In short, says Jensen, "their position is much like that of parents playing Santa Claus for their children: they know of the mask, but hide it from them". The men tell the women gruesome tales about the goings-on in the sacred bush. The attitude of the neophytes alternates between ecstasy, feigned madness, flesh-creeping and boyish swagger. Nor, in the last resort, are the women wholly duped. They know perfectly well who is hiding behind this mask or that. All the same they get fearfully excited when a mask comes up to them with minatory gestures, and fly shrieking in all directions. These expressions of terror, says Jensen, are in part quite genuine and spontaneous, and in part only acting up to a part imposed by tradition. It is "the done thing". The women are, as it were, the chorus to the play and they know that they must not be "spoil-sports".

In all this it is impossible to fix accurately the lower limit where holy earnest reduces itself to mere "fun". With us, a father of somewhat childish disposition might get seriously angry if his children caught him in the act of preparing Christmas presents. A Kwakiutl father in British Columbia killed his daughter who surprised him whilst carving things for a tribal ceremony.[13] The unstable nature of religious feeling among the Loango negroes is described by Pechuel-Loesche in terms similar to those used by Jensen. Their belief in the sanctities is a sort of half-belief, and goes with scoffing and pretended indifference. The really important thing is the *mood*, he concludes by saying.[14] R. R. Marett, in his chapter on "Primitive Credulity" in *The Threshold of Religion*, develops the idea that a certain element of "make-believe" is operative in all primitive religions. Whether one is sorcerer or sorcerized one is always knower and dupe at once. But one chooses to be the dupe. "The savage is a good actor who can be quite absorbed in his role, like a child at play; and, also like a child, a good spectator who can be frightened to death by the roaring of something he knows perfectly well to be no 'real' lion." The native, says Malinowski, feels and fears his belief rather than formulates it clearly to himself.[15] He uses certain terms and expressions, and these we must collect as documents of belief just as they are, without working them up into a consistent theory. The behaviour of those to whom the savage community attributes "supernatural" powers can often be best expressed by "acting up to the part".[16]

Despite this partial consciousness of things "not being real" in magic and supernatural phenomena generally, these authorities still warn against drawing the inference that the whole system of beliefs and practices is only a fraud invented by a group of "unbelievers" with a view to dominating the credulous. It is true that such an interpretation is given not only by many travellers but sometimes even by the traditions of the natives themselves. Yet it cannot be the right one. "The origin of any sacred act can only lie in the credulity of all, and the spurious maintaining of it in the interests of a special group can only be the final phase of a long line of development." As I see it, psychoanalysis tends to fall back on this antiquated interpretation of circumcision and puberty practices, so rightly rejected by Jensen.[17]

From the foregoing it is quite clear, to my mind at least, that where savage ritual is concerned we never lose sight of the play-concept for a single moment. To describe the phenomena we have to use the term "play" over and over again.

What is more, the unity and indivisibility of belief and unbelief, the indissoluble connection between sacred earnest and "make-believe" or "fun", are best understood in the concept of play itself. Jensen, though admitting the similarity of the child's world to that of the savage, still tries to distinguish in principle between the mentality of the two. The child, he says, when confronted with the figure of Santa Claus, has to do with a "ready-made concept", in which he "finds his way" with a lucidity and endowment of his own. But "the creative attitude of the savage with regard to the ceremonies here in question is quite another thing. He has to do not with ready-made concepts but with his natural surroundings, which themselves demand interpretation; he grasps their mysterious daemonism and tries to give it in representative form".[18] Here we recognize the views of Frobenius, who was Jensen's teacher. Still, two objections occur. Firstly, when calling the process in the savage mind "quite another thing" from that in the child-mind, he is speaking of the *originators* of the ritual on the one hand and of the child of *to-day* on the other. But we know nothing of these originators. All we can study is a ritualistic community which receives its religious imagery as traditional material just as "ready-made" as the child does, and responds to it similarly. Secondly, even if we ignore this, the process of "interpreting" the natural surroundings, of "grasping" them and "representing" them in a ritual image remains altogether inaccessible to our observation. It is only by fanciful metaphors that Frobenius and Jensen force an approach to it. The most we can say of the function that is operative in the process of image-making or imagination is that it is a poetic function; and we define it best of all by calling it a function of play—the *ludic* function, in fact.

So that the apparently quite simple question of what play really is, leads us deep into the problem of the nature and origin of religious concepts. As we all know, one of the most important basic ideas with which every student of comparative religion has to acquaint himself is the following. When a certain form of religion accepts a sacred identity between two things of a different order, say a human being and an animal, this relationship is not adequately expressed by calling it a "symbolical correspondence" as *we* conceive this. The identity, the essential oneness of the two goes far deeper than the correspondence between a substance and its symbolic image. It is a mystic unity. The one has *become* the other. In his magic dance the savage *is* a kangaroo. We must always be on our guard against the deficiencies and differences of our means of expression. In order to form any idea at all of the mental habits of the savage we are forced to give them in our terminology. Whether we will or not we are always transposing the savage's ideas of religion into the strictly logical modes of our own thought. We express the relationship between him and the animal he "identifies" himself with, as a "being" for him but a "playing" for us. He has taken on the "essence" of the kangaroo, says the savage; he is playing the kangaroo, say we. The savage, however, knows nothing of the conceptual distinctions between "being" and "playing"; he knows nothing of "identity", "image" or "symbol". Hence it remains an open question whether we do not come nearest to the mental attitude of the savage performing a ritual act, by adhering to this primary, universally understandable term "play".

In play as we conceive it the distinction between belief and make-believe breaks down. The concept of play merges quite naturally with that of holiness. Any Prelude of Bach, any line of tragedy proves it. By considering the whole sphere of so-called primitive culture as a play-sphere we pave the way to a more direct and more general understanding of its peculiarities than any meticulous psychological or sociological analysis would allow.

Primitive, or let us say, archaic ritual is thus sacred play, indispensable for the well-being of the community, fecund of cosmic insight and social development but always play in the sense Plato gave to it—an action accomplishing itself outside and above the necessities and seriousness of everyday life. In this sphere of sacred play the child and the poet are at home with the savage. His aesthetic sensibility has brought the modern man closer to this sphere than the "enlightened" man of the 18th century ever was. Think of the peculiar charm that the mask as an *objet d'art* has for the modern mind. People nowadays try to feel the essence of savage life. This kind of exoticism may sometimes be a little affected, but it goes a good deal deeper than the 18th century *engouement* for Turks, "Chinamen" and Indians. Modern man is very sensitive to the far-off and the strange. Nothing helps him so much in his understanding of savage society as his feeling for masks and disguise. While ethnology has demonstrated their enormous social importance, they arouse in the educated layman and art-lover an immediate aesthetic emotion compounded of beauty, fright, and mystery. Even for the cultured adult of to-day the mask still retains something of its terrifying power, although no religious emotions are attached to it. The sight of the masked figure, as a purely aesthetic experience, carries us beyond "ordinary life" into a world where something other than daylight reigns; it carries us back to the world of the savage, the child and the poet, which is the world of play.

Even if we can legitimately reduce our ideas on the significance of primitive ritual to an irreducible play-concept, one extremely troublesome question still remains. What if we now ascend from the lower religions to the higher? From the rude and outlandish ritual of the African, American or Australian aborigines our vision shifts to Vedic sacrificial lore, already, in the hymns of the *RigVeda*, pregnant with the wisdom of the Upanishads, or to the profoundly mystical identifications of god, man, and beast in Egyptian religion, or to the Orphic and Eleusinian mysteries. In form and practice all these are closely allied to the so-called primitive religions even to bizarre and bloody particulars. But the high degree of wisdom and truth we discern, or think we can discern in them, forbids us to speak of them with that air of superiority which, as a matter of fact, is equally out of place in "primitive" cultures. We must ask whether this formal similarity entitles us to extend the qualification "play" to the consciousness of the holy, the faith embodied in these higher creeds. If we accept the Platonic definition of play there is nothing preposterous or irreverent in doing so. Play consecrated to the Deity, the highest goal of man's endeavour—such was Plato's conception of religion. In following him we in no way abandon the holy mystery, or cease to rate it as the highest attainable expression of that which escapes logical understanding. The ritual act, or an important part of it, will always remain within the play category, but in this seeming subordination the recognition of its holiness is not lost.

Notes

1 For these theories see H. Zondervan, *Het Spel bij Dieren, Kinderen en Volwassen Menschen* (Amsterdam, 1928), and F. J. J. Buytendijk, *Het Spel van Mensch en Diet als openbaring van levensdriften* (Amsterdam, 1932).
2 Nature, kind, being, essence, etc. Trans.
3 M. Granet, *Festivals and Songs of Ancient China; Dances and Legends of Ancient China; Chinese Civilization* (Routledge).
4 Jane Harrison, *Themis: A Study of the Social Origins of Greek Religion* (Cambridge, 1912), p. 125.
5 R. R. Marett, *The Threshold of Religion*, 1912, p. 48.
6 Buytendijk, *Het Spel van Mensch en Dier als openbaring van levensdriften* (Amsterdam, 1932), pp. 70–71.
7 *Kultur geschichte Afrikas, Prolegomena zu einer historischen Gestaltlehre; Schicksalskunde im Sinne des Kulturwerdens* (Leipzig, 1932).
8 *Kulturgeschichte*, pp. 23, 122.
9 *Ibid*. p. 21.
10 Cf. *Laws*, vii, 796, where Plato speaks of the sacred dances of the Kouretes of Crete, calling them ἐνόπλια παιγνια.
11 *Vom Wesen des Festes*, Paideuma, Mitteilungen zur Kulturkunde I, Heft 2 (Dez., 1938), pp. 59–74.
12 *Beschneidung und Reifezeremonien bei Naturvölkern* (Stuttgart, 1933).
13 F. Boas, *The Social Organisation and the Secret Societies of the Kwakiutl Indians*, Washington, 1897, p. 435.
14 *Volkskunde von Loango*, Stuttgart, 1907, p. 345.
15 *The Argonauts of the Western Pacific*, London, 1922, p. 339.
16 *Ibid*. p. 240.
17 Jensen, *op. cit.* p. 152.
18 *Op. cit.* p. 149 f.

10

THE PLAY-ELEMENT IN CONTEMPORARY CIVILIZATION

Johan Huizinga

Source: *Homo Ludens: A Study of the Play-Element in Culture* (New York: Routledge, 1949), pp. 195–213. Originally published in Dutch, 1938.

Let us not waste time arguing about what is meant by "contemporary". It goes without saying that any time we speak of has already become an historical past, a past that seems to crumble away at the hinder end the further we recede from it. Phenomena which a younger generation is constantly relegating to "former days" are, for their elders, part of "our own day", not merely because their elders have a personal recollection of them but because their culture still participates in them. This different time-sense is not so much dependent on the generation to which one happens to belong as on the knowledge one has of things old and new. A mind historically focussed will embody in its idea of what is "modern" and "contemporary" a far larger section of the past than a mind living in the myopia of the moment. "Contemporary civilization" in our sense, therefore, goes deep into the 19th century.

The question to which we address ourselves is this: To what extent does the civilization we live in still develop in play-forms? How far does the play-spirit dominate the lives of those who share that civilization? The 19th century, we observed, had lost many of the play-elements so characteristic of former ages. Has this leeway been made up or has it increased?

It might seem at first sight that certain phenomena in modern social life have more than compensated for the loss of play-forms. Sport and athletics, as social functions, have steadily increased in scope and conquered ever fresh fields both nationally and internationally.

Contests in skill, strength and perseverance have, as we have shown, always occupied an important place in every culture either in connection with ritual or simply for fun and festivity. Feudal society was only really interested in the tournament; the rest was just popular recreation and nothing more. Now the tournament, with its highly dramatic staging and aristocratic embellishments, can hardly be called a sport. It fulfilled one of the functions of the theatre. Only a numerically small upper class took active part in it. This one-sidedness of mediaeval sporting life was due in large measure to the influence of the Church. The Christian ideal left but little room for the organized practice of sport and the cultivation of bodily exercise, except insofar as the latter contributed to gentle education. Similarly, the Renaissance affords fairly numerous examples of body-training cultivated for the sake of perfection, but only on the part of individuals, never groups or classes. If anything, the emphasis laid by the Humanists on learning and erudition tended to perpetuate the old under-estimation of the body, likewise the moral zeal and severe intellectuality of the Reformation and Counter-Reformation. The recognition of games and bodily exercises as important cultural values was withheld right up to the end of the 18th century.

The basic forms of sportive competition are, of course, constant through the ages. In some the trial of strength and speed is the whole essence of the contest, as in running and skating matches, chariot and horse races, weight-lifting, swimming, diving, marksmanship, etc.[1] Though human beings have indulged in such activities since the dawn of time, these only take on the character of organized games to a very slight degree. Yet nobody, bearing in mind the agonistic principle which animates them, would hesitate to call them games in the sense of play—which, as we have seen, can be very serious indeed. There are, however, other forms of contest which develop of their own accord into "sports". These are the ball-games.

What we are concerned with here is the transition from occasional amusement to the system of organized clubs and matches. Dutch pictures of the 17th century show us burghers and peasants intent upon their game of *kolf*; but, so far as I know, nothing is heard of games being organized in clubs or played as matches. It is obvious that a fixed organization of this kind will most readily occur when two groups play against one another. The great ballgames in particular require the existence of permanent teams, and herein lies the starting-point of modern sport. The process arises quite spontaneously in the meeting of village against village, school against school, one part of a town against the rest, etc. That the process started in 19th-century England is understandable up to a point, though how far the specifically Anglo-Saxon bent of mind can be deemed an efficient cause is less certain. But it cannot be doubted that the structure of English social life had much to do with it. Local self-government encouraged the spirit of association and solidarity. The absence of obligatory military training favoured the occasion for, and the need of, physical exercise. The peculiar form of education tended to work in the same direction, and finally the geography of the country and the nature of the terrain, on the whole flat and, in the ubiquitous commons, offering the most perfect playing-fields that could be desired, were of the greatest importance. Thus England became the cradle and focus of modern sporting life.

Ever since the last quarter of the 19th century games, in the guise of sport,[2] have been taken more and more seriously. The rules have become increasingly strict and elaborate. Records are established at a higher, or faster, or longer level than was ever conceivable before. Everybody knows the delightful prints from the first half of the 19th century, showing the cricketers in top-hats. This speaks for itself.

Now, with the increasing systematization and regimentation of sport, something of the pure play-quality is inevitably lost. We see this very clearly in the official distinction between amateurs and professionals (or "gentlemen and players" as used pointedly to be said). It means that the play-group marks out those for whom playing is no longer play, ranking them inferior to the true players in standing but superior in capacity. The spirit of the professional is no longer the true play-spirit; it is lacking in spontaneity and carelessness.[3] This affects the amateur too, who begins to suffer from an inferiority complex. Between them they push sport further and further away from the play-sphere proper until it becomes a thing *sui generis*: neither play nor earnest. In modern social life sport occupies a place alongside and apart from the cultural process. The great competitions in archaic cultures had always formed part of the sacred festivals and were indispensable as health and happiness-bringing activities. This ritual tie has now been completely severed; sport has become profane, "unholy" in every way and has no organic connection whatever with the structure of society, least of all when prescribed by the government. The ability of modern social techniques to stage mass demonstrations with the maximum of outward show in the field of athletics does not alter the fact that neither the Olympiads nor the organized sports of American Universities nor the loudly trumpeted international contests have, in the smallest degree, raised sport to the level of a culture-creating activity. However important it may be for the players or spectators, it remains sterile. The old play-factor has undergone almost complete atrophy.

This view will probably run counter to the popular feeling of to-day, according to which sport is the apotheosis of the play-element in our civilization. Nevertheless popular feeling is wrong. By way of emphasizing the fatal shift towards over-seriousness we would point out that it has also infected the non-athletic games where calculation is everything, such as chess and some card-games.

A great many board-games have been known since the earliest times, some even in primitive society, which attached great importance to them largely on account of their chanceful character. Whether they are games of chance or skill they all contain an element of seriousness. The merry play-mood has little scope here, particularly where chance is at a minimum as in chess, draughts, backgammon, halma, etc. Even so all these games remain within the definition of play as given in our first chapter. Only recently has publicity seized on them and annexed them to athletics by means of public championships, world tournaments, registered records and press reportage in a literary style of its own, highly ridiculous to the innocent outsider.

Card-games differ from board-games in that they never succeed in eliminating chance completely. To the extent that chance predominates they fall into the category of gambling and, as such, are little suited to club life and public competition. The more intellectual card-games, on the other hand, leave plenty of room for associative tendencies. It is in this field that the shift towards seriousness and over-seriousness is so striking. From the days of *ombre* and *quadrille* to whist and bridge, card-games have undergone a process of increasing refinement, but only with bridge have the modern social techniques made themselves master of the game. The paraphernalia of handbooks and systems and professional training has made bridge a deadly earnest business. A recent newspaper article estimated the yearly winnings of the Culbertson couple at more than two hundred thousand dollars. An enormous amount of mental energy is expended in this universal craze for bridge with no more tangible result than the exchange of relatively unimportant sums of money. Society as a whole is neither benefited nor damaged by this futile activity. It seems difficult to speak of it as an elevating recreation in the sense of Aristotle's *diagoge*. Proficiency at bridge is a sterile excellence, sharpening the mental faculties very one-sidedly without enriching the soul in any way, fixing and consuming a quantity of intellectual energy that might have been better applied. The most we can say, I think, is that it might have been applied worse. The status of bridge in modern society would indicate, to all appearances, an immense increase in the play-element to-day. But appearances are deceptive. Really to play, a man must play like a child. Can we assert that this is so in the case of such an ingenious game as bridge? If not, the virtue has gone out of the game.

The attempt to assess the play-content in the confusion of modern life is bound to lead us to contradictory conclusions. In the case of sport we have an activity nominally known as play but raised to such a pitch of technical organization and scientific thoroughness that the real play-spirit is threatened with extinction. Over against this tendency to over-seriousness, however, there are other phenomena pointing in the opposite direction. Certain activities whose whole *raison d'être* lies in the field of material interest, and which had nothing of play about them in their initial stages, develop what we can only call play-forms as a secondary characteristic. Sport and athletics showed us play stiffening into seriousness but still being felt as play; now we come to serious business degenerating into play but still being called serious. The two phenomena are linked by the strong agonistic habit which still holds universal sway, though in other forms than before.

The impetus given to this agonistic principle which seems to be carrying the world back in the direction of play derives, in the main, from external factors independent of culture proper—in a word, communications, which have made intercourse of every sort so extraordinarily easy for mankind as a whole. Technology, publicity and propaganda everywhere promote the competitive spirit and afford means of satisfying it on an unprecedented scale. Commercial competition does not, of course, belong to the immemorial sacred play-forms. It only appears when trade begins to create fields of activity within which each must try to surpass and outwit his neighbour. Commercial rivalry soon makes limiting rules imperative, namely the trading customs. It remained primitive in essence until quite late, only becoming really intensive with the advent of modern communications, propaganda and statistics. Naturally a certain play-element had entered into business competition at an early stage. Statistics stimulated it with an idea that had originally arisen in sporting life, the idea, namely, of trading records. A record, as the word shows, was once simply a memorandum, a note which the innkeeper scrawled on the walls of his inn to say that such and such a rider or traveller had been the first to arrive after covering so and so many miles. The statistics of trade and production could not fail to introduce a sporting element into economic life. In consequence, there is now a sporting side to almost every triumph of commerce or technology: the highest turnover, the biggest tonnage, the fastest crossing, the greatest altitude, etc. Here a purely ludic element has, for once, got the better of utilitarian considerations, since the experts inform us that smaller units—less monstrous steamers and aircraft, etc.—are more efficient in the long run. Business becomes play. This process goes so far that some of the great business concerns deliberately instil the play-spirit into their workers so as to step up production. The trend is now reversed: play becomes business. A captain of industry, on whom the Rotterdam Academy of Commerce had conferred an honorary degree, spoke as follows:

> "Ever since I first entered the business it has been a race between the technicians and the sales department. One tried to produce so much that the sales department would never be able to sell it, while the other tried to sell so much that the technicians would never be able to keep pace. This race has always continued: sometimes one is ahead, sometimes the other. Neither my brother nor myself has regarded the business as a task, but always as a game, the spirit of which it has been our constant endeavour to implant into the younger staff."

These words must, of course, be taken with a grain of salt. Nevertheless there are numerous instances of big concerns forming their own Sports Societies and even engaging workers with a view not so much to their professional capacities as to their fitness for the football eleven. Once more the wheel turns.

It is less simple to fix the play-element in contemporary art than in contemporary trade. As we tried to make clear in our tenth chapter, a certain playfulness is by no means lacking in the process of creating and "producing" a work of art. This was obvious enough in the arts of the Muses or "music" arts, where a strong play-element may be called fundamental, indeed, essential to them. In the plastic arts we found that a play-sense was bound up with all forms of decoration; in other words, that the play-function is especially operative where mind and hand move most freely. Over and above this it asserted itself in the master-piece or show-piece expressly commissioned, *the tour de force*, the wager in skill or ability. The question that now arises is whether the play-element in art has grown stronger or weaker since the end of the 18th century.

A gradual process extending over many centuries has succeeded in de-functionalizing art and making it more and more a free and independent occupation for individuals called artists. One of the landmarks of this emancipation was the victory of framed canvases over panels and murals, likewise of prints over miniatures and illuminations. A similar shift from the social to the individual took place when the Renaissance saw the main task of the architect no longer in the building of churches and palaces but of dwelling-houses; not in splendid galleries but in

159

drawing-rooms and bed-rooms. Art became more intimate, but also more isolated; it became an affair of the individual and his taste. In the same way chamber music and songs expressly designed for the satisfaction of personal aestheticisms began to surpass the more public forms of art both in importance and often in intensity of expression.

Along with these changes in form there went another, even more profound, in the function and appreciation of art. More and more it was recognized as an independent and extremely high cultural value. Right into the 18th century art had occupied a subordinate place in the scale of such values. Art was a superior ornament in the lives of the privileged. Aesthetic enjoyment may have been as high as now, but it was interpreted in terms of religious exaltation or as a sort of curiosity whose purpose was to divert and distract. The artist was an artisan and in many cases a menial, whereas the scientist or scholar had the status at least of a member of the leisured classes.

The great shift began in the middle of the 18th century as a result of new aesthetic impulses which took both romantic and classical form, though the romantic current was the more powerful. Together they brought about an unparalleled rise in aesthetic enjoyment all the more fervent for having to act as a substitute for religion. This is one of the most important phases in the history of civilization. We must leap over the full story of this apotheosis of art and can only point out that the line of art-hierophants runs unbroken from Winckelmann to Ruskin and beyond. All the time, art-worship and connoisseurship remained the privilege of the few. Only towards the end of the 19th century did the appreciation of art, thanks largely to photographic reproduction, reach the broad mass of the simply educated. Art becomes public property, love of art *bon ton*. The idea of the artist as a superior species of being gains acceptance, and the public at large is washed by the mighty waves of snobbery. At the same time a convulsive craving for originality distorts the creative impulse. This constant striving after new and unheard-of forms impels art down the steep slope of Impressionism into the turgidities and excrescences of the 20th century. Art is far more susceptible to the deleterious influences of modern techniques of production than is science. Mechanization, advertising, sensation-mongering have a much greater hold upon art because as a rule it works directly for a market and has a free choice of all the techniques available.

None of these conditions entitles us to speak of a play-element in contemporary art. Since the 18th century art, precisely because recognized as a cultural factor, has to all appearances lost rather than gained in playfulness. But is the net result a gain or a loss? One is tempted to feel, as we felt about music, that it was a blessing for art to be largely unconscious of its high purport and the beauty it creates. When art becomes self-conscious, that is, conscious of its own grace, it is apt to lose something of its eternal child-like innocence.

From another angle, of course, we might say that the play-element in art has been fortified by the very fact that the artist is held to be above the common run of mortals. As a superior being he claims a certain amount of veneration for his due. In order to savour his superiority to the full he will require a reverential public or a circle of kindred spirits, who will pour forth the requisite veneration more under-standingly than the public at large with its empty phrases. A certain esotericism is as necessary for art to-day as it was of old. Now all esoterics presuppose a conven-tion: we, the initiates, agree to take such and such a thing thus and thus, so we will understand it, so admire it. In other words, esoterics requires a play-community which shall steep itself in its own mystery. Wherever there is a catch-word end-ing in -*ism* we are hot on the tracks of a play-community. The modern apparatus of publicity with its puffy art-criticism, exhibitions and lectures is calculated to heighten the play-character of art.

It is a very different thing to try to determine the play-content of modern sci-ence, for it brings us up against a fundamental difficulty. In the case of art we took play as a primary datum of experience, a generally accepted quantity; but when it comes to science we are constantly being driven back on our definition of that quantity and having to question it afresh. If we apply to science our definition of play as an activity occurring within certain limits of space, time and meaning, according to fixed rules, we might arrive at the amazing and horrifying conclusion that all the branches of science and learning are so many forms of play because each of them is isolated within its own field and bounded by the strict rules of its own methodology. But if we stick to the full terms of our definition we can see at once that, for an activity to be called play, more is needed than limitations and rules. A game is time-bound, we said; it has no contact with any reality outside itself, and its performance is its own end. Further, it is sustained by the conscious-ness of being a pleasurable, even mirthful, relaxation from the strains of ordinary life. None of this is applicable to science. Science is not only perpetually seek-ing contact with reality by its usefulness, i.e. in the sense that it is *applied*, it is perpetually trying to establish a universally valid pattern of reality, i.e. as *pure* science. Its rules, unlike those of play, are not unchallengeable for all time. They are constantly being belied by experience and undergoing modification, whereas the rules of a game cannot be altered without spoiling the game itself.

The conclusion, therefore, that all science is merely a game can be discarded as a piece of wisdom too easily come by. But it is legitimate to enquire whether a science is not liable to indulge in play within the closed precincts of its own method. Thus, for instance, the scientist's continued penchant for systems tends in the direction of play. Ancient science, lacking adequate foundation in empiri-cism, lost itself in a sterile systematization of all conceivable concepts and prop-erties. Though observation and calculation act as a brake in this respect they do not altogether exclude a certain capriciousness in scientific activities. Even the most delicate experimental analysis can be, not indeed manipulated while actu-ally in progress, but played in the interests of subsequent theory. True, the mar-gin of play is always detected in the end, but this detection proves that it exists. Jurists have of old been reproached with similar manoeuvres. Philologists too are not altogether blameless in this respect, seeing that ever since the Old Testament and the Vedas they have delighted in perilous etymologies, a favour-ite game to this day for those whose curiosity outstrips their knowledge. And is it so certain that the new schools of psychology are not being led astray by the frivolous and facile use of Freudian terminology at the hands of competents and incompetents alike?

Apart from the possibility of the scientific worker or amateur juggling with his own method he may also be seduced into the paths of play by the competitive impulse proper. Though competition in science is less directly conditioned by economic factors than in art, the logical development of civilization which we call science is more inextricably bound up with dialectics than is the aesthetic. In an earlier chapter we discussed the origins of science and philosophy and found that they lay in the agonistic sphere. Science, as some one has not unjustly said, is polemical. But it is a bad sign when the urge to forestall the other fellow in discovery or to annihilate him with a demonstration, looms too large in the work done. The genuine seeker after truth sets little store by triumphing over a rival.

By way of tentative conclusion we might say that modern science, so long as it adheres to the strict demands of accuracy and veracity, is far less liable to fall into play as we have defined it, than was the case in earlier times and right up to the Renaissance, when scientific thought and method showed unmistakable play-characteristics.

These few observations on the play-factor in modern art and science must suffice here, though much has been left unsaid. We are hastening to an end, and it only remains to consider the play element in contemporary social life at large and especially in politics. But let us be on our guard against two misunderstandings from the start. Firstly, certain play-forms may be used consciously or unconsciously to cover up some social or political design. In this case we are not dealing with the eternal play-element that has been the theme of this book, but with false play. Secondly, and quite independently of this, it is always possible to come upon phenomena which, to a superficial eye, have all the appearance of play and might be taken for permanent play-tendencies, but are, in point of fact, nothing of the sort. Modern social life is being dominated to an ever-increasing extent by a quality that has something in common with play and yields the illusion of a strongly developed play-factor. This quality I have ventured to call by the name of Puerilism,[4] as being the most appropriate appellation for that blend of adolescence and barbarity which has been rampant all over the world for the last two or three decades.

It would seem as if the mentality and conduct of the adolescent now reigned supreme over large areas of civilized life which had formerly been the province of responsible adults. The habits I have in mind are, in themselves, as old as the world; the difference lies in the place they now occupy in our civilization and the brutality with which they manifest themselves. Of these habits that of gregariousness is perhaps the strongest and most alarming. It results in puerilism of the lowest order: yells or other signs of greeting, the wearing of badges and sundry items of political haberdashery, walking in marching order or at a special pace and the whole rigmarole of collective voodoo and mumbo-jumbo. Closely akin to this, if at a slightly deeper psychological level, is the insatiable thirst for trivial recreation and crude sensationalism, the delight in mass-meetings, mass-demonstrations, parades, etc. The club is a very ancient institution, but it is a disaster when whole nations turn into clubs, for these, besides promoting the precious qualities of friendship and loyalty, are also hotbeds of sectarianism, intolerance, suspicion, superciliousness and quick to defend any illusion that flatters self-love or group-consciousness. We have seen great nations losing every shred of honour, all sense of humour, the very idea of decency and fair play. This is not the place to investigate the causes, growth and extent of this world-wide bastardization of culture; the entry of half-educated masses into the international traffic of the mind, the relaxation of morals and the hypertrophy of technics undoubtedly play a large part.

One example of official puerilism must suffice here. It is, as we know from history, a sign of revolutionary enthusiasm when governments play at nine-pins with names, the venerable names of cities, persons, institutions, the calendar, etc. *Pravda*[5] reported that as a result of their arrears in grain deliveries three *kolkhoq* in the district of Kursk, already christened Budenny, Krupskaya and the equivalent of Red Cornfield, has been re-christened Sluggard, Saboteur and Do-Nothing by the local soviet. Though this *trop de zèle* received an official rebuff from the Central Committee and the offensive soubriquets were withdrawn, the puerilistic attitude could not have been more clearly expressed.

Very different is the great innovation of the late Lord Baden-Powell. His aim was to organize the social force of boyhood as such and turn it to good account. This is not puerilism, for it rests on a deep understanding of the mind and aptitudes of the immature; also the Scout Movement expressly styles itself a game. Here, if anywhere, we have an example of a game that comes as close to the culture-creating play of archaic times as our age allows. But when Boy-Scoutism in degraded form seeps through into politics we may well ask whether the puerilism that flourishes in present-day society is a play-function or not. At first sight the answer appears to be a definite yes, and such has been my interpretation of the phenomenon in other studies.[6] I have now come to a different conclusion. According to our definition of play, puerilism is to be distinguished from playfulness. A child playing is not puerile in the pejorative sense we mean here. And if our modern puerilism were genuine play we ought to see civilization returning to the great archaic forms of recreation where ritual, style and dignity are in perfect unison. The spectacle of a society rapidly goose-stepping into helotry is, for some, the dawn of the millennium. We believe them to be in error.

More and more the sad conclusion forces itself upon us that the play-element in culture has been on the wane ever since the 18th century, when it was in full flower. Civilization to-day is no longer played, and even where it still seems to play it is false play—I had almost said, it plays false, so that it becomes increasingly difficult to tell where play ends and non-play begins. This is particularly true of politics. Not very long ago political life in parliamentary democratic form was full of unmistakable play features. One of my pupils has recently worked up my observations on this subject into a thesis on parliamentary eloquence in France and England, showing how, ever since the end of the 18th century, debates in the House of Commons have been conducted very largely according to the rules of a game and in the true play-spirit. Personal rivalries are always at work, keeping up a continual match between the players whose object is to checkmate one another, but without prejudice to the interests of the country which they serve with all seriousness. The mood and manners of parliamentary democracy were, until recently, those of fair play both in England and in the countries that had adopted the English model with some felicity. The spirit of fellowship would allow the bitterest opponents a friendly chat even after the most virulent debate. It was in this style that the "Gentleman's Agreement" arose. Unhappily certain parties to it were not always aware of the duties implicit in the word gentleman. There can be no doubt that it is just this play-element that keeps parliamentary life healthy, at least in Great Britain, despite the abuse that has lately been heaped upon it. The elasticity of human relationships underlying the political machinery permits it to "play", thus easing tensions which would otherwise be unendurable or dangerous—for it is the decay of humour that kills. We need hardly add that this play-factor is present in the whole apparatus of elections.

In American politics it is even more evident. Long before the two-party system had reduced itself to two gigantic teams whose political differences were hardly discernible to an outsider, electioneering in America had developed into a kind of national sport. The presidential election of 1840 set the pace for all subsequent elections. The party then calling itself Whig had an excellent candidate, General Harrison of 1812 fame, but no platform. Fortune gave them something infinitely better, a symbol on which they rode to triumph: the log cabin which was the old warrior's modest abode during his retirement. Nomination by majority vote, i.e. by the loudest clamour, was inaugurated in the election of 1860 which brought Lincoln to power. The emotionality of American politics lies deep in the origins of the American nation itself: Americans have ever remained true to the rough and tumble of pioneer life. There is a great deal that is endearing in American politics, something naïve and spontaneous for which we look in vain in the dragoonings and drillings, or worse, of the contemporary European scene.

Though there may be abundant traces of play in domestic politics there would seem, at first sight, to be little opportunity for it in the field of international relationships. The fact, however, that these have touched the nadir of violence and precariousness does not in itself exclude the possibility of play. As we have seen from numerous examples, play can be cruel and bloody and, in addition, can often be false play. Any law-abiding community or community of States will have characteristics linking it in one way or another to a play-community. International law between States is maintained by the mutual recognition of certain principles which, in effect, operate like play-rules despite the fact that they may be founded in metaphysics. Were it otherwise there would be no need to lay down the *pacta sunt servanda* principle, which explicitly recognizes that the integrity of the system rests on a general willingness to keep to the rules. The moment that one or the other party withdraws from this tacit agreement the whole system of international law must, if only temporarily, collapse unless the remaining parties are strong enough to outlaw the "spoilsport".

The maintenance of international law has, at all stages, depended very largely on principles lying outside the strict domain of law, such as honour, decency, and good form. It is not altogether in vain that the European rules of warfare developed out of the code of honour proper to chivalry. International law tacitly assumed that a beaten Power would behave like a gentleman and a good loser, which unhappily it seldom did. It was a point of international decorum to declare your war officially before entering upon it, though the aggressor often neglected to comply with this awkward convention and began by seizing some outlying colony or the like. But it is true to say that until quite recently war was conceived as a noble game—the sport of kings—and that the absolutely binding character of its rules rested on, and still retained, some of the formal play-elements we found in full flower in archaic warfare.

A cant phrase in current German political literature speaks of the change from peace to war as "das Eintreten des Ernstfalles"—roughly, "the serious development of an emergency". In strictly military parlance, of course, the term is correct. Compared with the sham fighting of manoeuvres and drilling and training, real war is undoubtedly what seriousness is to play. But German political theorists mean something more. The term "Ernstfall" avows quite openly that foreign policy has not attained its full degree of seriousness, has not achieved its object or proved its efficiency, until the stage of actual hostilities is reached. The true relation between States is one of war. All diplomatic intercourse, insofar as it moves in the paths of negotiation and agreement, is only a prelude to war or an interlude between two wars. This horrible creed is accepted and indeed professed by many. It is only logical that its adherents, who regard war and the preparations for it as the sole form of serious politics, should deny that war has any connection with the contest and hence with play. The agonistic factor, they tell us, may have been operative in the primitive stages of civilization, it was all very well then, but war nowadays is far above the competitiveness of mere savages. It is based on the "friend-foe principle". All "real" relationships between nations and States, so they say, are dominated by this ineluctable principle.[7] Any "other" group is always either your friend or your enemy. Enemy, of course, is not to be understood as *inimicus* or ἐχθρός, i.e. a person you hate, let alone a wicked person, but purely and simply as *hostis* or πολέμιος, i.e. the stranger or foreigner who is in your group's way. The theory refuses to regard the enemy even as a rival or adversary. He is merely in your way and is thus to be made away with. If ever anything in history has corresponded to this gross over-simplification of the idea of enmity, which reduces it to an almost mechanical relationship, it is precisely that primitive antagonism between phratries, clans or tribes where, as we saw, the play-element was hypertrophied and distorted. Civilization is supposed to have carried us beyond this stage. I know of no sadder or deeper fall from human reason than Schmitt's barbarous and pathetic delusion about the friend-foe principle. His inhuman cerebrations do not even hold water as a piece of formal logic. For it is not war that is serious, but peace.

War and everything to do with it remains fast in the daemonic and magical bonds of play. Only by transcending that pitiable friend-foe relationship will mankind enter into the dignity of man's estate. Schmitt's brand of "seriousness" merely takes us back to the savage level.

Here the bewildering antithesis of play and seriousness presents itself once more. We have gradually become convinced that civilization is rooted in noble play and that, if it is to unfold in full dignity and style, it cannot afford to neglect the play-element. The observance of play-rules is nowhere more imperative than in the relations between countries and States. Once they are broken, society falls into barbarism and chaos. On the other hand we cannot deny that modern warfare has lapsed into the old agonistic attitude of playing at war for the sake of prestige and glory.

Now this is our difficulty: modern warfare has, on the face of it, lost all contact with play. States of the highest cultural pretensions withdraw from the comity of nations and shamelessly announce that "pacta non sunt setvanda". By so doing they break the play-rules inherent in any system of international law. To that extent their playing at war, as we have called it, for the sake of prestige is not true play; it, so to speak, plays the play-concept of war false. In contemporary politics, based as they are on the utmost preparedness if not actual preparation for war, there would seem to be hardly any trace of the old play-attitude. The code of honour is flouted, the rules of the game are set aside, international law is broken, and all the ancient associations of war with ritual and religion are gone. Nevertheless the methods by which war-policies are conducted and war-preparations carried out still show abundant traces of the agonistic attitude as found in primitive society. Politics are and have always been something of a game of chance; we have only to think of the challenges, the provocations, the threats and denunciations to realize that war and the policies leading up to it are always, in the nature of things, a gamble, as Neville Chamberlain said in the first days of September 1939. Despite appearances to the contrary, therefore, war has not freed itself from the magic circle of play.

Does this mean that war is still a game, even for the aggressed, the persecuted, those who fight for their rights and their liberty? Here our gnawing doubt whether war is really play or earnest finds unequivocal answer. It is the *moral* content of an action that makes it serious. When the combat has an ethical value it ceases to be play. The way out of this vexing dilemma is only closed to those who deny the objective value and validity of ethical standards. Carl Schmitt's acceptance of the formula that war is the "serious development of an emergency" is therefore correct—but in a very different sense from that which he intended. His point of view is that of the aggressor who is not bound by ethical considerations. The fact remains that politics and war are deeply rooted in the primitive soil of culture played in and as contest. Only through an ethos that transcends the friend-foe relationship and recognizes a higher goal than the gratification of the self, the group or the nation will a political society pass beyond the "play" of war to true seriousness.

So that by a devious route we have reached the following conclusion: real civilization cannot exist in the absence of a certain play-element, for civilization presupposes limitation and mastery of the self, the ability not to confuse its own tendencies with the ultimate and highest goal, but to understand that it is enclosed within certain bounds freely accepted. Civilization will, in a sense, always be played according to certain rules, and true civilization wili always demand fair play. Fair play is nothing less than good faith expressed in play terms. Hence the cheat or the spoil-sport shatters civilization itself. To be a sound culture-creating force this play-element must be pure. It must not consist in the darkening or debasing of standards set up by reason, faith or humanity. It must not be a false seeming, a masking of political purposes behind the illusion of genuine play-forms. True play knows no propaganda; its aim is in itself, and its familiar spirit is happy inspiration.

In treating of our theme so far we have tried to keep to a play-concept which starts from the positive and generally recognized characteristics of play. We took play in its immediate everyday sense and tried to avoid the philosophical short-circuit that would assert all human action to be play. Now, at the end of our argument, this point of view awaits us and demands to be taken into account.

"Child's play was what he called all human opinions", says late Greek tradition of Heraclitus.[8] As a pendant to this lapidary saying let us quote at greater length the profound words of Plato which we introduced into our first chapter: "Though human affairs are not worthy of great seriousness it is yet necessary to be serious; happiness is another thing . . . . I say that a man must be serious with the serious, and not the other way about. God alone is worthy of supreme seriousness, but man is made God's plaything, and that is the best part of him. Therefore every man and woman should live life accordingly, and play the noblest games, and be of another mind from what they are at present. For they deem war a serious thing, though in war there is neither play nor culture worthy the name, which are the things *we* deem most serious. Hence all must live in peace as well as they possibly can. What, then, is the right way of living? Life must be lived as play, playing certain games, making sacrifices, singing and dancing, and then a man will be able to propitiate the gods, and defend himself against his enemies, and win in the contest". Thus "men will live according to Nature since in most respects they are puppets, yet having a small part in truth". To which Plato's companion rejoins: "You make humanity wholly bad for us, friend, if you say that". And Plato answers: "Forgive me. It was with my eyes on God and moved by Him that I spoke so. If you like, then, humanity is not wholly bad, but worthy of some consideration."[9]

The human mind can only disengage itself from the magic circle of play by turning towards the ultimate. Logical thinking does not go far enough. Surveying all the treasures of the mind and all the splendours of its achievements we shall still find, at the bottom of every serious judgement, something problematical left. In our heart of hearts we know that none of our pronouncements is absolutely conclusive. At that point, where our judgement begins to waver, the feeling that the world is serious after all wavers with it. Instead of the old saw: "All is vanity", the more positive conclusion forces itself upon us that "all is play". A cheap metaphor, no doubt, mere impotence of the mind; yet it is the wisdom Plato arrived at when he called man the plaything of the gods. In singular imagery the thought comes back again in the *Book of Proverbs*, where Wisdom says: "The Lord possessed me in the beginning of his ways, before he made anything from the beginning. I was set up from eternity, and of old before the earth was made . . . I was with him forming all things: and was delighted every day, playing before him at all times; playing in the world. And my delights were to be with the children of men."[10]

Whenever we are seized with vertigo at the ceaseless shuttlings and spinnings in our mind of the thought: What is play? What is serious? We shall find the fixed, unmoving point that logic denies us, once more in the sphere of ethics. Play, we began by saying, lies outside morals. In itself it is neither good nor bad. But if we have to decide whether an action to which our will impels us is a serious duty or is licit as play, our moral conscience will at once provide the touchstone. As soon as truth and justice, compassion and forgiveness have part in our resolve to act, our anxious question loses all meaning. One drop of pity is enough to lift our doing beyond intellectual distinctions. Springing as it does from a belief in justice and divine grace, conscience, which is moral awareness, will always whelm the question that eludes and deludes us to the end, in a lasting silence.

Notes

1 A happy variation of the natatorial contest is found in *Beowulf*, where the aim is to hold your opponent under water until he is drowned.

2 It is probably significant that we no longer speak of "games" but of "sport". Our author may not have been sufficiently familiar with the development of "sport" in the last ten or twenty years, here and in America, to stress the all-important point that sport has become a business, or, to put it bluntly, a commercial racket. Trans.

3 Note G. K. Chesterton's dictum: If a thing is worth doing at all it is worth doing badly! Trans.

4 Cf. *In the Shadow of To-morrow*, Heinemann, 1936, ch. 16.

5 January 9th, 1935.

6 *Over de grenzen van spel en ernst in de cultuur*, p. 25, and *In the Shadow of To-morrow*, ch. 16.

7 Carl Schmitt, *Der Begriff des Politischen*, Hamburg, 1933.

8 *Fragments*, 70.

9 *Laws*, 803–4; cf. also 685. Plato's words echo sombrely in Luther's mouth when he says: "All creatures are God's masks and mummeries" (Erlanger Ausgabe, xi, p. 115).

10 viii, 22–3, 30–1. This is the Douay translation, based on the Vulgate. The text of the English A.V. and R.V. does not bring out the idea of "play".

11

'THE DEFINITION OF PLAY' AND 'THE CLASSIFICATION OF GAMES'

Roger Caillois

Source: *Man, Play and Games* (Paris: Librairie Gallimard, 1958), pp. 3–11; 11–37.

Context

The ideas that reached fruition in *Man, Play and Games* began as an appendix to Caillois' 1959 book *Man and the Sacred*. Much of Caillois' work on play and games is a direct critique of Johan Huizinga's *Homo Ludens*. In *Man, Play and Games*, he expands Huizinga's more contest-oriented notion of play to include a range of cultural forms. Driven by a desire to study play in and of itself, during the two chapters included here Caillois establishes his well-known taxonomy of play forms. In the rest of the book, Caillois applies this taxonomy to play activities from a range of world cultures. "The Definition of Play," and "The Classification of Games" come from *Man, Play and Games*, copyright 1958 by Librairie Gallimard. English translation by Meyer Barash, copyright 1961 by the Free Press of Glencoe, Inc.

The definition of play

In 1933, the rector of the University of Leyden, J. Huizinga, chose as the theme of an important oration, "The Cultural Limits of Play and the Serious." He took up and developed this topic in an original and powerful work published in 1938, *Homo Ludens*. This work, although most of its premises are debatable, is nonetheless capable of opening extremely fruitful avenues to research and reflection. In any case, it is permanently to J. Huizinga's credit that he has masterfully analyzed several of the fundamental characteristics of play and has demonstrated the importance of its role in the very development of civilization. First, he sought an exact definition of the essence of play; second, he tried to clarify the role of play present in or animating the essential aspects of all culture: in the arts as in philosophy, in poetry as well as in juridical institutions and even in the etiquette of war.

Huizinga acquitted himself brilliantly in this task, but even if he discovers play in areas where no one before him had done so, he deliberately omits, as obvious, the description and classification of games themselves, since they all respond to the same needs and reflect, without qualification, the same psychological attitude. His work is not a study of games, but an inquiry into the creative quality of the play principle in the domain of culture, and more precisely, of the spirit that rules certain kinds of games—those which are competitive. The examination of the criteria used by Huizinga to demarcate his universe of discourse is helpful in understanding the strange gaps in a study which is in every other way remarkable. Huizinga defines play as follows:

> Summing up the formal characteristics of play we might call it a free activity standing quite consciously outside "ordinary" life as being "not serious," but at the same time absorbing the player intensely and utterly. It is an activity connected with no material interest, and no profit can be gained by it. It proceeds within its own proper boundaries of time and space according to fixed rules and in an orderly manner. It promotes the formation of social groupings which tend to surround themselves with secrecy and to stress their difference from the common world by disguise or other means.[1]

Such a definition, in which all the words are important and meaningful, is at the same time too broad and too narrow. It is meritorious and fruitful to have grasped the affinity which exists between play and the secret or mysterious, but this relationship cannot be part of the definition of play, which is nearly always spectacular or ostentatious. Without doubt, secrecy, mystery, and even travesty can be transformed into play activity, but it must be immediately pointed out that this transformation is necessarily to the detriment of the secret and mysterious, which play exposes, publishes, and somehow *expends*. In a word, play tends to remove the very nature of the mysterious. On the other hand, when the secret, the mask, or the costume fulfills a sacramental function one can be sure that not play, but an institution is involved. All that is mysterious or make-believe by nature approaches play: moreover, it must be that the function of fiction or diversion is to remove the mystery; i.e. the mystery may no longer be awesome, and the counterfeit may not be a beginning or symptom of metamorphosis and possession.

In the second place, the part of Huizinga's definition which views play as action denuded of all material interest, simply excludes bets and games of chance—for example, gambling houses, casinos, racetracks, and lotteries—which, for better or worse, occupy an important part in the economy and daily life of various cultures. It is true that the kinds of games are almost infinitely varied, but the constant relationship between chance and profit is very striking. Games of chance played for money have practically no place in Huizinga's work. Such an omission is not without consequence.

It is certainly much more difficult to establish the cultural functions of games of chance than of competitive games. However, the influence of games of chance is no less considerable, even if deemed unfortunate, and not to consider them leads to a definition of play which affirms or implies the absence of economic interest. Therefore a distinction must be made.

In certain of its manifestations, play is designed to be extremely lucrative or ruinous. This does not preclude the fact that playing for money remains completely unproductive. The sum of the winnings at best would only equal the losses of the other players. Nearly always the winnings are less, because of large overhead, taxes, and the profits of the entrepreneur. He alone does not play, or if he plays he is protected against loss by the law of averages. In effect, he is the only one who cannot take pleasure in gambling.

Property is exchanged, but no goods are produced. What is more, this exchange affects only the players, and only to the degree that they accept, through a free decision remade at each game, the probability of such transfer. A characteristic of play, in fact, is that it creates no wealth or goods, thus differing from work or art. At the end of the game, all can and must start over again at the same point. Nothing has been harvested or manufactured, no masterpiece has been created, no capital has accrued. Play is an occasion of pure waste: waste of time, energy, ingenuity, skill, and often of money for the purchase of gambling equipment or eventually to pay for the establishment. As for the professionals—the boxers, cyclists, jockeys, or actors who earn their living in the ring, track, or hippodrome or on the stage, and who must think in terms of prize, salary, or title—it is clear that they are not players but workers. When they play, it is at some other game.

There is also no doubt that play must be defined as a free and voluntary activity, a source of joy and amusement. A game which one would be forced to play would at once cease being play. It would become constraint, drudgery from which one would strive to be freed. As an obligation or simply an order, it would lose one of its basic characteristics: the fact that the player devotes himself spontaneously to the game, of his free will and for his pleasure, each time completely free to choose retreat, silence, meditation, idle solitude, or creative activity. From this is derived Valéry's proposed definition of play: it occurs when *"l'ennui peut délierce que l'entrain avait lié."*[2] It happens only when the players have a desire to play, and play the most absorbing, exhausting game in order to find diversion, escape from responsibility and routine. Finally and above all, it is necessary that they be free to leave whenever they please, by saying: "I am not playing any more."

In effect, play is essentially a separate occupation, carefully isolated from the rest of life, and generally is engaged in with precise limits of time and place. There is place for play: as needs dictate, the space for hopscotch, the board for checkers or chess, the stadium, the racetrack, the list, the ring, the stage, the arena, etc. Nothing that takes place outside this ideal frontier is relevant. To leave the enclosure by mistake, accident, or necessity, to send the ball out of bounds, may disqualify or entail a penalty.

The game must be taken back within the agreed boundaries. The same is true for time: the game starts and ends at a given signal. Its duration is often fixed in advance. It is improper to abandon or interrupt the game without a major reason (in children's games, crying "I give up," for example). If there is occasion to do so, the game is prolonged, by agreement between the contestants or by decision of an umpire. In every case, the game's domain is therefore a restricted, closed, protected universe: a pure space.

The confused and intricate laws of ordinary life are replaced, in this fixed space and for this given time, by precise, arbitrary, unexceptionable rules that must be accepted as such and that govern the correct playing of the game. If the cheat violates the rules, he at least pretends to respect them. He does not discuss them: he takes advantage of the other players' loyalty to the rules. From this point of view, one must agree with the writers who have stressed the fact that the cheat's dishonesty does not destroy the game. The game is ruined by the nihilist who denounces the rules as absurd and conventional, who refuses to play because the game is meaningless. His arguments are irrefutable. The game has no other but an intrinsic meaning. That is why its rules are imperative and absolute, beyond discussion. There is no reason for their being as they are, rather than otherwise. Whoever does not accept them as such must deem them manifest folly.

One plays only if and when one wishes to. In this sense, play is free activity. It is also uncertain activity. Doubt must remain until the end, and hinges upon the denouement. In a card game, when the outcome is no longer in doubt, play stops and the players lay down their hands. In a lottery or in roulette, money is placed on a number which may or may not win. In a sports contest, the powers of the contestants must be equated, so that each may have a chance until the end. Every game of skill, by definition, involves the risk for the player of missing his stroke, and the threat of defeat, without which the game would no longer be pleasing. In fact, the game is no longer pleasing to one who, because he is too well trained or skillful, wins effortlessly and infallibly.

An outcome known in advance, with no possibility of error or surprise, clearly leading to an inescapable result, is incompatible with the nature of play. Constant and unpredictable definitions of the situation are necessary, such as are produced by each attack or counterattack in fencing or football, in each return of the tennis ball, or in chess, each time one of the players moves a piece. The game consists of the need to find or continue at once a response *which is free within the limits set by the rules.* This latitude of the player, this margin accorded to his action is essential to the game and partly explains the pleasure which it excites. It is equally accountable for the remarkable and meaningful uses of the term "play," such as are reflected in such expressions as the *playing* of a performer or the *play* of a gear, to designate in the one case the personal style of an interpreter, in the other the range of movement of the parts of a machine.

Many games do not imply rules. No fixed *or* rigid rules exist for playing with dolls, for playing soldiers, cops and robbers, horses, locomotives, and airplanes—games, in general, which presuppose free improvisation, and the chief attraction of which lies in the pleasure of playing a role, of acting as *if* one were someone or something else, a machine for example. Despite the assertion's paradoxical character, I will state that in this instance the fiction, the sentiment of as if, replaces and performs the same function as do rules. Rules themselves create fictions. The one who plays chess, prisoner's base, polo, or baccara, by the very fact of complying with their respective rules, is separated from real life where there is no activity that literally corresponds to any of these games. That is why chess, prisoner's base, polo, and baccara are played *for real*. *As if* is not necessary. On the contrary, each time that play consists in imitating life, the player on the one hand lacks knowledge of how to invent and follow rules that do not exist in reality, and on the other hand the game is accompanied by the knowledge that the required behavior is pretense, or simple mimicry. This awareness of the basic unreality of the assumed behavior is separate from real life and from the arbitrary legislation that defines other games. The equivalence is so precise that the one who breaks up a game, the one who denounces the absurdity of the rules, now becomes the one who breaks the spell, who brutally refuses to acquiesce in the proposed illusion, who reminds the boy that he is not really a detective, pirate, horse, or submarine, or reminds the little girl that she is not rocking a real baby or serving a real meal to real ladies on her miniature dishes.

Thus games are not ruled and make-believe. Rather, they are ruled or make-believe. It is to the point that if a game with rules seems in certain circumstances like a serious activity and is beyond one unfamiliar with the rules, i.e. if it seems to him like real life, this game can at once provide the framework for a diverting make-believe for the confused and curious layman. One easily can conceive of children, in order to imitate adults, blindly manipulating real or imaginary pieces on an imaginary chessboard, and by pleasant example, playing at "playing chess."

This discussion, intended to define the nature and the largest common denominator of all games, has at the same time the advantage of placing their diversity in relief and enlarging very meaningfully the universe ordinarily explored when games are studied. In particular, these remarks tend to add two new domains to this universe: that of wagers and games of chance, and that of mimicry and interpretation. Yet there remain a number of games and entertainments that still have imperfectly defined characteristics—for example, kite-flying and top-spinning, puzzles such as crossword puzzles, the game of patience, horsemanship, seesaws, and certain carnival attractions. It will be necessary to return to this problem.

But for the present, the preceding analysis permits play to be defined as an activity which is essentially:

1   *Free:* in which playing is not obligatory; if it were, it would at once lose its attractive and joyous quality as diversion;
2   *Separate:* circumscribed within limits of space and time, defined and fixed in advance;

3   *Uncertain:* the course of which cannot be determined, nor the result attained beforehand, and some latitude for innovations being left to the player's initiative;

4   *Unproductive:* creating neither goods, nor wealth, nor new elements of any kind; and, except for the exchange of property among the players, ending in a situation identical to that prevailing at the beginning of the game;

5   *Governed by rules:* under conventions that suspend ordinary laws, and for the moment establish new legislation, which alone counts;

6   *Make-believe:* accompanied by a special awareness of a second reality or of a free unreality, as against real life.

These diverse qualities are purely formal. They do not prejudge the content of games. Also, the fact that the two last qualities—rules and make-believe—may be related, shows that the intimate nature of the facts that they seek to define implies, perhaps requires, that the latter in their turn be subdivided. This would attempt to take account not of the qualities that are opposed to reality, but of those that are clustered in groups of games with unique, irreducible characteristics.

The classification of games

The multitude and infinite variety of games at first causes one to despair of discovering a principle of classification capable of subsuming them under a small number of well-defined categories. Games also possess so many different characteristics that many approaches are possible. Current usage sufficiently demonstrates the degree of hesitance and uncertainty: indeed, several classifications are employed concurrently. To oppose card games to games of skill, or to oppose parlor games to those played in a stadium is meaningless. In effect, the implement used in the game is chosen as a classificatory instrument in the one case; in the other, the qualifications required; in a third the number of players and the atmosphere of the game, and lastly the place in which the contest is waged. An additional over-all complication is that the same game can be played alone or with others. A particular game may require several skills simultaneously, or none.

Very different games can be played in the same place. Merry-go-rounds and the diabolo are both open-air amusements. But the child who passively enjoys the pleasure of riding by means of the movement of the carousel is not in the same state of mind as the one who tries as best he can to correctly whirl his diabolo. On the other hand, many games are played without implements or accessories. Also, the same implement can fulfill different functions, depending on the game played. Marbles are generally the equipment for a game of skill, but one of the players can try to guess whether the marbles held in his opponent's hand are an odd or even number. They thus become part of a game of chance.

This last expression must be clarified. For one thing, it alludes to the fundamental characteristic of a very special kind of game. Whether it be a bet, lottery, roulette, or baccara, it is clear that the player's attitude is the same. He does nothing, he merely awaits the outcome. The boxer, the runner, and the player of chess or hopscotch, on the contrary, work as hard as they can to win. It matters little that some games are athletic and others intellectual. The player's attitude is the same: he tries to vanquish a rival operating under the same conditions as himself. It would thus appear justified to contrast games of chance with competitive games. Above all, it becomes tempting to investigate the possibility of discovering other attitudes, no less fundamental, so that the categories for a systematic classification of games can eventually be provided.

After examining different possibilities, I am proposing a division into four main rubrics, depending upon whether, in the games under consideration, the role of competition, chance, simulation, or vertigo is dominant. I call these *agôn, alea, mimicry,* and *ilinx*, respectively. All four indeed belong to the domain of play. One *plays* football, billiards, or chess (*agôn*); roulette or a lottery (*alea*); pirate, Nero, or Hamlet (*mimicry*); or one produces in oneself, by a rapid whirling or falling movement, a state of dizziness and disorder (*ilinx*). Even these designations do not cover the entire universe of play. It is divided into quadrants, each governed by an original principle. Each section contains games of the same kind. But inside each section, the different games are arranged in a rank order of progression. They can also be placed on a continuum between two opposite poles. At one extreme an almost indivisible principle, common to diversion, turbulence, free improvisation, and carefree gaiety is dominant. It manifests a kind of uncontrolled fantasy that can be designated by the term *paidia*. At the opposite extreme, this frolicsome and impulsive exuberance is almost entirely absorbed or disciplined by a complementary, and in some respects inverse, tendency to its anarchic and capricious nature: there is a growing tendency to bind it with arbitrary, imperative, and purposely tedious conventions, to oppose it still more by ceaselessly practicing the most embarrassing chicanery upon it, in order to make it more uncertain of attaining its desired effect. This latter principle is completely impractical, even though it requires an ever greater amount of effort, patience, skill, or ingenuity. I call this second component *ludus*.

I do not intend, in resorting to these strange concepts, to set up some kind of pedantic, totally meaningless mythology. However, obligated as I am to classify diverse games under the same general category, it seemed to me that the most economical means of doing so was to borrow, from one language or another, the most meaningful and comprehensive term possible, so that each category examined should avoid the possibility of lacking the particular quality on the basis of which the unifying concept was chosen. Also, to the degree that I will try to establish the classification to which I am committed, each concept chosen will not relate too directly to concrete experience, which in turn is to be divided according to an as yet untested principle.

In the same spirit, I am compelled to subsume the games most varied in appearance under the same rubric, in order to better demonstrate their fundamental kinship. I have mixed physical and mental games, those dependent upon force with those requiring skill or reasoning. Within each class, I have not distinguished between children's and adults' games, and wherever possible I have sought instances of homologous behavior in the animal world. The point in doing this was to stress the very principle of the proposed classification. It would be less burdensome if it were perceived that the divisions set up correspond to essential and irreducible impulses.

1. Fundamental categories

Agôn

A whole group of games would seem to be competitive, that is to say, like a combat in which equality of chances is artificially created, in order that the adversaries should confront each other under ideal conditions, susceptible of giving precise and incontestable value to the winner's triumph. It is therefore always a question of a rivalry which hinges on a single quality (speed, endurance, strength, memory, skill, ingenuity, etc.], exercised, within defined limits and without outside assistance, in such a way that the winner appears to be better than the loser in a certain category of exploits. Such is the case with sports contests and the reason for their very many subdivisions. Two individuals or two teams are in opposition (polo, tennis, football, boxing, fencing, etc.), or there may be a varying number of contestants (courses of every kind, shooting matches, golf, athletics, etc.]. In the same class belong the games in which, at the outset, the adversaries divide the elements into equal parts and value. The games of checkers, chess, and billiards are perfect examples. The search for equality is so obviously essential to the rivalry that it is re-established by a handicap for players of different classes; that is, within the equality of chances originally established, a secondary inequality, proportionate to the relative powers of the participants, is dealt with. It is significant that such a usage exists in the *agôn* of a physical character (sports) just as in the more cerebral type (chess games for example, in which the weaker player is given the advantage of a pawn, knight, castle, etc.).

As carefully as one tries to bring it about, absolute equality does not seem to be realizable. Sometimes, as in checkers or chess, the fact of moving first is an advantage, for this priority permits the favored player to occupy key positions or to impose a special strategy. Conversely, in bidding games, such as bridge, the last bidder profits from the clues afforded by the bids of his opponents. Again, at croquet, to be last multiplies the player's resources. In sports contests, the exposure, the fact of having the sun in front or in back; the wind which aids or hinders one or the other side; the fact, in disputing for positions on a circular track, of finding oneself in the inside or outside lane constitutes a crucial test, a trump or disadvantage whose influence may be considerable. These inevitable imbalances are negated or modified by drawing lots at the beginning, then by strict alternation of favored positions.

The point of the game is for each player to have his superiority in a given area recognized. That is why the practice of *agôn* presupposes sustained attention, appropriate training, assiduous application, and the desire to win. It implies discipline and perseverance. It leaves the champion to his own devices, to evoke the best possible game of which he is capable, and it obliges him to play the game within the fixed limits, and according to the rules applied equally to all, so that in return the victor's superiority will be beyond dispute.

In addition to games, the spirit of *agôn* is found in other cultural phenomena conforming to the game code: in the duel, in the tournament, and in certain constant and noteworthy aspects of so-called courtly war.

In principle, it would seem that *agôn* is unknown among animals, which have no conception of limits or rules, only seeking a brutal victory in merciless combat. It is clear that horse races and cock fights are an exception, for these are conflicts in which men make animals compete in terms of norms that the former alone have set up. Yet, in considering certain facts, it seems that animals already have the competitive urge during encounters where limits are at least implicitly accepted and spontaneously respected, even if rules are lacking. This is notably the case in kittens, puppies, and bear cubs, which take pleasure in knocking each other down yet not hurting each other.

Still more convincing are the habits of bovines, which, standing face to face with heads lowered, try to force each other back. Horses engage in the same kind of friendly dueling: to test their strength, they rear up on their hind legs and press down upon each other with all their vigor and weight, in order to throw their adversaries off balance. In addition, observers have noted numerous games of pursuit that result from a challenge or invitation. The animal that is overtaken has nothing to fear from the victor. The most impressive example is without doubt that of the little ferocious "fighting" willow wrens. "A moist elevation covered with short grass and about two meters in diameter is chosen for the arena," says Karl Groos.[3] The males gather there daily. The first to arrive waits for an adversary, and then the fight begins. The contenders tremble and bow their heads several times. Their feathers bristle. They hurl themselves at each other, beaks advanced, and striking at one another. *Never is there any pursuit or conflict outside the space delimited for the journey.* That is why it seems legitimate for me to use the term *agôn* for these cases, for the goal of the encounters is not for the antagonist to cause serious injury to his rival, but rather to demonstrate his own superiority. Man merely adds refinement and precision by devising rules.

In children, as soon as the personality begins to assert itself, and before the emergence of regulated competition, unusual challenges are frequent, in which the adversaries try to prove their greater endurance. They are observed competing to see which can stare at the sun, endure tickling, stop breathing, not wink his eye, etc., the longest. Sometimes the stakes are more serious, where it is a question of enduring hunger or else pain in the form of whipping, pinching, stinging, or burning. Then these ascetic games, as they have been called, involve severe ordeals. They anticipate the cruelty and hazing which adolescents must undergo during their initiation. This is a departure from *agôn*, which soon finds its perfect form, be it in legitimately competitive games and sports, or in those involving feats of prowess (hunting, mountain climbing, crossword puzzles, chess problems, etc.) in which champions, without directly confronting each other, are involved in ceaseless and diffuse competition.

Alea

This is the Latin name for the game of dice. I have borrowed it to designate, in contrast to *agôn*, all games that are based on a decision independent of the player, an outcome over which he has no control, and in which winning is the result of fate rather than triumphing over an adversary. More properly, destiny is the sole artisan of victory, and where there is rivalry, what is meant is that the winner has been more favored by fortune than the loser. Perfect examples of this type are provided by the games of dice, roulette, heads or tails, baccara, lotteries, etc. Here, not only does one refrain from trying to eliminate the injustice of chance, but rather it is the very capriciousness of chance that constitutes the unique appeal of the game.

Alea signifies and reveals the favor of destiny. The player is entirely passive; he does not deploy his resources, skill, muscles, or intelligence. All he need do is await, in hope and trembling, the cast of the die. He risks his stake. Fair play, also sought but now taking place under ideal conditions, lies in being compensated exactly in proportion to the risk involved. Every device intended to equalize the competitors' chances is here employed to scrupulously equate risk and profit.

In contrast to *agôn, alea* negates work, patience, experience, and qualifications. Professionalization, application, and training are eliminated. In one instant, winnings may be wiped out. *Alea* is total disgrace or absolute favor. It grants the lucky player infinitely more than he could procure by a lifetime of labor, discipline, and fatigue. It seems an insolent and sovereign insult to merit. It supposes on the player's part an attitude exactly opposite to that reflected in *agôn*. In the latter, his only reliance is upon himself; in the former, he counts on everything, even the vaguest sign, the slightest outside occurrence, which he immediately takes to be an omen or token—in short, he depends on everything except himself.

Agôn is a vindication of personal responsibility; *alea* is a negation of the will, a surrender to destiny. Some games, such as dominoes, backgammon, and most card games, combine the two. Chance determines the distribution of the hands dealt to each player, and the players then play the hands that blind luck has assigned to them as best they can. In a game like bridge, it is knowledge and reasoning that constitute the player's defense, permitting him to play a better game with the cards that he has been given. In games such as poker, it is the qualities of psychological acumen and character that count.

The role of money is also generally more impressive than the role of chance, and therefore is the recourse of the weaker player. The reason for this is clear: *Alea* does not have the function of causing the more intelligent to win money, but tends rather to abolish natural or acquired individual differences, so that all can be placed on an absolutely equal footing to await the blind verdict of chance.

Since the result of *agôn* is necessarily uncertain and paradoxically must approximate the effect of pure chance, assuming that the chances of the competitors are as equal as possible, it follows that every encounter with competitive characteristics and ideal rules can become the object of betting, or *alea*, e.g. horse or greyhound races, football, basketball, and cock fights. It even happens that table stakes vary unceasingly during the game, according to the vicissitudes of *agôn*.[4]

Games of chance would seem to be peculiarly human. Animals play games involving competition, stimulation, and excess. K. Groos, especially, offers striking examples of these. In sum, animals, which are very much involved in the immediate and enslaved by their impulses, cannot conceive of an abstract and inanimate power, to whose verdict they would passively submit in advance of the game. To await the decision of destiny passively and deliberately, to risk upon it wealth proportionate to the risk of losing, is an attitude that requires the possibility of foresight, vision, and speculation, for which objective and calculating reflection is needed. Perhaps it is in the degree to which a child approximates an animal that games of chance are not as important to children as to adults. For the child, play is active. In addition, the child is immune to the main attraction of games of chance, deprived as he is of economic independence, since he has no money of his own. Games of chance have no power to thrill him. To be sure, marbles are money to him. However, he counts on his skill rather than on chance to win them.

Agôn and *alea* imply opposite and somewhat complementary attitudes, but they both obey the same law—the creation for the players of conditions of pure equality denied them in real life. For nothing in life is clear, since everything is confused from the very beginning, luck and merit too. Play, whether *agôn or alea*, is thus an attempt to substitute perfect situations for the normal confusion of contemporary life. In games, the role of merit or chance is clear and indisputable. It is also implied that all must play with exactly the same possibility of proving their superiority or, on another scale, exactly the same chances of winning. In one way or another, one escapes the real world and creates another. One can also escape himself and become another. This is *mimicry*.

Mimicry

All play presupposes the temporary acceptance, if not of an illusion (indeed this last word means nothing less than beginning a game: *in-lusio*), then at least of a closed, conventional, and, in certain respects, imaginary universe. Play can consist not only of deploying actions or submitting to one's fate in an imaginary milieu, but of becoming an illusory character oneself, and of so behaving. One is thus confronted with a diverse series of manifestations, the common element of which is that the subject makes believe or makes others believe that he is someone other than himself. He forgets, disguises, or temporarily sheds his personality in order to feign another. I prefer to designate these phenomena by the term *mimicry*, the English word for mimetism, notably of insects, so that the fundamental, elementary, and quasi-organic nature of the impulse that stimulates it can be stressed.

The insect world, compared to the human world, seems like the most divergent of solutions provided by nature. This world is in contrast in all respects to that of man, but it is no less elaborate, complex, and surprising. Also, it seems legitimate to me at this point to take account of mimetic phenomena of which insects provide most perplexing examples. In fact, corresponding to the free, versatile, arbitrary, imperfect, and extremely diversified behavior of man, there is in animals, especially in insects, the organic, fixed, and absolute adaptation which characterizes the species and is infinitely and exactly reproduced from generation to generation in billions of individuals: e.g. the caste system of ants and termites as against class conflict, and the designs on butterflies' wings as compared to the history of painting. Reluctant as one may be to accept this hypothesis, the temerity of which I recognize, the inexplicable mimetism of insects immediately affords an extraordinary parallel to man's penchant for disguising himself, wearing a mask, or *playing a part*—except that in the insect's case the mask or guise becomes part of the body instead of a contrived accessory. But it serves the same purposes in both cases, viz. to change the wearer's appearance and to inspire fear in others.[5]

Among vertebrates, the tendency to imitate first appears as an entirely physical, quasi-irresistible contagion, analogous to the contagion of yawning, running, limping, smiling, or almost any movement. Hudson seems to have proved that a young animal "follows any object that is going away, and flees any approaching object." Just as a lamb is startled and runs if its mother turns around and moves toward the lamb without warning, the lamb trails the man, dog, or horse that it sees moving away. Contagion and imitation are not the same as simulation, but they make possible and give rise to the idea or the taste for mimicry. In birds, this tendency leads to nuptial parades, ceremonies, and exhibitions of vanity in which males or females, as the case may be, indulge with rare application and evident pleasure. As for the oxyrhinous crabs, which plant upon their carapaces any alga or polyp that they can catch, their aptitude for disguise leaves no room for doubt, whatever explanation for the phenomenon may be advanced.

Mimicry and travesty are therefore complementary acts in this kind of play. For children, the aim is to imitate adults. This explains the success of the toy weapons and miniatures which copy the tools, engines, arms, and machines used by adults. The little girl plays her mother's role as cook, laundress, and ironer. The boy makes believe he is a soldier, musketeer, policeman, pirate, cowboy, Martian,[6] etc. An airplane is made by waving his arms and making the noise of a motor. However, acts of mimicry tend to cross the border between childhood and adulthood. They cover to the same degree any distraction, mask, or travesty, in which one participates, and which stresses the very fact that the play is masked or otherwise disguised, and such consequences as ensue. Lastly it is clear that theatrical presentations and dramatic interpretations rightly belong in this category.

The pleasure lies in being or passing for another. But in games the basic intention is not that of deceiving the spectators. The child who is playing train may well refuse to kiss his father while saying to him that one does not embrace locomotives, but he is not trying to persuade his father that he is a real locomotive. At a carnival, the masquerader does not try to make one believe that he is really a marquis, toreador, or Indian, but rather tries to inspire fear and take advantage of the surrounding license, a result of the fact that the mask disguises the conventional self and liberates the true personality. The actor does not try to make believe that he is "really" King Lear or Charles V. It is only the spy and the fugitive who disguise themselves to really deceive because they are not playing.

Activity, imagination, interpretation, and *mimicry* have hardly any relationship to *alea*, which requires immobility and the thrill of expectation from the player, but *agôn* is not excluded. I am not thinking of the masqueraders' competition, in which the relationship is obvious. A much more subtle complicity is revealed. For nonparticipants, every *agôn* is a spectacle. Only it is a spectacle which, to be valid, excludes simulation. Great sports events are nevertheless special occasions for *mimicry*, but it must be recalled that the simulation is now transferred from the participants to the audience. It is not the athletes who mimic, but the spectators. Identification with the champion in itself constitutes *mimicry* related to that of the reader with the hero of the novel and that of the moviegoer with the film star. To be convinced of this, it is merely necessary to consider the perfectly symmetrical functions of the champion and the stage or screen star. Champions, winners at *agôn*, are the stars of sports contests. Conversely, stars are winners in a more diffuse competition in which the stakes are popular favor. Both receive a large fan-mail, give interviews to an avid press, and sign autographs.

In fact, bicycle races, boxing or wrestling matches, football, tennis, or polo games are intrinsic spectacles, with costumes, solemn overture, appropriate liturgy, and regulated procedures. In a word, these are dramas whose vicissitudes keep the public breathless, and lead to denouements which exalt some and depress others. The nature of these spectacles remains that of an *agôn*, but their outward aspect is that of an exhibition. The audience are not content to encourage the efforts of the athletes or horses of their choice merely by voice and gesture. A physical contagion leads them to assume the position of the men or animals in order to help them, just as the bowler is known to unconsciously incline his body in the direction that he would like the bowling ball to take at the end of its course. Under these conditions, paralleling the spectacle, a competitive *mimicry* is born in the public, which doubles the true *agôn* of the field or track.

With one exception, *mimicry* exhibits all the characteristics of play: liberty, convention, suspension of reality, and delimitation of space and time. However, the continuous submission to imperative and precise rules cannot be observed— rules for the dissimulation of reality and the substitution of a second reality. *Mimicry* is incessant invention. The rule of the game is unique: it consists in the actor's fascinating the spectator, while avoiding an error that might lead the spectator to break the spell. The spectator must lend himself to the illusion without first challenging the decor, mask, or artifice which for a given time he is asked to believe in as more real than reality itself.

181

Ilinx

The Last kind of game includes those which are based on the pursuit of vertigo and which consist of an attempt to momentarily destroy the stability of perception and inflict a kind of voluptuous panic upon an otherwise lucid mind. In all cases, it is a question of surrendering to a kind of spasm, seizure, or shock which destroys reality with sovereign brusqueness.

The disturbance that provokes vertigo is commonly sought for its own sake. I need only cite as examples the actions of whirling dervishes and the Mexican *voladores*. I choose these purposely, for the former, in technique employed, can be related to certain children's games, while the latter rather recall the elaborate maneuvers of high-wire acrobatics. They thus touch the two poles of games of vertigo. Dervishes seek ecstasy by whirling about with movements accelerating as the drumbeats become ever more precipitate. Panic and hypnosis are attained by the paroxysm of frenetic, contagious, and shared rotation.[7] In Mexico, the *voladores*—Huastec or Totonac—climb to the top of a mast sixty-five to one hundred feet high. They are disguised as eagles with false wings hanging from their wrists. The end of a rope is attached to their waists. The rope then passes between their toes in such a way that they can manage their entire descent with head down and arms outstretched. Before reaching the ground, they make many complete turns, thirty according to Torquemada, describing an ever-widening spiral in their downward flight. The ceremony, comprising several flights and beginning at noon, is readily interpreted as a dance of the setting sun, associated with birds, the deified dead. The frequency of accidents has led the Mexican authorities to ban this dangerous exercise.[8]

It is scarcely necessary to invoke these rare and fascinating examples. Every child very well knows that by whirling rapidly he reaches a centrifugal state of flight from which he regains bodily stability and clarity of perception only with difficulty. The child engages in this activity playfully and finds pleasure thereby. An example is the game of teetotum[9] in which the player pivots on one foot as quickly as he is able. Analogously, in the Haitian game of *maïs d'or* two children hold hands, face to face, their arms extended. With their bodies stiffened and bent backward, and with their feet joined, they turn until they are breathless, so that they will have the pleasure of staggering about after they stop. Comparable sensations are provided by screaming as loud as one can, racing downhill, and tobogganing; in horsemanship, provided that one turns quickly; and in swinging.

Various physical activities also provoke these sensations, such as the tightrope, falling or being projected into space, rapid rotation, sliding, speeding, and acceleration of vertilinear movement, separately or in combination with gyrating movement. In parallel fashion, there is a vertigo of a moral order, a transport that suddenly seizes the individual. This vertigo is readily linked to the desire for disorder and destruction, a drive which is normally repressed. It is reflected in crude and brutal forms of personality expression. In children, it is especially observed in the games of hot cockles, "winner-take-all," and leapfrog in which they rush and spin pell-mell. In adults, nothing is more revealing of vertigo than the strange excitement that is felt in cutting down the tall prairie flowers with a switch, or in creating an avalanche of the snow on a rooftop, or, better, the intoxication that is experienced in military barracks—for example, in noisily banging garbage cans.

To cover the many varieties of such transport, for a disorder that may take organic or psychological form, I propose using the term *ilinx*, the Greek term for whirlpool, from which is also derived the Greek word for vertigo (*ilingos*).

This pleasure is not unique to man. To begin with, it is appropriate to recall the gyrations of certain mammals, sheep in particular. Even if these are pathological manifestations, they are too significant to be passed over in silence. In addition, examples in which the play element is certain are not lacking. In order to catch their tails dogs will spin around until they fall down. At other times they are seized by a fever for running until they are exhausted. Antelopes, gazelles, and wild horses are often panic-stricken when there is no real danger in the slightest degree to account for it; the impression is of an overbearing contagion to which they surrender in instant compliance.[10]

Water rats divert themselves by spinning as if they were being drawn by an eddy in a stream. The case of the chamois is even more remarkable. According to Karl Groos, they ascend the glaciers, and with a leap, each in turn slides down a steep slope, while the other chamois watch.

The gibbon chooses a flexible branch and weighs it down until it unbends, thus projecting him into the air. He lands catch as catch can, and he endlessly repeats this useless exercise, inexplicable except in terms of its seductive quality. Birds especially love games of vertigo. They let themselves fall like stones from a great height, then open their wings when they are only a few feet from the ground, thus giving the impression that they are going to be crushed. In the mating season they utilize this heroic flight in order to attract the female. The American nighthawk, described by Audubon, is a virtuoso at these impressive acrobatics.[11]

Following the teetotum, *maïs d'or*, sliding, horsemanship, and swinging of their childhood, men surrender to the intoxication of many kinds of dance, from the common but insidious giddiness of the waltz to the many mad, tremendous, and convulsive movements of other dances. They derive the same kind of pleasure from the intoxication stimulated by high speed on skis, motorcycles, or in driving sports cars. In order to give this kind of sensation the intensity and brutality capable of shocking adults, powerful machines have had to be invented. Thus it is not surprising that the Industrial Revolution had to take place before vertigo could really become a kind of game. It is now provided for the avid masses by thousands of stimulating contraptions installed at fairs and amusement parks.

These machines would obviously surpass their goals if it were only a question of assaulting the organs of the inner ear, upon which the sense of equilibrium is dependent. But it is the whole body which must submit to such treatment as anyone would fear undergoing, were it not that everybody else was seen struggling to do the same. In fact, it is worth watching people leaving these vertigo-inducing machines. The contraptions turn people pale and dizzy to the point of nausea.

They shriek with fright, gasp for breath, and have the terrifying impression of visceral fear and shrinking as if to escape a horrible attack. Moreover the majority of them, before even recovering, are already hastening to the ticket booth in order to buy the right to again experience the same pleasurable torture.

It is necessary to use the word "pleasure," because one hesitates to call such a transport a mere distraction, corresponding as it does more to a spasm than to an entertainment. In addition, it is important to note that the violence of the shock felt is such that the concessionaires try, in extreme cases, to lure the naive by offering free rides. They deceitfully announce that "this time only" the ride is free, when this is the usual practice. To compensate, the spectators are made to pay for the privilege of calmly observing from a high balcony the terrors of the cooperating or surprised victims, exposed to fearful forces or strange caprices.

It would be rash to draw very precise conclusions on the subject of this curious and cruel assignment of roles. This last is not characteristic of a kind of game, such as is found in boxing, wrestling, and in gladiatorial combat. Essential is the pursuit of this special disorder or sudden panic, which defines the term vertigo, and in the true characteristics of the games associated with it: viz. the freedom to accept or refuse the experience, strict and fixed limits, and separation from the rest of reality. What the experience adds to the spectacle does not diminish but reinforces its character as play.

2. From turbulence to rules

Rules are inseparable from play as soon as the latter becomes institutionalized. From this moment on they become part of its nature. They transform it into an instrument of fecund and decisive culture. But a basic freedom is central to play in order to stimulate distraction and fantasy. This liberty is its indispensable motive power and is basic to the most complex and carefully organized forms of play. Such a primary power of improvisation and joy, which I call *paidia*, is allied to the taste for gratuitous difficulty that I propose to call *ludus*, in order to encompass the various games to which, without exaggeration, a civilizing quality can be attributed. In fact, they reflect the moral and intellectual values of a culture, as well as contribute to their refinement and development.

I have chosen the term *paidia* because its root is the word for child, and also because of a desire not to needlessly disconcert the reader by resorting to a term borrowed from an antipodal language. However, the Sanskrit *kredati* and the Chinese *wan* seem both richer and more expressive through the variety and nature of their connotations. It is true that they also present the disadvantages of over-abundance—a certain danger of confusion, for one. *Kredati* designates the play of adults, children, and animals. It applies more specifically to gamboling, i.e., to the sudden and capricious movements provoked by a superabundance of gaiety and vitality. It applies equally to illicit sex relationships, the rise and fall of waves, and anything that undulates with the wind. The word *wan* is even more explicit, as much for what it defines as for what it avoids defining, i.e. specifying games of skill, competition, simulation, and chance. It manifests many refinements of meaning to which I will have occasion to return.

In view of these relationships and semantic qualifications, what can be the connotations and denotations of the term *paidia*? I shall define it, for my purposes, as a word covering the spontaneous manifestations of the play instinct: a cat entangled in a ball of wool, a dog sniffing, and an infant laughing at his rattle represent the first identifiable examples of this type of activity. It intervenes in every happy exuberance which effects an immediate and disordered agitation, an impulsive and easy recreation, but readily carried to excess, whose impromptu and unruly character remains its essential if not unique reason for being. From somersaults to scribbling, from squabble to uproar, perfectly clear illustrations are not lacking of the comparable symptoms of movements, colors, or noises.

This elementary need for disturbance and tumult first appears as an impulse to touch, grasp, taste, smell, and then drop any accessible object. It readily can become a taste for destruction and breaking things. It explains the pleasure in endlessly cutting up paper with a pair of scissors, pulling cloth into thread, breaking up a gathering, holding up a queue, disturbing the play or work of others, etc. Soon comes the desire to mystify or to defy by sticking out the tongue or grimacing while seeming to touch or throw the forbidden object. For the child it is a question of expressing himself, of feeling he is the *cause*, of forcing others to pay attention to him. In this manner, K. Groos recalls the case of a monkey which took pleasure in pulling the tail of a dog that lived with it, each time that the dog seemed to be going to sleep. The primitive joy in destruction and upset has been notably observed by the sister of G. J. Romanes in precise and most meaningful detail.[12]

The child does not stop at that. He loves to play with his own pain, for example by probing a toothache with his tongue. He also likes to be frightened. He thus looks for a physical illness, limited and controlled, of which he is the cause, or sometimes he seeks an anxiety that he, being the cause, can stop at will. At various points, the fundamental aspects of play are already recognizable, i.e. voluntary, agreed upon, isolated, and regulated activity.

Soon there is born the desire to invent rules, and to abide by them whatever the cost. The child then makes all kinds of bets—which, as has been seen, are the elementary forms of *agôn*—with himself or his friends. He hops, walks backwards with his eyes closed, plays at who can look longest at the sun, and will suffer pain or stand in a painful position.

In general, the first manifestations of *paidia* have no name and could not have any, precisely because they are not part of any order, distinctive symbolism, or clearly differentiated life that would permit a vocabulary to consecrate their autonomy with a specific term. But as soon as conventions, techniques, and utensils emerge, the first games as such arise with them: e.g. leapfrog, hide and seek, kite-flying, teetotum, sliding, blindman's buff, and doll-play. At this point the contradictory roads of *agôn*, *alea*, *mimicry*, and *ilinx* begin to bifurcate. At the same time, the pleasure experienced in solving a problem arbitrarily designed for this purpose also intervenes, so that reaching a solution has no other goal than personal satisfaction for its own sake.

This condition, which is *ludus* proper, is also reflected in different kinds of games, except for those which wholly depend upon the cast of a die. It is complementary to and a refinement of *paidia*, which it disciplines and enriches. It provides an occasion for training and normally leads to the acquisition of a special skill, a particular mastery of the operation of one or another contraption or the discovery of a satisfactory solution to problems of a more conventional type.

The difference from *agôn* is that in ludus the tension and skill of the player are not related to any explicit feeling of emulation or rivalry: the conflict is with the obstacle, not with one or several competitors. On the level of manual dexterity there can be cited games such as cup-and-ball, diabolo, and yo-yo. These simple instruments merely utilize basic natural laws, e.g. gravity and rotation in the case of the yo-yo, where the point is to transform a rectilinear alternating motion into a continuous circular movement. Kite-flying, on the contrary, relies on the exploitation of a specific atmospheric condition. Thanks to this, the player accomplishes a kind of auscultation upon the sky from afar. He projects his presence beyond the limits of his body. Again, the game of blindman's buff offers an opportunity to experience the quality of perception in the absence of sight.[13] It is readily seen that the possibilities of *ludus* are almost infinite.

Games such as solitaire or the ring puzzle, although part of the same species, already belong to another group of games, since they constantly appeal to a spirit of calculation and contrivance. And lastly, crossword puzzles, mathematical recreations, anagrams, olorhymes[14] and obscure poetry, addiction to detective stories (trying to identify the culprit], and chess or bridge problems constitute, even in the absence of gadgets, many varieties of the most prevalent and pure forms of *ludus*.

It is common knowledge that what to begin with seems to be a situation susceptible to indefinite repetition turns out to be capable of producing ever new combinations. Thus the player is stimulated to emulate himself, permitting him to take pride in his accomplishment, as against those who share his taste. There is a manifest relationship between *ludus* and *agôn*. In addition, it can happen that the same game may possess both, e.g. chess or bridge.

The combination of ludus and alea is no less frequent: it is especially recognizable in games of patience, in which ingenious maneuvers have little influence upon the result, and in playing slot machines in which the player can very crudely calculate the impulsion given to the ball at various points in directing its course. In both these examples, chance is still the deciding factor. Moreover, the fact that the player is not completely helpless and that he can at least minimally count on his skill or talent is sufficient reason to link *ludus* with *alea*.[15]

Ludus is also readily compatible with *mimicry*. In the simplest cases, it lends aspects of illusion to construction games such as the animals made out of millet stalks by Dogon children, the cranes or automobiles constructed by fitting together perforated steel parts and pullies from an Erector set, or the scale-model planes or ships that even adults do not disdain meticulously constructing. However, it is the theater which provides the basic connection between the two, by disciplining mimicry until it becomes an art rich in a thousand diverse routines, refined techniques, and subtly complex resources. By means of this fortunate development, the cultural fecundity of play is amply demonstrated.

In contrast, just as there could be no relationship between *paidia*, which is tumultuous and exuberant, and *alea*, which is passive anticipation of and mute immobility pending the outcome of the game, there also can be no connection between *ludus*, which is calculation and contrivance, and *ilinx*, which is a pure state of transport. The desire to overcome an obstacle can only emerge to combat vertigo and prevent it from becoming transformed into disorder or panic. It is, therefore, training in self-control, an arduous effort to preserve calm and equilibrium. Far from being compatible with *ilinx*, it provides the discipline needed to neutralize the dangerous effects of *ilinx*, as in mountain climbing or tightrope walking.

Ludus, in itself, seems incomplete, a kind of makeshift device intended to allay boredom. One becomes resigned to it while awaiting something preferable, such as the arrival of partners that makes possible the substitution of a contest for this solitary pleasure. Moreover, even in games of skill or contrivance (e.g. patience, crossword and other puzzles) which exclude or regard as undesirable the intervention of another person, *ludus* no less inspires in the player the hope of succeeding the next time when he may obtain a higher score. In this way, the influence of *agôn* is again manifested. Indeed, it enriches the pleasure derived from overcoming an arbitrarily chosen obstacle. In fact, even if each of these games is played alone and is not replaced by an openly competitive one, it can easily and quickly be converted into a contest, with or without prizes, such as newspapers organize on occasion.

There is also an aspect of *ludus* that, in my opinion, is explained by the presence of *agôn* within it: that is, that it is strongly affected by fashion. The yo-yo, cup-and-ball, diabolo, and ring puzzle appear and disappear as if by magic and soon are replaced by other games. In parallel fashion, the vogues for amusements of a more intellectual nature are no less limited in time; e.g. the rebus, the anagram, the acrostic, and the charade have had their hours. It is probable that crossword puzzles and detective stories will run the same course. Such a phenomenon would be enigmatic if *ludus* were an individual amusement, as seems superficially to be the case. In reality, it is permeated with an atmosphere of competition. It only persists to the degree that the fervor of addicts transforms it into virtual *agôn*. When the latter is missing, *ludus* cannot persist independently. In fact, it is not sufficiently supported by the spirit of organized competition, which is not essential to it, and does not provide the substance for a spectacle capable of attracting crowds. It remains transient and diffuse, or else it risks turning into an obsession for the isolated fanatic who would dedicate himself to it absolutely and in his addiction would increasingly withdraw from society.

Industrial civilization has given birth to a special form of *ludus*, the hobby, a secondary and gratuitous activity, undertaken and pursued for pleasure, e.g. collecting, unique accomplishments, the pleasure in billiards or inventing gadgets, in a word any occupation that is primarily a compensation for the injury to personality caused by bondage to work of an automatic and picayune character. It has been observed that the hobby of the worker-turned- artisan readily takes the form of constructing *complete* scale models of the machines in the fabrication of which he is fated to cooperate by always repeating the same movement, an operation demanding no skill or intelligence on his part. He not only avenges himself upon reality, but in a positive and creative way. The hobby is a response to one of the highest functions of the play instinct. It is not surprising that a technical civilization contributes to its development, even to providing compensations for its more brutal aspects. Hobbies reflect the rare qualities that make their development possible.

In a general way, *ludus* relates to the primitive desire to find diversion and amusement in arbitrary, perpetually recurrent obstacles. Thousands of occasions and devices are invented to satisfy simultaneously the desire for relaxation and the need, of which man cannot be rid, to utilize purposefully the knowledge, experience, and intelligence at his disposal, white disregarding self-control and his capacity for resistance to suffering, fatigue, panic, or intoxication.

What I call *ludus* stands for the specific element in play the impact and cultural creativity of which seems most impressive. It does not connote a psychological attitude as-precise as that of *agôn, alea, mimicry* or *ilinx*, but in disciplining the *paidia*, its general contribution is to give the fundamental categories of play their purity and excellence.

Besides, *ludus* is not the only conceivable metamorphosis of *paidia*. A civilization like that of classical China worked out a different destiny for itself. Wisely and circumspectly, Chinese culture is less directed toward purposive innovation. The need for progress and the spirit of enterprise generally seem to them a kind of compulsion that is not particularly creative. Under these conditions the turbulence and surplus of energy characteristic of *paidia* is channelized in a direction better suited to its supreme values. This is the place to return to the term *wan*. According to some, it would etymologically designate the act of indefinitely caressing a piece of jade while polishing it, in order to savor its smoothness or as an accompaniment to reverie. Perhaps this origin clarifies another purpose of *paidia*. The reservoir of free movement that is part of its original definition seems in this case to be oriented not toward process, calculation, or triumph over difficulties but toward calm, patience, and idle speculation. The term wan basically designates all kinds of semiautomatic activities which leave the mind detached and idle, certain complex games which are part of *ludus*, and at the same time, nonchalant meditation and lazy contemplation.

Tumult and din are covered by the expression *jeou-nao*, which means literally "passion-disorder." When joined to the term *nao*, the term *wan* connotes any exuberant or joyous behavior. But this term *wan* must be present. With the character *tchouang* (to pretend), it means "to find pleasure in simulating." Thus *wan* coincides fairly exactly with the various possible manifestations of *paidia*, although when used alone it may designate a particular kind of game. It is not used for competition, dice, or dramatic interpretation. That is to say, it excludes the various kinds of games that I have referred to as institutional.

Table 1 Classification of games

	AGÔN (Competition)	ALEA (Chance)	MIMICRY (Simulation)	ILINX (Vertigo)
PAIDIA ↑				
Tumult				
Agitation				
Immoderate laughter	Racing ⎫	Counting-out rhymes	Children's initiations	Children "whirling"
	Wrestling ⎬ not	Heads or tails	Games of illusion	Horseback riding
	Etc. ⎬ regulated		Tag, Arms Masks, Disguises	Swinging
	Athletics ⎭			Waltzing
Kite-flying	Boxing, Billiards	Betting		Volador
Solitaire	Fencing, Checkers	Roulette		Traveling carnivals
Patience	Football, Chess			Skiing
Crossword puzzles	Contests, Sports in general	Simple, complex, and continuing lotteries*	Theater Spectacles in general	Mountain climbing
				Tightrope walking
LUDUS ↓				

N.B. In each vertical column games are classified in such an order that the *paidia* element is constantly decreasing while the *ludus* element is ever increasing.

*A simple lottery consists of the one basic drawing. In a complex lottery there are many possible combinations. A continuing lottery (e.g. Irish Sweepstakes) is one consisting of two or more stages, the winner of the first stage being granted the opportunity to participate in a second lottery. [From correspondence with Caillois. M.B.]

The latter are designated by more specialized terms. The character *hsi* corresponds to games of disguise or simulation, covering the domain of the theater and the spectacle. The character *choua* refers to games involving skill and ability; however, it is also used for contests involving jokes or puns, for fencing, and for perfection in practicing a difficult art. The character *teou* refers to conflict as such, cock fighting or dueling. It is also used for card games. Lastly, the character *tou*, not to be applied to children's games, covers games of chance, feats of daring, bets, and ordeals. It also is the name for blasphemy, for to tempt chance is considered a sacrilegious wager against destiny.[16]

The vast semantic area of the term *wan* makes it even more deserving of interest. To begin with, it includes child's play and all kinds of carefree and frivolous diversion such as are suggested by the verbs to frolic, to romp, to trifle, etc. It is used to describe casual, abnormal, or strange sex practices. At the same time, it is used for games demanding reflection and *forbidding haste*, such as chess, checkers, puzzles *(tai Kiao)*, and the game of nine rings.[17] It also comprises the pleasure of appreciating the savor of good food or the bouquet of a wine, the taste for collecting works of art or even appreciating them, voluptuously handling and even fashioning delicate curios, comparable to the Occidental category of the hobby, collecting or puttering. Lastly, the transitory and relaxing sweetness of moonlight is suggested, the pleasure of a boat ride on a limpid lake or the prolonged contemplation of a waterfall.[18]

The example of the word *wan* shows that the destinies of cultures can be read in their games. The preference for *agôn, alea, mimicry,* or *ilinx* helps decide the future of a civilization. Also, the channeling of the free energy in *paidia* toward invention or contemplation manifests an implicit but fundamental and most significant choice.

Notes

1 J. Huizinga, *Homo Ludens* (English translation; New York: Roy Publishers, 1950, p. 13). On p. 28 there is another definition not quite as eloquent, but less restricted: "Play is a voluntary activity or occupation executed within certain fixed limits of time and place, according to rules freely accepted but absolutely binding, having its aim in itself and accompanied by a feeling of tension, joy, and consciousness that it is different from ordinary life."

2 Paul Valéry, *Tel quel*, II (Paris, 1943), p. 21.

3 Karl Groos, *The Play of Animals* (English translation; New York: D. Appleton & Co., 1898, p. 151).

4 For example, in the Balearic Islands for jai-alai, and cockfights in the Antilles. It is obvious that it is not necessary to take into account the cash prizes that may motivate jockeys, owners, runners, boxers, football players, or other athletes. These prizes, however substantial, are not relevant to *alea*. They are a reward for a well-fought victory. This recompense for merit has nothing to do with luck or the result of chance, which remain the uncertain monopoly of gamblers; in fact it is the direct opposite.

5 Terrifying examples of mimicry or structural dissimulation among insects (the spectral attitude of the mantis and the fright offered by *Smerinthus ocellata*) will be found in my study entitled "*Mimétisme et psychasténie,* "in *Le Mythe et L'Homme* (Paris, 1938),

pp. 101–143. Unfortunately, this study treats the problem with a perspective that today seems fantastic to me. Indeed I no longer view mimetism as a disturbance of space perception and a tendency to return to the inanimate, but rather, as herein proposed, as the insect equivalent of human games of simulation. The examples utilized in *Le Mythe et L'Homme* nevertheless retain their value [translated by M. B. from French text):

"In order to protect itself, an inoffensive animal assumes the appearance of a ferocious animal; for example the bee-shaped butterfly *Trochilium* and the wasp *Vespa crabro*: even to the smoky wings, brown feet and antennae, yellow-and-black striped abdomens and thoraxes, and the same impressive noisy flight in broad day. Sometimes the mimetic animal has a further goal. The caterpillar *Choerocampa elpenor*, for example, has two eyelike black- bordered spots on its fourth and fifth segments. When disturbed it retracts its anterior segments. The fourth swells enormously. The effect obtained is the illusion of a snake's head, a frightening apparition to lizards and small birds [L. Cuénot, *La génèse des espèces animatles*, Paris, 1911, pp. 470 and 473). According to Weismann [*Vorträge über Descendenztheorie*, Vol. 1, pp. 78–79) *Smerinthus ocellata*, which like all sphinxes at rest hides its lower wings, when in danger suddenly masks them with two large blue eyes on a red background, thus unexpectedly frightening the aggressor. [This terrifying transformation is automatic. It is approximated in cutaneous reflexes which, although they do not extend as far as a change of color designed to transform the animal, sometimes result in lending it a terrifying quality. A cat, confronted by a dog, is frightened; its hair stands on end, thus causing the cat to become frightening. Le Dantec by this analogy (*Lamarckiens et Darwiniens*, 3rd ed.; Paris, 1908, p. 139) explains the human phenomenon known as "goose pimples," a common result of extreme fright. Even though rendered dysfunctional by the comparative hairlessness of man, the reflex still persists.] This act is accompanied by a kind of nervousness. At rest, the animal resembles a thin, dessicated leaf. When disturbed, it clings to its perch, extends its antennae, inflates its thorax, retracts its head, exaggerates the curve of its abdomen, while its whole body shakes and shivers. The crisis past, it slowly returns to immobility. Standfuss' experiments have demonstrated the efficacy of this behavior in frightening the tomtit, the robin, the common nightingale and frequently the grey nightingale. [Cf. Standfuss, "Beispiel von Schutz and Trutzfärbung," *Mitt. Schweitz. Entomol. Ges.*, XI (1906), 155–157; P. Vignon, *Introduction a la biologie expérimentale*, Paris, 1930 (Encycl. Biol., Vol. VIII), p. 356), The moth, with extended wings, seems in fact like the head of an enormous bird of prey . . . .

"Examples of homomorphism are not lacking: the *calappes* and round pebbles, the *chlamys* and seeds, the *moenas* and gravel, the prawns and fucus. The fish *Phylopteryx* of the Sargasso Sea is only an 'alga cut into the shape of a floating lanner' (L. Murat, *Les merveilles du monde animal*, 1914, pp. 37–38) like *Antennarius* and *Pterophryne* (L. Cuénot, *op. cit.*, p. 453). The polyp retracts its tentacles, crooks its back, and adapts its color so that it resembles a pebble. The white and green lower wings of *catocala nupta* resemble the umbelliferae. The embossments, nodes, and streaks of the pieridine, *Aurora*, make it identical with the bark of the poplars on which it lives. The lichens of *Lithinus nigrocristinus* of Madagascar and the Flatides cannot be distinguished (*ibid.*, Fig. 114). The extent of mimetism among the mantidae is known. Their paws simulate petals or are rounded into corollae, which resemble flowers, imitating the effects of the wind upon the flowers through a delicate mechanical balance (A. Lefèbvre, *Ann. de la Soc. entom. de France*,

Vol. IV; Léon Binet, *La vie de la mante religieuse*, Paris, 1931; P. Vignon, *op. cit.*, pp. 374 ff.). *Cilix compressa* resembles a type of bird dung, and the *Ceroxeylus laceratus* with its foliated, light olive-green excrescences resembles a stick covered with moss. This last insect belongs to the phasmidae family which generally hang from bushes in the forest and have the bizarre habit of letting their paws hang irregularly thus making the error even easier (Alfred R. Wallace, *Natural Selection and Tropical Nature*, London: Macmillan, 1895,' p. 47). To the same family belong even the bacilli which resemble twigs. *Ceroys* and *Heteropteryx* resemble thorny dessicated branches; and the *membracides*, hemiplera of the Tropics, resemble buds or thorns, such as the impressive thorn-shaped insect, *Umbonia orozimbo*. Measuring worms, erect and rigid, can scarcely be distinguished from bush sprouts, equipped as they are with appropriate tegumentary wrinkles. Everyone is familiar with the insect of the genus *Phyllium* which resembles leaves. From here, the road leads to the perfect homomorphism of certain butterflies: *Oxydia*, above all, which perches perpendicularly from the tip of a branch, upper wings folded over, so that it looks like a terminal leaf. This guise is accentuated by a thin, dark line continuing across the four wings in such a way that the main vein of a leaf is simulated (Rabaud, *Éléments de biologie générale*, 2nd ed., Paris, 1928, p. 412, Fig. 54).

"Other species are even more perfected, their lower wings being provided with a delicate appendix used as a petiole, thus obtaining 'a foothold in the vegetable world' (Vignon, *loc. cit.*). The total impression of the two wings on each side is that of the lanceolate oval characteristic of the leaf. There is also a longitudinal line, continuing from one wing to the other, a substitute for the median vein of the leaf; 'the organic driving force has had to design and cleverly organize each of the wings so that it should attain a form not self-determined, but through union with the other wing' (*ibid.*). The main examples are *Coenophlebia archidona* of Central America (Delage and Goldsmith, *Les théories de l'évolution*, Paris, 1909, Fig. 1, p. 74) and the various types of *Kallima* in India and Malaysia."

Additional examples: *Le Mythe et L'Homme*, pp. 133–136.

6 As has been aptly remarked, girls' playthings are designed to imitate practical, realistic, and domestic activities, while those of boys suggest distant, romantic, inaccessible, or even obviously unreal actions.

7 O. Depont and X. Coppolani, *Les confréries religieuses musulmanes* (Algiers, 1887), pp. 156–159, 329–339.

8 Description and photographs in Helga Larsen, "Notes on the Volador and Its Associated Ceremonies and Superstitions." *Ethnos*. 2, No. 4 (July, 1937), 179–192, and in Guy Stresser-Péan, "Les origines du volador et du comelagatoazte," *Actes du XXVIIIe Congres International des Américanistes* (Paris, 1947), 327–334. I quote part of the description of the ceremony from this article [translated by M. B. from French text]:

"The chief of the dance or *K'ohal*, clad in a red and blue tunic, ascends in his turn and sits on the terminal platform. Facing east, he first invokes the benevolent deities, while extending his wings in their direction and using a whistle which imitates the puling of eagles. Then he climbs to the top of the mast. Facing the four points of the compass in succession, he offers them a chalice of calabash wrapped in white linen just like a bottle of brandy, from which he sips and spits some more or less vaporized mouthfuls. Once this symbolic offering has been made, he puts on his headdress of red feathers and dances, facing all four directions while beating his wings.

"These ceremonies executed at the summit of the mast mark what the Indians consider the most moving phase of the ritual, because it involves mortal risk. But the next stage of the 'flight' is even more spectacular. The four dancers, attached by the waist, pass underneath the structure, then let themselves go from behind. Thus suspended, they slowly descend to the ground, describing a grand spiral in proportion to the unrolling of the ropes. The difficult thing for these dancers is to seize this rope between their toes in such a way as to keep their heads down and arms outspread just like descending birds which soar in great circles in the sky. As for the chief, first he waits for some moments, then he lets himself glide along one of the four dancers' ropes."

9 [*Toton* in the French text. M. B.]
10 Groos, *op. cit*, p. 208.
11 *Ibid.*, p. 259.
12 Observation cited by Groos, *ibid.*, pp. 92–93:

"I notice that the love of mischief is very strong in him. Today he got hold of a wineglass and an egg cup. The glass he dashed on the floor with all his might and of course broke it. Finding, however, that the egg cup would not break when thrown down, he looked round for some hard substance against which to dash it. The post of the brass bedstead appearing to be suitable for the purpose, he raised the egg cup high above his head and gave it several hard blows. When it was completely smashed he was quite satisfied. He breaks a stick by passing it down between a heavy object and the wall and then hanging onto the end, thus breaking it across the heavy object. He frequently destroys an article of dress by carefully pulling out the threads (thus unraveling it) before he begins to tear it with his teeth in a violent manner.

"In accordance with his desire for mischief he is, of course, very fond of upsetting things, but he always takes great care that they do not fall on himself. Thus he will pull a chair toward him till it is almost overbalanced, then he intently fixes his eyes on the top bar of the back, and when he sees it coming over his way, darts from underneath and watches the fall with great delight; and similarly with heavier things. There is a washstand, for example, with a heavy marble top, which he has with great labor upset several times, but always without hurting himself." (G. J. Romanes, *Animal Intelligence*, New York, D. Appleton & Co., 1897, p. 484.)

13 This had already been observed by Kant. Cf. Y. Hirn, *Les jeux d'enfants* (French translation; Paris, 1926), p. 63.
14 [Olorimes (in French) are two lines of poetry in which each syllable of the first line rhymes with the corresponding syllable of the second line. Caillois suggested the following couplet from Victor Hugo as an example:

Gal, amant de la reine, alle, tour magnanime
Galamment de l'arène a la Tour Magne, a Nimes
From correspondence with Caillois, M. B.]

15 The development of slot machines in the modern world and the fascination or obsessive behavior that they cause is indeed astonishing. The vogue for playing slot machines is often of unsuspected proportions. It causes true obsessions and sometimes is a contributing factor to a youth's entire way of life. The following account appeared in the press on March 25, 1957, occasioned by the investigation conducted by the United States Senate that same month:

"Three hundred thousand slot machines manufactured by 15,000 employees in 50 factories, most of which are located in the environs of Chicago, were sold in 1956. These machines are popular not only in Chicago, Kansas City, or Detroit—not to speak of Las Vegas, the capital of gambling—but also in New York. All day and all night in Times Square, the heart of New York, Americans of all ages, from schoolboy to old man, spend their pocket money or weekly pension in an hour, in the vain hope of winning a free game. At 1485 Broadway, 'Play-land' in gigantic neon letters eclipses the sign of a Chinese restaurant. In an immense room without a door dozens of multicolored slot machines are aligned in perfect order. In front of each machine a comfortable leather stool, reminiscent of the stools in the most elegant bars on the Champs-Elysées, allows the player with enough money to sit for hours. He even has an ash tray and a special place for his hot dog and Coca Cola, the national repast of the poor in the United States, which he can order without budging from his place. With a dime or quarter, he tries to add up enough points to win a carton of cigarettes. In New York State it is illegal to pay off in cash. An infernal din muffles the recorded voice of Louis Armstrong or Elvis Presley which accompanies the efforts of the small-time gamblers. Youths in blue jeans and leather jackets rub shoulders with old ladies in flowered hats. The boys choose the atomic bomber or guided-missile machines and the women put their hand on the 'love meter' that reveals whether they are still capable of having a love affair, while little children for a nickel are shaken, almost to the point of heart failure, on a donkey that resembles a zebu. There are also the marines or aviators who listlessly fire revolvers."
[D. Morgaine, translated by M.B.]

The four categories of play are represented: *agôn* and *alea* involved in most of the machines, mimicry and illusion in the imaginary maneuvering of the atomic bomber or guided missile, ilinx on the shaking dookey.

It is estimated that Americans spend $400 million a year for the sole purpose of projecting nickel-plated balls against luminous blocks through various obstacles. In Japan, after the war, the mania was worse. It is estimated that about 12 per cent of the national budget was swallowed up annually by slot machines. There were some installed even in doctors' waiting rooms. Even today, in the shadow of the viaducts, in Tokyo, between the trains "is heard the piercing noise of the *pachencos*, the contraptions in which the player strikes a steel ball which gropingly traverses various tricky obstacles and then is lost forever. An absurd game, in which one can only lose, but which seduces those in whom the fury rages. That is why there are no less than 600,000 *pachencos* in Japan. I gaze at these rows of dark heads fascinated by a ball that gambols against some nails. The player holds the apparatus in both hands, no doubt so that his will to win shall pass into the machine. The most compulsive do not even wait for one ball to run its course before hitting another. It is a painful spectacle." [James de Coquet, Le Figaro, Feb. 18, 1957, translated by M.B.]

This seduction is so strong that it contributes to the rise of juvenile delinquency. Thus, in April of 1957, the American newspapers reported the arrest in Brooklyn of a gang of juveniles led by a boy of ten and a girl of twelve. They burglarized neighborhood stores of about one thousand dollars. They were only interested in dimes and nickels, which could be used in slot machines. Bills were used merely for wrapping their loot, and were later thrown away as refuse.

Julius Siegal, in a recent article entitled "The Lure of Pinball" [*Harper's* 215, No. 1289 [Oct. 1957], 44–47] has tried to explain the incredible fascination of the game. His study emerges as both confession and analysis. After the inevitable allusions to sexual symbolism, the author especially stresses a feeling of victory over modern technology in the pleasure derived from slot machines. The appearance of calculation that the player reflects before projecting the ball has no significance, but to him it seems sublime. "It seems to me that when a pinballer invests his nickel he pits himself—his own skill—against the combined skills of American industry (p. 45)." The game is therefore a kind of competition between individual skill and an immense anonymous mechanism. For one (real) coin, he hopes to win (fictive) million, for scores are always expressed in numbers with multiple zeros.

Finally, the possibility must exist of cheating the apparatus. "Tilt" indicates only an outer limit. This is a delicious menace, an added risk, a kind of secondary game grafted onto the first.

Curiously, Siegal admits that when depressed, he takes a half-hour's detour in order to find his favorite machine. Then he plays, confident that the game " . . . assumes positively therapeutic proportions—if I win (p. 46)." He leaves reassured as to his skill and chances of success. His despair is gone, and his aggression has been sublimated.

He deems a player's behavior at a slot machine to be as revealing of his personality as is the Rorschach test. Each player is generally trying to prove that he can beat the machine on its own ground. He masters the mechanism and amasses an enormous fortune shown in the luminous figures inscribed on the screen. He alone has succeeded, and can renew his exploit at will. " . . . He has freely expressed his irritation with reality, and made the world behave. All for only a nickel (p. 47)." The responsibility for such an ambitious conclusion is the author's. What is left is that the inordinate success of slot machines (in which nothing is won but the possibility of playing again] appears to be one of the most disconcerting enigmas posed by contemporary amusements.

16 The Chinese also use the word *yeou* to designate idling and games in space, especially kite-flying, and also great flights of fancy, mystic journeys of shamans, and the wanderings of ghosts and the damned.

17 Game analogous to ring puzzles: nine links form a chain and are traversed by a rod attached to a base. The point of the game is to unlink them. With experience, one succeeds at it, careful not to call attention to a quite delicate, lengthy, and complicated-manipulation where the least error makes it necessary to start again from the beginning.

18 From data provided by Duyvendak in Huizinga (*op. cit.*, p. 32), a study by Chou Ling, the valuable observations of Andre d'Hormon, and Herbert A. Giles' *Chinese-English Dictionary*, 2nd ed. (London, 1912), pp. 510–511 (*hsi*), 1250 (*choua*), 1413 (*teou*), 1452 (*wan*), 1487–1488 (*tou*), 1662–1663 (*yeou*).

12

DEEP PLAY

Notes on the Balinese cockfight

Clifford Geertz

Source: *Daedalus*, 101(1), *Myth, Symbol, and Culture* (Winter, 1972), 1–37.

Early in April of 1958, my wife and I arrived, malarial and diffident, in a Balinese village we intended, as anthropologists, to study. A small place, about five hundred people, and relatively remote, it was its own world. We were intruders, professional ones, and the villagers dealt with us as Balinese seem always to deal with people not part of their life who yet press themselves upon them: as though we were not there. For them, and to a degree for ourselves, we were nonpersons, specters, invisible men.

We moved into an extended family compound (that had been arranged before through the provincial government) belonging to one of the four major factions in village life. But except for our landlord and the village chief, whose cousin and brother-in-law he was, everyone ignored us in a way only a Balinese can do. As we wandered around, uncertain, wistful, eager to please, people seemed to look right through us with a gaze focused several yards behind us on some more actual stone or tree. Almost nobody greeted us; but nobody scowled or said anything unpleasant to us either, which would have been almost as satisfactory. If we ventured to approach someone (something one is powerfully inhibited from doing in such an atmosphere), he moved, negligently but definitively, away. If, seated or leaning against a wall, we had him trapped, he said nothing at all, or mumbled what for the Balinese is the ultimate nonword-"yes." The indifference, of course, was studied; the villagers were watching every move we made and they had an enormous amount of quite accurate information about who we were and what we were going to be doing. But they acted as if we simply did not exist, which, in fact, as this behavior was designed to inform us, we did not, or anyway not yet.

My wife and I were still very much in the gust of wind stage, a most frustrating, and even, as you soon begin to doubt whether you are really real after all, unnerving one, when, ten days or so after our arrival, a large cockfight was held in the public square to raise money for a new school.

Now, a few special occasions aside, cockfights are illegal in Bali under the Republic (as, for not altogether unrelated reasons, they were under the Dutch), largely as a result of the pretensions to puritanism radical nationalism tends to bring with it. The elite, which is not itself so very puritan, worries about the poor, ignorant peasant gambling all his money away, about what foreigners will think, about the waste of time better devoted to building up the country. It sees cock-fighting as "primitive," "backward," "unprogressive," and generally unbecoming an ambitious nation. And, as with those other embarrassments – opium smoking, begging, or uncovered breasts it seeks, rather unsystematically, to put a stop to it.

As a result, the fights are usually held in a secluded corner of a village in semisecrecy, a fact which tends to slow the action a little – not very much, but the Balinese do not care to have it slowed at all. In this case, however, perhaps because they were raising money for a school that the government was unable to give them, perhaps because raids had been few recently, perhaps, as I gathered from subsequent discussion, there was a notion that the necessary bribes had been paid, they thought they could take a chance on the central square and draw a larger and more enthusiastic crowd without attracting the attention of the law.

They were wrong. In the midst of the third match, with hundreds of people, including, still transparent, myself and my wife, fused into a single body around the ring, a superorganism in the literal sense, a truck full of policemen armed with machine guns roared up. Amid great screeching cries of "pulisi! pulisi!" from the crowd, the policemen jumped out, and, springing into the center of the ring, began to swing their guns around like gangsters in a motion picture, though not going so far as actually to fire them. The superorganism came instantly apart as its compo-nents scattered in all directions. People raced down the road, disappeared head first over walls, scrambled under platforms, folded themselves behind wicker screens, scuttled up coconut trees. Cocks armed with steel spurs sharp enough to cut off a finger or run a hole through a foot were running wildly around. Everything was dust and panic.

On the established anthropological principle, When in Rome, my wife and I decided, only slightly less instantaneously than everyone else, that the thing to do was run too. We ran down the main village street, northward, away from where we were living, for we were on that side of the ring. About half-way down another fugitive ducked suddenly into a compound – his own, it turned out – and we, see-ing nothing ahead of us but rice fields, open country, and a very high volcano, fol-lowed him. As the three of us came tumbling into the courtyard, his wife, who had apparently been through this sort of thing before, whipped out a table, a tablecloth, three chairs, and three cups of tea, and we all, without any explicit communication whatsoever, sat down, commenced to sip tea, and sought to compose ourselves.

A few moments later, one of the policemen marched importantly into the yard, looking for the village chief. (The chief had not only been at the fight, he had arranged it. When the truck drove up he ran to the river, stripped off his sarong, and plunged in so he could say, when at length they found him sitting there pouring water over his head, that he had been away bathing when the whole affair had occurred and was ignorant of it. They did not believe him and fined him three hundred rupiah, which the village raised collectively.) Seeing my wife and I, "White Men," there in the yard, the policeman performed a classic double take. When he found his voice again he asked, approximately, what in the devil did we think we were doing there. Our host of five minutes leaped instantly to our defense, producing an impassioned description of who and what we were, so detailed and so accurate that it was my turn, having barely communicated with a living human being save my landlord and the village chief for more than a week, to be astonished. We had a perfect right to be there, he said, looking the Javanese upstart in the eye. We were American professors; the government had cleared us; we were there to study culture; we were going to write a book to tell Americans about Bali. And we had all been there drinking tea and talking about cultural matters all afternoon and did not know anything about any cockfight. Moreover, we had not seen the village chief all day, he must have gone to town. The policeman retreated in rather total disarray. And, after a decent interval, bewildered but relieved to have survived and stayed out of jail, so did we.

The next morning the village was a completely different world for us. Not only were we no longer invisible, we were suddenly the center of all attention, the object of a great outpouring of warmth, interest, and, most especially, amusement. Everyone in the village knew we had fled like everyone else. They asked us about it again and again (I must have told the story, small detail by small detail, fifty times by the end of the day), gently, affectionately, but quite insistently teasing us: "Why didn't you just stand there and tell the police who you were?" "Why didn't you just say you were only watching and not betting?" "Were you really afraid of those little guns?" As always, kinesthetically minded and, even when fleeing for their lives (or, as happened eight years later, surrendering them), the world's most poised people, they gleefully mimicked, also over and over again, our graceless style of running and what they claimed were our panic-stricken facial expressions. But above all, everyone was extremely pleased and even more surprised that we had not simply "pulled out our papers" (they knew about those too) and asserted our Distinguished Visitor status, but had instead demonstrated our solidarity with what were now our covillagers. (What we had actually demonstrated was our cowardice, but there is fellowship in that too.) Even the Brahmana priest, an old, grave, half-way-to-Heaven type who because of its associations with the under-world would never be involved, even distantly, in a cockfight, and was difficult to approach even to other Balinese, had us called into his courtyard to ask us about what had happened, chuckling happily at the sheer extraordinariness of it all.

In Bali, to be teased is to be accepted. It was the turning point so far as our relationship to the community was concerned, and we were quite literally "in." The whole village opened up to us, probably more than it ever would have otherwise (I might actually never have gotten to that priest and our accidental host became one of my best informants), and certainly very much faster. Getting caught, or almost caught, in a vice raid is perhaps not a very generalizable recipe for achieving that mysterious necessity of anthropological field work, rapport, but for me it worked very well. It led to a sudden and unusually complete acceptance into a society extremely difficult for outsiders to penetrate. It gave me the kind of immediate, inside view grasp of an aspect of "peasant mentality" that anthropologists not fortunate enough to flee headlong with their subjects from armed authorities normally do not get. And, perhaps most important of all, for the other things might have come in other ways, it put me very quickly on to a combination emotional explosion, status war, and philosophical drama of central significance to the society whose inner nature I desired to understand. By the time I left I had spent about as much time looking into cockfights as into witchcraft, irrigation, caste, or marriage.

Of cocks and men

As much of America surfaces in a ball park, on a golf links, at a race track, or around a poker table, much of Bali surfaces in a cock ring. For it is only apparently cocks that are fighting there. Actually, it is men.

To anyone who has been in Bali any length of time, the deep psychological identification of Balinese men with their cocks is unmistakable. The double entendre here is deliberate. It works in exactly the same way in Balinese as it does in English, even to producing the same tired jokes, strained puns, and uninventive obscenities. Bateson and Mead have even suggested that, in line with the Balinese conception of the body as a set of separately animated parts, cocks are viewed as detachable, self-operating penises, ambulant genitals with a life of their own. And while I do not have the kind of unconscious material either to confirm or disconfirm this intriguing notion, the fact that they are masculine symbols par excellence is about as indubitable, and to the Balinese about as evident, as the fact that water runs downhill.

The language of everyday moralism is shot through, on the male side of it, with roosterish imagery. Sabung, the word for cock (and one which appears in inscriptions as early as A.D. 922), is used metaphorically to mean "hero," "warrior," "champion," "man of parts," "political candidate," "bachelor," "dandy," "lady-killer," or "tough guy." A pompous man whose behavior presumes above his station is compared to a tailless cock who struts about as though he had a large, spectacular one. A desperate man who makes a last, irrational effort to extricate himself from an impossible situation is likened to a dying cock who makes one final lunge at his tormentor to drag him along to a common destruction. A stingy man, who promises much, gives little, and begrudges that is compared to a cock which, held by the tail, leaps at another without in fact engaging him. A marriageable young man still shy with the opposite sex or someone in a new job anxious to make a good impression is called "a fighting cock caged for the first time." Court trials, wars, political contests, inheritance disputes, and street arguments are all compared to cockfights. Even the very island itself is perceived from its shape as a small, proud cock, poised, neck extended, back taut, tail raised, in eternal challenge to large, feckless, shapeless Java.

But the intimacy of men with their cocks is more than metaphorical. Balinese men, or anyway a large majority of Balinese men, spend an enormous amount of time with their favorites, grooming them, feeding them, discussing them, trying them out against one another, or just gazing at them with a mixture of rapt admiration and dreamy self-absorption. Whenever you see a group of Balinese men squatting idly in the council shed or along the road in their hips down, shoulders forward, knees up fashion, half or more of them will have a rooster in his hands, holding it between his thighs, bouncing it gently up and down to strengthen its legs, ruffling its feathers with abstract sensuality, pushing it out against a neighbor's rooster to rouse its spirit, withdrawing it toward his loins to calm it again. Now and then, to get a feel for another bird, a man will fiddle this way with someone else's cock for a while, but usually by moving around to squat in place behind it, rather than just having it passed across to him as though it were merely an animal.

In the houseyard, the high-walled enclosures where the people live, fighting cocks are kept in wicker cages, moved frequently about so as to maintain the optimum balance of sun and shade. They are fed a special diet, which varies somewhat according to individual theories but which is mostly maize, sifted for impurities with far more care than it is when mere humans are going to eat it and offered to the animal kernel by kernel. Red pepper is stuffed down their beaks and up their anuses to give them spirit. They are bathed in the same ceremonial preparation of tepid water, medicinal herbs, flowers, and onions in which infants are bathed, and for a prize cock just about as often. Their combs are cropped, their plumage dressed, their spurs trimmed, their legs massaged, and they are inspected for flaws with the squinted concentration of a diamond merchant. A man who has a passion for cocks, an enthusiast in the literal sense of the term, can spend most of his life with them, and even those, the overwhelming majority, whose passion though intense has not entirely run away with them, can and do spend what seems not only to an outsider, but also to themselves an inordinate amount of time with them. "I am cock crazy," my landlord, a quite ordinary aficionado by Balinese standards, used to moan as he went to move another cage, give another bath, or conduct another feeding. "We're all cock crazy."

The madness has some less visible dimensions, however, because although it is true that cocks are symbolic expressions or magnifications of their owner's self, the narcissistic male ego writ out in Aesopian terms, they are also expressions – and rather more immediate ones – of what the Balinese regard as the direct inversion, aesthetically, morally, and metaphysically, of human status: animality.

The Balinese revulsion against any behavior as animal-like can hardly be overstressed. Babies are not allowed to crawl for that reason. Incest, though hardly approved, is a much less horrifying crime than bestiality. (The appropriate punishment for the second is death by drowning, for the first being forced to live like an animal.) Most demons are represented – in sculpture, dance, ritual, myth – in some real or fantastic animal form. The main puberty rite consists in filing the child's teeth so they will not look like animal fangs. Not only defecation but eating is regarded as a disgusting, almost obscene activity, to be conducted hurriedly and privately, because of its association with animality. Even falling down or any form of clumsiness is considered to be bad for these reasons. Aside from cocks and a few domestic animals – oxen, ducks – of no emotional significance, the Balinese are aversive to animals and treat their large number of dogs not merely callously but with a phobic cruelty. In identifying with his cock, the Balinese man is identifying not just with his ideal self, or even his penis, but also, and at the same time, with what he most fears, hates, and ambivalence being what it is, is fascinated by – The Powers of Darkness.

The connection of cocks and cockfighting with such Powers, with the animalistic demons that threaten constantly to invade the small, cleared off space in which the Balinese have so carefully built their lives and devour its inhabitants, is quite explicit. A cockfight, any cockfight, is in the first instance a blood sacrifice offered, with the appropriate chants and oblations, to the demons in order to pacify their ravenous, cannibal hunger. No temple festival should be conducted until one is made. (If it is omitted someone will inevitably fall into a trance and command with the voice of an angered spirit that the oversight be immediately corrected.) Collective responses to natural evils – illness, crop failure, volcanic eruptions – almost always involve them. And that famous holiday in Bali, The Day of Silence (Njepi), when everyone sits silent and immobile all day long in order to avoid contact with a sudden influx of demons chased momentarily out of hell, is preceded the previous day by large-scale cockfights (in this case legal) in almost every village on the island.

In the cockfight, man and beast, good and evil, ego and id, the creative power of aroused masculinity and the destructive power of loosened animality fuse in a bloody drama of hatred, cruelty, violence, and death. It is little wonder that when, as is the invariable rule, the owner of the winning cock takes the carcass of the loser – often torn limb from limb by its enraged owner – home to eat, he does so with a mixture of social embarrassment, moral satisfaction, aesthetic disgust, and cannibal joy.

The fight

Cockfights (tetadjen; sabungan) are held in a ring about fifty feet square. Usually they begin toward late afternoon and run three or four hours until sunset. About nine or ten separate matches (sehet) comprise a program. Each match is precisely like the others in general pattern: there is no main match, no connection between individual matches, no variation in their format, and each is arranged on a completely ad hoc basis. After a fight has ended and the emotional debris is cleaned away – the bets paid, the curses cursed, the carcasses possessed – seven, eight, perhaps even a dozen men slip negligently into the ring with a cock and seek to find there a logical opponent for it. This process, which rarely takes less than ten minutes, and often a good deal longer, is conducted in a very subdued, oblique, even dissembling manner. Those not immediately involved give it at best but disguised, sidelong attention; those who, embarrassedly, are, attempt to pretend somehow that the whole thing is not really happening.

A match made, the other hopefuls retire with the same deliberate indifference, and the selected cocks have their spurs (tadji) affixed – razor sharp, pointed steel swords, four or five inches long. This is a delicate job which only a small proportion of men, a half-dozen or so in most villages, know how to do properly. The man who attaches the spurs also provides them, and if the rooster he assists wins its owner awards him the spur-leg of the victim. The spurs are affixed by winding a long length of string around the foot of the spur and the leg of the cock. For reasons I shall come to, it is done somewhat differently from case to case, and is an obsessively deliberate affair. The lore about spurs is extensive – they are sharpened only at eclipses and the dark of the moon, should be kept out of the sight of women, and so forth. And they are handled, both in use and out, with the same curious combination of fussiness and sensuality the Balinese direct toward ritual objects generally.

The spurs affixed, the two cocks are placed by their handlers (who may or may not be their owners) facing one another in the center of the ring. A coconut pierced with a small hole is placed in a pail of water, in which it takes about twenty-one seconds to sink, a period known as a tjeng and marked at beginning and end by the beating of a slit gong. During these twenty-one seconds the handlers (pengangkeb) are not permitted to touch their roosters. If, as sometimes happens, the animals have not fought during this time, they are picked up, fluffed, pulled, prodded, and otherwise insulted, and put back in the center of the ring and the process begins again. Sometimes they refuse to fight at all, or one keeps running away, in which case they are imprisoned together under a wicker cage, which usually gets them engaged.

Most of the time, in any case, the cocks fly almost immediately at one another in a wing beating, head-thrusting, leg-kicking explosion of animal fury so pure, so absolute, and in its own way so beautiful, as to be almost abstract, a Platonic concept of hate. Within moments one or the other drives home a solid blow with his spur. The handler whose cock has delivered the blow immediately picks it up so that it will not get a return blow, for if he does not the match is likely to end in a mutually mortal tie as the two birds wildly hack each other to pieces. This is particularly true if, as often happens, the spur sticks in its victim's body, for then the aggressor is at the mercy of his wounded foe.

With the birds again in the hands of their handlers, the coconut is now sunk three times after which the cock which has landed the blow must be set down to show that he is firm, a fact he demonstrates by wandering idly around the rink for a coconut sink. The coconut is then sunk twice more and the fight must recommence.

During this interval, slightly over two minutes, the handler of the wounded cock has been working frantically over it, like a trainer patching a mauled boxer between rounds, to get it in shape for a last, desperate try for victory. He blows in its mouth, putting the whole chicken head in his own mouth and sucking and blowing, fluffs it, stuffs its wounds with various sorts of medicines, and generally tries anything he can think of to arouse the last ounce of spirit which may be hidden somewhere within it. By the time he is forced to put it back down he is usually drenched in chicken blood, but, as in prize fighting, a good handler is worth his weight in gold. Some of them can virtually make the dead walk, at least long enough for the second and final round.

In the climactic battle (if there is one; sometimes the wounded cock simply expires in the handler's hands or immediately as it is placed down again), the cock who landed the first blow usually proceeds to finish off his weakened opponent. But this is far from an inevitable outcome, for if a cock can walk he can fight, and if he can fight, he can kill, and what counts is which cock expires first. If the wounded one can get a stab in and stagger on until the other drops, he is the official winner, even if he himself topples over an instant later.

Surrounding all this melodrama – which the crowd packed tight around the ring follows in near silence, moving their bodies in kinesthetic sympathy with the movement of the animals, cheering their champions on with wordless hand motions, shiftings of the shoulders, turnings of the head, falling back en masse as the cock with the murderous spurs careens toward one side of the ring (it is said that spectators sometimes lose eyes and fingers from being too attentive), surging forward again as they glance off toward another – is a vast body of extraordinarily elaborate and precisely detailed rules.

These rules, together with the developed lore of cocks and cockfighting which accompanies them, are written down in palm leaf manuscripts (lontar; rontal) passed on from generation to generation as part of the general legal and cultural tradition of the villages. At a fight, the umpire (saja konong; djuru kembar) – the man who manages the coconut – is in charge of their application and his authority is absolute. I have never seen an umpire's judgment questioned on any subject, even by the more despondent losers, nor have I ever heard, even in private, a charge of unfairness directed against one, or, for that matter, complaints about umpires in general. Only exceptionally well-trusted, solid, and, given the complexity of the code, knowledgeable citizens perform this job, and in fact men will bring their cocks only to fights presided over by such men. It is also the umpire to whom accusations of cheating, which, though rare in the extreme, occasionally arise, are referred; and it is he who in the not infrequent cases where the cocks expire virtually together decides which (if either, for, though the Balinese do not care for such an outcome, there can be ties) went first. Likened to a judge, a king, a priest, and a policeman, he is all of these, and under his assured direction the animal passion of the fight proceeds within the civic certainty of the law. In the dozens of cockfights I saw in Bali, I never once saw an altercation about rules. Indeed, I never saw an open altercation, other than those between cocks, at all.

This crosswise doubleness of an event which, taken as a fact of nature, is rage untrammeled and, taken as a fact of culture, is form perfected, defines the cockfight as a sociological entity. A cockfight is what, searching for a name for something not vertebrate enough to be called a group and not structureless enough to be called a crowd, Erving Goffman has called a "focused gathering" – a set of persons engrossed in a common flow of activity and relating to one another in terms of that flow. Such gatherings meet and disperse; the participants in them fluctuate; the activity that focuses them is discreet – a particulate process that reoccurs rather than a continuous one that endures. They take their form from the situation that evokes them, the floor on which they are placed, as Goffman puts it; but it is a form, and an articulate one, nonetheless. For the situation, the floor is itself created, in jury deliberations, surgical operations, block meetings, sit-ins, cockfights, by the cultural preoccupations – here, as we shall see, the celebration of status rivalry – which not only specify the focus but, assembling actors and arranging scenery, bring it actually into being.

In classical times (that is to say, prior to the Dutch invasion of 1908) when there were no bureaucrats around to improve popular morality, the staging of a cockfight was an explicitly societal matter. Bringing a cock to an important fight was, for an adult male, a compulsory duty of citizenship; taxation of fights, which were usually held on market day, was a major source of public revenue; patronage of the art was a stated responsibility of princes; and the cock ring, or wantilan, stood in the center of the village near those other monuments of Balinese civility – the council house, the origin temple, the marketplace, the signal tower, and the banyan tree. Today, a few special occasions aside, the newer rectitude makes so open a statement of the connection between the excitements of collective life and those of blood sport impossible, but, less directly expressed, the connection itself remains intimate and intact. To expose it, however, it is necessary to turn to the aspect of cockfighting around which all the others pivot, and through which they exercise their force, an aspect I have thus far studiously ignored. I mean, of course, the gambling.

Odds and even money

The Balinese never do anything in a simple way that they can contrive to do in a complicated one, and to this generalization cockfight wagering is no exception.

In the first place, there are two sorts of bets, or toh. There is the single axial bet in the center between the principals (toh ketengah), and there is the cloud of peripheral ones around the ring between members of the audience (toh kesasi). The first is typically large; the second typically small. The first is collective, involving coalitions of bettors clustering around the owner; the second is individual, man to man. The first is a matter of deliberate, very quiet, almost furtive arrangement by the coalition members and the umpire huddled like conspirators in the center of the ring; the second is a matter of impulsive shouting, public offers, and public acceptances by the excited throng around its edges. And most curiously, and as we shall see most revealingly, where the first is always, without exception, even money, the second, equally without exception, is never such. What is a fair coin in the center is a biased one on the side.

The center bet is the official one, hedged in again with a webwork of rules, and is made between the two cock owners, with the umpire as overseer and public witness. This bet, which, as I say, is always relatively and sometimes very large, is never raised simply by the owner in whose name it is made, but by him together with four or five, sometimes seven or eight, allies – kin, village mates, neighbors, close friends. He may, if he is not especially well-to-do, not even the major contributor, though, if only to show that he is not involved in any chicanery, he must be a significant one.

Of the fifty-seven matches for which I have exact and reliable data on the center bet, the range is from fifteen ringgits to five hundred, with a mean at eighty-five and with the distribution being rather noticeably trimodal: small fights (15 ringgits either side of 35) accounting for about 45 per cent of the total number; medium ones (20 ringgits either side of 70) for about 25 per cent; and large (75 ringgits either side of 175) for about 20 per cent, with a few very small and very large ones out at the extremes. In a society where the normal daily wage of a manual labourer – a brickmaker, an ordinary farmworker, a market porter – was about three ringgits a day, and considering the fact that fights were held on the average about every two-and-a-half days in the immediate area I studied, this is clearly serious gambling, even if the bets are pooled rather than individual efforts.

The side bets are, however, something else altogether. Rather than the solemn, legalistic pactmaking of the center, wagering takes place rather in the fashion in which the stock exchange used to work when it was out on the curb. There is a fixed and known odds paradigm which runs in a continuous series from ten-to-nine at the short end to two-to-one on the long: 10–9, 9–8, 8–7, 7–6, 6–5, 5–4, 4–3, 3–2, 2–1. The man who wants the underdog cock shouts the short-side number indicating the odds he wants to be given. That is, if he shouts gasal, "five," he wants the underdog at five-to-four (or, for him, four-to-five); if he shouts "four," he wants it at four-to-three (again, he putting up the "three"), if "nine" at nine-to-eight, and so on. A man backing the favorite, and thus considering giving odds if he can get them short enough, indicates the fact by crying out the color-type of that cock – "brown," "speckled," or whatever.

Almost always odds calling starts off toward the long end of the range – five-to-four or four-to-three- and then moves toward the shorter end with greater or less speed and to a greater and lesser degree. Men crying "five" and finding themselves answered only with cries of "brown" start crying "six." If the change is made and partners are still scarce, the procedure is repeated in a move to "seven," and so on. Occasionally, if the cocks are clearly mismatched, there may be no upward movement at all, or even movement down the scale to four-to-three, three-to-two, very, very rarely to two-to-one, a shift which is accompanied by a declining number of bets as a shift upward is accompanied by an increasing number. But the general pattern is for the betting to move a shorter or longer distance up the scale toward the, for sidebets, nonexistent pole of even money, with the overwhelming majority of bets falling in the four-to-three to eight-to-seven range.

The higher the center bet, the more likely the match will in actual fact be an even one. In a large-bet fight the pressure to make the match a genuinely fifty-fifty proposition is enormous, and is consciously felt as such. For medium fights the pressure is somewhat less, and for small ones less yet, though there is always an effort to make things at least approximately equal, for even at fifteen ringgits (five days work) no one wants to make an even money bet in a clearly unfavorable situation. And, again, what statistics I have tend to bear this out. In my fifty-seven matches, the favorite won thirty-three times over-all, the underdog twenty-four, a 1.4 to 1 ratio. But if one splits the figures at sixty ringgits center bets, the ratios turn out to be 1.1 to 1 (twelve favorites, eleven underdogs) for those above this line, and 1.6 to 1 (twenty-one and thirteen) for those below it. Or, if you take the extremes, for very large fights, those with center bets over a hundred ringgits the ratio is 1 to 1 (seven and seven); for very small fights, those under forty ringgits, it is 1.9 to 1 (nineteen and ten).

The paradox of fair coin in the middle, biased coin on the outside is thus a merely apparent one. The two betting systems, though formally incongruent, are not really contradictory to one another, but part of a single larger system in which the center bet is, so to speak, the "center of gravity," drawing, the larger it is the more so, the outside bets toward the short-odds end of the scale. The center bet thus "makes the game," or perhaps better, defines it, signals what, following a notion of Jeremy Bentham's, I am going to call its "depth."

The Balinese attempt to create an interesting, if you will, "deep," match by making the center bet as large as possible so that the cocks matched will be as equal and as fine as possible, and the outcome, thus, as unpredictable as possible. They do not always succeed. Nearly half the matches are relatively trivial, relatively uninteresting – in my borrowed terminology, "shallow" – affairs. But that fact no more argues against my interpretation than the fact that most painters, poets, and playwrights are mediocre argues against the view that artistic effort is directed toward profundity and, with a certain frequency, approximates it. The image of artistic technique is indeed exact: the center bet is a means, a device, for creating "interesting," "deep" matches, not the reason, or at least not the main reason, why they are interesting, the source of their fascination, the substance of their depth. The question why such matches are interesting – indeed, for the Balinese, exquisitely absorbing – takes us out of the realm of formal concerns into more broadly sociological and social-psychological ones, and to a less purely economic idea of what "depth" in gaming amounts to.

Playing with fire

Bentham's concept of "deep play" is found in his The Theory of Legislation. By it he means play in which the stakes are so high that it is, from his utilitarian standpoint, irrational for men to engage in it at all.

This, I must stress immediately, is not to say that the money does not matter, or that the Balinese is no more concerned about losing five hundred ringgits than fifteen. Such a conclusion would be absurd. It is because money does, in this hardly unmaterialistic society, matter and matter very much that the more of it one risks the more of a lot of other things, such as one's pride, one's poise, one's dispassion, one's masculinity, one also risks, again only momentarily but again very publicly as well. In deep cockfights an owner and his collaborators, and, as we shall see, to a lesser but still quite real extent also their backers on the outside, put their money where their status is.

It is in large part because the marginal disutility of loss is so great at the higher levels of betting that to engage in such betting is to lay one's public self, allusively and metaphorically, through the medium of one's cock, on the line. And though to a Benthamite this might seem merely to increase the irrationality of the enterprise that much further, to the Balinese what it mainly increases is the meaningfulness of it all. And as (to follow Weber rather than Bentham) the imposition of meaning on life is the major end and primary condition of human existence, that access of significance more than compensates for the economic costs involved. Actually, given the even-money quality of the larger matches, important changes in material fortune among those who regularly participate in them seem virtually nonexistent, because matters more or less even out over the long run.

This graduated correlation of "status gambling" with deeper fights and, inversely, "money gambling" with shallower ones is in fact quite general. Bettors themselves form a sociomoral hierarchy in these terms. As noted earlier, at most cockfights there are, around the very edges of the cockfight area, a large number of mindless, sheer-chance type gambling games (roulette, dice throw, coin-spin, pea-under-the-shell) operated by concessionaires. Only women, children, adolescents, and various other sorts of people who do not (or not yet) fight cocks – the extremely poor, the socially despised, the personally idiosyncratic – play at these games, at, of course, penny ante levels. Cockfighting men would be ashamed to go anywhere near them. Slightly above these people in standing are those who, though they do not themselves fight cocks, bet on the smaller matches around the edges. Next, there are those who fight cocks in small, or occasionally medium matches, but have not the status to join in the large ones, though they may bet from time to time on the side in those. And finally, there are those, the really substantial members of the community, the solid citizenry around whom local life revolves, who fight in the larger fights and bet on them around the side. The focusing element in these focused gatherings, these men generally dominate and define the sport as they dominate and define the society. When a Balinese male talks, in that almost venerative way, about "the true cockfighter," the bebatoh ("bettor") or djuru kurung ("cage keeper"), it is this sort of person, not those who bring the mentality of the pea-and-shell game into the quite different, inappropriate context of the cockfight, the driven gambler (potet, a word which has the secondary meaning of thief or reprobate), and the wistful hanger-on, that they mean. For such a man, what is really going on in a match is something rather closer to an affaire d'honneur (though, with the Balinese talent for practical fantasy, the blood that is spilled is only figuratively human) than to the stupid, mechanical crank of a slot machine.

What makes Balinese cockfighting deep is thus not money in itself, but what, the more of it that is involved the more so, money causes to happen: the migration of the Balinese status hierarchy into the body of the cockfight. Psychologically an Aesopian representation of the ideal/demonic, rather narcissistic, male self, sociologically it is an equally Aesopian representation of the complex fields of tension set up by the controlled, muted, ceremonial, but for all that deeply felt, interaction of those selves in the context of everyday life. The cocks may be surrogates for their owners' personalities, animal mirrors of psychic form, but the cockfight is – or more exactly, deliberately is made to be – a simulation of the social matrix, the involved system of crosscutting, overlapping, highly corporate groups – villages, kingroups, irrigation societies, temple congregations, "castes" – in which its devotees live. And as prestige, the necessity to affirm it, defend it, celebrate it, justify it, and just plain bask in it (but not given the strongly ascriptive character of Balinese stratification, to seek it), is perhaps the central driving force in the society, so also – ambulant penises, blood sacrifices, and monetary exchanges aside – is it of the cockfight. This apparent amusement and seeming sport is, to take another phrase from Erving Goffman, "a status bloodbath."

The easiest way to make this clear, and at least to some degree to demonstratee it, is to invoke the village whose cockfighting activities I observed the closest – the one in which the raid occurred and from which my statistical data are taken.

Consider, then, as support of the general thesis that the cockfight, and especially the deep cockfight, is fundamentally a dramatization of status concerns, the following facts:

1 A man virtually never bets against a cock owned by a member of his own kingroup. Usually he will feel obliged to bet for it, the more so the closer the kin tie and the deeper the fight. If he is certain in his mind that it will not win, he may just not bet at all, particularly if it is only a second cousin's bird or if the fight is a shallow one. But as a rule he will feel he must support it and, in deep games, nearly always does. Thus the great majority of the people calling "five" or "speckled" so demonstratively are expressing their allegiance to their kinsman, not their evaluation of his bird, their understanding of probability theory, or even their hopes of unearned income.

2 This principle is extended logically. If your kin group is not involved you will support an allied kingroup against an unallied one in the same way, and so on through the very involved networks of alliances which, as I say, make up this, as any other, Balinese village.

3 So, too, for the village as a whole. If an outsider cock is fighting any cock from your village you will tend to support the local one. If, what is a rarer circumstance but occurs every now and then, a cock from outside your cockfight circuit is fighting one inside it you will also tend to support the "home bird."

4 Cocks which come from any distance are almost always favorites, for the theory is the man would not have dared to bring it if it was not a good cock, the more so the further he has come. His followers are, of course, obliged to support him, and when the more grand-scale legal cockfights are held (on holidays and so on) the people of the village take what they regard to be the best cocks in the village, regardless of ownership, and go off to support them, although they will almost certainly have to give odds on them and to

make large bets to show that they are not a cheapskate village. Actually, such "away games," though infrequent, tend to mend the ruptures between village members that the constantly occurring "home games," where village factions are opposed rather than united, exacerbate.

5 Almost all matches are sociologically relevant. You seldom get two outsider cocks fighting, or two cocks with no particular group backing, or with group backing which is mutually unrelated in any clear way. When you do get them, the game is very shallow, betting very slow, and the whole thing very dull, with no one save the immediate principals and an addict gambler or two at all interested.

6 By the same token, you rarely get two cocks from the same group, even more rarely from the same subfaction, and virtually never from the same sub-subfaction (which would be in most cases one extended family) fighting. Similarly, in outside village fights two members of the village will rarely fight against one another, even though, as bitter rivals, they would do so with enthusiasm on their home grounds.

7 On the individual level, people involved in an institutionalized hostility rela-tionship, called puik, in which they do not speak or otherwise have anything to do with each other (the causes of this formal breaking of relations are many: wife-capture, inheritance arguments, political differences) will bet very heavily, sometimes almost maniacally, against one another in what is a frank and direct attack on the very masculinity, the ultimate ground of his status, of the opponent.

8 The center bet coalition is, in all but the shallowest games, always made up by structural allies – no "outside money" is involved. What is "outside" depends upon the context, of course, but given it, no outside money is mixed in with the main bet; if the principals cannot raise it, it is not made. The center bet, again especially in deeper games, is thus the most direct and open expression of social opposition, which is one of the reasons why both it and match making are surrounded by such an air of unease, furtiveness, embarrassment, and so on.

9 The rule about borrowing money – that you may borrow for a bet but not in one – stems (and the Balinese are quite conscious of this) from similar con-siderations: you are never at the economic mercy of your enemy that way. Gambling debts, which can get quite large on a rather short-term basis, are always to friends, never to enemies, structurally speaking.

10 When two cocks are structurally irrelevant or neutral so far as you are con-cerned (though, as mentioned, they almost never are to each other) you do not even ask a relative or a friend whom he is betting on, because if you know how he is betting and he knows you know, and you go the other way, it will lead to strain. This rule is explicit and rigid; fairly elaborate, even rather arti-ficial precautions are taken to avoid breaking it. At the very least you must pretend not to notice what he is doing, and he what you are doing.

11 There is a special word for betting against the grain, which is also the word for "pardon me" (mpura). It is considered a bad thing to do, though if the

center bet is small it is sometimes all right as long as you do not do it too often. But the larger the bet and the more frequently you do it, the more the "pardon me" tack will lead to social disruption.

12　In fact, the institutionalized hostility relation, puik, is often formally initiated (though its causes always lie elsewhere) by such a "pardon me" bet in a deep fight, putting the symbolic fat in the fire. Similarly, the end of such a relationship and resumption of normal social intercourse is often signalized (but, again, not actually brought about) by one or the other of the enemies supporting the other's bird.

13　In sticky, cross-loyalty situations, of which in this extraordinarily complex social system there are of course many, where a man is caught between two more or less equally balanced loyalties, he tends to wander off for a cup of coffee or something to avoid having to bet, a form of behavior reminiscent of that of American voters in similar situations.

14　The people involved in the center bet are, especially in deep fights, virtually always leading members of their group – kinship, village, or whatever. Further, those who bet on the side (including these people) are, as I have already remarked, the more established members of the village – the solid citizens. Cockfighting is for those who are involved in the everyday politics of prestige as well, not for youth, women, subordinates, and so forth.

15　So far as money is concerned, the explicitly expressed attitude toward it is that it is a secondary matter. It is not, as I have said, of no importance; Balinese are no happier to lose several weeks' income than anyone else. But they mainly look on the monetary aspects of the cockfight as self-balancing, a matter of just moving money around, circulating it among a fairly well-defined group of serious cockfighters. The really important wins and losses are seen mostly in other terms, and the general attitude toward wagering is not any hope of cleaning up, of making a killing (addict gamblers again excepted), but that of the horseplayer's prayer: "Oh, God, please let me break even." In prestige terms, however, you do not want to break even, but, in a momentary, punctuate sort of way, win utterly. The talk (which goes on all the time) is about fights against such-and-such a cock of So-and-So which your cock demolished, not on how much you won, a fact people, even for large bets, rarely remember for any length of time, though they will remember the day they did in Pan Loh's finest cock for years.

16　You must bet on cocks of your own group aside from mere loyalty considerations, for if you do not people generally will say, "What! Is he too proud for the likes of us? Does he have to go to Java or Den Pasar [the capital town] to bet, he is such an important man?" Thus there is a general pressure to bet not only to show that you are important locally, but that you are not so important that you look down on everyone else as unfit even to be rivals. Similarly, home team people must bet against outside cocks or the outsiders will accuse it – a serious charge – of just collecting entry fees and not really being interested in cockfighting, as well as again being arrogant and insulting.

17   Finally, the Balinese peasants themselves are quite aware of all this and can and, at least to an ethnographer, do state most of it in approximately the same terms as I have. Fighting cocks, almost every Balinese I have ever discussed the subject with has said, is like playing with fire only not getting burned. You activate village and kingroup rivalries and hostilities, but in "play" form, coming dangerously and entrancingly close to the expression of open and direct interpersonal and intergroup aggression (something which, again, almost never happens in the normal course of ordinary life), but not quite, because, after all, it is "only a cockfight."

More observations of this sort could be advanced, but perhaps the general point is, if not made, at least well-delineated, and the whole argument thus far can be usefully summarized in a formal paradigm:

THE MORE A MATCH IS . . .

1   Between near status equals (and/or personal enemies)
2   Between high status individuals

THE DEEPER THE MATCH.

THE DEEPER THE MATCH IS

1   The closer the identification of cock and man (or: more properly, the deeper the match the more the man will advance his best, most closely-identified-with cock).
2   The finer the cocks involved and the more exactly they will be matched.
3   The greater the emotion that will be involved and the more the general absorption in the match.
4   The higher the individual bets center and outside, the shorter the outside bet odds will tend to be, and the more betting there will be over-all.
5   The less an economic and the more a "status" view of gaming will be involved, and the "solider" the citizens who will be gaming.

Inverse arguments hold for the shallower the fight, culminating, in a reversed-signs sense, in the coin-spinning and dice-throwing amusements. For deep fights there are no absolute upper limits, though there are of course practical ones, and there are a great many legend-like tales of great Duel-in-the-Sun combats between lords and princes in classical times (for cockfighting has always been as much an elite concern as a popular one), far deeper than anything anyone, even aristocrats, could produce today anywhere in Bali.

Indeed, one of the great culture heroes of Bali is a prince, called after his passion for the sport, "The Cockfighter," who happened to be away at a very deep cock-fight with a neighboring prince when the whole of his family – father, brothers, wives, sisters – were assassinated by commoner usurpers. Thus spared, he returned to dispatch the upstarts, regain the throne, reconstitute the Balinese high tradition, and build its most powerful, glorious, and prosperous state. Along with everything else that the Balinese see in fighting cocks – themselves, their social order, abstract hatred, masculinity, demonic power – they also see the archetype of status virtue, the arrogant, resolute, honor-mad player with real fire, the ksatria prince.

Conclusion

What sets the cockfight apart from the ordinary course of life, lifts it from the realm of everyday practical affairs, and surrounds it with an aura of enlarged importance is not, as functionalist sociology would have it, that it reinforces status discriminations (such reinforcement is hardly necessary in a society where every act proclaims them), but that it provides a metasocial commentary upon the whole matter of assorting human beings into fixed hierarchical ranks and then organizing the major part of collective existence around that assortment. Its function, if you want to call it that, is interpretive: it is a Balinese reading of Balinese experience; a story they tell themselves about themselves.

What the cockfight says it says in a vocabulary of sentiment – the thrill of risk, the despair of loss, the pleasure of triumph. Yet what it says is not merely that risk is exciting, loss depressing, or triumph gratifying, banal tautologies of affect, but that it is of these emotions, thus exampled, that society is built and individuals put together. Attending cockfights and participating in them is, for the Balinese, a kind of sentimental education. What he learns there is what his culture's ethos and his private sensibility (or, anyway, certain aspects of them) look like when spelled out externally in a collective text; that the two are near enough alike to be articulated in the symbolics of a single such text; and – the disquieting part – that the text in which this revelation is accomplished consists of a chicken hacking another mindlessly to bits.

Every people, the proverb has it, loves its own form of violence. The cock-fight is the Balinese reflection on theirs: on its look, its uses, its force, its fascination. Drawing on almost every level of Balinese experience, it brings together themes – animal savagery, male narcissism, opponent gambling, status rivalry, mass excitement, blood sacrifice – whose main connection is their involvement with rage and the fear of rage, and, binding them into a set of rules which at once contains them and allows them play, builds a symbolic structure in which, over and over again, the reality of their inner affiliation can be intelligibly felt. If, to quote Northrop Frye again, we go to see Macbeth to learn what a man feels like after he has gained a kingdom and lost his soul, Balinese go to cockfights to find out what a man, usually composed, aloof, almost obsessively self-absorbed, a kind of moral autocosm, feels like when, attacked, tormented, challenged, insulted, and driven in result to the extremes of fury, he has totally triumphed or been brought totally low.

13

PLAY AND AMBIGUITY

Brian Sutton-Smith

Source: *The Ambiguity of Play* (Cambridge, MA: Harvard University Press, 1997), pp. 1–17.

Context

The Ambiguity of Play (Harvard University Press, 1997) known
also as **The Rhetorics of Play** from which this essay is taken, is a
deconstructive account of the play theories of the past 100 years.
It demonstrates that there has been little universal science but
rather a series of arguments favoring the views (the rhetorics) that
play should be conceptualized as about Progress (largely meaning
cognition), or about Fate (games of chance); about Power (sports
contests); about Identity (festivals); about self or narcissim (peak
experience). The book concludes with the suggestion that what all
of these rhetorics may have in common is their relative resonance
of adaptive variability.

A nip is but a nip
And a boojum
Is but a buttercup.
after Lewis Carroll

We all play occasionally, and we all know what playing feels like. But when
it comes to making theoretical statements about what play is, we fall into silliness. There is little agreement among us, and much ambiguity. Some of the most
outstanding scholars of children's play have been concerned by this ambiguity.
For example, classical scholar Mihail Spariosu (1989) calls play "amphibolous,"
which means it goes in two directions at once and is not clear. Victor Turner
(1969), the anthropologist, calls play "liminal" or "liminoid," meaning that it
occupies a threshold between reality and unreality, as if, for example, it were
on the beach between the land and the sea. Geoffrey Bateson (1956), biologist,
suggests that play is a paradox because it both is and is not what it appears to be.
Animals at play bite each other playfully, knowing that the playful nip connotes a
bite, but not what a bite connotes. In turn, Richard Schechner (1988), dramaturge,
suggests that a playful nip is not only not a bite, it is also *not* not a bite. That is, it

is a positive, the sum of two negatives. Which is again to say that the playful nip may not be a bite, but it is indeed what a bite means.

Kenneth Burke's works suggest that play is probably what he terms a "dramatistic negative," which means that for animals who do not have any way of saying "no," it is a way of indicating the negative through an affirmative action that is clearly not the same as that which it represents (thus, again, nipping rather than biting). He says that prior to the evolutionary emergence of words, the negative could be dramatized only by the presentation of stylized and gestural forms of the positive (Burke, 1966, p. 423). "The most irritating feature of play," says Robert Fagen (1981), leading animal play theorist, "is not the perceptual incoherence, as such, but rather that play taunts us with its inaccessibility. We feel that something is behind it all, but we do not know, or have forgotten how to see it."

If we seek greater definitional clarity by analyzing the meaning of ambiguity itself, following William Empson's classic *Seven Types of Ambiguity* (1955), then we can say that play involves all of his seven types, which are as follows, with the play examples in parentheses:

1   the ambiguity of reference (is that a pretend gun sound, or are you choking?);
2   the ambiguity of the referent (is that an object or a toy?);
3   the ambiguity of intent (do you mean it, or is it pretend?);
4   the ambiguity of sense (is this serious, or is it nonsense?);
5   the ambiguity of transition (you said you were only playing);
6   the ambiguity of contradiction (a man playing at being a woman);
7   the ambiguity of meaning (is it play or playfighting?).

And finally, as if all these paradoxes were not enough, Stephen Jay Gould, evolutionist, says that there are some human traits that are just side effects of more fundamental genetic functions and really deserve no functional explanation themselves. The quotation that heads this chapter, and those in the chapters that follow, would suggest that, if that is the case, there are nevertheless many interesting things about our so-called junk genes. The quotations at the beginning of each chapter also often bring up interesting rhetorics from much earlier times. Many authors use children's play as a metaphor for the ephemerality of life, for what quickly passes, or for what is innocent, infantile, or foolish. Others who are quoted render adult life as a very serious mortal game in which foul play is possible. The diversity of this metaphoric playfulness would seem to suggest that, whether junk or not, play takes on multiple forms in somber discourse.[1]

This chapter is a search for some of the more obvious possible reasons for the ambiguity, as well as an introduction to the particular focus of the volume as a whole: the ideological underpinnings of play theories, and what an understanding of them can contribute to clearing up these confusions. The ambiguity is most obvious, however, in the multiple forms of play and the diversity of the kinds of play scholarship they have instigated. Obviously the word *play* stands for a category of very diverse happenings, though the same could be said about most omnibus categories, such as, for example, religion, art, war, politics, and culture.

The diversity of play forms and experiences

The diversity of play is well illustrated by the varied kinds of play that are to be found within the larger menagerie of the "play" sphere. Almost anything can allow play to occur within its boundaries, as is illustrated, for example, by works on tourism as play (McCannell, 1976), television as play (Stephenson, 1967), daydreaming as play (Caughey, 1984), sexual intimacy as play (Betcher, 1987), and even gossip as play (Spack, 1986). Travel can be a playful competition to see who can go to the most places or have the most authentic encounters. "Have you done London, the Eiffel Tower, Ayres Rock, Palmer Station, and Easter Island?" Watching television can be watching and identifying with other people at play, whether in fiction or in real life—and, after all, one can turn it off or on, which makes it like play and not like real life. Viewers can control their involvement just as if the "play" belongs to them, as in "playing" with the channels. Even the news, which is "live at five," is only an account from a studio with theatric backdrops. All of us carry dozens of characters around in our daydreams with whom we carry on imaginary encounters and conversations, none of which are real in the usual sense. Many of the characters in our heads are also people on television or in films, but most are everyday acquaintances. Sexual intimates are said to play with each other in innumerable ways, painting each other's bodies, eating food off of each other, playing hide the thimble with bodily crevices, communicating in public with their own esoteric vocabulary, and, in general, teasing and testing each other with playful impropriety. Gossip, by contrast, can be a playfully irreverent game of denigrating those who are not present.

A list of activities that are often said to be play forms or play experiences themselves is presented below. The terms illustrate the great diversity of play phenomena, although they do not indicate the even wider extension of informal play through all other spheres of life. This list itself awaits both adequate description and adequate play theorizing, because the items that it contains are often typically called by other names, such as entertainments, recreations, pastimes, and hobbies, as if it would be an embarrassment to admit that they can also be called play. Each of these states of mind, activities, or events could be described as I have described with travel and gossip, above. The boundaries between them are never as discrete as listing them here might imply. They are arranged in order from the mostly more private to the mostly more public.

> *Mind or subjective play:* dreams, daydreams, fantasy, imagination, ruminations, reveries, Dungeons and Dragons, metaphors of play, and playing with metaphors.
> *Solitary play:* hobbies, collections, (model trains, model airplanes, model power boats, stamps), writing to pen pals, building models, listening to records

215

and compact discs, constructions, art projects, gardening, flower arranging, using computers, watching videos, reading and writing, novels, toys, travel, Civil War reenactments, music, pets, reading, woodworking, yoga, antiquing, flying, auto racing, collecting and rebuilding cars, sailing, diving, astrology, bicycling, handicrafts, photography, shopping, backpacking, fishing, needlework, quilting, bird watching, crosswords, and cooking.

Playful behaviors: playing tricks, playing around, playing for time, playing up to someone, playing a part, playing down to someone, playing upon words, making a play for someone, playing upon others as in tricking them, playing hob, putting something into play, bringing it into play, holding it in play, playing fair, playing by the rules, being played out, playing both ends against the middle, playing one's cards well, playing second fiddle.

Informal social play: joking, parties, cruising, travel, leisure, dancing, rollerskating, losing weight, dinner play, getting laid, potlucks, malls, hostessing, babysitting, Saturday night fun, rough and tumble, creative anachronism, amusement parks, intimacy, speech play (riddles, stories, gossip, jokes, nonsense), singles clubs, bars and taverns, magic, ham radio, restaurants, and the Internet.

Vicarious audience play: television, films, cartoons, concerts, fantasy-lands, spectator sports, theater, jazz, rock music, parades (Rose Bowl, mummers', Thanksgiving), beauty contests, stock-car racing, Renaissance festivals, national parks, comic books, folk festivals, museums, and virtual reality.

Performance play: playing the piano, playing music, being a play actor, playing the game for the game's sake, playing New York, playing the fishes, playing the horses, playing Iago, play voices, play gestures, playbills, playback, play by play, player piano, playgoing, playhouses, playlets.

Celebrations and festivals: birthdays, Christmas, Easter, Mother's Day, Halloween, gifting, banquets, roasts, weddings, carnivals, initiations, balls, Mardi Gras, Fastnacht, Odunde.

Contests (games and sports): athletics, gambling, casinos, horses, lotteries, pool, touch football, kite fighting, golf, parlor games, drinking, the Olympics, bullfights, cockfights, cricket, Buzkashi, poker, gamesmanship, strategy, physical skill, chance, animal contests, archery, arm wrestling, board games, card games, martial arts, gymnastics

Risky or deep play: caving, hang gliding, kayaking, rafting, snowmobiling, orienteering, snowballing, and extreme games such as bungee jumping, windsurfing, sport climbing, skateboarding, mountain biking, kite skiing, street luge, ultrarunning, and sky jumping.

The diversity of players, play agencies, and play scenarios

The ambiguity of play, as well as lying in this great diversity of play forms, owes some of its force to the parallel diversity of the players. There are infant, preschool, childhood, adolescent, and adult players, all of whom play somewhat differently.

216

There are male and female players. There are gamblers, gamesters, sports, and sports players, and there are playboys and play-girls, playfellows, playful people, playgoers, playwrights, playmakers, and playmates. There are performers who play music and act in plays and perhaps play when they paint, sing, or sculpt. There are dilettantes, harlequins, clowns, tricksters, comedians, and jesters who represent a kind of characterological summit of playfulness. There are even playful scholars, such as Paul Feyerabend (1995), Jacques Derrida (1980), and Mikhail Bakhtin (1981). Playful persons in literature and the arts are countless.

Then there is the diversity of multiple kinds of play equipment, such as balls, bats, goals, cards, checkers, roulettes, and toys. Practically anything can become an agency for some kind of play. The scenarios of play vary widely also, from playpens, playrooms, playhouses, and playgrounds to sports fields, circuses, parade grounds, and casinos. Again, while some playfulness is momentary, other kinds, with their attendant preparations, can last throughout a season (as in many festivals and team sports) and, in some cases, over periods of years, as in the World Cup and the Olympics. Play has temporal diversity as well as spatial diversity.

The diversity of play scholarship

Although most people throughout history have taken for granted their own play, and in some places have not even had a word for it, since about 1800 in Western society, intellectuals of various kinds have talked more or less systematically and more or less scientifically about play, and have discovered that they have immense problems in conceptualizing it. Presumably this is in part because there are multiple kinds of play and multiple kinds of players, as described above. Different academic disciplines also have quite different play interests. Some study the body, some study behavior, some study thinking, some study groups or individuals, some study experience, some study language—and they all use the word *play* for these quite different things. Furthermore their play theories, which are the focus of this present work, rather than play itself, come to reflect these various diversities and make them even more variable.

For example, biologists, psychologists, educators, and sociologists tend to focus on how play is adaptive or contributes to growth, development, and socialization. Communication theorists tell us that play is a form of metacommunication far preceding language in evolution because it is also found in animals. Sociologists say that play is an imperial social system that is typically manipulated by those with power for their own benefit. Mathematicians focus on war games and games of chance, important in turn because of the data they supply about strategy and probability. Thermonuclear war games, it appears, can be either a hobby or deadly serious. Anthropologists pursue the relationships between ritual and play as these are found in customs and festivals, while folklorists add an interest in play and game traditions. Art and literature, by contrast, have a major focus on play as a spur to creativity. In some mythology scholarship, play is said to be the sphere of the gods, while in the physical sciences it is sometimes another name for the indeterminacy or chaos of basic matter. In psychiatry, play offers a way to diagnose and provide therapy for the inner conflicts of young and old patients alike. And in the leisure sciences, play is about qualities of personal experience, such as intrinsic motivation, fun, relaxation, escape, and so on. No discipline is, however, so homogeneous that all its members are tunneled into only one such way of theorizing. Nevertheless the diversity exists, and it makes reconciliation difficult.

Finally there are the ambiguities that seem particularly problematic in Western society, such as why play is seen largely as what children do but not what adults do; why children play but adults only recreate; why play is said to be important for children's growth but is merely a diversion for adults. The most reviled form of play, gambling, is also the largest part of the national play budget. How can it be that such ecstatic adult play experiences, which preoccupy so much emotional time, are only diversions? And why do these adult play preoccupations, which seem like some vast cultural, even quasi-religious subconsciousness, require us to deny that this kind of play may have the same meaning for children?

The rhetorical solution

It is the intent of the present work to bring some coherence to the ambiguous field of play theory by suggesting that some of the chaos to be found there is due to the lack of clarity about the popular cultural rhetorics that underlie the various play theories and play terms. The word *rhetoric* is used here in its modern sense, as being a persuasive discourse, or an implicit narrative, wittingly or unwittingly adopted by members of a particular affiliation to persuade others of the veracity and worthwhileness of their beliefs. In a sense, whenever identification is made with a belief or a cause or a science or an ideology, that identification reveals itself by the words that are spoken about it, by the clothes and insignia worn to celebrate it, by the allegiances adopted to sustain it, and by the hard work and scholarly devotion to it, as well as by the theories that are woven within it (Burke, 1950). Authors seek to persuade us in innumerable ways that their choice and their direction of research or study is sound. These identifications of theirs, and their persuasiveness, implicit or otherwise, are the intellectual odor that is to be known here as their rhetoric. It needs to be stressed that what is to be talked about here as rhetoric, therefore, is not so much the substance of play or of its science or of its theories, but rather the way in which the underlying ideological values attributed to these matters are both subsumed by the theorists and presented persuasively to the rest of us. As the term is used here, the rhetorics of play express the way play is placed in context within broader value systems, which are assumed by the theorists of play rather than studied directly by them. Having said that, however, it must be admitted that it is still almost impossible to suppress the desire to ask the question: "Yes, all right, but what is play itself?"—an impulse that the reader needs to stifle for now, though it will not go untrifled with before this work is played out.

It follows that all the sciences, physical and social, whatever their empirical virtues, are presented here as being maintained by rhetorical means, whether these be seen optimistically, for example, as the "scientific attitude," or somewhat more cynically, as the way in which disciplines, through controlling a knowledge base, enhance their own political power (Foucault, 1973). In what follows, the rhetorics that are the focus of this work will be called popular ideological rhetorics, and where necessary, these will be distinguished from what are called scientific or scholarly rhetorics, as well as from disciplinary rhetorics and personal rhetorics. The popular rhetorics are large-scale cultural "ways of thought" in which most of us participate in one way or another, although some specific groups will be more strongly advocates for this or that particular rhetoric. The larger play rhetorics are part of the multiple broad symbolic systems—political, religious, social, and educational—through which we construct the meaning of the cultures in which we live. It should be made clear that I do not assume these value presuppositions to be necessarily in vain or negative, nor to be without considerable value to those committed to them. In fact, it is impossible to live without them. The issue is only whether, by becoming confused with our play theories, they set us in pursuit of false explanations or false grandiosity. One promise of such an analysis as I propose is that, by revealing these rhetorical underpinnings of the apparently diverse theoretical approaches to play, there is the possibility of bridging them within some more unifying discourse. *The Recovery of Rhetoric* (Roberts and Good, 1993) offers much optimism for the possibilities of a more genuinely interdisciplinary organization of any subject matter, not excluding that of play. However, opinion has to be reserved on the integrating promise of rhetorical analysis until there is an examination of the present popular rhetorics specific to play and their interaction with the scholarly studies that have arisen around them. It is just as possible that the rhetorics, when explicated, will be revealed to be themselves a deceptive gloss over other, far more fundamental cultural disagreements. For example, play's supposed frivolity may itself be a mask for play's use in more widespread systems for denigrating the play of other groups, as has been done characteristically throughout history by those of higher status against the recreations of those of lower status (Armitage, 1977).

Seven rhetorics

The seven rhetorics to be presented in this work are characterized as follows.

The rhetoric of play as progress, usually applied to children's play, is the advocacy of the notion that animals and children, but not adults, adapt and develop through their play. This belief in play as progress is something that most Westerners cherish, but its relevance to play has been more often assumed than demonstrated. Most educators over the past two hundred years seem to have so needed to represent playful imitation as a form of children's socialization and moral, social, and cognitive growth that they have seen play as being primarily about development rather than enjoyment.

The rhetoric of play as fate is usually applied to gambling and games of chance, and it contrasts totally with the prior rhetoric. It is probably the oldest of all of the rhetorics, resting as it does on the belief that human lives and play are controlled by destiny, by the gods, by atoms or neurons, or by luck, but very little by ourselves, except perhaps through the skillful use of magic or astrology. This rhetoric enjoys only an underground advocacy in the modern world. It is no longer a widespread and conscious value system among the intellectual elites, though it remains popular among lower socioeconomic groups. It contrasts most strongly also with those modern theories of leisure that argue that the distinguishing feature of play is that it is an exercise of free choice.

The rhetoric of play as power, usually applied to sports, athletics, and contests, is—like fate, community identity, and frivolity—a rhetoric of ancient hue. These four all predate modern times and advocate collectively held community values rather than individual experiences. Recently these ancient rhetorics have been given much less philosophical attention than the modern three, progress, the imaginary, and the self, though they are more deep seated as cultural ideologies. The rhetoric of play as power is about the use of play as the representation of conflict and as a way to fortify the status of those who control the play or are its heroes. This rhetoric is as ancient as warfare and patriarchy. It is an anathema to many modern progress- and leisure-oriented play theorists.

The rhetoric of play as identity, usually applied to traditional and community celebrations and festivals, occurs when the play tradition is seen as a means of confirming, maintaining, or advancing the power and identity of the community of players. Because so much twentieth-century attention has been given to children's play as a form of progress, I have found it valuable to present a more balanced rhetorical advocacy of the character of their play from the point of view of these other rhetorics, power and fantasy.

The rhetoric of play as the imaginary, usually applied to playful improvisation of all kinds in literature and elsewhere, idealizes the imagination, flexibility, and creativity of the animal and human play worlds. This rhetoric is sustained by modern positive attitudes toward creativity and innovation. The rhetoric of progress, the rhetoric of the self, and the rhetoric of the imaginary constitute the modern set of rhetorics, with a history largely elaborated ideologically only in the past two hundred years.

The rhetoric of the self is usually applied to solitary activities like hobbies or high-risk phenomena like bungee jumping, but it need not be so proscribed. These are forms of play in which play is idealized by attention to the desirable experiences of the players—their fun, their relaxation, their escape—and the intrinsic or the aesthetic satisfactions of the play performances. Here the central advocacies of the secular and consumerist manner of modern life invade the interpretations of play and are questioned because of their twentieth-century relativity.

The rhetoric of play as frivolous is usually applied to the activities of the idle or the foolish. But in modern times, it inverts the classic "work ethic" view of play, against which all the other rhetorics exist as rhetorics of rebuttal. But frivolity, as used here, is not just the puritanic negative, it is also a term to be applied more to historical trickster figures and fools, who were once the central and carnivalesque persons who enacted playful protest against the orders of the ordained world. This chapter is placed last in this work because of its largely reflexive character, as commentary on all the other rhetorics. Historically frivolity belongs with the ancient set that includes fate, power, and identity.

  I should note that although each of these rhetorics is discussed in the singular, there are multiple variants within each category, so that it might be more proper to speak of the plural *rhetorics* throughout. To repeat, each is called a rhetoric because its ideological values are something that the holders like to persuade others to believe in and to live by. Much of the time such values do not even reach a level of conscious awareness. People simply take it for granted, for example, that children develop as a result of their playing; or that sports are a part of the way in which different states and nations compete with each other; or that festivals are a way in which groups are bonded together; or that play is a desirable modern form of creativity or personal choice; or that, contrary to all of these, play is a waste of time. By seeing how the play descriptions and play theories can be tied in with such broad patterns of ideological value, one has greater hope of coming to understand the general character of play theory, which is the ultimate objective here.

A scale of rhetorics

These seven play rhetorics can be illuminated by contrasting them, on the one hand, with rhetorics that are broader than they are, and on the other, with rhetorics that are narrower. Of the broader kind are those that derive from beliefs about religion, politics, social welfare, crime, and morality—that is, from all the matters that priests, politicians and salespersons constantly harangue folks about. These are the rhetorics that fill the airwaves of daily life, in churches, in schools, and in the community. People cannot live without them, even if they often can't stand some of them. They constitute the incessant discourse about who we are and how we should live. The group of rhetorics for the particular subject matter play are of the same broad kind, being about progress and power, but they are more limited in the present usage because they are applied only to the specific subject of play theories. The rhetorics of science are generally of a narrower and more explicit kind. Science, after all, has its own epistemological rhetorics of reliability, validity, and prediction. Scholarship in general has its required consistency, coherence, and authenticity. All of these scientific and scholarly tenets are also rhetorics, because they assume and propagate the view that there is a knowable world, or a knowable text, and then, acting as if that assumption is real (a hypothetical fiction), proceed to their methodological undertakings. As Pepper (1961) has shown, even philosophical scholars must make arbitrary distinctions about which part of the world they seek to study, some focusing on the structures or forms of reality, some on the causes of reality and behavior, others on the changing historical context in which these things occur, and yet others on the kinds of integration or organicism that they can discover. What is added here to any such "scientific" (play) rhetorics is that the subject-matter rhetorics (those seven listed above) may be able to suggest why the scientific rhetorics take the direction they do—and also suggest why that direction may often have limitations deriving not so much from the science or scholarship, but from the presuppositions of the value systems in which the science is embedded. Parenthetically, the present focus on such presuppositions is not meant to suggest that "objective" social science is without value, or that "objectivity" is not fruitful within the ideological frames being presented. My aim here is much more modest, it seeks only for the sources of ambiguity in play rhetoric.

In the past several decades the claims of scholarship or science for sheer objectivity have been frequently challenged. The limitations of the claims for scholarly literature's independence from propaganda are challenged by Burke in such works as *The Rhetoric of Motives* (1950) and *Language as Symbolic Action* (1966). The same orientation is made a criticism of general scientific objectivity by Kuhn's now famous *The Structure of Scientific Revolutions* (1970), in which he points out the role played by human motivation in the development of science, particularly in respect to the way in which accepted theories often are not displaced until a new generation of thinkers finds them irrelevant. Science is not as cumulative or as autonomously objective in the growth of its knowledge as has often been supposed. But the roots of the present enterprise can be found in the work of many other scholars as well, from Wittgenstein's emphasis on the meaning of language relying on its context of usage, for example, to Foucault's stricture that knowledge is always an exercise of power, never merely information. Those who create information are those who decide how others shall think about their lives. Leading play theorists who quite explicitly see themselves talking about the rhetorics of play in order to talk about play theory at all include Helen Schwartzman (1978), Margaret Duncan (1988), and Mihail Spariosu (1989).

Between the historically based subject-matter rhetorics that will be presented here (progress, power, and so on) and the most general scientific epistemological rhetorics, which involve, for example, the metaphysical assumptions underlying the expectancy of causal regularities in nature, a host of other disciplinary rhetorics also play their part in the amalgam that is social science. Elsewhere, for example, I have described rhetorics that are applied to childhood in modern life, with children variously being seen as: the child of god, the child as the future, the predictable child, the imaginary child, the child as consumer, and the gender androgynous child (Sutton-Smith, 1994).

But the physical scientists are not immune to such rhetorics either, and there are disputes about how the public should interpret the personality of their science in the culture. These can be called questions about the ontological rhetorics of the scientists. They may be seen as "objective" or "cautious," but at times they are also seen as rebels, subversives, Frankensteins, relentless creatures of reason, conquerors of nature, empirical reductionists, mathematical formalists, artists, philosophers, secular saints, or irresponsible devils. And as Dyson (1995) shows, these kinds of rhetorics, when personal to the scientists, make an enormous difference in the direction of their inquiries. One might conclude that all scholars are creatures of their personal disposition, which may become a motivating rhetoric for them, and they are also, historically, inheritors of larger ideological or cultural patterns that affect their scholarship. They are the legatees as well of the rhetorics of disciplinary assumptions and disciplinary methodologies.

What needs most emphasis at this initial point is that rhetorical involvement at some or all of these levels is inescapable. Scholarly objectivity always exists within such contexts as broad cultural rhetorics (political, religious, moral), disciplinary rhetorics (sciences, humanities, arts), epistemological rhetorics (validity, reliability, causalism, formism), subject-matter rhetorics (in the present case, play rhetorics), general ontological rhetorics (objectivity, scientific caution), and personal rhetorics (idiosyncratic dispositions).

Within the subject of the present inquiry (play), the major emphasis is on the way in which the theories within this scholarly domain are underlain by the seven rhetorics outlined above. As William Kessen, a leading scholar of such reflexive self-consciousness in developmental psychology, states that we should

> recognize that, deeply carved into our professional intention is a desire to change the lives of our readers, to have them believe something that we believe. In grand nineteenth-century style, we can call this the Unspoken Intention that is hidden by the wonderful devices all of us have learned to speak with the voice of certain authority . . . .
>
> Our work is packed with our values, our intentions for our small part of the world: a great deal would be gained by a critical analysis and display of those intentions, [but] the governing principle for evidence in both psychology and history [is that] we do not seek proofs; we do not attempt demonstrations. We all want to tell plausible stories. (1993, p. 229)

Validating the existence of the seven rhetorics

Though it is not difficult to assert in a general way that the science of play is underlain by these seven subject-matter narratives, or rhetorics, the assertion itself has fairly vague "scientific" or "scholarly" cogency without some criteria of coherence that can be used to affirm their presence. The criteria I use to frame the rhetorical contentions are as follows:

1   That the assumed seven rhetorics can be shown to have a clear basis in well known cultural attitudes of a contemporary or historical kind. This historical context, although not dealt with in great detail here, is the most basic source of their cultural construction (Glassie, 1982).
2   That the rhetorics have their own specific groups of advocates, a necessary precondition if these phenomena are to be seen as not just narratives but also rhetorics of persuasion.

3   That each rhetoric applies primarily to a distinct kind of play or playfulness. If this is so, it suggests some kind of epistemological affinity between the rhetorics and their ludic subject matter. They are not accidentally correlated.

4   That each rhetoric applies primarily to distinct kinds of players.

5   That there is an affinity between the rhetoric and particular scholarly or scientific disciplines, and between particular play theories and play theorists.

6   That (following criteria 2 through 5), there is a "matching" interplay between the nature of the rhetorical assertions and the character of the forms of play to which they are applied. Thus a rhetoric of progress might find partial substantiation in the finding that some kinds of skill during play can take "progressive" forms. In addition it may be possible to show that the rhetoric itself is often the way in which the play passes into the culture, because the play practice is thus justified ideologically. In this way, the two, play and rhetoric, have an impact on each other. The recommendation that the interplay between play and nonplay should be more carefully studied was made by the famous play theorist Erik Erikson in his book *Toys and Reasons* (1977). But this recommendation is also the constant beguilement of all those who study the interrelationships between play and nonplay to try to puzzle out how they reciprocally affect each other (Abrahams, 1977).

7   That the group that maintains the rhetoric benefits by the exercise of hegemony over the players, over their competitors, or over those who are excluded from the play. This postulate makes explicit why the present approach to play centers on the rhetorics of the theorists rather than, more simply, on the narratives they tell themselves. Rhetorics are narratives that have the intent to persuade because there is some kind of gain for those who are successful in their persuasion. Telling plausible stories would not be enough.

8   That the way in which the scholarly disciplines define the subject matter of play may or may not make sense in terms of the rhetorics that are being proposed in this work. This is open to investigation. Three kinds of play definitions will be considered where they are available:

   a   The definitions by players of their own *play experiences* and functions. What do the players reckon to be the character of and the reasons for their own participation? Obviously there is not much research to be referred to here, although there is a considerable amount of anecdotal opinion to be cited. It is useful to discover that there can be—and often is—very little relationship between the players' own play definitions and those of the theorists.

   b   The definitions by theorists of *intrinsic play functions*. These are definitions drawn from the research literature, or new ones arising out of the present analysis, that are supposed to account scientifically for the play's functioning by pointing to the players' game-related motives for playing.

   c   The definitions by the theorists of *extrinsic play functions*, which account for the forms of play in terms of functions they are supposed to serve in the larger culture.

It is with the two last types of definitions (b and c) that this study is preoccupied. It is quite possible, for example, for players to have one rhetoric while "experts" have another. But it is also possible for experts to use one rhetoric when talking about the players' responses and another rhetoric when discussing theoretically what they think is the underlying function of the forms of play. A description of the players' enjoyments, after all, need not be the same as an account of the supposed adaptive functions of those enjoyments. More important, finding the relationship between accounts of play in terms of intrinsic and extrinsic functions is yet another way of talking about the interplay of play and nonplay. There is promise here of some clarification of the causalities of play and life.

As a final point of each chapter, it will be necessary to return to the issue of play's ambiguity, with which this work begins. My aim is to establish to what extent ambiguity is an outcome of the seven rhetorics, or if it must instead be attributed to the character of play itself.

Note

1 Play-related quotations here and throughout the rest of this work are, for the most part, from *Bartlett's Familiar Quotations*, 16th ed. (Boston: Little, Brown, 1992) Playful quotes, noted as "after" are of fictional status. Dr. Frech is frivolous.

Bibliography

Abrahams, R. D. 1977. *Towards an enactment-centered theory of folklore.* American Association for the Advancement of Science. Boulder, Colo.: Westview Press, 19–20.

Armitage, J. 1977 *Man at play.* London: Frederic Warne.

Bakhtin, M. M. 1981. *The dialogic imagination.* Austin: University of Texas Press.

Bateson, G. 1956. The message, "This is play." In *Group processes*, ed. B. Shaffner. New York: Josiah Macy.

Burke, K. 1950. *The rhetoric of motives.* New York: Prentice Hall.

——. 1996. Language as symbolic action. Berkeley: University of California Press.

Caughey, J. 1984. *Imaginary source worlds: A cultural approach.* Lincoln: University of Nebraska Press.

Derrida, J. 1980. *The archeology of the frivolous.* Lincoln: University of Nebraska Press.

Duncan, M. 1988. Play discourse and the rhetorical turn: A semiological analysis of *Homo Ludens. Play and Culture*, 1 (1): 28–42.

Dyson, F. 1995. The scientist as rebel. *The New York Review of Books* 42(9): 31–33.

Empson, W. 1955. *Seven types of ambiguity.* New York: Meridian Books.

Erikson, E. 1977. *Toys and* reasons. New York: Norton.

Fagen, R. 1981. *Animal play behavior.* New York: Oxford University Press.

Feyerabend, P. 1995. *Killing time.* Chicago: University of Chicago Press.

——. 1973. Madness and civilization. New York: Vintage.

Glassie, H. 1982. *Passing time in Ballymenone.* Philadelphia: University of Pennsylvania Press.

Kessen, W. 1993. A developmentalist's reflections. In *Children in time and place*, ed. G. H. Elder et al. New York: Cambridge University Press, 226–229.

Kuhn, T. S. 1970. *The structure of scientific revolutions.* Chicago: University of Chicago Press.

MacCannell, Dean. 1976. *The tourist: A new theory of the leisure class.* New York: Schocken Books.

Pepper, S. 1961. *World hypotheses.* Berkeley: University of California Press.

Roberts, R. H., and Good, J. M. M. 1993. *The recovery of rhetoric.* Charlottesville: University Press of Virginia.

Schechner, R. 1988. Playing. *Play and Culture* 1 (1): 3–27.

Schwartzman, H. B. 1978. *Transformations: The anthropology of children's play.* New York: Plenum.

Spack, P. 1986. *Gossip.* Chicago: University of Chicago Press.

Spariosu, M. 1989. *Dionysus reborn.* Ithaca, N.Y.: Cornell University Press.

Stephenson, W. 1967. *The play theory of mass communication.* Chicago: University of Chicago Press.

Sutton-Smith, B. 1994. Paradigms of intervention. In *Play and intervention,* ed. J. Hellendorn et al. Albany: State University of New York Press.

Turner, V. 1969. *The ritual process.* New York: Aldine.

14

THE LESSONS OF LUCASFILM'S *HABITAT*

F. Randall Farmer and Chip Morningstar

Source: Michael Benedikt (ed.), *Cyberspace: First Steps* (Cambridge, MA: The MIT Press, 1990), pp. 273–301.

Context

This paper was presented at The First Annual International Conference on Cyberspace in 1990. It was published in **Cyberspace: First Steps,** Michael Benedikt [ed.] [MIT Press, 1990].

Introduction

Lucasfilm's *Habitat* was created by Lucasfilm Games, a division of LucasArts Entertainment Company, in association with Quantum Computer Services, Inc. It was arguably one of the first attempts to create a very large scale commercial multi-user virtual environment. A far cry from many laboratory research efforts based on sophisticated interface hardware and tens of thousands of dollars per user of dedicated compute power, *Habitat* is built on top of an ordinary commercial online service and uses an inexpensive—some would say "toy"—home computer to support user interaction. In spite of these somewhat plebeian underpinnings, *Habitat* is ambitious in its scope. The system we developed can support a population of thousands of users in a single shared cyberspace. *Habitat* presents its users with a real-time animated view into an online simulated world in which users can communicate, play games, go on adventures, fall in love, get married, get divorced, start businesses, found religions, wage wars, protest against them, and experiment with self-government.

The *Habitat* project proved to be a rich source of insights into the nitty-gritty reality of actually implementing a serious, commercially viable cyberspace environment. Our experiences developing the *Habitat* system, and managing the virtual world that resulted, offer a number of interesting and important lessons for prospective cyberspace architects. The purpose of this paper is to discuss some of these lessons. We hope that the next generation of builders of virtual worlds can benefit from our experiences and (especially) from our mistakes.

227

Due to space limitations, we won't be able to go into as much technical detail as we might like; this will have to be left to a future publication. Similarly, we will only be able to touch briefly upon some of the history of the project as a business venture, which is a fascinating subject of its own. Although we will conclude with a brief discussion of some of the future directions for this technology, a more detailed exposition on this topic will also have to wait for a future article.

The essential lesson that we have abstracted from our experiences with *Habitat* is that a cyberspace is defined more by the interactions among the actors within it than by the technology with which it is implemented. While we find much of the work presently being done on elaborate interface technologies— Data Gloves, head-mounted displays, special-purpose rendering engines, and so on—both exciting and promising, the almost mystical euphoria that currently seems to surround all this hardware is, in our opinion, both excessive and somewhat misplaced. We can't help having a nagging sense that it's all a bit of a distraction from the really pressing issues. At the core of *our* vision is the idea that cyberspace is necessarily a *multiple-participant environment.* It seems to us that the things that are important to the inhabitants of such an environment are the capabilities available to them, the characteristics of the other people they encounter there, and the ways these various participants can affect one another. Beyond a foundation set of communications capabilities, the technology used to present this environment to its participants, while sexy and interesting, is a peripheral concern.

What is *Habitat?*

Habitat is a "multi-player online virtual environment" (its purpose is to be an entertainment medium; consequently, the users are called "players"). Each player uses his or her home computer as a front end, communicating over a commercial packet-switching data network to a centralized backend system. The front end provides the user interface, generating a real-time animated display of what is going on and translating input from the player into requests to the backend. The backend maintains the world model, enforcing the rules and keeping each player's front end informed about the constantly changing state of the universe. The backend enables the players to interact not only with the world but also with each other.

Habitat was inspired by a long tradition of "computer hacker science fiction", notably Vernor Vinge's novel, True Names (Vinge, 1981), as well as many fond childhood memories of games of make-believe, more recent memories of role-playing games and the like, and numerous other influences too thoroughly blended to pinpoint. To this we add a dash of silliness, a touch of cyberpunk (Gibson, 1984; Sterling, 1986), and a predilection for object-oriented programming (Sussman and Abelson, 1985).

The initial incarnation of *Habitat* uses a Commodore 64 for the frontend[1]. The largest part of the screen is devoted to the graphics display. This is an animated view of the player's current location in the *Habitat* world. The scene consists of various objects arrayed on the screen, such as the houses and tree you see here. The players are represented by animated figures that we call "Avatars." Avatars are usually, though not exclusively, humanoid in appearance. In this scene you can see two of them, carrying on a conversation.

A typical *Habitat* scene

Avatars can move around, pick up, put down and manipulate objects, talk to each other, and gesture, each under the control of an individual player. Control is through the joystick, which enables the player to point at things and issue commands. Talking is accomplished by typing on the keyboard. The text that a player types is displayed over his or her Avatar's head in a cartoon-style "word balloon".

The *Habitat* world is made up of a large number of discrete locations that we call "regions." In its prime, the prototype *Habitat* world consisted of around 20,000 of them. Each region can adjoin up to four other regions, which can be reached simply by walking your Avatar to one or another edge of the screen. Doorways and other passages can connect to additional regions. Each region contains a set of objects which define the things that an Avatar can do there and the scene that the player sees on the computer screen.

Some of the objects are structural, such as the ground or the sky. Many are just scenic, such as the tree or the mailbox. Most objects, however, have some function that they perform. For example, doors transport Avatars from one region to another and may be opened, closed, locked and unlocked. ATMs (Automatic Token Machines) enable access to an Avatar's bank account [2]. Vending machines dispense useful goods in exchange for *Habitat* money.

Many objects are portable and may be carried around in an Avatar's hands or pockets. These include various kinds of containers, money, weapons, tools, and exotic magical implements. Listed here are some of the most important types of objects and their functions. The complete list of object types numbers in the hundreds.

Object class	Function
ATM	Automatic Token Machine; access to an Avatar's bank account
Avatar	Represents the player in the *Habitat* world
Bag, Box	Containers in which things may be carried
Book	Document for Avatars to read (e.g., the daily newspaper)
Bureaucrat-in-a-box	Communication with system operators
Change-o-matic	Device to change Avatar gender
Chest, Safe	Containers in which things can be stored
Club, Gun, Knife	Various weapons
Compass	Points direction to West Pole
Door	Passage from one region to another; can be locked
Drugs	Various types; changes Avatar body state, e.g., cure wounds
Elevator	Transportation from one floor of a tall building to another
Flashlight	Provides light in dark places
Fountain	Scenic highlight; provides communication to system designers
Game piece	Enables various board games: *backgammon, checkers, chess*, etc.
Garbage can	Disposes of unwanted objects
Glue	System building tool; attaches objects together
Ground, Sky	The underpinnings of the world
Head	An Avatar's head; comes in many styles; for customization
Key	Unlocks doors and other containers
Knick-knack	Generic inert object; for decorative purposes
Magic wand	Various types, can do almost anything
Paper	For writing notes, making maps, etc.; used in mail system
Pawn machine	Buys back previously purchased objects
Plant, Rock, Tree	Generic scenic objects
Region	The foundation of reality
Sensor	Various types, detects otherwise invisible conditions in the world
Sign	Allows attachment of text to other objects
Stun gun	Non-lethal weapon
Teleport booth	Means of quick long-distance transport; analogous to phone booth
Tokens	*Habitat* money
Vendroid	Vending machine; sells things

Implementation

The following, along with several programmer-years of tedious and expensive detail that we won't cover here, is how the system works:

At the heart of the *Habitat* implementation is an object-oriented model of the universe.

The front end consists of a system kernel and a collection of objects. The kernel handles memory management, display generation, disk I/O, telecommunications, and other "operating system" functions. The objects implement the semantics of the world itself. Each type of *Habitat* object has a definition consisting of a set of resources, including animation cels to drive the display, audio data, and executable code. An object's executable code implements a series of standard behaviors, each of which is invoked by a different player command or system event. The model is similar to that found in an object-oriented programming system such as Smalltalk (Goldberg and Robson, 1983), with its classes, methods and messages. These resources consume significant amounts of scarce front end memory, so we can't keep them all in core at the same time. Fortunately, their definitions are invariant, so we simply swap them in from disk as we need them, discarding less recently used resources to make room.

When an object is instantiated, we allocate a block of memory to contain the object's state. The first several bytes of an object's state information take the same form in all objects, and include such things as the object's screen location and display attributes. This standard information is interpreted by the system kernel as it generates the display and manages the run-time environment. The remainder of the state information varies with the object type and is accessed only by the object's behavior code.

Object behaviors are invoked by the kernel in response to player input. Each object responds to a set of standard verbs that map directly onto the commands available to the player. Each behavior is simply a subroutine that executes the indicated action; to do this it may invoke the behaviors of other objects or send request messages to the backend. Besides the standard verb behaviors, objects may have additional behaviors which are invoked by messages that arrive synchronously from the backend.

The backend also maintains an object-oriented representation of the world. As in the front end, objects on the backend possess executable behaviors and in-memory state information. In addition, since the backend maintains a persistent global state for the entire *Habitat* world, the objects are also represented by database records that may be stored on disk when not "in use". Backend object behaviors are invoked by messages from the front end. Each of these backend behaviors works in roughly the same way: a message is received from a player's front end requesting some action; the action is taken and some state changes to the world result; the backend behavior sends a response message back to the front end informing it of the results of its request and notification messages to the front ends of any other players who are in the same region, informing *them* of what has taken place.

The lessons

In order to say as much as we can in the limited space available, we will describe what we think we learned via a series of principles or assertions surrounded by supporting reasoning and illustrative anecdotes. A more formal and thorough exposition will have to come later in some other forum where we might have the space to present a more comprehensive and detailed model.

We mentioned our primary principle above:

A multi-user environment is central to the idea of cyberspace.

It is our deep conviction that a definitive characteristic of a cyberspace system is that it represents a multi-user environment. This stems from the fact that what (in our opinion) people seek in such a system is richness, complexity and depth. Nobody knows how to produce an automaton that even approaches the complexity of a real human being, let alone a society. Our approach, then, is not even to attempt this, but instead to use the computational medium to augment the communications channels between real people.

If what we are constructing is a multi-user environment, it naturally follows that some sort of communications capability must be fundamental to our system. However, we must take into account an observation that is the second of our principles:

Communications bandwidth is a scarce resource.

This point was rammed home to us by one of *Habitat's* nastier externally imposed design constraints, namely that it provide a satisfactory experience to the player over a 300 baud serial telephone connection (one, moreover, routed through commercial packet-switching networks that impose an additional, uncontrollable latency of 100 to 5000 milliseconds on each packet transmitted).

Even in a more technically advanced network, however, bandwidth remains scarce in the sense that economists use the term: available carrying capacity is not unlimited. The law of supply and demand suggests that no matter how much capacity is available, you always want more. When communications technology advances to the point were we all have multi-gigabaud fiber optic connections into our homes, computational technology will have advanced to match. Our processors' expanding appetite for data will mean that the search for ever more sophisticated data compression techniques will *still* be a hot research area (though what we are compressing may at that point be high-resolution volumetric time-series or something even more esoteric) (Drexler, 1986).

Computer scientists tend to be reductionists who like to organize systems in terms of primitive elements that can be easily manipulated within the context of a simple formal model. Typically, you adopt a small variety of very simple primitives which are then used in large numbers. For a graphics-oriented cyberspace system, the temptation is to build upon bit-mapped images or polygons or some other *graphic* primitive. These sorts of representations, however, are invitations to disaster. They arise from an inappropriate fixation on display technology, rather than on the underlying purpose of the system.

However, the most significant part of what we wish to be communicating is human behaviors. These, fortunately, can be represented quite compactly, provided we adopt a relatively abstract, high-level description that deals with behavioral concepts directly. This leads to our third principle:

An object-oriented data representation is essential

Taken at its face value, this assertion is unlikely to be controversial, as object-oriented programming is currently the methodology of choice among the software engineering cognoscenti. However, what we mean here is not only that you should adopt an object-oriented approach, but that the basic objects from which you build the system should correspond more-or-less to the objects in the user's conceptual model of the virtual world, that is, people, places, and artifacts. You could, of course, use object-oriented programming techniques to build a system based on, say, polygons, but that would not help to cope with the fundamental problem.

The goal is to enable the communications between machines to take place primarily at the behavioral level (what people and things are doing) rather than at the presentation level (how the scene is changing). The description of a place in the virtual world should be in terms of what is there rather than what it looks like. Interactions between objects should be described by functional models rather than by physical ones. The computation necessary to translate between these higher-level representations and the lower-level representations required for direct user interaction is an essentially local function. At the local processor, display-rendering techniques may be arbitrarily elaborate and physical models arbitrarily sophisticated. The data channel capacities required for such computations, however, need not and should not be squeezed into the limited bandwidth available between the local processor and remote ones. Attempting to do so just leads to disasters such as NAPLPS (ANSI, 1983; Alber, 1985) which couples dreadful performance with a display model firmly anchored in the technology of the 1970s.

Once we begin working at the conceptual rather than the presentation level, we are struck by the following observation:

The implementation platform is relatively unimportant.

The presentation level and the conceptual level cannot (and should not) be *totally* isolated from each other. However, defining a virtual environment in terms of the configuration and behavior of objects, rather than their presentation, enables us to span a vast range of computational and display capabilities among the participants in a system. This range extends both upward and downward. As an extreme example, a typical scenic object, such as a tree, can be represented by a handful of parameter values. At the lowest conceivable end of things might be an ancient Altair 8800 with a 300 baud ASCII dumb terminal, where the interface is reduced to fragments of text and the user sees the humble string so familiar to the players of text adventure games, "There is a tree here." At the high end, you might have a powerful processor that generates the image of the tree by growing a fractal model and rendering it three dimensions at high resolution, the finest details ray-traced in real-time, complete with branches waving in the breeze and the sound of wind in the leaves coming through your headphones in high-fidelity digital stereo. And these two users might be looking at the same tree in same the place in the same world and talking to each other as they do so. Both of these scenarios are implausible at the moment, the first because nobody would suffer with such a crude interface when better ones are so readily available, the second because the computational hardware does not yet exist. The point, however, is that this approach covers the ground between systems already obsolete and ones that are as yet gleams in their designers' eyes. Two consequences of this are significant. The first is that we can build effective cyberspace systems today. *Habitat* exists as ample proof of this principle. The second is that it is conceivable that with a modicum of cleverness and foresight you could start building a system with today's technology that could evolve smoothly as the tomorrow's technology develops. The availability of pathways for growth is important in the real world, especially if cyberspace is to become a significant communications medium (as we obviously think it should).

Given that we see cyberspace as fundamentally a communications medium rather than simply a user interface model, and given the style of object-oriented approach that we advocate, another point becomes clear:

Data communications standards are vital.

However, our concerns about cyberspace data communications standards center less upon data transport protocols than upon the definition of the data being transported. The mechanisms required for reliably getting bits from point A to point B are not terribly interesting to us. This is not because these mechanisms are not essential (they obviously are) nor because they do not pose significant research and engineering challenges (they clearly do). It is because we are focused on the unique communications needs of an object-based cyberspace. We are concerned with the protocols for sending messages between objects, that is, for communicating behavior rather than presentation, and for communicating object definitions from one system to another.

Communicating object definitions seems to us to be an especially important problem, and one that we really didn't have an opportunity to address in *Habitat*.

It *will* be necessary to address this problem if we are to have a dynamic system. The ability to add new classes of objects over time is crucial if the system is to be able to evolve.

While we are on the subject of communications standards, we would like to make some remarks about the ISO Reference Model of Open System Interconnection (ISO, 1986). This multilayered model has become a centerpiece of most discussions about data communications standards these days. Unfortunately, while the bottom 4 or 5 layers of this model provide a more or less sound framework for considering data transport issues, we feel that the model's Presentation and Application layers are not so helpful when considering cyberspace data communications.

We have two main quarrels with the ISO model: first, it partitions the general data communications problem in a way that is a poor match for the needs of a cyberspace system; second, and more importantly, we think it is an active source of confusion because it focuses the attention of system designers on the wrong set of issues and thus leads them to spend their time solving the wrong set of problems. We know because this happened to us. "Presentation" and "Application" are simply the wrong abstractions for the higher levels of a cyberspace communications protocol. A "Presentation" protocol presumes characteristics of the display are embedded in the protocol. The discussions above should give some indication why we feel such a presumption is both unnecessary and unwise. An "Application" protocol presumes a degree of foreknowledge of the message environment that is incompatible with the sort of dynamically evolving object system we envision.

A better model would be to substitute a different pair of top layers: a Message layer, which defines the means by which objects can address one another and standard methods of encapsulating structured data and encoding low-level data types (e.g., numbers); and a Definition layer built on top of the Message layer, which defines a standard representation for object definitions so that object classes can migrate from machine to machine. One might argue that these are simply Presentation and Application with different labels, but we don't think the differences are so easily reconciled. In particular, we think the ISO model has, however unintentionally, systematically deflected workers in the field from considering many of the issues that concern us.

World building

There were two sorts of implementation challenges that *Habitat* posed. The first was the problem of creating a working piece of technology—developing the animation engine, the object-oriented virtual memory, the message-passing pseudo operating system, and squeezing them all into the ludicrous Commodore 64 (the backend system also posed interesting technical problems, but its constraints were not as vicious). The second challenge was the creation and management of the *Habitat* world itself. It is the experiences from the latter exercise that we think will be most relevant to future cyberspace designers.

We were initially our own worst enemies in this undertaking, victims of a way of thinking to which we engineers are dangerously susceptible. This way of thinking is characterized by the conceit that all things may be planned in advance and then directly implemented according to the plan's detailed specification. For persons schooled in the design and construction of systems based on simple, well-defined and well-understood foundation principles, this is a natural attitude to have. Moreover, it is entirely appropriate when undertaking most engineering projects. It is a frame of mind that is an essential part of a good engineer's conceptual tool kit. Alas, in keeping with Maslow's assertion that, "to the person who has only a hammer, all the world looks like a nail", it is a tool that is easy to carry beyond its range of applicability. This happens when a system exceeds the threshold of complexity above which the human mind loses its ability to maintain a complete and coherent model.

One generally hears about systems crossing the complexity threshold when they become very large. For example, the Space Shuttle and the B-2 bomber are both systems above this threshold, necessitating extraordinarily involved, cumbersome and time-consuming procedures to keep the design under control—procedures that are at once vastly expensive and only partially successful. To a degree, the complexity problem can be solved by throwing money at it. However, such capital intensive management techniques are a luxury not available to most projects. Furthermore, although these dubious "solutions" to the complexity problem are out of reach of most projects, alas the complexity threshold itself is not. Smaller systems can suffer from the same sorts of problems. It is possible to push much smaller and less elaborate systems over the complexity threshold simply by introducing chaotic elements that are outside the designers' sphere of control or understanding. The most significant such chaotic elements are autonomous computational agents (e.g., other computers). This is why, for example, debugging even very simple communications protocols often proves surprisingly difficult. Furthermore, a special circle of living Hell awaits the implementers of systems involving that most important category of autonomous computational agents of all, groups of interacting human beings. This leads directly to our next (and possibly most controversial) assertion:

Detailed central planning is impossible; don't even try.

The constructivist prejudice that leads engineers into the kinds of problems just mentioned has received more study from economists and sociologists (e.g., Popper 1962, 1972; Hayek 1973, 1978, 1989; Sowell 1987) than from research-ers in the software engineering community. Game and simulation designers are experienced in creating virtual worlds for individuals and small groups. However, they have had no reason to learn to deal with large populations of simultaneous users. Since each user or group is unrelated to the others, the same world can be used over and over again. If you are playing an adventure game, the fact that thousands of other people elsewhere in the (real) world are playing the same game has no effect on your experience. It is reasonable for the creator of such a world to spend tens or even hundreds of hours crafting the environment for each hour that a user will spend interacting with it, since that user's hour of experience will be duplicated tens of thousands of times by tens of thousands of other individual users.

Builders of online services and communications networks are experienced in dealing with large user populations, but they do not, in general, create elaborate environments. Furthermore, in a system designed to deliver information or communications services, large numbers of users are simply a load problem rather than a complexity problem. All the users get the same information or services; the comments in the previous paragraph regarding duplication of experience apply here as well. It is not necessary to match the size and complexity of the information space to the size of the user population. While it may turn out that the quantity of information available on a service is a function of the size of the user population, this information can generally be organized into a systematic structure that can still be maintained by a few people. The bulk, wherein the complexity lies, is the product of the users themselves, rather than the system designers—the operators of the system do not have to create all this material. (This observation is the first clue to the solution to our problem.)

Our original specification for *Habitat* called for us to create a world capable of supporting a population of 20,000 Avatars, with expansion plans for up to 50,000. By any reckoning this is a large undertaking and complexity problems would certainly be expected. However, in practice we exceeded the complexity threshold very early in development. By the time the population of our online community had reached around 50 we were in over our heads (and these 50 were "insiders" who were prepared to be tolerant of holes and rough edges).

Moreover, a virtual world such as *Habitat* needs to scale with its population. For 20,000 Avatars we needed 20,000 "houses", organized into towns and cities with associated traffic arteries and shopping and recreational areas. We needed wilderness areas between the towns so that everyone would not be jammed together into the same place. Most of all, we needed things for 20,000 people to do. They needed interesting places to visit—and since they can't all be in the same place at the same time, they needed a *lot* of interesting places to visit—and things to do in those places. Each of those houses, towns, roads, shops, forests, theaters, arenas, and other places is a distinct entity that someone needs to design and create. We, attempting to play the role of omniscient central planners, were swamped.

Automated tools may be created to aid the generation of areas that naturally possess a high degree of regularity and structure, such as apartment buildings and road networks. We created a number of such tools, whose spiritual descendents will no doubt be found in the standard bag of tricks of future cyberspace architects. However, the very properties which make some parts of the world amenable to such techniques also make those same parts of the world among the least important. It is really not a problem if every apartment building looks pretty much like every other. It is a big problem if every enchanted forest is the same. Places whose value lies in their uniqueness, or at least in their differentiation from the places around them, need to be crafted by hand. This is an incredibly labor intensive and time consuming process. Furthermore, even very imaginative people are limited in the range of variation that they can produce, especially if they are working in a virgin environment uninfluenced by the works and reactions of other designers.

Running the world

The world design problem might still be tractable, however, if all players had the same goals, interests, motivations and types of behavior. Real people, however, are all different. For the designer of an ordinary game or simulation, human diversity is not a major problem, since he or she gets to establish the goals and motivations on the participants' behalf, and to specify the activities available to them in order to channel events in the preferred direction. *Habitat*, however, was deliberately open-ended and pluralistic. The idea behind our world was precisely that it did not come with a fixed set of objectives for its inhabitants, but rather provided a broad palette of possible activities from which the players could choose, driven by their own internal inclinations. It was our intent to provide a variety of possible experiences, ranging from events with established rules and goals (a treasure hunt, for example) to activities propelled by the players' personal motivations (starting a business, running the newspaper) to completely free-form, purely existential activities (hanging out with friends and conversing). Most activities, however, involved some degree of pre-planning and setup on our part—we were to be like the cruise director on an ocean voyage, but we were still thinking like game designers.

The first goal-directed event planned for *Habitat* was a rather involved treasure hunt called the "D'nalsi Island Adventure". It took us hours to design, weeks to build (including a 100-region island), and days to coordinate the actors involved. It was designed much like the puzzles in an adventure game. We thought it would occupy our players for days. In fact, the puzzle was solved in about 8 hours by a person who had figured out the critical clue in the first 15 minutes. Many of the players hadn't even had a chance to get into the game. The result was that one person had had a wonderful experience, dozens of others were left bewildered, and a huge investment in design and setup time had been consumed in an eye blink. We expected that there would be a wide range of "adventuring" skills in the *Habitat* audience. What wasn't so obvious until afterward was that this meant that most people didn't have a very good time, if for no other reason than that they never really got to participate. It would clearly be foolish and impractical for us to do things like this on a regular basis.

Again and again we found that activities based on often unconscious assumptions about player behavior had completely unexpected outcomes (when they were not simply outright failures). It was clear that we were not in control.

The more people we involved in something, the less in control we were. We could influence things, we could set up interesting situations, we could provide opportunities for things to happen, but we could not dictate the outcome. Social engineering is, at best, an inexact science (or, as some wag once said, "In the most carefully constructed experiment under the most carefully controlled conditions, the organism will do whatever it damn well pleases").

Propelled by these experiences, we shifted into a style of operations in which we let the players themselves drive the direction of the design. This proved far more effective. Instead of trying to push the community in the direction we thought it should go, an exercise rather like herding mice, we tried to observe what people were doing and aid them in it. We became facilitators as much as we were designers and implementers. This often meant adding new features and new regions to the system at a frantic pace, but almost all of what we added was used and appreciated, since it was well matched to people's needs and desires. We, as the experts on how the system worked, could often suggest new activities for people to try or ways of doing things that people might not have thought of. In this way we were able to have considerable influence on the system's development in spite of the fact that we didn't really hold the steering wheel—more influence, in fact, than we had had when we were operating under the illusion that we controlled everything.

Indeed, the challenges posed by large systems are prompting some research-ers to question the centralized, planning dominated attitude that we have criticized here, and to propose alternative approaches based on evolutionary and market principles (Miller and Drexler, 1988a, 1988b; Drexler and Miller 1988). These principles appear applicable to complex systems of all types, not merely those involving interacting human beings.

The great debate

Among the objects we made available to Avatars in *Habitat* were guns and various other sorts of weapons. We included these because we felt that players should be able to materially effect each other in ways that went beyond simply talking, ways that required real moral choices to be made by the participants. We recognized the age old story-teller's dictum that conflict is the essence of drama. Death in *Habitat* was, of course, not like death in the real world! When an Avatar is killed, he or she is teleported back home, head in hands (literally), pockets empty, and any object in hand at the time dropped on the ground at the scene of the crime. Any possessions carried at the time are lost. It was more like a setback in a game of "Chutes and Ladders" than real mortality. Nevertheless, the death metaphor had a profound effect on people's perceptions. This potential for murder, assault and other mayhem in *Habitat* was, to put it mildly, controversial. The controversy was further fueled by the potential for lesser crimes. For instance, one Avatar could steal something from another Avatar simply by snatching the object out its owner's hands and running off with it.

We had imposed very few rules on the world at the start. There was much debate among the players as to the form that *Habitat* society should take. At the core of much of the debate was an unresolved philosophical question: is an Avatar an extension of a human being (thus entitled to be treated as you would treat a real person) or a *Pac-Man-like* critter destined to die a thousand deaths or something else entirely? Is *Habitat* murder a crime? Should all weapons be banned? Or is it all "just a game"? To make a point, one of the players took to randomly shooting people as they roamed around. The debate was sufficiently vigorous that we took a systematic poll of the players. The result was ambiguous: 50% said that *Habitat* murder was a crime and shouldn't be a part of the world, while the other 50% said it was an important part of the fun.

We compromised by changing the system to allow thievery and gunplay only outside the city limits. The wilderness would be wild and dangerous while civilization would be orderly and safe. This did not resolve the debate, however. One of the outstanding proponents of the anti-violence point of view was motivated to open the first *Habitat* church, the Order of the Holy Walnut (in real life he was a Greek Orthodox priest). His canons forbid his disciples to carry weapons, steal, or participate in violence of any kind. His church became quite popular and he became a very highly respected member of the *Habitat* community.

Furthermore, while we had made direct theft impossible, one could still engage in indirect theft by stealing things set on the ground momentarily or otherwise left unattended. And the violence still possible in the outlands continued to bother some players. Many people thought that such crimes ought to be prevented or at least punished somehow, but they had no idea how to do so. They were used to a world in which law and justice were always things provided by somebody else. Somebody eventually made the suggestion that there ought to be a Sheriff. We quickly figured out how to create a voting mechanism and rounded up some volunteers to hold an election. A public debate in the town meeting hall was heavily attended, with the three Avatars who had chosen to run making statements and fielding questions. The election was held, and the town of Populopolis acquired a Sheriff.

For weeks the Sheriff was nothing but a figurehead, though he was a respected figure and commanded a certain amount of moral authority. We were stumped about what powers to give him. Should he have the right to shoot anyone anywhere? Give him a more powerful gun? A magic wand to zap people off to jail? What about courts? Laws? Lawyers? Again we surveyed the players, eventually settling on a set of questions that could be answered via a referendum. Unfortunately, we were unable to act on the results before the pilot operations ended and the system was shut down. It was clear, however, that there are two basic camps: anarchy and government. This is an issue that will need to be addressed by future cyberspace architects. However, our view is that a virtual world need not be set up with a "default" government, but can instead evolve one as needed.

A warning

Given the above exhortation that control should be released to the users, we need to inject a note of caution and present our next assertion:

You can't trust anyone.

This may seem like a contradiction of much of the preceding, but it really is not. Designers and operators of a cyberspace system must inhabit two levels of virtual world at once. The first we call the "infrastructure level", which is the implementation, where the laws that govern "reality" have their genesis. The second we call the "percipient level", which is what the users see and experience. It is important that there not be "leakage" between these two levels. The first level defines the physics of the world. If its integrity is breached, the consequences can range from aesthetic unpleasantness (the audience catches a glimpse of the scaffolding behind the false front) to psychological disruption (somebody does something "impossible", thereby violating users' expectations and damaging their fantasy) to catastrophic failure (somebody crashes the system). When we exhort you to give control to the users, we mean control at the percipient level. When we say that you can't trust anyone, we mean that you can't trust them with access to the infrastructure level. Some stories from *Habitat* will illustrate this.

When designing a piece of software, you generally assume that it is the sole intermediary between the user and the underlying data being manipulated (possibly multiple applications will work with the same data, but the principle remains the same). In general, the user need not be aware of how data are encoded and structured inside the application. Indeed, the very purpose of a good application is to shield the user from the ugly technical details. It is conceivable that a technically astute person who is willing to invest the time and effort could decipher the internal structure of things, but this would be an unusual thing to do as there is rarely much advantage to be gained. The purpose of the application itself is, after all, to make access to and manipulation of the data easier than digging around at the level of bits and bytes. There are exceptions to this, however. For example, most game programs deliberately impose obstacles on their players in order for play to be challenging. By tinkering around with the insides of such a program—dumping the data files and studying them, disassembling the program itself and possibly modifying it—it may be possible to "cheat." However, this sort of cheating has the flavor of cheating at solitaire: the consequences adhere to the cheater alone. There is a difference, in that disassembling a game program is a puzzle-solving exercise in its own right, whereas cheating at solitaire is pointless, but the satisfactions to be gained from it, if any, are entirely personal.

If, however, a computer game involves multiple players, delving into the program's internals can enable one to truly cheat, in the sense that one gains an

241

unfair advantage over the other players of which they may be unaware. *Habitat* is such a multi-player game. When we were designing the software, our "prime directive" was, "The backend shall not assume the validity of anything a player computer tells it." This is because we needed to protect ourselves against the possibility that a clever user had hacked around with his copy of the front end program to add "custom features." For example, we could not implement any of the sort of "skill and action" elements found in traditional video games wherein dexterity with the joystick determines the outcome of, say, armed combat, because you couldn't guard against someone modifying their copy of the program to tell the backend that they had "hit," whether they actually had or not. Indeed, our partners at QuantumLink warned us of this very eventuality before we even started—they already had users who did this sort of thing with their regular system. Would anyone actually go to the trouble of disassembling and studying 100K or so of incredibly tight and bizarrely threaded 6502 machine code just to tinker? As it turns out, the answer is yes. People have. We were not 100% rigorous in following our own rule. It turned out that there were a few features whose implementation was greatly eased by breaking the rule in situations where, in our judgment, the consequences would not be material if people "cheated" by hacking their own systems. Darned if people didn't hack their systems to cheat in exactly these ways.

Care must be taken in the design of the world as well. One incident that occurred during our pilot test involved a small group of players exploiting a bug in our world database which they interpreted as a feature. First, some background. Avatars are hatched with 2000 Tokens in their bank account, and each day that they login they receive another 100T. Avatars may acquire additional funds by engaging in business, winning contests, finding buried treasure, and so on. They can spend their Tokens on, among other things, various items that are for sale in vending machines called Vendroids. There are also Pawn Machines, which will buy objects back (at a discount, of course).

In order to make this automated economy a little more interesting, each Vendroid had its own prices for the items in it. This was so that we could have local price variation (i.e., a widget would cost a little less if you bought it at Jack's Place instead of The Emporium). It turned out that in two Vendroids across town from each other were two items for sale whose prices we had inadvertently set lower than what a Pawn Machine would buy them back for: Dolls (for sale at 75T, hock for 100T) and Crystal Balls (for sale at 18,000T, hock at 30,000T!). Naturally, a couple of people discovered this. One night they took all their money, walked to the Doll Vendroid, bought as many Dolls as they could, then took them across town and pawned them. By shuttling back and forth between the Doll Vendroid and the Pawn Shop for *hours*, they amassed sufficient funds to buy a Crystal Ball, whereupon they continued the process with Crystal Balls and a couple orders of magnitude higher cash flow. The final result was at least three Avatars with hundreds of thousands of Tokens each. We only discovered this the next morning when our daily database status report said that the money supply had quintupled overnight.

We assumed that the precipitous increase in "T1" was due to some sort of bug in the software. We were puzzled that no bug report had been submitted. By poking around a bit we discovered that a few people had suddenly acquired enormous bank balances. We sent *Habitat* mail to the two richest, inquiring as to where they had gotten all that money overnight. Their reply was, "We got it fair and square! And we're not going to tell you how!" After much abject pleading on our part they eventually did tell us, and we fixed the erroneous pricing. Fortunately, the whole scam turned out well, as the nouveau rich Avatars used their bulging bankrolls to underwrite a series of treasure hunt games which they conducted on their own initiative, much to the enjoyment of many other players on the system.

Keeping "reality" consistent

The urge to breach the boundary between the infrastructure level and the percipient level is not confined to the players. The system operators are also subject to this temptation, though their motivation is expediency in accomplishing their legitimate purposes rather than the gaining of illegitimate advantage. However, to the degree to which it is possible, we vigorously endorse the following principle:

Work within the system.

Wherever possible, things that can be done within the framework of the percipient level should be. The result will be smoother operation and greater harmony among the user community. This admonition applies to both the technical and the sociological aspects of the system.

For example, with the players in control, the *Habitat* world would have grown much larger and more diverse than it did had we ourselves not been a technical bottleneck. All new region generation and feature implementation had to go through us, since there was no means for players to create new parts of the world on their own. Region creation was an esoteric technical specialty, requiring a plethora of obscure tools and a good working knowledge of the treacherous minefield of limitations imposed by the Commodore 64. It also required a lot of behind-the-scenes activity that would probably spoil the illusion for many. One of the goals of a next generation *Habitat*-like system ought to be to permit far greater creative involvement by the participants without requiring them to ascend to full-fledged guru-hood to do so.

A further example of working within the system, this time in a social sense, is illustrated by the following experience. One of the more popular events in *Habitat* took place late in the test, the brainchild of one of the more active players who had recently become a QuantumLink employee. It was called the "Dungeon of Death".

For weeks, ads appeared in *Habitat's* newspaper, The Rant, announcing that that Duo of Dread, DEATH and THE SHADOW, were challenging all comers to enter their lair. Soon, on the outskirts of town, the entrance to a dungeon appeared. Out front was a sign reading, "Danger! Enter at your own risk!" Two system operators were logged in as DEATH and THE SHADOW, armed with specially concocted guns that could kill in one shot, rather than the usual twelve. These two characters roamed the dungeon blasting away at anyone they encountered. They were also equipped with special magic wands that cured any damage done to them by other Avatars, so that they wouldn't themselves be killed. To make things worse, the place was littered with dead ends, pathological connections between regions, and various other nasty and usually fatal features. It was clear that any explorer had better be prepared to "die" several times before mastering the dungeon. The rewards were pretty good: 1000 Tokens minimum and access to a special Vendroid that sold magic teleportation wands. Furthermore, given clear notice, players took the precaution of emptying their pockets before entering, so that the actual cost of getting "killed" was minimal.

One evening, one of us was given the chance to play the role of DEATH. When we logged in, we found him in one of the dead ends with four other Avatars who were trapped there. We started shooting, as did they. However, the last operator to run DEATH had not bothered to use his special wand to heal any accumulated damage, so the character of DEATH was suddenly and unexpectedly "killed" in the encounter. As we mentioned earlier, when an Avatar is killed, any object in his hands is dropped on the ground. In this case, said object was the special kill-in-one-shot gun, which was immediately picked up by one of the regular players who then made off with it. This gun was not something that regular players were supposed to have. What should we do?

It turned out that this was not the first time this had happened. During the previous night's mayhem the special gun was similarly absconded with. In this case, the person playing DEATH was one of the regular system operators, who, used to operating the regular Q-Link service, simply ordered the player to give the gun back. The player considered that he had obtained the weapon as part of the normal course of the game and balked at this, whereupon the operator threatened to cancel the player's account and kick him off the system if he did not comply. The player gave the gun back, but was quite upset about the whole affair, as were many of his friends and associates on the system. Their world model had been painfully violated.

When it happened to us, we played the whole incident within the role of DEATH. We sent a message to the Avatar who had the gun, threatening to come and kill her if she didn't give it back. She replied that all she had to do was stay in town and DEATH couldn't touch her (which was true, if we stayed within the system). OK, we figured, she's smart. We negotiated a deal whereby DEATH would ransom the gun for 10,000 Tokens. An elaborate arrangement was made to meet in the center of town to make the exchange, with a neutral third Avatar acting as an intermediary to ensure that neither party cheated. Of course, word got around and by the time of the exchange there were numerous spectators. We played the role of DEATH to the hilt, with lots of hokey melodramatic shtick. The event was a sensation. It was written up in the newspaper the next morning and was the talk of the town for days. The Avatar involved was left with a wonderful story about having cheated DEATH, we got the gun back, and everybody went away happy.

These two very different responses to an ordinary operational problem illustrate our point. Operating within the participants' world model produced a very satisfactory result. On the other hand, what seemed like the expedient course, which involved violating this model, provoked upset and dismay. Working within the system was clearly the preferred course in this case.

Current status

As of this writing, the North American incarnation of Lucasfilm's *Habitat*, QuantumLink's "Club Caribe," has been operating for almost two years. It uses our original Commodore 64 front end and a somewhat stripped-down version of our original Stratus backend software. Club Caribe now sustains a population of some 15,000 participants.

A technically more advanced version, called *Fujitsu Habitat*, has recently started pilot operations in Japan, available on Nifty Serve. The initial front end for this version is the new Fujitsu FM Towns personal computer, though ports to several other popular Japanese machines are anticipated. This version of the system benefits from the additional computational power and graphics capabilities of a newer platform, as well as the Towns' built-in CD-ROM for object imagery and sounds. However, the virtuality of the system is essentially unchanged and Fujitsu has not made significant alterations to the user interface or to any of the underlying concepts.

Future directions

There are several directions in which this work can be extended. Most obvious is to implement the system on more advanced hardware, enabling a more sophisticated display. A number of extensions to the user interface also suggest themselves. However, the line of development most interesting to us is to expand on the idea of making the development and expansion of the world itself part of the users' sphere of control. There are two major research areas in this. Unfortunately, we can only touch on them briefly here.

The first area to investigate involves the elimination of the centralized backend. The backend is a communications and processing bottleneck that will not withstand growth above too large a size. While we can support tens of thousands of users with this model, it is not really feasible to support millions. Making the system fully distributed, however, requires solving a number of difficult problems. The most significant of these is the prevention of cheating. Obviously, the owner of the network node that implements some part of the world has an incentive to tilt things in his favor there. We think that this problem can be addressed by secure operating system technologies based on public-key cryptographic techniques (Rivest, Shamir and Adelman, 1978; Miller et al, 1987).

The second fertile area of investigation involves user configuration of the world itself. This requires finding ways to represent the design and creation of regions and objects as part of the underlying fantasy. Doing this will require changes to our conception of the world. In particular, we don't think it will be possible to conceal all of the underpinnings to those who work with them. However, all we really need to do is find abstractions for those underpinnings that fit into the fantasy itself. Though challenging, this is, in our opinion, eminently feasible.

Conclusions

We feel that the defining characteristic of cyberspace is the shared virtual environment, not the display technology used to transport users into that environment. Such a cyberspace is feasible today, if you can live without head-mounted displays and other expensive graphics hardware. *Habitat* serves as an existence proof of this contention.

It seems clear to us that an object-oriented world model is a key ingredient in any cyberspace implementation. We feel we have gained some insight into the data representation and communications needs of such a system. While we think that it may be premature to start establishing detailed technical standards for these things, it is time to begin the discussions that will lead to such standards in the future.

Finally, we have come to believe that the most significant challenge for cyberspace developers is to come to grips with the problems of world creation and management. While we have only made the first inroads onto these problems, a few things have become clear. The most important of these is that managing a cyberspace world is not like managing the world inside a single-user application or even a conventional online service. Instead, it is more like governing an actual nation. Cyberspace architects will benefit from study of the principles of sociology and economics as much as from the principles of computer science. We advocate an agoric, evolutionary approach to worldbuilding rather than a centralized, socialistic one.

We would like to conclude with a final admonition, one that we hope will not be seen as overly contentious:

Get real.

In a discussion of cyberspace on Usenet, one worker in the field dismissed Club Caribe (*Habitat's* current incarnation) as uninteresting, with a comment to the effect that most of the activity consisted of inane and trivial conversation. Indeed, the observation was largely correct. However, we hope some of the anecdotes recounted above will give some indication that more is going on than those inane and trivial conversations might indicate. Further, to dismiss the system on this basis is to dismiss the users themselves. *They* are paying money for this service. They don't view what they do as inane and trivial, or they wouldn't do it. To insist this presumes that one knows better than they what they should be doing. Such presumption is another manifestation of the omniscient central planner who dictates all that happens, a role that this entire article is trying to deflect you from seeking. In a real system that is going to be used by real people, it is a mistake to assume that the users will all undertake the sorts of noble and sublime activities which you created the system to enable. Most of them will not. Cyberspace may indeed change humanity, but only if it begins with humanity as it really is.

Acknowledgements

We would like to acknowledge the contributions of some of the many people who helped make *Habitat* possible. At Lucasfilm, Aric Wilmunder wrote much of the Commodore 64 frontend software; Ron Gilbert, Charlie Kelner, and Noah Falstein also provided invaluable programming and design support; Gary Winnick and Ken Macklin were responsible for all the artwork; Chris Grigg did the sounds; Steve Arnold provided outstanding management support; and George Lucas gave us the freedom to undertake a project that for all he knew was both impossible and insane. At Quantum, Janet Hunter wrote the guts of the backend; Ken Huntsman and Mike Ficco provided valuable assistance with communications protocols. Kazuo Fukuda and his crew at Fujitsu have carried our vision of *Habitat* to Japan and made it their own. Phil Salin, our boss at AMiX, let us steal the time to write this paper and even paid for us to attend the First Conference on Cyberspace, even though its immediate relevance to our present business may have seemed a bit obscure at the time. We'd also like to thank Michael Benedikt, Don Fussell and their cohorts for organizing the Conference and thereby prompting us to start putting our thoughts and experiences in writing.

Notes

1 One of the questions we are asked most frequently is, "Why the Commodore 64?" Many people somehow get the impression that this was a technical decision, but the real explanation has to do with business, not technology. *Habitat* was initially developed by Lucasfilm as commercial product for QuantumLink, an online service (then) exclusively for owners of the Commodore 64. At the time we started (1985), the Commodore 64 was the mainstay of the recreational computing market. Since then it has declined dramatically in both its commercial and technical significance. However, when we began the project, we didn't get a choice of platforms. The nature of the deal was such that both the Commodore 64 for the frontend and the existing QuantumLink host system (a brace of Stratus fault-tolerant minicomputers) for the backend were givens.

2 *Habitat* contains its own fully-fledged economy, with money, banks, and so on. *Habitat's* unit of currency is the Token, reflecting the fact that it is a token economy and to acknowledge the long and honorable association between tokens and video games. Incidently, the *Habitat* Token is a 23-sided plastic coin slightly larger than an American quarter, with a portrait of Vernor Vinge and the motto "Fiat Lucre" on its face, and the text "Good for one fare" on the back; these details are difficult to make out on the Commodore 64 screen.

References

Alber, Antone F., *Videotex/Teletext: Principles and Practices* (McGraw-Hill, New York, 1985).

American National Standards Institute, *Videotex/Teletext Presentation Level Protocol Syntax*, North American PLPS (ANSI, December 1983).

Drexler, K. Eric, *Engines of Creation* (Anchor Press, Doubleday, Garden City, New York, 1986).

Drexler, K. Eric, and Miller, Mark S., "Incentive Engineering for Computational Resource Management", in Huberman, B.A., ed., *The Ecology of Computation* (Elsevier Science Publishers, Amsterdam, 1988).

Gibson, William, *Neuromancer* (Ace Books, New York, 1984).

Goldberg, Adele, and Robson, David, *Smalltalk-80: The Language and Its Implementation* (Addison- Wesley, Reading, Mass, 1983).

Hayek, Friedrich A., *Law Legislation and Liberty*, Volume I: Rules and Order (University of Chicago Press, Chicago, 1973).

Hayek, Friedrich A., *New Studies in Philosophy, Politics, Economics, and the History of Ideas* (University of Chicago Press, Chicago, 1978).

Hayek, Friedrich A., *The Fatal Conceit* (University of Chicago Press, Chicago, 1989).

International Standards Organization, *Information Processing Systems—Open System Interconnection–Transport Service Definition*, International Standard number 8072 (ISO, Switzerland, June 1986).

Miller, Mark S., Bobrow, Daniel G., Tribble, Eric Dean, and Levy, David Jacob, "Logical Secrets", in Shapiro, Ehud, ed., *Concurrent Prolog: Collected Papers* (MIT Press, Cambridge, 1987).

Miller, Mark S., and Drexler, K. Eric, "Comparative Ecology: A Computational Perspective", in Huberman, B.A., ed., *The Ecology of Computation* (Elsevier Science Publishers, Amsterdam, 1988a).

Miller, Mark S., and Drexler, K. Eric, "Markets and Computation: Agoric Open Systems", in Huberman, B.A., ed., *The Ecology of Computation* (Elsevier Science Publishers, Amsterdam, 1988b).

Popper, Karl R., *The Open Society and Its Enemies* (fifth edition) (Princeton University Press, Princeton, New Jersey, 1962).

Popper, Karl R., *Objective Knowledge: An Evolutionary Approach* (Oxford University Press, Oxford, 1972).

Rivest, R., Shamir, A., and Adelman, L., "A Method for Obtaining Digital Signatures and Public- Key Cryptosystems", in *Communications of the ACM*, Vol. 21, No. 2 (February 1978).

Sowell, Thomas, *A Conflict of Visions* (William Morrow, New York, 1987).

Sterling, Bruce, ed., *Mirrorshades: The Cyberpunk Anthology* (Arbor House, New York, 1986).

Sussman, Gerald Jay, and Abelson, Harold, *Structure and Interpretation of Computer Programs* (MIT Press, Cambridge, 1985).

Vinge, Vernor, "True Names", *Binary Star* #5 (Dell Publishing Company, New York, 1981).

15

HEARTS, CLUBS, DIAMONDS, SPADES

Players who suit MUDs

Richard Bartle[1]

Source: *Journal of MUD Research*, 1(1), 1996 (available online).

Abstract

Four approaches to playing MUDs are identified and described. These approaches may arise from the inter-relationship of two dimensions of playing style: action versus interaction, and world-oriented versus player-oriented. An account of the dynamics of player populations is given in terms of these dimensions, with particular attention to how to promote balance or equilibrium. This analysis also offers an explanation for the labelling of MUDs as being either "social" or "gamelike".

Preface

Most MUDs can trace their lineage directly back to Trubshaw's 1978 game (Bartle, 1990b; Burka, 1995) and, perhaps because of this heritage, the vast majority are regarded as "games" by their "players". For the convenience of its readers, this paper continues to view MUDs in this tradition; however, it should be noted that MUDs can be of considerable value in nongame (ie. "serious") applications (Bruckman, 1994a; Kort, 1991; Bruckman & Resnick, 1993; Curtis & Nichols, 1993; Evard, 1993; Fanderclai, 1995; Riner & Clodius, 1995; Moock, 1996). Indeed, the thrust of this paper emphasises those factors which should be borne in mind when attempting to create a stable MUD in general, whatever the application; it is only the terminology which is that of "fun" MUDs, not the subject matter. In any case, even those MUDs which are built, from the ground up, to be absolutely straight are still treated by users as if they were games in some respects, eg. by choosing whimsical names rather than using their real ones (Roush, 1993).

It is worthwhile considering for a moment whether MUDs (as they are generally played) really are games, or whether they're something else. People have many recreational activities available to them, and perhaps MUDs fit some other category better? Looking up the word "game" in a dictionary of synonyms (Urdang & Manser, 1980) elicits three related nouns: "pastime", "sport" and "entertainment" (a fourth, "amusement", is the general class of which the others are all examples). So it might be useful to ask:

Are MUDs

- games? Like chess, tennis, AD&D?
- pastimes? Like reading, gardening, cooking?
- sports? Like huntin', shootin', fishin'?
- entertainments? Like nightclubs, TV, concerts?

Or are they a combination of all four? Perhaps individual players even see the *same* MUD differently from each another?

These questions will be returned to at the end of this paper, along with some proposed answers.

A simple taxonomy

This work grew out of a long, heated discussion which ran from November 1989 to May 1990 between the wizzes (ie. highly experienced players, of rank wizard or witch) on one particular commercial MUD in the UK (Bartle, 1985). The debate was sparked by the question "What do people want out of a MUD?", and comprised several hundred bulletinboard postings, some of considerable length, typically concerning what the players liked, what they didn't like, why they played, and changes they would like to see to "improve" the game. Some 15 individuals took a major part, with perhaps another 15 adding their comments from time to time; this comprised almost the entire set of active wizzes during that period. Although at times the debate became quite intense, never did it lapse into the flaming which typically ends most open-ended, multi-speaker, online discussions.

The fact that the people contributing to this argument were the most advanced players in a MUD which allowed player-killing might, on the face of it, be taken as evidence that they would probably prefer more "gamelike" aspects over "social" ones. However, this was not the case: the MUD in question had players of all types in it, even at wiz level. (Later in this paper, an analysis is given as to how such a MUD can come to be).

When the participants had finally run out of new things to say, it became time for me (as senior administrator) to summarise. Abstracting the various points that had been raised, a pattern emerged; people habitually found the same kinds of thing about the game "fun", but there were several (four, in fact) sub-groupings into which opinion divided. Most players leaned at least a little to all four, but each tended to have some particular overall preference. The summary was generally well received by those who had participated in the debate.

Note that although this MUD was one in which player-killing was allowed, the taxonomy which is about to be described does (as will be explained later) apply equally to "social" MUDs. The advice concerning changes which can be made to affect the player make-up of a MUD is, however, less useful to social MUDs, or to ones with a heavy role-playing component. Also, the original discussion concerned only non-administrative aspects of MUDding; people who might play MUDs to learn object-oriented programming, for example, are therefore not addressed by this paper.

The four things that people typically enjoyed personally about MUDs were:

i   Achievement within the game context.

Players give themselves game-related goals, and vigorously set out to achieve them. This usually means accumulating and disposing of large quantities of high-value treasure, or cutting a swathe through hordes of mobiles (ie. monsters built in to the virtual world).

ii   Exploration of the game.

Players try to find out as much as they can about the virtual world. Although initially this means mapping its topology (ie. exploring the MUD's breadth), later it advances to experimentation with its physics (ie. exploring the MUD's depth).

iii   Socialising with others.

Players use the game's communicative facilities, and apply the role-playing that these engender, as a context in which to converse (and otherwise interact) with their fellow players.

iv   Imposition upon others.

Players use the tools provided by the game to cause distress to (or, in rare circumstances, to help) other players. Where permitted, this usually involves acquiring some weapon and applying it enthusiastically to the persona of another player in the game world.

So, labelling the four player types abstracted, we get: achievers, explorers, socialisers and killers. An easy way to remember these is to consider suits in a conventional pack of cards: achievers are Diamonds (they're always seeking treasure); explorers are Spades (they dig around for information); socialisers are Hearts (they empathise with other players); killers are Clubs (they hit people with them).

Naturally, these areas cross over, and players will often drift between all four, depending on their mood or current playing style. However, my experience having observed players in the light of this research suggests that many (if not most) players do have a primary style, and will only switch to other styles as a (deliberate or subconscious) means to advance their main interest.

Looking at each player type in more detail, then:

i   Achievers regard points-gathering and rising in levels as their main goal, and all is ultimately subservient to this. Exploration is necessary only to find new sources of treasure, or improved ways of wringing points from it. Socialising is a relaxing method of discovering what other players know about the business of accumulating points, that their knowledge can be applied to the task of gaining riches. Killing is only necessary to eliminate rivals or people who get in the way, or to gain vast amounts of points (if points are awarded for killing other players).

Achievers say things like:

> "I'm busy."
> "Sure, I'll help you. What do I get?"
> "So how do YOU kill the dragon, then?"
> "Only 4211 points to go!"

ii   Explorers delight in having the game expose its internal machinations to them. They try progressively esoteric actions in wild, out-of-the-way places, looking for interesting features (ie. bugs) and figuring out how things work. Scoring points may be necessary to enter some next phase of exploration, but it's tedious, and anyone with half a brain can do it. Killing is quicker, and might be a constructive exercise in its own right, but it causes too much hassle in the long run if the deceased return to seek retribution. Socialising can be informative as a source of new ideas to try out, but most of what people say is irrelevant or old hat. The real fun comes only from discovery, and making the most complete set of maps in existence.

Explorers say things like:

> "Hmm . . . "
> "You mean you *don't know* the shortest route from <obscure room 1> to <obscure room 2>?"
> "I haven't tried that one, what's it do?"
> "Why is it that if you carry the uranium you get radiation sickness, and if you put it in a bag you still get it, but if you put it in a bag and drop it then wait 20 seconds and pick it up again, you don't?"

iii   Socialisers are interested in people, and what they have to say. The game is merely a backdrop, a common ground where things happen to players. Inter-player relationships are important: empathising with people, sympathising, joking, entertaining, listening; even merely observing people play can be rewarding – seeing them grow as individuals, maturing over time. Some exploration may be necessary so as to understand what everyone else is talking about, and points-scoring could be required to gain access to neat communicative spells available only to higher levels (as well as to obtain a certain status in the community). Killing, however, is something only ever to be excused if it's a futile, impulsive act of revenge, perpetrated upon someone who has caused intolerable pain to a dear friend. The only ultimately fulfilling thing is not how to rise levels or kill hapless drips; it's getting to *know* people, to understand them, and to form beautiful, lasting relationships.

Socialisers say things like:

"Hi!"
"Yeah, well, I'm having trouble with my boyfriend."
"What happened? I missed it, I was talking."
"Really? Oh no! Gee, that's terrible! Are you sure? Awful, just awful!"

iv Killers get their kicks from imposing themselves on others. This may be "nice", ie. busybody do-gooding, but few people practice such an approach because the rewards (a warm, cosy inner glow, apparently) aren't very substantial. Much more commonly, people attack other players with a view to killing off their personae (hence the name for this style of play). The more massive the distress caused, the greater the killer's joy at having caused it. Normal points-scoring is usually required so as to become powerful enough to begin causing havoc in earnest, and exploration of a kind is necessary to discover new and ingenious ways to kill people. Even socialising is sometimes worthwhile beyond taunting a recent victim, for example in finding out someone's playing habits, or discussing tactics with fellow killers. They're all just means to an end, though; only in the knowledge that a real person, somewhere, is very upset by what you've just done, yet can themselves do nothing about it, is there any true adrenalin-shooting, juicy fun.

Killers says things like:

"Ha!"
"Coward!"
"Die!"
"Die! Die! Die!"

(Killers are people of few words).

How many players typically fall within each area depends on the MUD. If, however, too many gravitate to one particular style, the effect can be to cause players of other persuasions to leave, which in turn may feed back and reduce the numbers in the first category. For example, too many killers will drive away the achievers who form their main prey; this in turn will mean that killers will stop playing, as they'll have no worthwhile victims (players considered by killers to be explorers generally don't care about death, and players considered to be socialisers are too easy to pose much of a challenge). These direct relationships are discussed in more detail towards the end of this paper.

For the most part, though, the inter-relationships between the various playing styles are more subtle: a sharp reduction in the number of explorers for whatever reason could mean a gradual reduction in achievers, who get bored if they're not occasionally told of different hoops they can jump through for points; this could affect the number of socialisers (the fewer players there are, the less there is to talk about), and it would certainly lower the killer population (due to a general lack of suitable victims).

Making sure that a game doesn't veer off in the wrong direction and lose players can be difficult; administrators need to maintain a balanced relationship between the different types of player, so as to guarantee their MUD's "feel". Note that I am not advocating any particular form of equalibrium: it is up to the game administrators themselves to decide what atmosphere they want their MUD to have, and thus define the point at which it is "balanced" (although the effort required to maintain this desired state could be substantial). Later, this paper considers means by which a MUD can be pushed in different directions, either to restore an earlier balance between the player types, to define a new target set of relationships between the player types, or to cause the interplay between the player types to break down entirely. However, first a means is required of formally linking the four principal playing styles into aspects of a unified whole; this helps account for different degrees of adherence to particular styles, and aids visualisation of what "altering the balance" of a MUD might actually *mean*.

Interest graph

Consider the following abstract graph:

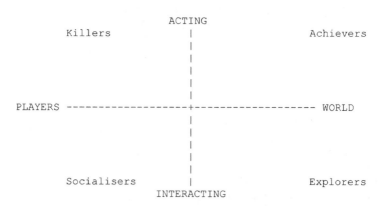

```
                          ACTING
           Killers          |              Achievers
                            |
                            |
                            |
                            |
                            |
   PLAYERS ----------------+------------------ WORLD
                            |
                            |
                            |
                            |
           Socialisers      |              Explorers
                       INTERACTING
```

The axes of the graph represent the source of players' interest in a MUD. The x-axis goes from an emphasis on players (left) to an emphasis on the environment (right); the y-axis goes from acting with (bottom) to acting on (top). The four extreme corners of the graph show the four typical playing preferences associated with each quadrant. To see how the graph works, it is appropriate to consider each of the four styles in detail:

i   Achievers are interested in doing things to the game, ie. in ACTING on the WORLD. It's the fact that the game environment is a fully-fledged world in which they can immerse themselves that they find compelling; its being shared with other people merely adds a little authenticity, and perhaps a competitive element. The point of playing is to master the game, and make it do what you want it to do; there's nothing intrinsically worthwhile in rooting out irrelevant details that will never be of use, or in idling away your life with gossip.

Achievers are proud of their formal status in the game's built-in level hierarchy, and of how short a time they took to reach it.

ii Explorers are interested in having the game surprise them, ie. in INTERACTING with the WORLD. It's the sense of wonder which the virtual world imbues that they crave for; other players add depth to the game, but they aren't essential components of it, except perhaps as sources of new areas to visit. Scoring points all the time is a worthless occupation, because it defies the very open-endedness that makes a world live and breathe. Most accomplished explorers could easily rack up sufficient points to reach the top, but such one-dimensional behaviour is the sign of a limited intellect.

Explorers are proud of their knowledge of the game's finer points, especially if new players treat them as founts of all knowledge.

iii Socialisers are interested in INTERACTING with other PLAYERS. This usually means talking, but it can extend to more exotic behaviour. Finding out about people and getting to know them is far more worthy than treating them as fodder to be bossed around. The game world is just a setting; it's the characters that make it so compelling.

Socialisers are proud of their friendships, their contacts and their influence.

iv Killers are interested in doing things to people, ie. in ACTING on other PLAYERS. Normally, this is not with the consent of these "other players" (even if, objectively, the interference in their play might appear "helpful"), but killers don't care; they wish only to demonstrate their superiority over fellow humans, preferably in a world which serves to legitimise actions that could mean imprisonment in real life. Accumulated knowledge is useless unless it can be applied; even when it is applied, there's no fun unless it can affect a real person instead of an emotionless, computerised entity.

Killers are proud of their reputation and of their oft-practiced fighting skills.

The "interest graph" is a representational structure which can chart what players find of interest in a MUD. The axes can be assigned a relative scale reflecting the ratio of an individual's interest between the two extremes that it admits. Thus, for example, someone who thinks that the people who are in the world are maybe twice as important as the the world itself would lie on a vertical line intersecting the x-axis at a point 1/6 of the distance from the origin to the left edge; if they had little interest in bending the game to their will, preferring their actions to have some give and take, then they would also lie on a horizontal line at the bottom of the y-axis. The intersection of the two lines would put them in the socialiser quadrant, with leanings to explorer.

It is, of course, possible to analyse the behaviour of individual players quantitatively by processing transcripts of their games. Unfortunately, this is very difficult to do except for very limited domains (eg. forms of communication (Cherny, 1995a; Cherny, 1995b)). An alternative approach might simply be to ask the players what they themselves like about a particular MUD: even a short questionnaire, completed anonymously, can give a fair indication of what players find enjoyable (Emert, 1993). Such information can then be used to determine the make-up of the MUD's player base, so that in times of falling player numbers the current composition could be compared against some earlier ideal, and remedial action taken to redress the imbalance. This "ideal" configuration would, however, be specific to that particular MUD, and its precise form is therefore not addressed here. Instead, the more general issue of how to alter the balance between player types is considered, along with the gross effects that can be expected to follow from having done so.

Changing the player type balance

A stable MUD is one in which the four principal styles of player are in equilibrium. This doesn't imply that there are the same number of players exhibiting each style; rather, it means that over time the proportion of players for each style remains roughly constant, so that the balance between the the various types remains the same. Other factors *are* important, to do with the rate at which new players arrive and overall player numbers, but their consideration is not within the brief of this paper; the interaction between players of different types *is* within its brief, however, and is discussed in some detail later.

The actual point of balance (ie. whereabouts in the interest graph the centre of gravity of the individual players' points lies) can vary quite enormously; it is up to individual administrators to determine where they want it to lie, and to make any programming or design changes necessary to ensure that this is where it actually does. What kind of strategies, though, can be employed to achieve this task?

In order to answer this question, consider the interest graph. If it is regarded as a plane in equilibrium, it can be tilted in a number of ways to favour different areas. Usually, this will be at the expense of some other (opposite) area, but not necessarily. Although tilting can in theory occur along any line in the plane, it makes sense (at least initially) to look at what happens when the tilt lines coincide with the x and y axes if the graph.

What follows, then, is a brief examination of means by which a MUD can be adjusted so as to favour the various extremes of the interest graph, and what would happen if each approach were taken to the limit:

Players

Putting the emphasis on players rather than the game is easy – you just provide the system with lots of communication commands and precious little else. The more the scales are tipped towards players, though, the less of a MUD you have and the more of a CB-style chatline. Beyond a certain point, the game can't provide a context for communication, and it ceases to be a viable virtual world: it's just a comms channel for the real world. At this stage, when all sense of elsewhere-presence is lost, you no longer have a MUD.

World

Tilting the game towards the world rather than its inhabitants is also easy: you simply make it so big and awkward to traverse that no-one ever meets anyone in it; alternatively, you can ensure that if they do meet up, then there are very few ways in which they an interact. Although this can result in some nice simulations, there's a loss of motivation implicit within it: anyone can rack up points given time, but there's not the same sense of achievement as when it's done under pressure from competing players. And what use is creating beautifully-crafted areas anyway, if you can't show them to people? Perhaps if computer-run personae had more AI a MUD could go further in this direction (Mauldin, 1994), but it couldn't (yet) go all the way (as authors of single-player games have found (Caspian-Kaufman, 1995)). Sometimes, you just *do* want to tell people real-world things – you have a new baby, or a new job, or your cat has died. If there's no-one to tell, or no way to tell them, you don't have a MUD.

Interacting

Putting the emphasis on interaction rather than action can also go a long way. Restricting the freedom of players to choose different courses of action is the mechanism for implementing it, so they can only follow a narrow or predetermined development path. Essentially, it's MUD-as-theatre: you sit there being entertained, but not actually participating much. You may *feel* like you're in a world, but it's one in which you're paralysed. If the bias is only slight, it can make a MUD more "nannyish", which newcomers seem to enjoy, but pushing it all the way turns it into a radio set. Knowledge may be intrinsically interesting (ie. trivia), but it's meaningless unless it can be applied. If players can't play, it's not a MUD.

Acting

If the graph is redrawn to favour doing-to over doing-with, the game quickly becomes boring. Tasks are executed repeatedly, by rote. There's always monotony, never anything new, or, if these *is* something new, it's of the "man versus random number generator" variety. People do need to be able to put into practice what they've learned, but they also need to be able to learn it in the first place! Unless the one leads to the other, it's only a matter of time before patience is exhausted and the players give up. Without depth, you have no MUD.

From the above list of ways to tilt the interest graph, a set of stratagems can be composed to help MUD administrators shift the focus of their games in whatever particular direction they choose. Some of these stratagems are simply a question of management: if you don't tell people what communication commands there are, for example, people will be less likely to use them all. Although such approaches are good for small shifts in the way a MUD is played, the more powerful and absolute method is to consider *programming* changes (programming being the "nature" of a MUD, and administration being the "nurture").

Here, then, are the programming changes which administrators might wish to consider in order to shape their MUD:

Ways to emphasise PLAYERS over WORLD:

- add more communication facilities
- add more player-on-player commands (eg. transitive ones like TICKLE or CONGRATULATE, or commands to form and maintain closed groups of personae)
- make communication facilities easy and intuitive
- decrease the size of the world
- increase the connectivity between rooms
- maximise the number of simultaneous players
- restrict building privileges to a select few
- cut down on the number of mobiles

Ways to emphasise WORLD over PLAYERS:

- have only basic communication facilities
- have few ways that players can do things to other players
- make building facilities easy and intuitive
- maximise the size of the world (ie. add *breadth*)
- use only "rational" room connections in most cases
- grant building privileges to many
- have lots of mobiles

Ways to emphasise INTERACTING over ACTING:

- make help facilities produce vague information
- produce cryptic hints when players appear stuck
- maximise the effects of commands (ie. add *depth*)
- lower the rewards for achievement
- have only a shallow level/class system
- produce amusing responses for amusing commands

258

- edit all room descriptions for consistent atmosphere
- limit the number of commands available in any one area
- have lots of small puzzles that can be solved easily
- allow builders to add completely new commands

Ways to emphasise ACTING over INTERACTING:

- provide a game manual
- include auto-map facilities
- include auto-log facilities
- raise the rewards for achievement
- have an extensive level/class system
- make commands be applicable wherever they might reasonably have meaning
- have large puzzles, that take over an hour to complete
- have many commands relating to fights
- only allow building by top-quality builders

These strategies can be combined to encourage or discourage different styles of play. To appeal to achievers, for example, one approach might be to introduce an extensive level/class system (so as to provide plenty of opportunity to reward investment of time) and to maximise the size of the world (so there is more for them to achieve). Note that the "feel" of a MUD is derived from the position on the interest graph of the MUD's players, from which a "centre of gravity" can be approximated. It is therefore sometimes possible to make two changes simultaneously which have "opposite" effects, altering how some individuals experience the MUD but not changing how the MUD feels overall. For example, adding large puzzles (to emphasise ACTING) and adding small puzzles (to emphasise INTERACTING) would encourage both pro-ACTING and pro-INTERACTING players, thereby keeping the MUD's centre of gravity in the same place while tending to increase total player numbers. In general, though, these strategems should not be used as a means to attract new players; strategems should only be selected from one set per axis.

The effects of the presence (or lack of it) of other types of player are also very important, and can be used as a different way to control relative population sizes. The easiest (but, sadly, most tedious) way to discuss the interactions which pertain between the various player types is to enumerate the possible combinations and consider them independently; this is the approach adopted by this paper.

First, however, it is pertinent to discuss the ways that players generally categorise MUDs today.

The social versus gamelike debate

Following the introduction of TinyMUD (Aspnes, 1989), in which combat wasn't even implemented, players now tend to categorise individual MUDs as either "social" or "gamelike" (Carton, 1995). In terms of the preceding discussion, "social" means that the games are heavily weighted to the area below the x-axis, but whether "gamelike" means the games are weighted heavily above the x-axis, or merely balanced on it, is a moot point. Players of social MUDs might suggest that "gamelike" means a definite bias on and above the x-axis, because from their perspective any explicit element of competitiveness is "too much". Some (but not most) players of gamelike MUDs could disagree, pointing out that their MUDs enjoy rich social interactions between the players despite the fact that combat is allowed.

So strongly is this distinction felt, particularly among social MUDders, that many of their newer participants don't regard themselves as playing "MUDs" at all, insisting that this term refers only to combat-oriented games, with which they don't wish to be associated. The rule-of-thumb applied is server type, so, for example, LPMUD => gamelike, MOO => social; this is despite the fact that each of these systems is of sufficient power and flexibility that it could probably be used to implement an interpreter for the other one!

Consequently, there are general Internet-related books with chapter titles like "Interactive Multiuser Realities: MUDs, MOOs, MUCKs and MUSHes" (Poirier, 1994) and "MUDs, MUSHes, and Other Role-Playing Games" (Eddy, 1994). This fertile ground is where the term "MU*" (Norrish, 1995) originates - as an attempt to fill the void left by assigning the word "MUD" to gamelike (or "player-killing") MUDs; its deliberate use can therefore reasonably be described as a political act (Bruckman, 1992).

This attitude misses the point, however. Although social MUDs may be a major branch on the MUD family tree, they are, nevertheless, still on it, and are therefore still MUDs. If another overarching term is used, then it will only be a matter of time before someone writes a combat-oriented surver called "KillerMU*" or whatever, and cause the wound to reopen. Denial of history is not, in general, a wise thing to do.

Besides, social MUDs do have their killers (ie. people who fall into that area of the interest graph). Simply because explicit combat is prohibited, there is nevertheless plenty of opportunity to cause distress in other ways. To list a few: virtual rape (Dibbell, 1993; Reid, 1994); general sexual harrassment (Rosenberg, 1992); deliberate fracturing of the community (Whitlock, 1994a); vexatious litigancy (Whitlock, 1994b). Indeed, proper management of a MUD insists that contingency plans and procedures are already in place such that antisocial behaviour can be dealt with promptly when it occurs (Bruckman, 1994b).

Social MUDs do have their achievers, too: people who regard building as a competitive act, and can vie to have the "best" rooms in the MUD (Clodius, 1994), or who seek to acquire a large quota for creating ever-more objects (Farmer, Morningstar & Crockford, 1994). The fact that a MUD might not itself reward such behaviour should, of course, naturally foster a community of players who are primarily interested in talking and listening, but there nevertheless *will* still be killers and achievers around – in the same way that there will be socialisers and explorers in even the most bloodthirsty of MUDs.

Researchers have tended to use a more precise distinction than the players, in terms of a MUD's similarity to (single-user) adventure games. Amy Bruckman's observation that:

> "there are two basic types [of MUD]: those which are like adventure games, and those which are not"
>
> (Bruckman, 1992)

is the most succinct and unarguable expression of this dichotomy. However, in his influential paper on MUDs, Pavel Curtis states:

> "Three major factors distinguish a MUD from an Adventure-style computer game, though:
>
> • A MUD is not goal-oriented; it has no beginning or end, no 'score', and no notion of 'winning' or 'success'. In short, even though users of MUDs are commonly called players, a MUD isn't really a game at all.
> • A MUD is extensible from within; a user can add new objects to the database such as rooms, exits, 'things', and notes. [. . .]
> • A MUD generally has more than one user connected at a time. All of the connected users are browsing and manipulating the same database and can encounter the new objects created by others. The multiple users on a MUD can communicate with each other in real time."
>
> (Curtis, 1992)

This definition explicitly rules out MUDs as adventure games – indeed, it claims that they are not games at all. This is perhaps too tight a definition, since the very first MUD was most definitely programmed to be a game (I know, because I programmed it to be one!). The second point, which states that MUDs must involve building, is also untrue of many MUDs; in particular, commercial MUDs often aim for a high level of narrative consistency (which isn't conducive to letting players add things unchecked), and, if they have a graphical frontend, it is also inconvenient if new objects appear that generate no images. However, the fact that Curtis comes down on the side of "social" MUDs to bear the name "MUD" at least recognises that these programs *are* MUDs, which is more than many "MU*" advocates are prepared to admit.

This issue of "social or gamelike" will be returned to presently, with an explanation of exactly *why* players of certain MUDs which are dubbed "gamelike" might find a binary distinction counter-intuitive.

Player interactions

What follows is a brief explanation of how players predominantly of one type view those other players whom they perceive to be predominantly of one type. Warning: these notes concern *stereotypical* players, and are not to be assumed to be true of any individual player who might otherwise exhibit the common traits of one or more of the player classes.

The effects of increasing and decreasing the various populations is also discussed, but this does *not* take into account physical limitations on the amount of players involved. Thus, for example, if the number of socialisers is stated to have "no effect" on the number of achievers, that disregards the fact that there may be an absolute maximum number of players that the MUD can comfortably hold, and the socialisers may be taking up slots which achievers could otherwise have filled. Also, the knock-on effects of other interactions are not discussed at this stage: a game with fewer socialisers means the killers will seek out more achievers, for example, so there is a secondary effect of having fewer achievers even though there is no primary effect. This propogation of influences is, however, examined in detail afterwards, when the first-level dynamics have been laid bare.

Achievers v. achievers

Achievers regard other achievers as competition to be beaten (although this is typically friendly in nature, rather than cut-throat). Respect is given to those other achievers who obviously are extraordinarily good, but typically achievers will cite bad luck or lack of time as reasons for not being as far advanced in the game as their contemporaries.

That said, achievers do often co-operate with one another, usually to perform some difficult collective goal, and from these shared experiences can grow deep, enduring friendships which may surpass in intensity those commonly found among individuals other groups. This is perhaps analagous to the difference between the bond that soldiers under fire share and the bond that friends in a bar share.

Achievers do not need the presence of any other type of player in order to be encouraged to join a MUD: they would be quite happy if the game were empty but for them, assuming it remained a challenge (although some do feel a need to describe their exploits to anyone who will listen). Because of this, a MUD can't have too many achievers, physical limitations excepted.

Achievers v. explorers

Achievers tend to regard explorers as losers: people who have had to resort to tinkering with the game mechanics because they can't cut it as a player. Exceptionally good explorers may be elevated to the level of eccentric, in much the same way that certain individuals come to be regarded as gurus by users of large computer installations: what they do is pointless, but they're useful to have around when you need to know something obscure, fast. They can be irritating, and they rarely tell the whole truth (perhaps because they don't know it?), but they do have a place in the world.

The overall number of explorers has only a marginal effect on the population of achievers. In essence, more explorers will mean that fewer of the really powerful objects will be around around for the achievers to use, the explorers having used their arcane skills to obtain them first so as to use them in their diabolical experiments . . . This can cause achievers to become frustrated, and leave. More importantly, perhaps, the number of explorers affects the *rate of advancement* of achievers, because it determines whether or not they have to work out all those tiresome puzzles themselves. Thus, more explorers will lead to a quicker rise through the ranks for achievers, which will tend to encourage them (if not overdone).

Achievers v. socialisers

Achievers merely tolerate socialisers. Although they are good sources of general hearsay on the comings and goings of competitors, they're nevertheless pretty much a waste of space as far as achievers are concerned. Typically, achievers will regard socialisers with a mixture of contempt, disdain, irritation and pity, and will speak to them in either a sharp or patronising manner. Occasionally, flame wars between different cliques of socialisers and achievers may break out, and these can be among the worst to stop: the achievers don't want to lose the argument, and the socialisers don't want to stop talking!

Changing the number of socialisers in a MUD has no effect on the number of achievers.

Achievers v. killers

Achievers don't particularly like killers. They realise that killers as a concept are necessary in order to make achievement meaningful and worthwhile (there being no way to "lose" the game if any fool can "win" just by plodding slowly unchallenged), however they don't pesonally like being attacked unless it's obvious from the outset that they'll win. They also object to being interrupted in the middle of some grand scheme to accumulate points, and they don't like having to arm themselves against surprise attacks every time they start to play. Achievers will, occasionally, resort to killing tactics themselves, in order to cause trouble for a rival or to reap whatever rewards the game itself offers for success, however the risks are usually too high for them to pursue such options very often.

Increasing the number of killers will reduce the number of achievers; reducing the killer population will increase the achiever population. Note, however, that those general MUDs which nevertheless allow player-killing tend to do so in the belief that in small measure it is good for the game: it promotes cameraderie, excitement and intensity of experience (and it's the only method that players will accept to ensure that complete idiots don't plod inexorably through the ranks to acquire a degree of power which they aren't really qualified to wield). As a consequence, reducing the number of killers *too* much will be perceived as cheapening the game, making high achievement commonplace, and it will put off those achievers who are alarmed at the way any fool can "do well" just by playing poorly for long enough.

Explorers v. achievers

Explorers look on achievers as nascent explorers, who haven't yet figured out that there's more to life than pursuing meaningless goals. They are therefore willing to furnish them with information, although, like all experts, they will rarely tell the full story when they can legitimately give cryptic clues instead. Apart from the fact that they sometimes get in the way, and won't usually hand over objects that are needed for experiments, achievers can live alongside explorers without much friction.

Explorers' numbers aren't affected by the presence of achievers.

Explorers v. explorers

Explorers hold good explorers in great respect, but are merciless to bad ones. One of the worst things a fellow explorer can do is to give out incorrect information, believing it to be true. Other than that, explorers thrive on telling one another their latest discoveries, and generally get along very well. Outwardly, they will usually claim to have the skill necessary to follow the achievement path to glory, but have other reasons for not doing so (eg. time, tedium, or having proven themselves already with a different persona). There are often suspicions, though, that explorers are too theoretical in most cases, and wouldn't be able to put their ideas into practice on a day-to-day basis if they were to recast themselves in the achiever or killer mould.

Explorers enjoy the company of other explorers, and they will play more often if they have people around them to whom they can relate. Unfortunately, not many people have the type of personality which finds single-minded exploring a riveting subject, so numbers are notoriously difficult to increase. If you have explorers in a game, hold on to them!

Explorers v. socialisers

Explorers consider socialisers to be people whom they can impress, but who are otherwise pretty well unimportant. Unless they can appreciate the explorer's talents, they're not really worth spending time with. There *are* some explorers who treat conversation as their specialist explorer subject, but these are very rare indeed; most will be polite and attentive, but they'll find some diversion if the conversation isn't MUD-related or if their fellow interlocutor is clearly way below them in the game-understanding stakes.

The explorer population is not directly affected by the size of the socialiser population.

Explorers v. killers

Explorers often have a grudging respect for killers, but they do find their behaviour wearisome. It's just *so* annoying to be close to finishing setting up something when a killer comes along and attacks you. On the other hand, many killers do know their trade well, and are quite prepared to discuss the finer details of it with explorers. Sometimes, an explorer may try attacking other players as an exercise, and they can be extremely effective at it. Explorers who are particularly riled by a killer may even decide to "do something about it" themselves. If they make such a decision, then it can be seriously bad news for the killer concerned: being jumped and trashed by a low-level (in terms of game rank) explorer can have a devastating effect on a killer's reputation, and turn them into a laughing stock overnight. Explorers do not, however, tend to have the venom or malice that true killers possess, nor will they continue the practice to the extent that they acquire a reputation of their own for killing.

The affect of killers on the explorer population is fairly muted, because most explorers don't particularly care if they get killed (or at least they profess not not). However, if it happens too often then they will become disgruntled, and play less frequently.

Socialisers v. achievers

Socialisers like achievers, because they provide the running soap opera about which the socialisers can converse. Without such a framework, there is no uniting cause to bring socialisers together (at least not initially). Note that socialisers don't particularly enjoy talking *to* achievers (not unless they can get them to open up, which is very difficult); they do, however, enjoy talking *about* them. A cynic might suggest that the relationship between socialisers and achievers is similar to that between women and men . . .

Increasing the achiever/socialiser ratio has only a subtle effect: socialisers may come to feel that the MUD is "all about" scoring points and killing mobiles, and some of them may therefore leave before matters "get worse". Decreasing it has little effect unless the number of active achievers drops to near zero, in which case new socialisers might find it difficult to break into established conversational groups, and thus decide to take their play elsewhere.

Note: although earlier it was stated that this paper does not address people who play MUDs for meta-reasons, eg. to learn how to program, I believe that their empirical behaviour with regard to the actions of other players is sufficiently similar to that of socialisers for the two groups to be safely bundled together when considering population dynamics.

Socialisers v. explorers

Socialisers generally consider explorers to be sad characters who are desperately in need of a life. Both groups like to talk, but rarely about the same things, and if they do get together it's usually because the explorer wants to sound erudite and the socialiser has nothing better to do at the time.

The number of explorers in a MUD has no effect on the number of socialisers.

Socialisers v. socialisers

A case of positive feedback: socialisers can talk to one another on any subject for hours on end, and come back later for more. The key factor is whether there is an open topic of conversation: in a game-like environment, the MUD itself provides the context for discussion, whether it be the goings-on of other players or the feeble attempts of a socialiser to try playing it; in a non-game environment, some other subject is usually required to structure conversations, either within the software of the MUD itself (eg. building) or without it (eg. "This is a support MUD for the victims of cancer"). Note that this kind of subject setting is only required as a form of ice-breaker: once socialisers have acquired friends, they'll invariably find other things that they can talk about.

The more socialisers there are in a game, the more new ones will be attracted to it.

Socialisers v. killers

This is perhaps the most fractious relationship between player group types. The hatred that some socialisers bear for killers admits no bounds. Partly, this is the killers' own fault: they go out of their way to rid MUDs of namby-pamby socialisers who wouldn't know a weapon if one came up and hit them (an activity that killers are only too happy to demonstrate), and they will generally hassle socialisers at every opportunity simply because it's so easy to get them annoyed. However, the main reason that socialisers tend to despise killers is that they have completely antisocial motives, whereas socialisers have (or like to think they have) a much more friendly and helpful attitude to life. The fact that many socialisers take attacks on their personae personally only compounds their distaste for killers.

It could be argued that killers do have a positive role to play from the point of view of socialisers. There are generally two defences made for their existence: 1) without killers, socialisers would have little to talk about; 2) without evil as a contrast, there is no good. The former is patently untrue, as socialisers will happily talk about anything and everything; it may be that it helps provide a catalyst for long conversations, but only if it isn't an everyday occurrence. The second argument is more difficult to defend against (being roughly equivalent to the reason why God allows the devil to exist), however it presupposes that those who attack other players are the only example of nasty people in a MUD. In fact, there is plenty of opportunity for players of all persuasions to behave obnoxiously to one another; killers merely do it more openly, and (if allowed) in the context of the game world.

Increasing the number of killers will decrease the number of socialisers by a much greater degree. Decreasing the number of killers will likewise greatly encourage (or, rather, fail to discourage) socialisers to play the MUD.

Killers v. achievers

Killers regard achievers as their natural prey. Achievers are good fighters (because they've learned the necessary skills against mobiles), but they're not quite as good as killers, who are more specialised. This gives the "thrill of the chase" which many killers enjoy - an achiever may actually be able to escape, but will usually succumb at some stage, assuming they don't see sense and quit first. Achievers also dislike being attacked, which makes the experience of attacking them all the more fun; furthermore, it is unlikely that they will stop playing after being set back by a killer, and thus they can be "fed upon" again, later. The main disadvantage of pursuing achievers, however, is that an achiever can get so incensed at being attacked that they decide to take revenge. A killer may thus innocently enter a game only to find a heavily-armed achiever lying in wait, which rather puts the boot on the other foot . . .

Note that there is a certain sub-class of killers, generally run by wiz-level players, who have a more ethical point to their actions. In particular, their aim is to "test" players for their "suitability" to advance to the higher levels themselves. In general, such personae should not be regarded as falling into the killer category, although in some instances the ethical aspect is merely an excuse to indulge in killing sprees without fear of sanction. Rather, these killers tend to be run by people in either the achievement category (protecting their own investment) or the explorer category (trying to teach their victims how to defend themselves against *real* killers).

Increasing the number of achievers will, over time, increase the number of killers in a typically Malthusian fashion.

Killers v. explorers

Killers tend to leave explorers alone. Not only can explorers be formidable fighters (with many obscure, unexpected tactics at their disposal), but they often don't fret about being attacked - a fact which is very frustrating for killers. Sometimes, particularly annoying explorers will simply ignore a killer's attack, and make no attempt whatsoever to defend against it; this is the ultimate in cruelty to killers. For more long-term effects, though, a killer's being beaten by an explorer has more impact on the game: the killer will feel shame, their reputation will suffer, and the explorer will pass on survival tactics to everyone else. In general, then, killers will steer well clear of even half-decent explorers, except when they have emptied a game of everyone else and are so desperate for a fix that even an explorer looks tempting . . .

Increasing the number of explorers will slightly decrease the number of killers.

Killers v. socialisers

Killers regard socialisers with undisguised glee. It's not that socialisers are in any way a challenge, as usually they will be pushovers in combat; rather, socialisers feel a dreadful hurt when attacked (especially if it results in the loss of their persona), and it is this which killers enjoy about it. Besides, killers tend to like to have a bad reputation, and if there's one way to get people to talk about you, it's to attack a prominent socialiser . . .

Increasing the number of socialisers will increase the number of killers, although of course the number of socialisers wouldn't remain increased for very long if that happened.

Killers v. killers

Killers try not to cross the paths of other killers, except in pre-organised challenge matches. Part of the psychology of killers seems to be that they wish to be viewed as somehow superior to other players; being killed by a killer in open play would undermine their reputation, and therefore they avoid risking it (compare Killers v Explorers). This means that nascent or wannabe killers are often put off their chosen particular career path because they themselves are attacked by more experienced killers and soundly thrashed. For this reason, it can take a very long time to increase the killer population in a MUD, even if all the conditions are right for them to thrive; killer numbers rise grindingly slowly, unless competent killers are imported from another MUD to swell the numbers artificially.

Killers will occasionally work in teams, but only as a short-term exercise; they will usually revert to stalking their victims solo in the next session they play.

There are two cases where killers might be attacked by players who, superficially, look like other killers. One of these is the "killer killer", usually run by wiz-level players, which has been discussed earlier. The other is in the true hack-and-slash type of MUD, where the whole aim of the game is to kill other personae, and no-one particularly minds being killed because they weren't expecting to last very long anyway. This type of play does not appeal to "real" killers, because it doesn't cause people emotional distress when their personae are deleted (indeed, socialisers prefer it more than killers do). However, it's better than nothing.

The only effect that killers have on other killers is in reducing the number of potential victims available. This, in theory, should keep the number of killers down, however in practice killers will simply attack less attractive victims instead. It takes a very drastic reduction in the number of players before established killers will decide to stop playing a MUD and move elsewhere, by which time it is usually too late to save the MUD concerned.

Dynamics

From the discussion in the previous section, it is possible to summarise the interactions between player types as follows:

To increase the number of achievers:

- reduce the number of killers, but not by too much.
- if killer numbers are high, increase the number of explorers.

To decrease the number of achievers:

- increase the number of killers.
- if killer numbers are low, reduce the number of explorers.

To increase the number of explorers:

- increase the number of explorers.

To decrease the number of explorers:

- massively increase the number of killers.

To increase the number of socialisers:

- slightly decrease the number of killers.
- increase the number of socialisers.

To decrease the number of socialisers:

- slightly increase the number of killers.
- massively increase the number of achievers.
- massively decrease the number of achievers.
- decrease the number of socialisers.

To increase the number of killers:

- increase the number of achievers.
- massively decrease the number of explorers.
- increase the number of socialisers.

To decrease the number of killers

- decrease the number of achievers.
- massively increase the number of explorers.
- decrease the number of socialisers.

What are the dynamics of this model? In other words, if players of each type were to trickle into a system, how would it affect the overall make-up of the player population?

The following diagram illustrates the flow of influence. Each arrow shows a relationship, from the blunt end to the pointed end. Ends are marked with a plus or minus to show an increase or decrease respectively; the symbols are doubled up to indicate a massive increase or decrease. Example: the line killers + ------------------> – achievers

means that increasing the number of killers will decrease the number of achievers.

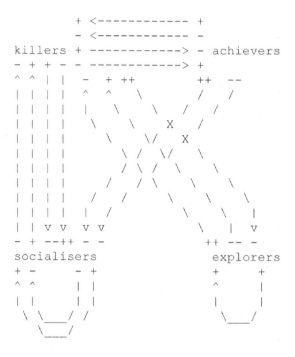

A graphical version of the figure appears at the end of the paper.[2]

From this, it can be seen that the numbers of killers and achievers is basically an equilibrium: increasing the number of achievers will increase the number of killers, which will in turn dampen down the increase in the number of achievers and thereby reduce the number of excess killers.

The explorer population is almost inert: only huge numbers of killers will reduce it. It should be noted, however, that massively increasing the number of explorers is the *only* way to reduce the number of killers without also reducing the player numbers in other groups. Because increasing the number of explorers in a MUD generally encourages others to join (and non-explorers to experiment with exploration), this gives a positive feedback which will eventually reduce the killer population (although recall the earlier point concerning how few people are, by nature, explorers).

The most volatile group of people is that of the socialisers. Not only is it highly sensitive to the number of killers, but it has both positive and negative feedback on itself, which amplifies any changes. An increase in the number of socialisers will lead to yet more socialisers, but it will also increase the number of killers; this, in turn, will reduce the number of socialisers drastically, which will feed back into a yet greater reduction. It is possible for new socialisers to arrive in large enough quantities for a downward spiral in numbers not to be inevitable, but it is unlikely that such a system could remain viable in over a long period of time.

This analysis of the dynamics of the relationships between players leads naturally to a consideration of what configurations could be considered stable. There are four:

1 Killers and achievers in equilibrium. If the number of killers gets too high, then the achievers will be driven off, which will cause the number of killers to fall also (through lack of victims). If there aren't enough killers, then achievers feel the MUD isn't a sufficient challenge (there being no way to "lose" in it), and they will gradually leave; new killers could appear, attracted by the glut of potential prey, however this happens so slowly that its impact is less than that of the disaffection among achievers. Socialisers who venture out of whatever safe rooms are available eventually fall prey to killers, and leave the game. Those who stay find that there aren't many interesting (to them) people around with whom to talk, and they too drift off. Explorers potter around, but are not a sufficient presence to affect the number of killers.

2 A MUD dominated by socialisers. Software changes to the MUD are made which prevent (or at least seriously discourage) killers from practising their craft on socialisers; incoming socialisers are encouraged by those already there, and a chain reaction starts. There are still achievers and explorers, but they are swamped by the sheer volume of socialisers. The number of socialisers is limited only by external factors, or the presence of killers masquerading as socialisers. If the population of socialisers drops below a certain critical level, then the chain reaction reverses and almost all the players will leave, however only events outside the MUD would cause that to happen once the critical mass had been reached.

3 A MUD where all groups have a similar influence (although not necessarily similar numbers). By nurturing explorers using software means (ie. giving the game great depth or "mystique", or encouraging non-explorers to dabble for a while by regularly adding new areas and features), the overall population of explorers will gradually rise, and the killer population will be held in check by them. The killers who remain do exert an influence on the number of socialisers, sufficient to stop them from going into fast-breeder mode, but insufficient to initiate an exodus. Achievers are set upon by killers often enough to feel that their achievements in the game have meaning. This is perhaps the most balanced form of MUD, since players can change their position on the interest graph far more freely: achievers can become explorers, explorers can become socialisers, socialisers can become achievers - all without sacrificing stability. However, actually attaining that stability in the first place is very difficult indeed; it requires not only a level of game design beyond

what most MUDs can draw on, but time and player management skills that aren't usually available to MUD administrators. Furthermore, the administrators need to recognise that they are aiming for a player mix of this kind in advance, because the chances of its occurring accidentally are slim.

4   A MUD with no players. The killers have killed/frightened off everyone else, and left to find some other MUD in which to ply their trade. Alternatively, a MUD structured expressly for socialisers never managed to acquire a critical mass of them.

Other types could conceivably exist, but they are very rare if they do. The dynamics model is, however, imprecise: it takes no account of outside factors which may influence player types or the relationships between then. It is thus possible that some of the more regimented MUDs (eg. role-playing MUDs, educational MUDs, group therapy MUDs) have an external dynamic (eg. fandom interest in a subject, instructions from a teacher/trainer, tolerance of others as a means to advance the self) which adds to their cohesion, and that this could make an otherwise flaky configuration hold together. So other stable MUD forms may, therefore, still be out there.

It might be argued that "role-playing" MUDs form a separate category, on a par with "gamelike" and "social" MUDs. However, I personally favour the view that role-playing is merely a strong framework within which the four types of player still operate: some people will role-play to increase their power over the game (achievers); others will do so to explore the wonder of the game world (explorers); others will do so because they enjoy interacting and co-operating within the context that the role-playing environment offers (socialisers); others will do it because it gives them a legitimate excuse to hurt other players (killers). I have not, however, undertaken a study of role-playing MUDs, and it could well be that there is a configuration of player types peculiar to many of them which would be unstable were it not for the order imposed by enforcing role-play. It certainly seems likely that robust roleplaying rules could make it easier for a MUD to achieve type 3) stability, whatever.

At this point, we return to the social/gamelike MUD debate.

Ignoring the fourth (null) case from the above, it is now much easier to see why there is a schism. Left to market forces, a MUD will either gravitate towards type 1) ("gamelike") or type 2) ("social"), depending on its administrators' line on player-killing (more precisely: how much being "killed" annoys socialisers). However, the existence of type 3) MUDs, albeit in smaller numbers because of the difficulty of reaching the steady state, does show that it is possible to have both socialisers and achievers co-existing in significant numbers in the same MUD.

It's very easy to label a MUD as either "hack-and-slash" or "slack-and-hash", depending on whether or not player-killing is allowed. However, using player-killing as the only defining factor in any distinction is an over-generalisation, as it groups together type 1) and type 3) MUDs. These two types of MUD should *not* be considered as identical forms: the socialising which occurs in a type 3)

MUD simply isn't possible in a type 1), and as a result the sense of community in type 3)s is very strong. It is no accident that type 3) MUDs are the ones preferred commercially, because they can hold onto their players for far longer than the other two forms. A type 1) MUD is only viable commercially if there is a sufficiently large well of potential players to draw upon, because of the much greater churn rate these games have. Type 2)s have a similarly high turnover; indeed, when TinyMUD first arrived on the scene it was almost slash-and-burn, with games lasting around six months on university computers before a combination of management breakdown (brought on by player boredom) and resource hogging would force them to close down - with no other MUDs permitted on the site for perhaps years afterwards.

This explains why some MUDs perceived by socialisers to be "gamelike" can actually be warm, friendly places, while others are nasty and vicious: the former are type 3), and the latter are type 1). Players who enter the type 3)s, expecting them to be type 1)s, may be pleasantly surprised (Bruckman, 1993). However, it should be noted that this initial warm behaviour is sometimes the approach used by administrators to ensure a new player's further participation in their particular MUD, and that, once hooked, a player may find that attitudes undergo a subtle change (Epperson, 1995).

As mentioned earlier, this paper is not intended to promote any one particular style of MUD. Whether administrators aim for type 1), 2) or 3) is up to them – they're all MUDs, and they address different needs. However, the fact that they *are* all MUDs, and not "MU*s" (or any other abbreviation-of-the-day), really should be emphasised.

To summarise: "gamelike" MUDs are the ones in which the killer-achiever equilibrium has been reached, ie. type 1); "social" MUDs are the ones in which the pure-social stability point has been reached, ie. type 2), and this is the basis upon which they differ. There is a type 3) "all round" (my term) MUD, which exhibits both social and gamelike traits, however such MUDs are scarce because the conditions necessary to reach the stable point are difficult or time-consuming to arrange.

Overbalancing a mud

Earlier, the effect of taking each axis on the interest graph to its extremes was used to give an indication of what would happen if a MUD was pushed so far that it lost its MUDness. It was noted, though, that along the axes was not the only way a MUD could be tilted.

What would happen if, in an effort to appeal to certain types of player, a MUD was overcompensated in their favour?

Tilting a MUD towards achievers would make it obsessed with gameplay. Players would spend their time looking for tactics to improve their position, and the presence of other players would become unnecessary. The result would be effectively a single-player adventure game (SUD?).

Tilting towards explorers would add depth and interest, but remove much of the activity. Spectacle would dominate over action, and again there would be no need for other players. The result of this is basically an online book.

Tilting towards socialisers removes all gameplay, and centres on communication. Eventually, all sense of the virtual world is lost, and a chatline or IRC-style CB program results.

Tilting towards killers is more difficult, because this type of player is parasitic on the other three types. The emphasis on causing grief has to be sacrificed in favour of the thrill of the chase, and bolstered by the use of quick-thinking and skill to overcome adversity in clever (but violent) ways. In other words, this becomes an arcade ("shoot 'em up") type of game.

It's a question of balance: if something is added to a MUD to tilt the graph one way, other mechanisms will need to be in place to counterbalance it (preferably automatically). Otherwise, what results is a SUD, book, chatline or arcade game. It's the *combination* that makes MUDs unique - and special. It *is* legitimate to say that anything which goes too far in any direction is not a MUD; it is *not* legitimate to say that something which doesn't go far enough in any direction is not a MUD. So long as a system is a (text-based) multi-user virtual world, that's enough.

Summary

To answer the questions posed in the preface:

Are MUDs

- games? Like chess, tennis, D&D?
  Yes - to achievers.
- pastimes? Like reading, gardening, cooking?
  Yes - to explorers.
- sports? Like huntin', shootin', fishin'?
  Yes - to killers.
- entertainments? Like nightclubs, TV, concerts?
  Yes - to socialisers.

Notes

1 This paper is an April 1996 extension of an earlier article, "Who Plays MUAs" (Bartle, 1990a). As a result of this, and of the fact that I am not a trained psychologist, do not expect a conventionally rigorous approach to the subject matter. Permission to redistribute freely for academic purposes is granted provided that no material changes are made to the text.

2 In the figure below, green indicates increasing numbers and red indicates decreasing numbers. A red line with a green arrowhead means that decreasing numbers of the box pointed from lead to increasing numbers of the box pointed to; a red line with a red

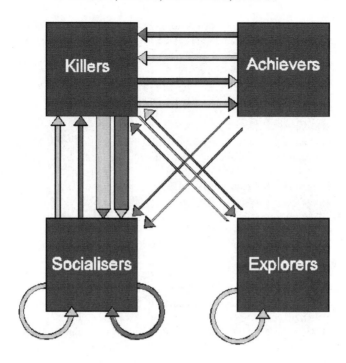

arrowhead would mean that a decrease in one leads to a decrease in the other, and so on. The thickness of the line shows the strength of the effect: thin lines mean there's only a small effect; medium lines mean there's an effect involving roughly equal numbers of players from both boxes; thick lines means there's a great effect, magnifying the influence of the origin box.

References

Aspnes, J. (1989). TinyMUD [C] http://ftp.tcp.com/ftp/pub/mud/TinyMUD/tinymudpc. 1.0.tar.gz

Bartle, R. A. (1985). MUD2 [MUDDLE] MUSE Ltd, Colchester, Essex, UK.

Bartle, R. A. (1990a). Who Plays MUAs? Comms Plus!, October/November 1990 18–19.

Bartle, R. A. (1990b). Interactive Multi-Player Computer Games. MUSE Ltd, Colchester, Essex, UK ftp://ftp.lambda.moo.mud.org/pub/MOO/papers/mudreport.txt

Bruckman, A. S. (1992). Identity Workshop: Emergent Social and Psychological Phenomena in Text-Based Virtual Reality. MIT Media Laboratory, Cambridge, Massachusetts. ftp:// media.mit.edu/pub/asb/papers/identity-workshop.ps

Bruckman, A. S. (1993). Gender Swapping on the Internet Proc. INET-93 ftp://media.mit. edu/pub/asb/papers/gender-swapping.txt

Bruckman, A. S. & Resnick, M. (1993). Virtual Professional Community: Results from the MediaMOO Project. MIT Media Laboratory, Cambridge, Massachusetts. ftp://media. mit.edu/pub/asb/papers/convergence.txt

Bruckman, A. S. (1994a). Workshop: "Serious" Uses of MUDs? Proc. DIAC-94 ftp:// media.mit.edu/pub/asb/papers/serious-diac94.txt

Bruckman, A. S. (1994b). Approaches to Managing Deviant Behaviour in Virtual Communities. MIT Media Laboratory, Cambridge, Massachusetts. ftp://media.mit.edu/pub/asb/deviance-chi94.txt

Burka, L. P. (1995). The MUDline. http://www.ccs.neu.edu/home/lpb/mudline.html

Carton, S. (1995). Internet Virtual Worlds Quick Tour: MUDs, MOOs and MUSHes: Interactive games, Conferences and Forums Ventana Press, Chapel Hill, North Carolina.

Caspian-Kaufman, J. (1995). Sid Meier's CivNET: Instruction Manual Microprose, Hunt Valley, Maryland.

Cherny, L. (1995a). The Modal Complexity of Speech Events in a Social MUD. Electronic Journal of Communication, Summer 1995. ftp://bhasha.stanford.edu/pub/cherny/ejc.txt

Cherny, L. (1995b). The Situated Behaviour of MUD Back Channels. Dept. Linguistics, Stanford University, California. ftp://bhasha.stanford.edu/pub/cherny/aaai.ps

Clodius, J. A. (1994). Concepts of Space in a Virtual Community. http://tinylondon.ucsd.edu/~jen/space.html

Curtis, P. (1992). Mudding: Social Phenomena in Text-Based Virtual Realities. Proc. DIAC92 ftp://ftp.lambda.moo.mud.org/pub/MOO/papers/DIAC92.txt

Curtis, P. & Nichols, D. A. (1993). MUDs Grow Up: Social Virtual Reality in the Real World. Xerox PARC, Palo Alto, California. ftp://ftp.lambda.moo.mud.org/pub/MOO/papers/MUDsGrowUp.txt

Dibbell, J. (1993). A Rape in Cyberspace. The Village Voice, December 21, 1993. ftp://ftp.lambda.moo.mud.org/pub/MOO/papers/VillageVoice.txt

Emert, H. G. (1993). "X" Marks the Spot. East Stroudsburg University, Pennsylvania. http://www-f.rrz.uni-koeln.de/themen/cmc/text/emert.n01.txt

Eddy, A. (1994). Internet After Hours Prima, Rocklin, California.

Epperson, H. L. (1995). Patterns of Social Behaviour in Computer-Mediated Communications. Dept. Sociology, Rice University. http://www.eff.org/pub/Net_culture/Misc_net_culture/ web_social_behaviour.paper

Evard, R. (1993). Collaborative Networked Communication: MUDs as System Tools. Proc. LISA-93 http://www.ccs.neu.edu/home/remy/documents/cncmast.html

Fanderclai, T. F. (1995). MUDs in Education: New Environments, New Pedagogies. Computer-Mediated Communication Magazine, 2(1), 8.

Farmer, F. R., Morningstar, C. & Crockford, D. (1994). From Habitat to Global Cyberspace. Proc. CompCon-94, IEEE http://www.communities.com/paper/hab2cybr.html

Kort, B. (1991). The MUSE as an Educational Medium BBN Labs, Cambridge, Massachusetts. ftp://musenet.bbn.com/pub/micromuse

Mauldin, M. L. (1994). Chatterbots, TinyMUDs and the Turing Test: Entering the Loebner Prize Competition. Proc. AAAI-94 http://fuzine.mt.cs.cmu.edu/mlm/aaai94.html

Moock, C. (1996). Virtual Campus at the University of Waterloo. http://arts.uwaterloo.ca:80/~camoock/virtual_classroom.htm

Norrish, J. (1995). MU*s. http://www.vuw.ac.nz/~jamie/mud/mud.html

Poirier, J. R. (1994). Interactive Multiuser Realities: MUDs, MOOs, MUCKs, and MUSHes. The Internet Unleashed, 1192–1127. SAMS Publishing, Indianapolis, Indiana.

Reid, E. (1994). Cultural Formations in Text-Based Virtual Realities. Dept. English, University of Melbourne, Australia. ftp://ftp.lambda.moo.mud.org/pub/MOO/papers/CulturalFormations.txt

Riner, R. D. & Clodius, J. A. (1995). Simulating Future Histories: The NAU Solar System Simulation and Mars Settlement. Anthropology & Education Quarterly 26(1):95–104. http://tinylondon.ucsd.edu/~jen/solsys.html

Rosenberg, M. S. (1992). Virtual Reality: Reflections of Life, Dreams and Technology. An Ethnography of a Computer Society. ftp://ftp.lambda.moo.mud.org/pub/MOO/papers/ethnography.txt

Roush, W. (1993). The Virtual STS Centre on MediaMOO: Issues and Challenges as NonTechnical Users Enter Social Virtual Spaces. MIT Media Laboratory, Cambridge, Massachusetts. ftp://media.mit.edu/pub/MediaMOO/Papers/STS-Centre

Urdang, L. & Manser, M. (1980). The Pan Dictionary of Synonyms and Antonyms Pan Reference, London, UK.

Whitlock, T. D. (1994). Fuck Art, Let's Kill!: Towards a Post Modern Community. gopher://actlab.rtf.utexas.edu/00/art_and_tech/rtf_papers/pmc.terrorism

Whitlock, T. D. (1994b). Technological Hierarchy in MOO: Reflections on Power in Cyberspace http://www.actlab.utexas.edu/~smack/papers/TechHier.txt

16

ENVIRONMENTAL STORYTELLING

Creating immersive 3D worlds using lessons learned from the theme park industry

Don Carson

Source: *Gamasutra*, March 2000, available at http://www.gamasutra.com/features/20000301/carson_pfv.htm.

For the past 15 years I have worked as a designer for many theme park, computer gaming, and software companies. In every project I undertake, I am faced with the same challenge, "How do I draw my audience into my imagined world and make them want to stay?" Whether it's a 100 million dollar Disney ride, a 3D shooter, or a kid's entertainment title, it is my objective to tell a story through the experience of traveling through a real, or imagined physical space. Unlike a linear movie, my audience will have choices along their journey. They will have to make decisions based on their relationship to the virtual world I have created, as well as their everyday knowledge of the physical world. Most important of all, their experience is going to be a "spatial" one.

If I have an all encompassing desire for any computer game I play or themed attraction I visit, it is this:

Take me to a place that:

Lets me go somewhere I could never go.
Lets me be someone I could never be.
Lets me do things I could never do!

The evolution of 3D gaming

Quake 3 Arena demonstrates the increasingly dramatic and realistic nature of 3D technology. Within the past decade we have been witness to the evolution of the 3D gaming universe. In games such as Wolfenstien, Doom, and now Quake 3 Arena, we can visit and explore worlds on our computer screens that are increasingly dramatic and realistic. The notion of walking through theatrical environments like those found in Cyan's Myst and Riven, real time, are not that far fetched. Yet, despite our staggering leaps in technology, the game play remains relatively unchanged. We may be transported into ever engrossing and elaborate theatrically lighted cathedrals, but the fact is, we are still simply killing each other. Please understand, I have nothing against 3D shooters. I have spent countless hours with a rocket launcher in my hands and know the glories of a low Ping rate. This doesn't change the fact that on many occasions I have been blown to bits because I dared hesitate to admire a beautiful piece of virtual architecture.

Despite these technological miracles, the audience that experiences these worlds are relatively small. Bloodshed and mayhem rein supreme, with many a computer savvy cyber gladiator having to wrestle a 3D accelerator card into the guts of their increasingly obsolete PC. But, times are changing, and it seems that we are on the brink of an untapped market potential. With more PC's coming onto the market with 3D accelerators built in, it is quite possible that your everyday Joe will have the power to visit increasingly realistic worlds from their desktop.

Theme parks and the virtual world

Prior to the mid-1990's, my experience and interest in the computer gaming world was marginal. Not until the release of games like Myst and Doom did I fully see a potential bridge between the theme park world I was working in and the world of the computer on my desktop. As my professional computer experience has grown, so has my belief that the two worlds are not that far apart. True, their audience demographics may be slightly different, but in many ways they face the same challenge: How to bring people into their created worlds and keep them immersed and entertained. Now with the growing popularity of multiplayer and internet games, computer environments are treading on a realm, until now, reserved for the physical world. Many thousands of people are connecting and participating in these virtual worlds with total strangers for one reason . . . . namely, the allure of the "shared" experience. A chance to make a human connection in these new worlds and to be able to say, "HEY! Did you see THAT!?"

One of the trade secrets behind the design of entertaining themed environments is that the story element is infused into the physical space a guest walks or rides through.

Because of this, there is a lot of knowledge that should be shared between these two seemingly different industries. Amusement parks have been entertaining people for over a 150 years. In the past 50 years theme parks like Disneyland, have taken the art of spatially entertaining people to new heights. No longer are rides simply a short lived thrill, now guests are fully immersed in stories, where they play the main character. Over the years these designers have developed tricks and trade secrets that (from experience) they know will work.

Environmental storytelling

One of the trade secrets behind the design of entertaining themed environments is that the story element is infused into the physical space a guest walks or rides through. In many respects, it is the physical space that does much of the work of conveying the story the designers are trying to tell. Color, lighting and even the texture of a place can fill an audience with excitement or dread.

Much of this is done by manipulating an audience's expectations, which they have based on their own experiences of the physical world. Armed only with their own knowledge of the world, and those visions collected from movies and books, the audience is ripe to be dropped into your adventure. The trick is to play on those memories and expectations to heighten the thrill of venturing into your created universe.

The importance of story

The first secret is "story." When I say story I am not talking about a linear "once upon a time" type story. I am talking about an all encompassing notion, a "big picture" idea of the world that is being creating. A set of rules that will guide, the design and the project team to a common goal. It is this first step that will insure the created world will be seamless. If you are creating a game or attraction based on, let's say "pirates", you'll need to play your audiences expectation like a violin. You want to pamper them by fulfilling every possible expectation of what it must be like to be a pirate. Every texture you use, every sound you play, every turn in the road should reinforce the concept of "pirates!" If you successfully establish a strong enough "story" early on in your design process, you will have little trouble keeping your team focused. If you break any of the rules, more often than not your team will argue, "we can't put that in there, that's not at all 'piratey'!"

Most important of all is once you have created this story, or the rules by which your imagined universe exists, you do not break them! These rules can be broad, but if they are broken your visitors will feel cheated. They will be slapped in the face with the contradiction and never again allow themselves to be as lost in your world as they may have been at the onset.

"Where am I?"

In the telling of your "story," the next most important task is to answer your audiences first question . . . . "Where am I?" No matter how well designed your environments are, if your audience can not answer this question in the first 15 seconds, you are already lost. This can be as simple as "Oh, I am in a dark warehouse." or "Ah, I am in the hold of a ship." Wherever it is, your first job is to present your audience with the opportunity to answer this question for themselves.

Your next question to answer is "What is my relationship to this place?" No matter how gorgeous your medieval castle, or abandoned space station might be, if they can't figure out what their role is in this place, you have missed out on a marvelous opportunity to pull your audience deeper into your world. This need not be done with lengthy CD liner notes or costly Intro AVIs. Clues can be left throughout your environment. Although you may not know who you are, you should be able to begin to have a notion based on your initial location. Valve's Half Life does an award winning job of playing with the player's desire for self identity, but only lets them come to a conclusion through their experience of the physical space and random encounters with peripheral game characters.

Self discovery can be even more enjoyable than having the story spelled out for you in the opening credits. There are lots of ways designers can place story elements throughout their environments to lead their audience to conclusions designed into the games plot.

Storytelling through cause and effect

One of the most successful methods for pulling your audience into your story environment is through the use of "cause and effect" vignettes. These are staged areas that lead the game player to come to their own conclusions about a previous event or to suggest a potential danger just up ahead. Some examples of "cause and effect" elements include, doors that have been broken open, traces of a recent explosion, a crashed vehicle, a piano dropped from a great height, charred remains of a fire . . . etc. These "cause and effect" bits of storytelling can help the game player better understand where they are and what they might expect to experience further on. Putting in an element just because it is "cool" misses a vital opportunity to use that element to help further your story along.

Half Life is an excellent example of cause and effect elements triggered by actions of the game player.

"Cause and effect" elements can also depict the passage of time. A game character may return to a place that they had become familiar with earlier in the game, only to find it completely altered. This may be due to a cataclysmic event, or the disappearance of elements remembered from a previous visit. "Cause and effect" elements could also be triggered directly by the actions of the game player. The best examples are found in games like Half Life and Duke Nukem 3D. In the case of Duke Nukem, the game player reaks havoc on his environment, blasting toilets, setting fire to palm trees, and making Swiss cheese of many architectural elements. After a lengthy Deathmatch, there is no doubt as to what has transpired in Duke's futuristic Los Angeles.

Another example of "cause and effect" is the use of what I call "Following Saknussemm." Derived from the story Journey to the Center of the Earth by Jules Verne. In Verne's story the main characters follow a trail of symbols scratched into subterranean walls by their adventuring predecessor, a sixteenth century Icelandic scientist, Arne Saknussemm. In this way, the game player is pulled through the story by following "bread crumbs" left behind by a fictitious proceeding game character. Whether you create notes scattered throughout your environments, or have the game player follow the destructive path of some dangerous creature, "cause and effect" elements will only heighten the drama of the story you are trying to tell!

The power of designing the familiar

Another powerful trick is to use the familiar in your designs. If your goal is to create an environment that is totally alien, it pays to periodically give your audience something familiar to anchor them themselves to. All too often, game designers will create a level built entirely of pulsating walls of intestine like material. Although the concept of such a place may sound "cool," it does more to alienate the game player than draw them in. If you can periodically give them some reference point . . . such as, "Oh, I am in a spaceship" or "Hey, this must be the engine room" you will be doing them a great favor. Even something like "Wow! These look like alien toilets!?!" will bring your audience back to relating to the environment, and even lend a little humor.

Remember, this is a theatre!

The buildings in the "Pirates of the Caribbean" attraction at Disneyland, despite appearing solid are entirely made of painted stretched canvas and example of clever theatrical magic. On several occasions I have had a chance to walk through the "Pirates of the Caribbean" attraction in Disneyland, CA. During my first visit, I took a breather in the "Auction Scene." As I leaned back against one of the Caribbean stucco buildings I was shocked to discover they were entirely made of painted stretched canvas! All through my childhood I had just assumed that the buildings were solid, and even today it is hard to remember they are only clever theatrical magic. It is important to remember that the virtual world is no different than a theatre stage or a film set. Although we don't use canvas and paint, we can learn much from the tried and true tricks handed down to us by 2000 years of theatre. Texture maps are our canvas sets and how we choose to use them will make or destroy the story we are trying to convey. Texture maps are not wallpaper, but our tool to trick the eye. Even though dynamic lighting is one of the many luxuries of the new 3D technology, don't let lighting dictate how an environment appears to your audience. If your texture has architectural details that are carving into, or stick out of the two dimensional surface, it pays to paint in the necessary shadows to help heighten the illusion of depth an drama. The more you can achieve in your texture maps the fewer polygons you will waste on frivolous details.

The design mantra "Less Is More" applies. Refrain from cluttering your spaces with complicated, busy, or loudly patterned textures. Visual complexity is a luxury that should be used lightly. Pick and choose where you place your accenting textures, and down play simpler patterns. Use your details as architectural arrows that help lead your audience from one space to another. One trick is to save your most decorative elements for areas you wish to draw your audience to. Rather than cluttering an unimportant corridor with gorgeous ornamentation, simply save one detailed element for the end of the hallway and let it draw your audience, like a dangling carrot, into the next space.

Another pitfall to be weary of is the overly illuminated environment. After a map builder has painstakingly finished a level, it is understandable that he/she should want to show off every nook and cranny. Unfortunately, too many lights flooding an environment washes out and flattens the illusion of depth. Just like a flash photo removes all sense of mood or drama, so does a map that's lighted like a Walmart. Don't be afraid to loose large areas of your map in shadow. Of course it is important that you do not hide vital game elements in the gloom, but use your lights to draw attention to only those things that are most important to your story!

It is easy to see that lighting can create marvelous dramatic effects, but the same can be true of the placement of props and objects. A large room with a single shaft of light illuminating a solitary prop is more effective than a room filled with detailed elements. If you have an important "cause and effect" prop you wish to highlight, compose all other textures and props in the space as merely supporting players to the important Story element. Be careful not to confuse the game player with too many choices at any given time. Though it is you who has orchestrated the environment, when it is done right, the game player has the illusion that they are in complete control of their character's destiny.

Using contrasting elements to your advantage

If you have ever visited a medieval cathedral or even a large old church, there is a reason the vast interior is so awe inspiring. What you may not realize when you enter, is that the architects of these places have forced you to enter the church through a small confined space, before revealing the monumental interior of the main church. This in done quite on purpose, and it is the contrasting effect of having been confined in a small space that makes the adjacent room all the more dramatic.

Contrast is another tool in the environmental designer's bag of tricks. Whenever possible, create variety in your spaces. Force your audience to wander through a cool lighted space before dropping them into a hot one. Give them the experience of disorder before you deliver them into a place of order. And above all, give them asymmetry whenever possible. The world we live in is far from geometrically perfect, and spaces where every chair, desk, and potted plant is lined up in a grid only helps emphasize how fake your world really is! This is the same with your architectural interiors. Many architectural monuments can be perfectly symmetrical, but in our lives little else is. If you must create a long expanse of repeating pillars, or some such element, make one unique among the rest. Nudge it out slightly, or knock the thing right over, it will only add life to an otherwise mathematically perfect, but boring, environment.

The paradox of designing environments for "gamers"

One challenge to designing successful environments in the computer is working in and around the expectations of your main client . . . . mainly "gamers." I had an experience of art directing an Indiana Jones type game for a gaming company. After painstaking work on making the environments as realistic as possible, I walked into the lead programmers office to witness my carefully rendered torch flames flickering at an unrealistic lightening pace. When I complained, the Programmer proudly argued that he had done it for "the gamers." To be specific, he wished to show off the remarkable frame rate of the game, and felt that "gamers" would appreciate the visual effect of a high frame rate over the realism of my environments.

Needless to say, there is a fine line between fulfilling the desires of creating a beautiful game, and creating a game that people will want to play. No matter how stunning your environments might be, if it's no fun, no one will buy it! The same is true of the layout of a particular space. Designing environments that optimize the enjoyment of firing rockets, may not be one that tells a slowly evolving story. This does not mean that we should be left with spaces that are no more than strategically placed platforms, no matter how ornate the decor. It is within these challenges that a team can lean back on a strong story. If you are creating arenas for gladiators to blast each other to bits, play up the gladiator arena aspect of the game rather than guild it in unrelated ornate textures. Above all, make the game playable, but use your knowledge and story to support the enjoyment of your game rather than confusing it.

I have also had the experience of working with team leaders who can only articulate their desires as "Make it more 'edgy' or "It's not awesome yet, I will tell you when it is." Sadly, I do not have foolproof advice to combat such statements, it's a part of this industry. I do however know that if you can establish a strong story, one that your whole team can agree on, arguments are usually relegated to small details rather than gutting and overhauling the look of the game 3 months before it ships!

The advantages of computer environments over theme parks

In theme parks Tomb Raider style back flips off 10 story cliffs are out of the question. There are several things that virtual environments can give you that theme parks can not. Foremost is the expensive limitation of building in the physical world. Theme park designs need to take into consideration the necessity to push as many people an hour as they can through their various attractions. One attraction alone can cost a 100 million dollars to build, and takes millions more per year to just keep it clean and running. Theme Park experiences run from 30 seconds to 15 minutes in duration and could never rival the 40 hours spent wandering the islands of Myst. Theme parks must always be aware of safety, so my Lara Croft back flips off 10 story cliffs are out of the question.

As a theme park designer, I have had to battle hard and fast to add more expensive themed light fixtures to a particular attraction, while in my computer environments I can just cut and paste. In the computer I am only limited by the number of polygons my machine can crunch and how willing I am to slow my progress down in favor of a room full of themed lamps. I am also reassured that as technology and computer processors get faster, my environments will be even richer and more detailed.

One area the computer has yet to master, is the physical experience of sitting next to your friend, parent, or loved one, and truly "living" through your adventure together. Sure, we can holler over our cubical at Johnson in accounting as we nail him with a rail gun, or wander through EverQuest with players in Japan, Austrailia, and Moscow, but we still can't sit close to our loved ones and friends and experience our adventure together. Goodness knows, one day we will!

Missed opportunities

For the time being, the ability to create virtual worlds is relatively new to us. I have no doubt that in the years to come we will continue to blaze new trails deep into this entertainment medium. Although we break new technological ground with every year that passes, I still find that I am left wanting. I long for the day we break away from rambling labyrinths for their own sake, whether they are dungeon passages, back street alleys, or miles of sewer pipes. I look forward to visiting virtual places that tell me more about where I am and what I am supposed to do. I want to use my wits and knowledge to get myself out of tight spots, and never again have to twitch my way through timed puzzles that force me to repeat my actions over and over to simply reach another level of the game.

With the growing popularity of multiplayer games and the promise of higher band widths, I relish the day I can meet friends and explore these worlds together. Places where our success isn't measured only in frags, and our rewards aren't merely based on how many fire beetles we have killed. I look forward to the day when the act of exploration actually builds relationships between it's players. I want my character to be tested. I want to be given the choice of sacrificing myself for a higher cause, or sacrifice others for my own petty rewards. I want to be given choices that test my relationship with other players. Force us to work together for a common goal, pull us apart, then bring us together, and make us pool our mental and emotional resources to get through this adventure in one piece.

In closing, I want to say that I relish the years to come. I can't wait to see what virtual worlds you will have created for us to explore. Push that envelope and bravely challenge the "way it has always been done before." Use your environments to draw us in deep, and build on the strength of a good Story, making it the back bone of your project. You have the power. You are the storytellers. Now . . . . . .

Take us somewhere we could never go.
Let us be someone we could never be.
Let us do things we could never do.

Part 3

HISTORY AND HISTORIOGRAPHICAL CONCERNS

17

THE HISTORY OF VIDEO GAMES

Steven D. Bristow

Source: *IEEE Transactions on Consumer Electronics*, (1), February 1977, 58–68.

Coin operated amusement machines have been around a long time. Versions of the slot machine were popular well before the 1890's.

The coin operated jukebox was preceded by the coin operated player piano. Wurlitzer was a player piano manufactured before they started making jukeboxes. In the 1930's the first pinball machine was invented. They are still with us today. Electromechanical games have been with us at least as long as the slot machines.

Electromechanical games have the advantage that the graphics can be as good as the artist. 3-D effects are easy to generate using real models. The use of 1/2 silvered mirrors allows floating effects.

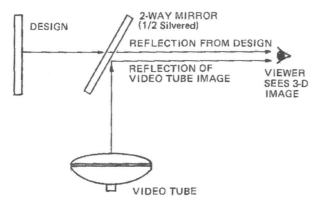

2-Way Mirror (1/2 Silvered)

These work by allowing the player to see the background directly. The object is seen through the 1/2 silvered mirror. Because it is painted in a fluorescent paint, it is seen while its supporting gear is invisible. Electromechanical games are limited in that:

A   Their use of mechanical brackets, motors, coins, linkages, etc. requires labor to assemble.

B   The cost of the electromechanical components has bottomed out years ago and is rising.

C   The kind of motions an object can have and the number of objects is limited by the cost and complexity of the components and labor needed to assemble them.

To get around these limitations and to allow better games, the first video games were created.

The first coupling of a computer with a graphics terminal to play games is unknown, but one of the very first applications occurred in Boston. There in the very early 1960's Steve Russell programmed a PDP-1 to play "Space War" From then on every computer center that had a graphics terminal had its games. "Space War" and its variants spread. The video games required a graphics terminal, but the word games only needed a teletype and a computer. They also spread even faster. The word games range in complexity from economic modeling situations to the games of "Wumpus" where you try to locate the "Wumpus" before he finds you. As computers spread so did the game playing spread, but not to the public. There were two problems keeping computer games away from the public. First of all, no one tried it. That is a basic, simple and easy to cure problem, but so are many fundamental problems, once you recognize them. Secondly, the cost of components was too high. To pay off a game that is being operated on 25¢ play, the operator can't spend over a few thousand dollars for the game. These economics rule out $5,000 terminals much less $100,000 vector drawing terminals or $3,000 to $10,000 computers.

Video games finally came to the public when the potential market of video games in both the coin-operated and consumer field was recognized, which solved the first basic problem, and when the circuit techniques and cost of components came down with the dawn of integrated circuits, which solved the second problem.

The video game first appeared before the public in two forms: coin-operated and consumer versions.

The first games I will talk about are the coin-operated ones. The first coin-operated video game was invented by Nolan Bushnell, Chairman of the Board of Atari, Inc. He had a background of operating games to finance his college education that allowed him to recognize the market. He was working in "Silicon Gulch" and saw the prices fall. He left Ampex and joined Nutting Associates in Mountain View, California, to finish his first design. It was "Computer Space". "Computer Space" was first shown to the public at a trade show in 1971 and was in production by 1972. It featured a cheap raster monitor (G.E. 19" TV with compactron tubes) and about 185 T^2L MSI and SSI IC's. Its design was feasible due to some innovative design by Nolan and by the plummeting cost of T^2L. It sold for $1,850 complete. Nolan left Nutting to form Atari, Inc., now a division of Warner Communications, Inc. Atari has come out with at least twelve new video games a year since 1972. Because the coin-operated game has lower volume and a higher price of sale than the consumer product, more products have been attempted in the coin-operated field. Now, with the advent of the microprocessor controlled consumer game, many manufacturers are looking at the coin-operated game hits and trying to apply them to the consumer field. This synergism will in all likelihood continue now that the coin-operated game manufacturers have switched to micro-processor designs: the 6800, 6502, F8, and 8080 seem to be the ones being used now. Because of the size and cost parameters of the coin-operated market, I believe that it will continue to be used as a test bed for consumer game ideas.

The consumer game was being introduced to the public about the same time as the coin-operated game. In 1972 Magnavox introduced Odyssey. It was a ball and paddle game using patented circuitry developed by Sanders Associates. The objects displayed were generated by the analog techniques of ramps, differentiators and slicers. Until fall of 1975, it was the only video game in town.

In the fall of 1975 Atari introduced through Sears, Roebuck and Company its PONG™ game. The Atari approach differed from that of Magnavox in that the PONG™ game's entire logic was on one digital IC. The only parts external to the chip were the controls, sound output stage, clock and RF output circuitry. The total test and adjustment time on a PONG™ game is less than a minute, using purely manual techniques. The switch to digital circuitry brought to the consumer games more precise, repeatable and reliable games than heretofore had been possible. The switch to digital techniques has been joined by most of the other entrants in the consumer game field.

Later, I will go into exactly how the PONG™ game works, but first, let me go into some of the special needs of the coin-operated video game. First of all, a coin-operated game must be reliable. The electronics exist in a locked box. A simple thing like a vertical hold control that might have to be adjusted once each ninety-six hours of use would be unacceptable as the game owner would have to make a service call in order to do this. A further incentive for the game manufacturer to eliminate adjustments is the fact that the game industry is just now getting out of relays. A game manufacturer just can't count on having a qualified person around to make any adjustments. For the manufacturer, it is best to have *NO* critical controls on a game. To illustrate another requirement let me quote an Atari design rule: "King Kong plays our games". The coin-operated games must be built to withstand intentional dropping, kicking and beating. In typical use the owner is far removed and the player has no interest in the machine's welfare. The game must be constructed so no beer or other liquid may reach the critical internal parts when poured intentionally onto or into the cabinet. Thirdly, the coin-operated game must be immune to power variations, transients, and static electricity. The same coin-operated game must be able to operate on 50 cycle – 90 volt, 60 cycle – 110 volt, and 50 cycle – 220 volt power. It must not lose regulation or lock. Many games are operated off of regulated AC power sources in locations like carnivals. The other power related problem of the coin-operated game is static. When hit with a 30KV discharge from the finger tip of a player who has just shuffled across a nylon carpet in the low humidity of Chicago in the winter. The coin-operated game must not give away a free game or be damaged. Grounding and safety are

PONG Block Diagram

also very important as many games are operated at seashore environments where the players are wet and conductive to the ground. All of these factors: reliability, abuse, static, and safety make the life of the game designer an interesting one.

What can be done on a TV game? Literally anything can be done. Games have ranged from PONG™, a simple ball and paddle game, to a four-player and sixteen-player ball and paddle game. There are battle games like TANK™, JETFIGHTER™, ANTI-AIRCRAFT™, PURSUIT™, TANK 8™, and COP'S 'N ROBBERS™. There are abstract games like GOTCHA™, a chase game in a maze, and CROSSFIRE™, a conservation of momentum game. There are driving games like TRAK 10™, TRAK 20™, LEMANS™, and SPRINT™. There are simulation games like STEEPLE-CHASE™, a horse race, STUNT CYCLE™, a motorcycle car jumping game, FLYBALL™, a baseball game, and WORLD CUP SOCCER™, a soccer game. Anything that is enjoyable and fun will or has been simulated for fun and profit on the screen of a TV game.

The preceding has been in the way of a lead in to dissecting and explaining the block diagram and circuitry of a coin-operated PONG™ game.

The PONG™ is basically composed of a sync, scoring, paddle generation, sound, ball generation and control, and credit sections. Each will now be explained in detail.

Description of blocks of PONG™ game sync section

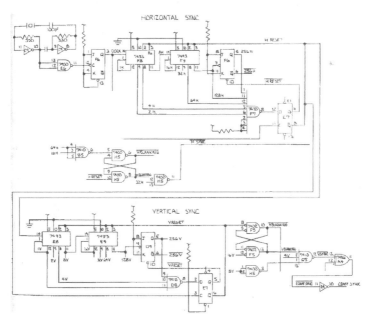

PONG Sync Section

293

The master oscillator for the game is implemented in two inverters back to back. The wave form from the oscillator is squared up by a logic gate E6, and is divided by 2, by a flip-flop F6. Starting from a 14 MHz crystal after being divided down the basic clock of the system is a 7 MHz signal. This clock is counted by a nine stage ripple counter composed of two 7493's and a single flip-flop. When a count of 454 is reached and detected by a gate on the next rising edge of the clock, the counter chain is reset by the signal from flip-flop E7. The counters operate on the falling edge of the clock and the reset detecting flip-flop operates on the rising edge of the clock, thus eliminating propagation problems with the ripple counters. The vertical sync counter counts the horizontal reset pulses. It is composed of two 7493 ripple counters and a JK flip-flop acting as divide by two. In a similar fashion to the horizontal system this chain detects a count of 261 and resets the system. The internal states of both the vertical and horizontal counters are used for timing signals throughout the system. Counts 0 through 80 are reserved for a horizontal blanking interval internally. They are created by cross-coupled nand-gates H5. *The horizontal* blanking signal is gated with the 32H function and this becomes horizontal sync. In a similar manner the vertical blanking signals are created by two cross-coupled NOR gates. The vertical blanking signal is anded with two more vertical functions 4V and 8V to create vertical sync bar. These signals are combined in an exclusive OR gate which not only has the function of both combining the vertical and horizontal sync, but also of inverting the polarity of the horizontal sync during the vertical blanking interval. This sync signal is inverted and summed into the vertical signal.

Coin detection

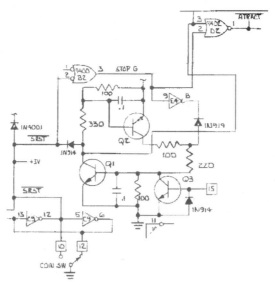

PONG Coin Detection

The coin switch is a single pole double throw micro-switch that is actuated by a coin passing by it. This signal is debounced by the coupled inverters C9. After being debounced it is used to pull down the set line of a discrete component flip-flop that controls the state of the game. This flip-flop is composed of transistors Q1 and Q2, and their associated components. This flip-flop also has a couple of unique features. It is always guaranteed to come up in a low state from power on. If the power ever drops below approximately 4 volts, it will revert from a high state if it was in one, to a low state. This flip-flop also has been built to be especially slow. Both base emitter functions of the transistors are bypassed with capacitors. All these features were designed in so that no one could get a free play by disconnecting and reconnecting the power or hitting the game with bolts of static. In addition to Q1 and Q2 there is one more component credit detection circuitry. Transistor Q3 acts upon the base of Q1 to turn Q1 off in case Q3 comes on. The base of Q3 is fed to the outside world by means of a two foot length of wire connected in the harness of the game but disconnected and hanging free at its extremity. This wire is a static detector. If a large enough static bolt happens that might tend to even upset the discrete flip-flop, Q3 will conduct and shut down or keep shut down the discrete flip-flop for some amount of time. The state of the discrete flip-flop is sensed at the collector of Q1, and is used to decide whether the game is in play or not. The flip-flop is reset by means of turning off Q1 by applying a stop game signal through a diode coupled to Q1's base.

Sound

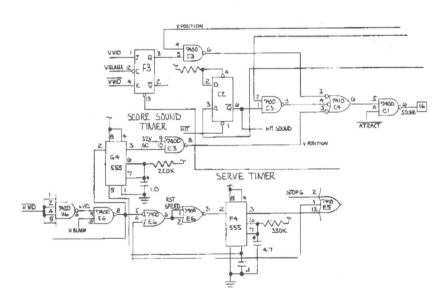

PONG Sound

All the sounds in the PONG™ game generated on board. They are all digital sounds. They emerge from the board as logic levels which are coupled into the sound amplifier in the monitor. The sounds are basically convenient sync sub-multiples that are gated out to the sound circuit. The miss sound is generated by a miss toggling the trigger pin of a 555 timer #G4. During the time that the output of the timer is high, the 32V tone frequency is gated out of gate C3. When there is a hit flip-flop C2 is set. Flip-flop C2 is reset the next time the ball position counter reaches the terminal count. This will be about one frame. During that time, one of the less significant bits of the ball vertical position counter is gated out through gate C3. When the ball reaches a vertical boundary, as on a bounce, flip-flop F3 is set. Flip-flop F3 is reset as soon as the ball bounces off the boundary. During the time the output of F3 is high, one of the ball vertical position signals is gated out through gate C3. All the sounds are then OR'd together in an OR gate (C4) and gated out to the monitor when the game is in play. When the game is not in play the attract signal on gate C1 prevents the sounds from appearing.

Score

Each player's score is accumulated in a counter composed of a 7490 decode counter and a flip-flop for the half digit overflow. Whenever a ball misses a paddle and exits the game, a score pulse is created. This is gated to the appropriate counter by a left-right signal. The signal is low on the left side of the screen for the left signal and low on the right side of the screen for the right signal. These signals then gate the score pulse to the appropriate 7490 counter. The digits of the scores (4) are multiplexed by two four to one multiplexers. The address to the multiplexer depends on where the TV scan is across the horizontal line. During the time any score is displayed the four bits of its data are outputed from the multiplexer. These multiplexers are C6 and D6. These four bits are decoded by a 7448 BCD to 7 segment decoder. The vertical and horizontal coarse decoding of windows in which the score should appear is done in the gates that AND and OR together the various horizontal and vertical functions to create the enable signal for the 7448. These coding gates are G1, F2, D2, and E3. The output of the 7448 is 7 bits of data, one for each segment of the score. Further gating combines the various fine detail horizontal and vertical signals to create the appropriate segment video. These seven segment bits from the decoder then act to gate these segments in gates D4, C4 and D5. The output of the individual segment gates is then combined in an OR gate. The output of the OR gate is the actual score video. This video is then summed into the monitor video along with the sync information.

Video summer

The video summer is simply composed of three resistors which resistively add together the video logic signals from the game video, sync, and score sections of the game. This signal is then AC coupled into the monitor.

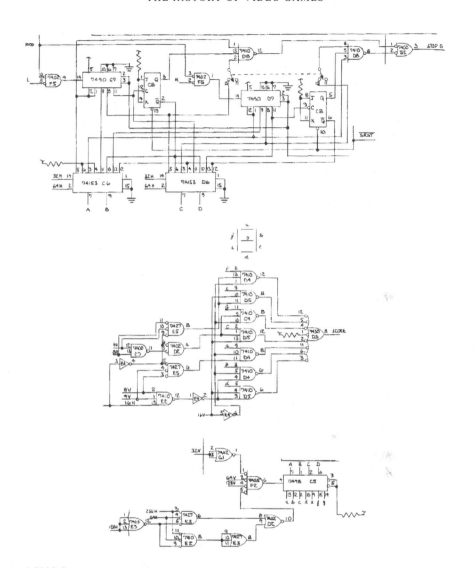

PONG Score

PONG Video Summer

297

Power supply

The power supply of the game is quite simple. A 16V AC signal is full wave rectified and roughly filtered. It then goes to a single three terminal voltage regulator. The output of the regulator is the regulated 5V supply for the whole game. The single three terminal regulator was picked because of its thermal protection, short circuit protection and pure simplicity.

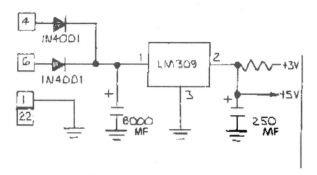

PONG Power Supply

Paddle generation

The paddles are generated by two identical circuits. A 555 timer is triggered at the start of every frame by the 256V signal. The player controls a paddle by manipulating the control voltage applied to pin 5 of the 555 timer. The player's input signal which is the signal off the wiper of a pot which has either end of the pot connected to +5 or ground, is isolated from the game circuitry by means of a 470Ω series resistor and a 0.1 μF bypass capacitor before the signal is applied to the 555 timer. The basic period of the 555 is set by RC combination connected to pin 6 and 7 of the 555. The output of the one shot is used to reset a 7493 paddle position counter when the output is high. When the one shot has timed out the 7493 counter is allowed to count. When the 7493 counter has reached an all one state, this fact is decoded by gate A7 and is used to prevent the 7493 from receiving any more clock pulses. The 7493 retains then the all one state until reset by the rising output of the 555 timer. When allowed to count, the 7493 counter counts horizontal sync pulses. Thus, during the time it is counting, the 7493's state will reflect the number of lines that have transpired since the player's paddle one shot timed out. The state of the 7493 counter will be used in the ball control section of the game to decide where the ball hit the paddle. The fact that the paddle is there vertically at all is decoded by gate B7, which outputs the signal when the condition exists that the 555 timer has timed out and the 7493 counter has not finished counting.

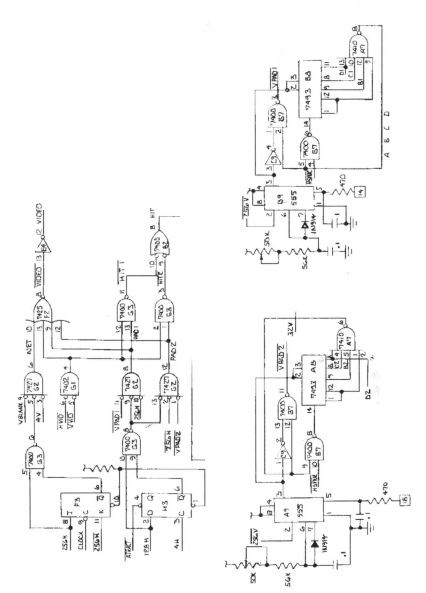

PONG Paddle Generation

Ball motion

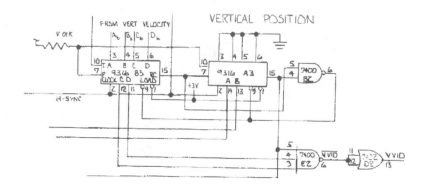

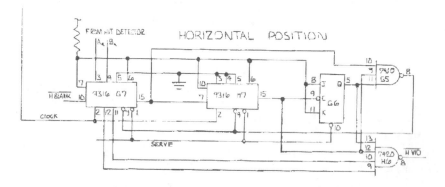

PONG Ball Motion

The method of motion used on PONG™ was invented by our Chairman, Nolan Bushnell. It allows the circuitry used to move the ball all over the screen to any one of roughly 64k positions with roughly eight (8) chips. The circuitry works by duplicating the horizontal and vertical sync counters for the ball. The division rate of the ball position counters is adjustable to be more than equal to or less than the corresponding sync counter. A state of the motion counter is decoded to become the ball. If the H-motion counter has the same rate as the H sync counter, the ball stands still on the screen. If the H-motion counter counts less than the H sync counter, the ball moves to the left as the counters slip in relation to each other. Motion to the right is accomplished by having the motion counter count longer than the sync counter.

The sync counter defines the position of the beam on the screen, while the ball counter defines when the ball occurs. If the counters slip, the ball moves.

The actual implementation follows. Four (4) bit counters G7 and H7 along with flip-flop GG comprise the H ball position counter. Its state is decoded by

300

gate G5. When G5's output goes low, the H position counter is not reset but loaded with a number. By varying this number, the counter can be made to run faster or slower than the H sync counter. A four (4) element wide state of this counter is decoded by gate HG and becomes the H video signal of the ball.

The vertical ball position counter works similarly to the H ball position counter. The counter is composed of counters B3 and A3. Gate B2 detects when to reload the counter. Gate E2 decodes the ball. The H ball video and V ball video are "anded" to produce ball video in gate G1.

Ball control

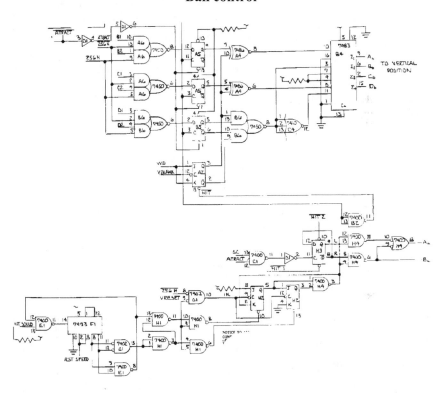

PONG Ball Control

Counter F1 counts the number of hits since the ball was served. Gate G1 decodes a count of 5 to 11, in this range its output causes a medium speed to the H speed of the ball. At speed 12 gate E1 decodes this number and causes the highest H speed of the ball and prevents any change of count, through gate E1, until the counter is reset.

Flip-flops H2 compose a variable pulse width one shot. Each frame V reset resets them in some combination determined by the H speed counter F1 and gates H1. They are then cleared out by 0, 1 or 2 256H pulses, the number depending on how they were reset. During the time the flip-flops are counting out the A and B bits are held to cause the motion counter to slip. The direction of slip is determined by which paddle last hit the ball, as determined by flip-flop H3. The A and B signals are used to lead the H ball motion counters.

The vertical ball motion is determined by:

A   Where it hit the last paddle or,
B   If it has hit a horizontal wall.

The paddle position information is gated by gates A6 and B6 from each paddle as determined by the 256 H signal. This information is latched when the paddle is contracted by the ball by flip-flops A5 and B5. This position signal is passed through or inverted by gates A4 and B6, depending on whether the ball has hit an upper or lower boundary or not, as determined by flip-flop A2. Adder B4 acts as a code converter to convert this speed code into the proper format to input to the vertical ball motion circuit.

That is how the PONG™ works. It is typical in a simple fashion of the coin-operated video game. The new designs that are microprocessor have just hit production in the last year or so and will have to be the subject of a later discussion.

Acknowledgment

I wish to acknowledge the contributions to this paper by George Opperman, Kathleen Mahoney, and Donna Mitchell. I wish to thank John Slusarski of Magnavox Company for the use of some of his slides.

References

Kam Li, Signetics Corporation, Sunnyvale, California. *Technical Aspects of Video Games.*

Kenneth D. Liston, Jr., and John F. Slusarski, Magnavox Company, Fort Wayne, Indiana. *Video Games – LSI Flexibility.*

E. D. Hill, Applied Microsystems, Sacramento, California. *Synthetic Color Signal Generation and Control for TV Games and Other Simple Applications.*

18

VIDEO GAMES CAUGHT UP IN HISTORY

Accessibility, teleological distortion, and other methodological issues

Carl Therrien

Source: Mark J. P. Wolf (ed.), *Before the Crash: Early Video Game History* (Detroit, MI: Wayne State University Press, 2012), pp. 9–29.

> One notices that each generation of historians performs a selection, neglects certain traces, on the contrary exhumes others, for which no one, for some time, or since the beginning, showed interest. Consequently, the view we have of this detritus is already subjective; it relies on a specific interrogation . . .
>
> —GEORGES DUBY[1]

At the foundation of history as a discipline, lies the necessity to synthesize vast bodies of information in order to represent the evolution of human cultures. The exclusion of sources and artifacts constitutes its inevitable shortcoming. The self-proclaimed objective accumulation of facts—thematically organized, chronologically ordered—associated with positivistic methodology fails to conceal the same unavoidable reality: the selection of relevant information is always subjected to the world vision of contemporary historians. Following Duby's introductory quote, a cautious and selfaware historical approach should be able to piece together a series of phenomena through a conceptual lens that can account for the complexity of its object, while remaining conscious of how this lens partially constructs the object. Gazing at the past thus becomes an inevitable window into our own contemporary fascinations. The current state of a given culture, its obsessions and its ideals, often acts as an implicit telos which already conditions the gaze, preselects relevant information in order to piece together a teleological causal chain. Whether to serve the glorification of a national identity or to create a comforting illusion of mastery over the informational chaos that surrounds us, these forms of exclusion only echo the selection carried out by any given period under examination; this chain of exclusions greatly complicates the work of historians. What holds true for historical science as a whole cannot be avoided by a more focused subfield like art history.

In an article that exposes the methodological problems encountered by early cinema historians, André Gaudreault notes the partial nature of his practice on two distinct levels.[2] First, only part of the early film strips is still accessible to today's historians; second, it is impossible for any historian to look back on such a distant object in an unbiased manner. For post-Brighton cinema historians, the emphasis on narrative figures in moving pictures before 1906 (and the corollary praise afforded to filmmakers such as Edwin Porter), at the expense of more widely spread practices, constitutes a teleological travesty; only after 1915 did cinema become the storytelling institution we now take for granted. Of course, such biases influenced film conservation and thus contributed to the accessibility problem underlined by Gaudreault. On the surface, things might appear simpler for video games historians. A strong community constantly feeds online documentation resources, seeking to preserve the memory of games, and some historians experienced the emergence of arcade games firsthand. The commodity of the computer age, with its data storage, organization and transcoding abilities, promises to solve accessibility problems. Yet in spite of these resources, and to a certain extent because of them, the challenges in bringing the young, new medium to history books are considerable. Moreover, this medium appears to constantly vie for perfection through the evolution of imaging techniques, processing power, and interactive devices. How is one to avoid a progress-laden teleological discourse when faced with an object that seems to be defined by its constant evolution? Drawing on historical research experience, notably field and conceptual work for Bernard Perron's research projects on interactive cinema and horror games, as well as a postdoctoral research project on the evolution of game design, this essay seeks to expose both the trivial and conceptual challenges pertaining to the methodology of video game history.

Look back in anger: accessibility issues in the computer age

Relatively little has appeared regarding older games and game systems, arcade games, or video game history in general. Part of the reason is that many of the old games are already gone or very hard to find and play; although this may make writing about them more difficult, it also suggests a greater need for historical research, before it is too late.

—Mark J. P. Wolf[3]

In spite of the vigorous wake of video game studies in the past 10 years, video game equivalents of film conservation institutions are merely starting to emerge. For many years, the closest approximation of such an essential resource came in the shape of the itinerant Videotopia exhibit. Acknowledging "the destruction of the majority of these games and fearing the loss of their historical importance,"[4] the Electronics Conservancy organization set out to find and restore

400 rare arcade cabinets, while also collecting home video game systems. The Computerspielemuseum opened in 1997 in Berlin; the new permanent exhibition "Computer Games: Evolution of a Medium" opened in January 2011 and features more than 300 exhibits. In 2007, following a proposition from major universities led by games researcher Henry Lowood from Stanford,[5] the Library of Congress announced it would preserve a "game canon" formed of the ten "most significant" titles.[6] Academia-related collections are emerging along dedicated games programs, but with obvious budget and conservation space limitations. Since the end of the 1990s, Stanford Libraries has amassed a significant number of video game artifacts as part of the "History of Science and Technology" collections, curated by Lowood; it features thousands of games on systems ranging from the Atari 2600 to the Microsoft Xbox. English Scholars from the Nottingham Trent University, in cooperation with the National Media Museum in Bradford, recently announced an ambitious conservation project; the National Video Game Archive specifically seeks to avoid "the 'mistakes' made in the film industry that lead to the loss of historically significant materials in the past."[7] Still, in the realm of video games today, the most exhaustive equivalents of conservation institutions are purely virtual ones. The following observations should not be seen as a rebuttal of the incredible contribution offered by online databases and emulation endeavors; rather, they seek to expose the almost inevitable drawbacks associated with such projects.

Little more than a decade after the worldwide explosion of the Internet, there is a staggering amount of general-purpose video game databases available online. Every major gaming publication on the web (IGN.com, 1Up.com, Gamespot.com, etc.) eventually incorporated titles that predate their own creation. However, these corporate databases only echo the most basic information (such as release date, platform, and genre) about older titles; with the exception of IGN.com's retro section (http://retro.ign.com), publications focus first and foremost on creating editorial content for new releases. Competing for the web-surfer's click, major gaming sites create an echo chamber of basic information, artificially multiplying results on search engines, which only burdens the work of the researcher. Thankfully, extensive data collecting projects have emerged. Founded in 1999, Mobygames.com officially set out to amass information about computer, console, and arcade games, such as release history, developer bios, screen captures, and box art. Limited to a few platforms before 2001, it eventually included most major home systems, all the way back to the Odyssey. As of 2011, it contains data about more than 56,000 games on 95 different platforms. More than 180,000 digitized visual elements (such as box covers and game media) also provide invaluable information.[8] To this day, the arcade portion of the database has not been developed. However, other dedicated projects have gained the respect and admiration of the community. The Killer List of Video Games (KLOV) database (http://www.klov.com) focuses exclusively on coin-operated arcade video games. Its origins can be traced back to the bulletin board system (BBS) era, where enthusiasts gathered to share information. The project eventually led to the creation of The International Arcade Museum and now encompasses the entire coin-operated entertainment phenomenon. The site has detailed pages with technical descriptions, gameplay information, cabinet pictures, and screenshots for more than 4,400 arcade video games. The Arcade History project is even larger and has information about arcade video games, pinballs, slot machines/pachislots, pachinkos, bat games, bingos, gun games, bowlers/shuffle alleys, jukeboxes, musical instruments, trade stimulators, fortune tellers, strength testers and much more.[9]

Literally dozens of smaller websites dedicated to a specific platform (Lemon Commodore 64/Lemon Amiga, PC Engine Catalog Project), developer (AtariAge, the Nintendo database at Gamespy.com, The LucasArts Museum), genre or theme (Dragon's Lair Project, Home of the Underdogs) supplement the larger databases.[10] These projects grew to considerable proportions by relying heavily on user-contributed content; similar in concept to a wiki, editing descriptions on Mobygames or the KLOV is a matter of being a registered user.[11] Closed editorial resources about older games do exist, and sometimes prove to be the only detailed source of information about rare or lesser-known games and systems. From short reviews on a great variety of consoles (The Video Game Critic) to extensive evaluation of graphic adventure games (JustAdventure+), amateur enthusiasts often spend incredible amounts of energy on these projects.[12] Clearly, the community's genuine concern and dedication to preserve the history of games is commendable. Both open contribution and restricted editorial resources, however, are ultimately amateur endeavors and face the same challenge of providing accurate information.

The appeal of retrogaming review projects lies precisely in the surrogate firsthand experience of rare or inaccessible objects. Despite the guarantee of an actual encounter with the object, however, game descriptions cannot always be taken at face value. Even with firsthand experience, one can misinterpret the actual algorithmic complexity of a game. This raises the fundamental question of the researcher's competence to examine historical objects; the ever-changing technical aspect of video games makes this medium even more demanding than cinema. As Wolf observes, "The history of video games now spans over four decades, and while this is a relatively short time compared to the histories of other more traditional media, it is fast moving and exciting, with innovations and advances occurring at a rate unparalleled in other media."[13]

Acute technical information about a game is not always readily available in the professional press, and relying on promotional material, which often overemphasizes or blatantly distorts technical features, is not an option. *Cruise for a Corpse* (Delphine Software, Amiga, 1991), *Axelay* (Konami, SNES, 1992), and *Doom* (Id Software, DOS, 1993) have all been promoted as achievements in 3-D graphics, even though neither the manipulation of vector shapes, the "mode 7" bitmap scaling, nor the "2.5-D" texture interpolation engine truly correspond to the contemporary definition of a 3-D game engine.[14] Moreover, the "omnidimension 4-D" touted on the box of *Beyond the Forbidden Forest* (Cosmi, Commodore 64, 1985) is highly suspicious.

The question is certainly legitimate: would a programmer or technician familiar with the various creation tools be the ideal video game historian? Researchers should possess sufficient knowledge to contextualize information given by the publishers or made available in databanks. A few noteworthy contributions that take into account these aspects have already been made. In "Video Games in Computer Space: The Complex History of Pong," Henry Lowood explains how the first arcade cabinets are often discussed as computer games, when to a large extent they were created by repurposing television technology.[15] Ian Bogost and Nick Montfort's *Racing the Beam* (2009) provides in-depth information about the Atari VCS 2600's inner workings and its decisive influence on game design. The author's Platform Studies collection seeks precisely to explain "how certain platforms facilitate certain types of computational expression and innovation."[16] Similarly, Noah Wardrip-Fruin makes a case for a closer inspection of the actual computational processes involved in the video game experience; in *Expressive Processing: Digital Fictions, Computer Games and Software Studies* (2009), he begins to trace the historical developments of this procedural reality—including authoring systems and A.I. routines.

Emulation and technical proficiency

Needless to say, all the previously listed resources are useful inasmuch as firsthand experience of the historical objects (both in their material aspect—the original boxes, manuals, cartridges—and the experience of the game itself) is not easily accessible. Some older systems and games can be bought in online auctions (prices are potentially restrictive, particularly in the case of arcade cabinets), but many early consoles and arcade games have already disappeared, and specific types of hardware (such as the first generation CD-ROM add-ons, consoles, and discs) are unlikely to be found in optimum functioning state. Thanks to the transcoding abilities of the computer medium, however, there is another opportunity for researchers to experience their object: emulation. An emulator attempts to duplicate on a recent system the functions and instruction sets associated with previous hardware. Dedicated software can be used directly (if the media reader, such as a disk or CD-ROM drive, is available in the host machine) or from digital copies (typically referred to as ROMs, from "read-only memory," or ISOs, from the ISO archive file system, in the case of CD games). Preservation of the software is taken very seriously by emulation enthusiast. The Old School Emulation Center project (TOSEC) established a clear protocol to archive and name ROM sets; users constantly update lists about software released on more than 200 platforms. Emulation remains a delicate issue, for the creation or appropriation of ROMs for games that have not been declared public domain by the copyright holder is considered illegal in many cases.

Classic computers and consoles tend to attract the most attention from the emulation community; four major emulators exist for the Atari 2600, and many projects associated with the Super Nintendo Entertainment System are being developed. Exclusion of lesser-known systems and games is just one of many issues raised by emulation. As a general rule, more accurate emulation of original components requires more powerful host machines,[17] and many consoles or specific hardware parts are difficult to emulate perfectly. Relatively old computers, like the Commodore Amiga (1985), already featured a complex assemblage of co-processing units that can be taxing to emulate even on modern computers. To recreate a playable experience, programmers sometimes rely on emulation shortcuts: leaving out nonessential hardware modules or functions, or using alternate computing methods that are more efficient on the host system. A potential pitfall resides not so much in the obvious performance disparities that occur in CCS64 (for Commodore 64 emulation) or the impossibility of using the original game controllers in Bliss (for Intellivision emulation), but rather the subtle differences in emulation speed or audiovisual output that are not readily apparent. Far from a simple blessing, a journey in the realm of emulation requires researchers to have even more proficiency with technical aspects.

Thankfully, the emulation community is very concerned about creating the most accurate emulation possible. Emulators are constantly updated by their creators. One of the most ambitious projects, Multiple Arcade Machine Emulator (MAME) emulates a number of arcade games. Since its initial release in 1997, over 4,000 unique games have been emulated, encompassing a great variety of chipsets (such as Capcom's CPS-1 or SNK's NeoGeo boards). The incredible variety of input devices used in arcade cabinets since the early days of the phenomenon adds to the complexity; trackballs, light guns, pedals, and more have to be mapped to present-day devices like keyboards, mouses, and third-party control pads. Display technology discrepancy, although not as apparent as previously discussed difficulties, can also be a significant issue. Beyond the theoretical specifications of the visual assets stored on the game disk or cartridge (e.g., resolution and color depth), display technologies affect how the actual image appears to the user. Different types of cathode-ray tubes have been used in arcade cabinets during the period covered by MAME (at the time of this writing: 1976–2007). Without getting into complicated technical details, we can observe that the phosphorescent end of cathode-ray tubes—the area scanned by an electron beam whose intensity is modulated to reproduce the signal—had specific characteristics that came to be associated with the video game experience. In an attempt to mimic screen artifacts such as scan lines and red/green/blue dots, MAME offers the possibility to overlay a visual representation of these artifacts on top of the emulated game (Figure 1).[18] Even with the use of these masks, an exact reproduction of original monitor effects on modern-day LCD panels, and even on the CRTs used with computers in the 1990s, is nearly impossible. The clarity of modern computer displays is making the blurriness associated with arcade monitors a thing of the past. This is not an improvement or a way to belatedly do justice to the original experience; this blurriness, resulting from less efficient luminance and color handling, often masked the imperfections and aliasing of the original source visuals or contributed to the illusion of deeper color depth with the use of dithering.[19]

Figure 1 Visual masks in MAME (blown-up sections of tiled patterns)

The incomplete object

It is now clear that the inaccessibility of objects and the palliative resources available to researchers open many methodological issues. Even when firsthand contact is possible, given the highly technical nature of the medium, it is the researcher's competency (or lack thereof) that can become a source of misinformation. The ultimate accessibility issue, however, goes beyond the availability of the object or the technical expertise of the researcher. Video games require nontrivial effort, and in many instances, actual proficiency in order to evaluate the object in its entirety. As Wolf points out, "Gameplaying skills may be required to advance beyond the first few levels, or some puzzle-solving ability may be needed just to enter a locked door encountered early on in the game."[20] It is technically possible for researchers to use cheat codes or other tricks, or to simply access later stages in the games. However, cheats are clearly a distortion that prevents proper evaluation of gameplay mechanics. Skipping to later stages is even more likely to push researchers to their limit because it will place them right in the middle of the learning curve. Most emulators offer a save-state functionality, allowing the user to create a marker that can complement the game's checkpoint, password, or save system. These various save points could be used to facilitate researchers' access, but the same proficiency issue would surface.

A dedicated community, yet again, has answered the call: thousands of hours of archived audiovisual playthroughs are available online, including "speedruns," where apt gamers record their fastest performance of any given game, and "longplays," where gamers try to expose the content of the game as thoroughly as possible. The commented playthrough is also a growing Internet meme; unrelated members of the gaming community compulsively started to produce content under the same "Let's Play . . . " name, with hundreds of examples to be found on YouTube. Quick-thrill classics such as *Jungle Hunt* (Taito, 1982) are of course well suited to this archival process, but the number of playthroughs of lengthier games, such as interactive movies and role-playing games, is surprisingly large. *Phantasmagoria: A Puzzle in Flesh* (Sierra On-Line, 1996) is divided into 25 ten-minute segments; the typical *Kingdom Hearts* (Square, 2002) playthrough lasts several hours. Needless to say, archived playthroughs should not act as a substitute for firsthand experience and, in themselves, are prone to misinterpretation. In the context of the *Ludiciné* research project on interactive cinema (http://www.ludicine.ca), Bernard Perron decided to invest resources in the archiving of an actual playthrough for many games. The database built for the project allows researchers to tag the videos with a consistent set of descriptors that seeks to dissipate any confusion regarding the gameplay. In conjunction with other information, audiovisual archives provide access to content that can take several hours to reach under normal circumstances, while minimizing the risk of distortion.

Teleological illusion: from early cinema to early video games

The significance of the accessibility problem cannot be overstated. The conceptual organization and presentation of a phenomenon's development over time, by definition, depends on the available historical traces. The ongoing and rapid technological evolution partly responsible for these accessibility problems also favors a teleological view of video game history. *Teleology* can be defined as the tendency to conceptualize the evolution of a phenomenon as a purposeful development toward a clear goal. From 1978 onward, cinema historians sought to evacuate teleological distortion from history books. André Gaudreault and Tom Gunning, among others, exposed the numerous manifestations of teleology in the work of traditional cinema historians. The primary form of exclusion is so readily apparent in the books of Sadoul and Mitry that it might not have been completely unconscious: cinema's recognition as a noble art form is strongly tied to the development of its storytelling abilities, and pre-Brighton historians were keen to underline the early manifestations of this very specific and noble practice,[21] while promptly discarding the residual information, a protean landscape of practices that truly defined early moving pictures. Gunning clearly summarized the problem:

> The history of early cinema, like the history of cinema generally, has been written and theorized under the hegemony of narrative films. Early filmmakers like Smith, Méliès and Porter have been studied primarily from the viewpoint of their contribution to film as a storytelling medium, particularly the evolution of narrative editing. Although such approaches are not totally misguided, they are one-sided and potentially distort both the work of these filmmakers and the actual forces shaping cinema before 1906.[22]

Focusing only on figures and codes that *retrospectively echo* those privileged by the institution of cinema—and the corollary obsession to establish a list of their first incidences—is clearly a teleological distortion. In this period of *primitive* cinema, not everything seems to be equally primitive. Incidentally, this very designation of "primitive" is not only a contemporary value judgment alien to the object studied, it also happens to be part of a biologic metaphor that reinforces the teleological illusion. By listing the first occurrences of these primitive figures— just like proud parents cataloguing their child's first footsteps and words—such historical discourse places the phenomenon on a pre-written progressive path going from naive infancy up to the great accomplishments of maturity. Is it any wonder, then, that historians kept looking for the fathers and forefathers of narrative editing? To paraphrase André Gaudreault: by putting early cinema in a crib, this historical account is rocking us with comforting illusions.

Through this teleological conception of history, each period simply becomes the antechamber of the following one. Post-Brighton cinema historians proposed some guidelines to avoid teleological pitfalls. Resorting to a falsely objective decoupage of time, for example by matching periods with decades, would constitute a naive abdication with respect to the historian's duty to conceptualize history. The main idea was not to completely abandon chronological periodization, but rather to emphasize the insurmountable heterogeneity of the early period by documenting the multiple ongoing, and often contradictory, practices. The end result was the promotion of a unique yet multifaceted concept to better understand the early days as a continuation of cultural series that existed prior to the invention of cinematography: the attraction. "The cinema of attractions directly solicits spectator attention, inciting visual curiosity, and supplying pleasure through an exciting spectacle . . . It is the direct address to the audience, in which an attraction is offered to the spectator by a cinema showman, that defines this approach to film making."[23] This exhibitionist mode of address contrasts most clearly with the voyeuristic aspect that Noël Burch and Christian Metz, among others, associate with narrative cinema. Interestingly, an attraction doesn't refer solely to the enticing content of the film strips (exotic travelogues, Hale's vehicle rides, saucy vignettes, etc.), but also to the apparatus itself or to new cinematographic tricks and innovations (splice effects, close-ups). Such a concept encompasses larger cultural manifestations and thus favors an historical account based on cultural paradigms that can overlap at any given time rather than discrete successive periods; attraction and narration both coexist during the early days, and the resurgence of attraction in later stages of the medium's development (musical numbers, special effects) is a frequent observation.[24]

The video game medium poses an interesting challenge in terms of historical conceptualization. The industry has grown to considerable proportions over the course of the past four decades, and in spite of the undeniable frailty one can observe in the constant acquisitions, mergers, and studio shutdowns, this growth has triggered the establishment of major players, production molds, specialized roles, and training. Many history books focus on the anecdote surrounding the development of the industry and the creation of landmark games. Steven L. Kent's *The Ultimate History of Video Games* was built from a previous account by Leonard Herman (*Phoenix: The Fall & Rise of Videogames*) and 500 interviews with major figures in the industry. The industrial account often provides a first convenient period marker for the history of video games: the Crash of 1983. Kent places the Golden Age of the medium right before the Crash, Van Burnham's account of classic games range from 1971 to 1984,[25] and *The Video Game Explosion*'s first major historical demarcation is titled "The Industry Rebounds (1985–94)." Not surprisingly, the great fathers of the medium are often pioneers of the exploitation aspect: Ralph Baer as "The Father of TV Games"[26] or "Home Video Games,"[27] and Nolan Bushnell (inventor of the first mass-produced coin-operated arcade video game, *Computer Space* in 1971) as the "Father of the Industry."[28] Video games have been put in a crib, and it's the promise of a great cultural industry that seems to call for paternity examination.

The classic paternity dispute between Willy Higinbotham (inventor of a table tennis game displayed on an oscilloscope, in 1958) and Steve Russell (who "hacked" the PDP-1 supercomputer to create *Spacewar!* in 1962) points toward the clearest source of teleological distortion in various video game accounts: technology. Since the original technical principle has been developed, a constant onslaught of seemingly perfected yet constantly perfectible machines has been associated with the medium. The first obvious consequence of this constant technological development is a tendency to give particular attention or significance to the hardware and games that represent a technological breakthrough. Symptomatically, on top of the obvious industry landmarks, the timelines integrated in history books put significant emphasis on the first occurrences of specific technological aspects. The launch of major consoles and computer systems are listed along *important* games: the first game integrating ROM chips to store graphical information (*Tank!*, Kee Games, 1974), the first game to use a microprocessor (*Gunman*, Taito, 1975), the first game to use a laserdisc (Electro Sport's *Quarter Horse*, 1981), the first full-color game (*Galaxian*, Namco, 1979).

The editor of *The Video Game Explosion* clearly expressed a desire to let the games take center stage. The games are thematically organized in accordance to a technical aspect in many instances: vector games, laserdisc games, CD-ROM games, handheld video game systems, online role-playing games, and so forth. Moreover, the temptation to use the multiple generations of hardware— associations of systems released around the same time frame—as historical period markers is very strong. On the *Wikipedia* account of video game history, generations play a major role: from the Magnavox Odyssey to the PlayStation 3, seven major generations have been outlined. In his 2001 account, Kent dedicates two chapters to "The 'Next' Generation" (the mid-1990s competition between the Sony PlayStation, Sega Saturn, and Nintendo 64), and further underlines the relative nature of this "next" phase in "And the Cycle Continues." *The Video Game Explosion*'s other major period distinction is titled "Advancing to the Next Level (1995–Present)"; Wolf notes that by the end of 1994, "the industry was booming again, providing the revenue to invest in new technological advances, like 32-bit home game systems, that were just around the corner."[29]

Technical aspects of early games are often described with adjectives such as *basic* and *primitive*.[30] Besides blatantly eclipsing the historical reception of objects that were appreciated as technological attractions, these references to the naive infancy of the medium also points the other way, toward an ideal apparatus. The true offspring of the forefathers, it seems, is not yet completed. To this day, hardware designers, game developers, and gamers have their eyes set on the future of games. In "L'appel de la simulation" (Therrien, 2005),[31] I outlined a game design tendency influenced by the simulation ideal: development of open-ended worlds (The *Grand Theft Auto* series), integration of complex physics algorithms (the Havok engine), refinements to artificial intelligence (*Halo: Combat Evolved*, Bungie, 2001), and so on. The marketing campaign for Nintendo's Wii console (code-named "Revolution" during its design phase) focuses on the seemingly perfect synchronism between the actual manipulation of the user and the resulting action in the game world. The frequent assumption that better game mechanics involve greater realism already traces a privileged path for the future of games.[32] Writing about immersion and presence in video games, Alison McMahan declares:

> A recent shift in computer game design involves a move away from 2-D level design in games like *Prince of Persia* (1992) [*sic*] to 3-D design and a first-person point of view. This shift increases the sense of immersion by replicating the aesthetic approaches of first-person shooter games in other types of games, such as adventure games, role-playing games, and even strategy games, which previously used 2-D levels or isometric views. *The shift in design is indicative of an overall trend to make desktop video games feel more like virtual reality.*[33]

The ongoing technological evolution generates an overarching narrative that defines the ideal stage of the medium in terms of immediacy,[34] feeding on actual techno-military devices (complex simulations, virtual reality interfaces) as much as fantasized versions of these experiments (the *Star Trek* Holodeck).

With its biological infancy metaphors and presentation of the great fathers, and historical periods chronologically organized and conceptualized in terms of progress, it is clear that video game history integrates the aspects of teleological discourse to a great extent. The focus on technological evolution contributes to the promotion of immediacy as a *telos*, potentially distorting historical inspections into the early days of the medium. What defining aspects of the video game experience are likely to be obscured by such a progress-laden organization of the past? Is there a way to account for the undeniable evolution of the medium while exploring other means to conceptualize its history?

Reconfiguring history

In their 2003 book *Digital Play*, Steven Kline, Nick Dyer-Witheford and Greig De Peuter suggest that a thorough historical examination should address the evolution and interactions of three circuits: technology, industry, and culture. The development of technological innovations and the establishment of the major industrial players that successfully marketed these innovations has taken the center stage so far in the young history of the new medium. But in order to better understand video games and conceptualize its history, the evolution of the cultural circuit, where games are created and consumed for the quality of the experience provided, deserves a lot more attention. Closer inspection reveals that any technological aspect is intertwined in a web of often conflicting design imperatives that go far beyond the fascination with immediacy. At the risk of aggravating the cultural bias toward vision, let's take the visual aspects of games as an example. Dozens of techniques have been developed over time to create in-game visuals, each strongly dependent on technological and production resources. Yet newer techniques don't simply replace those of older games; rather, they can be classified somewhere between the conflicting imperatives of increasing the representational potential of the image, its malleability (and potential reactivity to the player), and its readability for gameplay purposes. Early video game visuals didn't simply "remediate" older audiovisual media like cinema and television; because of their procedural nature, the visual elements to be assembled and reformulated have long trailed behind the visual realism of their predecessors. Yet this very abstraction is a decisive factor in just how engaging these early games can be. Very little resources are necessary to suggest useful or harmful elements: a few carefully arranged pixels (the scorpion in *Pitfall!*, 1982) or primary colors with culturally reinforced meanings are sufficient. Elements relevant to the goals of the game are clearly detached from the background. The growing proficiency of audiovisual techniques brought with it the question of readability, and game designers have used a wide variety of strategies to address it: cinema-influenced composition and framing, translucent rendering of 3-D objects that come between the player's virtual point of view and her avatar, and sometimes obvious directional arrows or other visual cues to indicate relevant information. In the early 1990s, the development of full-motion video (FMV)[35] represented the pinnacle of visual realism in video game graphics, yet the technique quickly lost momentum because these sequences could not be manipulated as easily as the 2-D bitmaps, and thus came to be seen as a step back in terms of reactivity. Filled-polygon 3-D graphics, a technique that was developed as early as 1983, became the center of interest even though it was a clear regression in terms of visual fidelity.

Finding inspiration in the long history of visual representation has been a great way for games to simply circumvent the fascination with verisimilitude: abstraction has been a recurring visual style (*Tetris*, Pajitnov, 1985; *Rez*, United Game Artists, 2001), and caricature dominates at certain periods and for certain game developers such as Nintendo.[36] Both styles clearly accommodate the readability imperative. The evolution of video game visuals cannot be seen as a simple linear progression toward greater immediacy. Moreover, the influence of previous media, most notably cinema, is clearly visible.[37] Even with the development of 3-D imagery, the visual experience of games, most interestingly, is far removed from the virtual reality utopia emphasized by McMahan: a majority of 3-D games propose to control an avatar from a third-person camera perspective, which can also be controlled to some extent. This highly mediated experience—*hypermediatic*, to use the expression coined by Bolter and Grusin— might have prospered out of the simple imperative to present visual problems relevant to the game's objectives as clearly as possible to facilitate gameplay. Similar observations can be made about the integration of complex physics, artificial intelligence algorithms, and other simulation elements in games. These developments should not overshadow the defining aspect of gaming experiences; the very nature of a game is to clearly prescribe relevant actions in order to limit the range of possibilities that the player has to consider. The purely conventional nature of certain rules and the qualitative spacing of the experience with regards to reality are major contributors to the incredibly satisfying nature of this experience. Even in simulation-inspired games, conventions abound and clear restrictions and objectives are put forward in order to maximize the potential gratification. Even when they wrap their rules in highly sophisticated and ever more realistic algorithms, games and the immersive journey they propose constitute a highly mediated experience.

Tom Gunning suggested that "every change in film history implies a change in its address to the spectator, and each period constructs its spectator in a new way."[38] Defining different modes of address requires acute knowledge of the rationales that shape the decisions of game creators at any given time. To define different modes of address and their relative importance at any given time, video game studies would benefit from an extensive account of gameplay mechanics. Academic books discussing gameplay are mostly synchronic affairs; historical accounts of gameplay evolution are hard to come by. *The Video Game Explosion* features a few chapters on specific genres ("Adventure Games," "Interactive Movies," etc.), and the development of genre studies might attract attention to the evolution of specific mechanics. In *Half-Real*, Juul outlines two types of games, two ways of creating challenges and regulating success. Emergence involves a simple system of interacting rules that can lead to infinite variations and many satisfying performances, and is said to be "historically dominant"; "progression games are a historically new game form where the game designer explicitly determines the possible ways in which the game can progress."[39] Yet this historical hypothesis is not developed further.

Similarly, conceptual propositions focused on player attitudes are seldom organized historically. Building on previous distinctions between play/game (Winnicott) and ludus/païdia (Caillois), Bernard Perron defined two major attitudes in the experience of video games: the *gamer* seeks to complete clearly defined objectives in order to win the game; the *player* can define his own objectives with no clear valorization of outcomes.[40] The integration of deeper simulation elements in games would seem to favor the player attitude,[41] yet the development of this tendency doesn't mean the progressive exclusion of the gamer attitude. In *Man, Play and Games* (1958), Roger Caillois proposed a typology of games based on psychological attitudes: competition (*agôn*), chance (*alea*), make-believe (*mimicry*), and vertigo (*ilinx*). The typology has often been criticized for being too broad,[42] and as Juul has argued, all these components can be found in a typical modern video game.[43] The historical dimension of Caillois's thesis is often overlooked, but the author did organize his typology historically by associating the rise of major civilizations with the promotion of chance and competition in games, at the expense of the make-believe and vertigo impulses.

Even if the abstract video games of early days had already strong representational undertones,[44] even if their audiovisual resources could overwhelm the senses to some extent, it is clear that the make-believe and vertigo components have been developed considerably in parallel with the technological evolution of the medium. From Pac-Man to Solid Snake, from the infinitely looping alien invasion of *Space Invaders* (Taito, 1978) to the takeover of Liberty City's criminal world, players are invited to project themselves into specific fictional characters and events that go beyond the arbitrary nature of rules; as Juul pointed out in *Half-Real*, the fictional element of games cannot be ignored. As for the vertigo component, the development of interactive imagery opened the door to vertigo-inducing effects that play a significant part in many genres (such as racing games and 3-D action games). Such an observation is rather trivial and seems to feed on the immediacy *telos* discussed in the context of this essay, with its promise of ever more realistic virtual worlds and ability to address the senses viscerally. Indeed, it should be complemented by another one, regarding the evolution of the agonistic component.

To great extent, early games correspond to Juul's definition of emergence, but his emphasis on a permissive regulation of success can potentially misrepresent the actual challenge of these games. Emergent rule systems in the early days are typically not static; as the player progresses through simple repetitive scenarios, the balance is constantly adjusted to be more competitive. Randomization (chance) did represent a low-cost means of introducing interesting variations from one playthrough to the next, but also played an essential part of increasing the difficulty level. Emergence games all obey the basic "easy to learn, hard to master" principle outlined by Salen and Zimmerman,[45] but early games appear harder to master than contemporary games. The notorious difficulty of titles such as *Donkey Kong* (Nintendo, 1981) and *Pac-Man* (Namco, 1980) encouraged a highly competitive environment where the display of proficiency in arcade parlors became an attraction in itself. As the industry progresses from this highly competitive model—where technological attractions are presented in the context of an arcade parlor in order to maximize the potential "attraction of the self"—to the domination of home-based entertainment geared toward the gratification of casual gamers, we might have witnessed already a major change in video games' mode of address that is echoed by the evolution of the industry as a whole.[46]

In order to investigate these aspects, video game historians would greatly benefit from the elaboration of a comparative tool that is precise enough to account for the great variety of interactive encounters, yet abstract enough to avoid listing all the actual manipulations on the various control devices and their effects in the game on a case-by-case scenario. A figure of interactivity such as "combat" can be procedurally implemented in many ways, including the simple combinations necessary to produce a few kicks and punches in *Karateka* (Mechner, 1984) and the impressive roster of blows, multiform combinations, and countering abilities involved in the contemporary fighting game *Dead or Alive 4* (Tecmo, 2005). Depending on the representation of space, "spatial exploration" could be carried out in first- or third-person perspective, by lateral scrolling, square-by-square, or on the depth axis through depth cues and interpolation of 2-D objects, or in a fully realized 3-D world; the world to be explored could be opened in many directions and organized in a linear or even circular fashion. The monitoring of vital resources might involve basic physical or psychological integrity, or each of these categories could be affected by many other variables (as in the ADD-inspired RPGs that include stats on endurance, strength, dexterity, intelligence, wisdom, charisma, etc.); players might be able to accumulate some capital for each variable, and the variation of these variables might affect gameplay in a binary fashion (life/death), through various distinct stages, or in a progressive manner. Along with manipulation complexity, the study of learning curves, satisfactory performance intervals, tutorials, in-game aids, save systems, and check points from a historical perspective would allow a better understanding of the prevalent modes of address at any given time and help refine the conceptualization of video game history.

Shifting the focus from technological evolution to concepts such as attraction, immersion, and mediation, this essay illustrates some of the components glossed over by utopian teleological conceptions of the medium. Most strikingly, the attraction of immediacy that one can observe in the constant evolution of illusion-making techniques and simulation algorithms is clearly counterbalanced by the gratification principle inherent to games; the evolution of game design in relation to player gratification represents a fruitful avenue for historical investigations. To properly lay out the history of the medium, one should also consider Hans Robert Jauss's call for the inclusion of reception as a way to reform traditional art history. Prevalent modes of address at any given time certainly help shape users' horizons of expectations, but other contextual information is also relevant.[47] Jauss listed three areas of investigation to define these frames of experience: preliminary experience with the norms of artistic forms/genres; relationship of the work with other works in the reception context; and comparison between the poetic and pragmatic uses of language. On top of prevalent genres/influential games and the evolution of their specific gameplay mechanics, a thorough historical examination will have to consider contexts of usage, reception of these games in specialized press and online communities, statistical information about players' preferences and rituals, and much more. If different modes of address can be largely defined through the study of structural elements such as game mechanics, it is the reception pole which ultimately determines usage. The greatest advantage of video game historians, after all, resides in this simple fact: whereas contemporary researchers of the "century of cinema" don't have a single living spectator of early moving pictures, video game historians still have access to early players. Only a closer inspection of the players through interviews and field studies will lead the way to a proper conceptualization of the medium's history. By integrating field work and theoretical propositions from sociology and psychology to reform the unavoidable techno-industrial account, video game history as a discipline can truly propose a synthesizing point of view living up to the complexity of its object.

Notes

The author would like to thank Henry Lowood for his comments and suggestions.

1 Quoted by André Gaudreault on page 115 in "Distance et Historicité: Problèmes de Méthode de la 'Reconstitution' historique," in *Le Cinéma en Histoire: Institutions Cinématographiques, Réception Filmique et Reconstitution Historique*, A. Gaudreault, G. Lacasse, and I. Raynauld, ed., (Québec: Nota Bene, 1999), 107–50. Translated by the author.
2 Ibid.
3 Mark J. P. Wolf, ed., *The Video Game Explosion: A History from PONG to PlayStation and Beyond*, (Westport, CT: Greenwood Press, 2007), 1.
4 "Electronics Conservency," Electronics Conservancy Inc., accessed October 18, 2011, http://www.videotopia.com/ec.htm.
5 Lowood was also responsible for the academic research project "How They Got Game: The History and Culture of Interactive Simulations and Video Games." The project led to the creation of a website and the course "History of Computer Game Design: Technology, Culture, Business" in the Science, Technology and Society program at Stanford University.
6 Heather Chaplin, "Is That Just Some Game? No, It's a Cultural Artifact," *New York Times*, March 12, 2007, http://www.nytimes.com.
7 Kris Pigna, "U.K. Launches First Official National Videogame Archive," *1up.com*, October 5, 2008, http://www.1up.com/do/newsStory?cId=3170366.
8 Each release of the same game on a different platform counts as one entry. Multiple box/media art from different countries can be stored for any game.
9 "Arcade History," accessed October 18, 2011, http://www.arcade-history.com.
10 See the following sites: http://www.lemonamiga.com; http://www.lemon64.com; http://www.pcecp.com; http://www.atariage.com; http://nindb.classicgaming.gamespy. com; http://lucasarts.vintagegaming.org; http://www.dragons-lair-project.com; and http://www.dragons-lair-project.com.
11 Which is not to say that the content is not reviewed by a core team member of each website; review procedures do exist, but are limited by obvious constraints.
12 See http://www.videogamecritic.net; and http://www.justadventure.com.
13 Wolf, *The Video Game Explosion*, xv.
14 Among other features promoted on their respective box art illustrations, *Cruise for a Corpse* lists "Completely interactive in full 3-D vision," the cover of *Axelay* mentions "six graphically shocking 3-D levels," and the SNES version of *Doom* boosts "FX2 Chip for screaming fast, real time 3D graphics."
15 Henry Lowood, "Videogames in Computer Space: The Complex History of Pong," *IEEE Annals of the History of Computing*, July-September (2009): 5–19.
16 Nick Montfort and Ian Bogost, *Racing the Beam: The Atari Video Computer System* (Cambridge, MA: The MIT Press, 2009), vii.
17 As of 2010, the PlayStation 2, GameCube, and Xbox consoles have been emulated to some extent.
18 The file names of the masks, from left to right: Apperture 3x6 Aaron; Apperture 2x4rb Aaron; Scanrez1 Althor; Scanlines75dx_j4.
19 Dithering is the juxtaposition of two colors in complex patterns in order to give the illusion of a greater color depth.
20 Wolf, *The Video Game Explosion*, 23.
21 The 1978 FIAF conference in Brighton represents a turning point for the history of cinema; it marks the beginning of a critical inspection of traditional accounts of cinema by a new generation of historians.

22 Tom Gunning, "The Cinema of Attractions: Early Film, Its Spectator, and the Avant-Garde," in *Early Cinema: Space-Frame-Narrative*, ed. Thomas Elsaesser, (London: British Film Institute, 1990), 56.

23 Ibid., 58–59.

24 In 2000, Gaudreault and Philippe Marion proposed a complex "birth" scenario to better understand the formation and evolution of media: the "integrative birth" corresponds to the advent of an apparatus and its appropriation by various cultural series (photography with the Lumière brothers, stage trickery in the case of Méliès, etc.); the "differential birth" refers to the advent of a dedicated institution and a clear hierarchy of practices for which the medium developed specific codes. See André Gaudreault and Philippe Marion, "Un média naît toujours deux fois . . . ," *Sociétés et Représentations*, 9 (2000): 21–36.

25 In the introduction, Burnham nuances the term classic, but refers to the selected era as the "Golden Age"; see Van Burnham, *Supercade: A Visual History of the Videogame Age 1971–1984* (Cambridge, MA: The MIT Press, 2003), 23.

26 Ibid., 18.

27 Steven L. Kent, *The Ultimate History of Video Games* (New York: Three Rivers Press, 2001), 21.

28 Ibid., 27.

29 Wolf, *The Video Game Explosion*, 107.

30 For example, "*Trak 10* had very basic graphics" (62) and "*Tank* had very primitive graphics" (67), in Kent, *The Ultimate History of Video Games*, 2001.

31 Carl Therrien, "L'appel de la simulation: deux approches du design vidéoludique," in *Le game design de jeux vidéo: approches de l'expression vidéoludique*, ed. Sébastien Genvo (Paris: L'Harmattan, 2005), 175–94.

32 Chris Crawford notoriously defined good game design in terms of consistency and coherence; Janet Murray, in her discussion on agency, proclaims that "the most dramatically satisfying puzzles are those that encourage the interactor to apply real-world thinking to the virtual world." (Janet Murray, *Hamlet on the Holodeck: The Future of Narrative in Cyberspace* (Cambridge, MA: The MIT Press, 1997), 139).

33 Allison McMahan, "Immersion, Engagement, and Presence" in *The Video Game Theory Reader*, ed. Mark J. P. Wolf and Bernard Perron (New York: Routledge, 2003), 67–86. Emphasis mine.

34 The concept of immediacy is central to Bolter and Grusin's media genealogy; it is one of the two logics of remediation, defined as "the way in which one medium is seen by our culture as reforming or improving upon another [. . .] Each new medium is justified because it fills a lack or repairs a fault in its predecessor, because it fulfills the unkept promise of an older medium." J. David Bolter and Richard Grusin, *Remediation: Understanding New Media* (Cambridge, MA: The MIT Press, 1999), 59–60).

35 FMV is the brand name of various techniques allowing the playback of fully animated sequences created from digitized live-action material or computer-generated assets. It doesn't stipulate strict norms in terms of frames per second, color depth, compression algorithms, or display size.

36 See Aki Jarvinen, "Gran Stylissimo: The Audiovisual Elements and Styles in Computer and Video Games" in *Proceedings of Computer Games and Digital Cultures Conference*, ed. Frans Mäyrä (Tampere, Finland: Tampere University Press, 2002), 113–28. Thanks to Martin Picard who brought this resource to my attention.

37 See Carl Therrien, "Graphics in Video Games" in *The Video Game Explosion: A History from PONG to PlayStation and Beyond*, ed. Mark J. P. Wolf Carl Therrien (Westport, Connecticut: Greenwood Press, 2007), 239–50.

38 Tom Gunning, "The Cinema of Attractions: Early Film, Its Spectator, and the Avant-Garde," in *Early Cinema: Space-Frame-Narrative*, ed. Thomas Elsaesser (London: British Film Institute, 1990), 61.

39 Jesper Juul, J., *Half-Real: Videogames between Real Rules and Fictional Worlds* (Cambridge, MA: The MIT Press, 2005), 56.

40 Bernard Perron, "From Gamers to Players and Gameplayers: The Example of Interactive Movies" in *The Video Game Theory Reader*, ed. Mark J. P. Wolf and Bernard Perron (New York: Routledge, 2003), 237–58.

41 The complex physics engine integrated in *Halo: Combat Evolved* (Bungie, 2001) incited many players to experiment with the power of accumulative deflagration on different world objects, for example by trying to catapult vehicles to otherwise unreachable parts of a given map. It is clearly this player attitude that Bungie wanted to cater to with the addition of Forge to *Halo 3* (2007); the mapeditor module allows direct control over object placement and can become a game in itself.

42 See Colas Duflo, *Jouer et Philosopher* (Paris: PUF, 1997).

43 Juul, *Half-Real: Videogames between Real Rules and Fictional Worlds*, 10.

44 The first arcade games, *Computer Space* (1971) and *PONG* (1972) had strikingly abstract universes that could nonetheless evoke specific referents (outer space and table tennis). In 1972, color overlays (such as tennis and hockey playfields), sold with Magnavox Odyssey games, added some representational value to the abstract shapes on screen.

45 Juul, *Half-Real: Videogames between Real Rules and Fictional Worlds*, 69.

46 Of course, this proposition should be nuanced by pointing out the tremendous development of competitive gaming in certain regions of the world. *StarCraft* (1998) tournaments in South Korea, to name but one example, have reached the level of professional sport in terms of popularity and sponsorship.

47 The aesthetic of reception is not only a plea for the exhaustive study of the interaction between art and its audience, but a strong case for the reformation of literary and art history. For Jauss, the historical approach should focus on the horizons of expectations that define the reception of art at any given time. See Hans Robert Jauss, *Toward an Aesthetic of Reception* (Minneapolis: University of Minnesota Press, 1982).

19

STRATEGIC SIMULATIONS AND OUR PAST

The bias of computer games in the presentation of history

Kevin Schut

Source: *Games and Culture*, 2(3), 2007, 213–235.

Abstract

Many popular digital games have historical themes or settings. Taking its cue from recent research emphasizing the educational value of computer and video games, this article investigates the bias of the medium in presenting history. Although sharing an appreciation for the cultural value of history simulations and games, the author argues that the digital game medium currently tends to result in stereotypically masculine, mechanical, and spatially oriented interactive presentations of history. This article does not take a technological determinist stance nor a simplistic view of interpretation. Nevertheless, the author believes that the weight and momentum of the historical development of the digital game medium, its technological structure, and its institutional character have encouraged certain patterns in digital games that should be critically examined.

History textbooks claim that Julius Caesar conquered Gaul in a series of campaigns stretching from 58 B.C. to 51 B.C. But when I did it, I used my general Quintus the Mighty, and I captured Alesia by 240 B.C. Of course, I myself have never ridden at the front of troops, but my digital minions have gone into battle for me time and again in the popular computer game Rome: Total War (Creative Assembly, 2004). In my travels through a reconstructed, hypothetical classical-era Mediterranean, I have encountered Gauls, Iberians, Germans, and Britons, crossed the mighty Rhone, sailed past the giant statue of Zeus at Olympia, and entered into diplomatic negotiations with the Macedonians.

War-gaming is an old pastime (King & Borland, 2003)—especially if you include games such as chess—but today's digital war games have entered new territory: the ability to visually and aurally immerse players in history. Although complex board games can certainly teach a great deal about the past to those who trouble themselves with the enormous rulebooks, they have a hard time providing the multifaceted, complicated, yet intuitive interaction with virtual worlds that computers make possible. Thus, digital games have opened up a whole new way for people to experience or learn about history.

In many ways, the digital game medium is an ideal tool for building historical knowledge and understanding. But if we want a balanced assessment, we need to consider some of the limitations and blind spots of historical computer games. In this article, I argue that the digital game medium, because of its cultural and technological construction, is predisposed toward presentations of history that are stereotypically masculine, highly systematic, and focused on spatially oriented interactivity.

Education and historical simulations

A growing number of educators are starting to champion the use of digital games as teaching tools.[1] Anyone who has played a substantial number of games probably already realizes that this new medium has several educational benefits. But aside from the obligatory copy of Oregon Trail (Learning Company, 1997) or other relatively simple and limited edutainment CD-ROMs hanging around the classroom computer, computer games have not been commonly used to teach in a systematic manner. Now an increasing number of voices are speaking up for just that.

In a recent guest editorial in *Wired* magazine, famed game designer Will Wright (2006), who designed SimCity (Maxis Software, 1989) and The Sims (Maxis Software, 2000), touts the ability of games to encourage scientific thinking. Likewise, writer Steven Johnson (2005), in his engaging book *Everything Bad Is Good for You*, argues that video games have been a perfect vehicle for encouraging increasingly complex thought patterns. This echoes recent publications in education theory. James Paul Gee's (2003) book *What Video Games Have to Teach Us About Learning and Literacy* is a very readable treatise on how good digital games model good learning practices. The book puts together a persuasive case for the ability of games to make meaning situated, to help create motivated, tailored, and incremental discoveries, and to encourage social sharing of knowledge, among other things. Although evidence-based research is still not available in large quantities—and much of what *is* available is methodologically questionable—Kurt Squire (2004b, 2005; Squire & Jenkins, 2003) is one prominent education researcher who has widely published about using the game Civilization III (described in more detail below) in actual classrooms. Although he sees potential drawbacks, Squire believes that digital games are potentially powerful teaching tools. Gee, Squire, and others do not argue that games are a panacea for all that ails schools today; rather, these theorists see computer and video games as valuable tools when coupled with proper guidance and other media resources.

Personally, I strongly support the idea of integrating games with teaching. As a lifelong game player, I have experienced many of the benefits of gaming that Squire, Gee, and others describe. But there is no such thing as a perfect tool. Games have significant strengths and limitations. This does not mean we should abstain from historical simulations; it simply means we should approach them with something of a critical eye. The current educational research on games certainly notes the pragmatic limitations of using them in standard school settings. These critiques focus on things such as cost, time involved and scheduling issues, technical problems, difficulty of teaching complex games, and more (Egenfeldt-Nielsen, 2004; Trotter, 2004, 2005). Some educators and critics also note some of the inherent limitations of simulations, something I discuss in more detail below (Salen & Zimmerman, 2004; Squire, 2004a; Starr, 1994; Thiagarajan, 1998; Trotter, 2004). Squire (2006), although focusing on the positives of games as teaching tools, also points out in a recent article that the educational ideology of games is at odds with established educational practices. I think, however, that these analyses could go a little further.

I take my cue for this article partly from a question asked in a recent article by the educators at the University of Wisconsin who are leading the charge for the use of games in classrooms (Shaffer, Squire, Halverson, & Gee, 2005). The authors end the piece with a call for more research on games, and specifically wonder "how inhabiting a virtual world develops situated knowledge—how playing a game like Civilization III, for example, mediates players' conceptions of world history" (p. 111). It is at this level that I think educators and players need to be aware of some of the limitations and tendencies of the medium.

Media ecology and the ideology of games

As games have moved from niche-culture status to mainstream, intellectuals have started to pay more attention to the ideologies that a game appears to support, in spite of the apparent freedom of play. Although a digital game may seem to give greater latitude to gamers than do other media, the procedural authors of games set limits and boundaries to activity (Frasca, 2003). As Shoshana Magnet (2006) argues in her critique of Tropico (PopTop Software, 2001), capitalist or ethnocentric assumptions can be built right into a game's virtual landscape (its "gamescape," as she puts it). Barkin (2002) and Chen (2003) likewise criticize Civilization III (Firaxis Games, 2001) for the problematic assumptions built into the game's model of culture. In their seminal textbook *Rules of Play*, Katie Salen and Eric Zimmerman (2004) also extensively talk about the possibility of specific games encoding ideologies.

Although this kind of single-game analysis is valuable, we can draw a larger picture: a consideration of the ideological implications of the medium as a whole. As Ted Friedman (1999) puts it, "Any medium . . . can teach you how to see life in new ways" (p. 133). By being able to "reorganize perception," to use Friedman's term, the digital game medium can have profound implications for how we understand the world and how it works. Educators and players in general would be well served to consider how computer and video games provide new ways to see and understand history.[2]

To address this question, I want to broadly rely on a media ecology perspective: the idea, in a nutshell, that the structure of a culture's dominant media is a major shaper of that very same culture. Media ecology studies how our tools and methods of communication form our cultural environments (Nystrom, 1973). The kinds of arguments and perspectives that media ecologists have used over the years vary quite widely. One of the key ideas developed and frequently employed in media ecology, however, is the concept of a medium's "bias." Innis (1950/1972, 1951) used this term to describe whether any given medium was better at communicating across time or space. Subsequent theorists, such as Postman (1985), developed the notion further, connecting the structure of a medium with a wider range of cultural issues. In other words, a medium is good at facilitating some kinds of communication and inhibits other kinds of communication; these strengths and weaknesses have cultural effects.

So does this mean the digital game medium has an ideological bias? This may seem like a ridiculous question to ask in a very broad manner. Various computer games could potentially contain numerous different and potentially quite contradictory ideologies. One game, for example, might be dedicated to utilizing natural resources specifically for capitalist gain, whereas another might be dedicated to sparing the environment from as much development as possible. Clearly, this medium has a great deal of ideological flexibility.

Even if we were to note some kind of consistent ideology in computer and video games, there are two common objections to talking about the bias of a medium. First, a wide range of cultural studies theorists have demonstrated that media users (readers, viewers, listeners, etc.) have more interpretive freedom than academics and marketers typically give them credit for. Just because a movie, television show, or book attempts to get the viewer or reader to buy into a specific way of thinking does not mean that this attempt is automatically successful. Media users can reinterpret, repurpose, or reject what they hear (e.g., Fiske, 1987; Jenkins, 1992). In fact, many cultural studies theorists would argue that studying texts in isolation is wasted time—the ultimate measure of communication is interpretation, so effective study of communication should be audience-focused, or at least based substantially upon audience research. Similarly, many game studies theorists have argued that games are configurative texts (Aarseth, 1997) and that we cannot understand games outside of how they are modified, talked about, and played (e.g., Salen & Zimmerman, 2004; Squire, 2006). Players and communities of players can take the same program and turn it into vastly different experiences. If this is the case, is it really worthwhile to talk about a medium's bias?

A second objection comes from the growing body of work on the social construction of technology. Historians and theorists of technology in the 20th century have often conceptualized our machines and techniques as virtually autonomous cultural actors (for a good overview of different technology studies, see Bijker, 1995b). The social construction of technology perspective seeks to counteract this way of thinking by stressing the absolute necessity of human involvement and intentionality for technology to have existence or meaning. A light bulb was not some Platonic form ready to be discovered—it was created through a thoroughly social process that was not predestined to happen the way it did. Once that light bulb did come into existence, its use was determined not by itself but by a whole series of social and cultural interactions—and in fact the light bulb is still being renegotiated today (e.g., Bijker, 1995a; Latour, 1996). If technology is so thoroughly created and recreated by social processes, does it make sense to talk about a medium's bias? If the medium has power, is that power not social and thus human? And cannot that medium be changed so that its perceived bias is no longer the same?

These are solid questions that require a clarification of the term *medium* and the concept of *medium bias*. It is crucial to recognize that a medium is not just technology, at least not in the typical use of the word that sees technology as a nonhuman machine. Television is a medium, but it is not just cameras and television sets. The medium of television includes that entire complex of institutions, machinery, and systems necessary for it to be a tool of communication. That means that the medium is constantly developing and redeveloping—it is not static, and it is not independent of human culture and society.

But to say this does not mean that the medium is completely fluid and instantly malleable—even purely human social forces are not easy to reshape. Television has evolved into what it is today because of extended historical cultural developments and because of material realities. Practices of broadcasting and the manufacturing of television machinery are unlikely to drastically change overnight because they have the weight of complex social developments beyond them. To say drastic change is possible is not the same thing as saying that it is likely. For example, switching to a completely noncommercial television broadcasting system in North America is certainly possible, but it would require massive economic and social reorganization or a very long and gradual process, both options requiring an enormous amount of social power and determination. In addition, certain material realities cannot be wished away. Batteries lose power when used, whether we want them to or not. In other words, to say that media are not static is not the same thing as saying they can have no bias. Biases may change, but that does not mean they are not present.[3]

Likewise, although it is clearly true that readers, viewers, and listeners have a great deal of interpretive flexibility and players have the ability to move beyond interpretation and actually configure a game, it is also true that the medium matters (as do texts). The audience can technically take a message in any possible direction: A radio listener could understand a racist joke as, say, an ironic commentary on the stupidity of hegemonic culture, even if that was seemingly not the intention. But to say that a message sender or the tool of communication have absolutely no effect on the interpretation of communication flies in the face of everyday experience. I suspect, for example, that most people do not randomly reinterpret the meaning of stop signs on a whim. A hardcore devotion to the interpretive power of the audience ignores the necessity of symbol creation for communication to occur. Media users do not receive just anything in the process of communication; what they receive has been created (often thoughtfully) and delivered with tools that have specific abilities and limitations.[4] Configurative practices have limitations as well. A community of players may share strategies, write fan fiction about a game, play alone or in groups, and even modify a game, all of which will significantly affect the experience of play. But they have to start with something, and it takes time and effort to change a game in unanticipated ways; certainly, someone with the requisite skills can modify crucial sequences of code in a game, but only at a cost of hours and/or dollars.

Any truly complete analysis of mediated communication must include audience studies (or a study of "performance"; Squire, 2006), a study of the medium, and research into textual production. If we keep this in mind, however, it should not be problematic to focus on one part of the process rather than the whole thing. Studying gameplay is not the only form of valuable game studies because gamers do not fully create the games they play. Thus, there is a place for game studies that seek to examine the medium of communication, as long as the researchers do not naively assume that their reading is the only possible one or that this is the only proper type of game research.

A good media ecology analysis, then, will avoid rigid technological determinism and an overly simplistic reading of texts that ignores what a reader, viewer, or player brings to or does to a text. This is not as difficult as it might sound. The metaphor that makes the most sense to me is that medium bias is like a hill. The slope (bias) of the ground is going to make moving in the direction of the top of the hill more difficult than moving down the hill (or across it). Of course, a determined hiker can go against the slope. People have mundane reasons to regularly walk against the slope; say, their home is on top of the hill and their work is at the bottom. But given no compelling reason to do otherwise, many, if not most, will take the path of least resistance and go with the slope—and even if they do not, it will take extra effort to climb. In addition, the hill is not truly stationary or immutable. Engineers and construction workers can reshape it, digging a tunnel through it or gouging a great slash through which to run a road or path. But all of this takes effort. Likewise, media are constructed in ways that change, but in their current existence, they have biases that encourage certain kinds of uses or certain kinds of interpretations.

So what kinds of factors affect the ideological bias of digital games—at least insofar as this bias affects the presentation of history? We could possibly make a very long list, but in this article, I want to focus on three factors: the masculine history and culture surrounding digital games, the systematic nature of both computers and games, and the ability of computers to create virtual, interactive game spaces. Each of these features will be analyzed by looking at a set of four historically themed series of games.

Terminology

Before launching into this examination, however, I want to clarify some important terminology used throughout the article. One key idea, of course, is that of *history*. History is not synonymous with the past—the latter is the unchangeable sequence of events and actions that have occurred, whereas the former is our record and conception of the past.[5] I want to reject the notion of objective history, at least in the modernist form of the notion (i.e., what really happened, regardless of anyone's opinion). In other words, all history is mediated through someone else's recollection and collection (usually, although not exclusively, via recording technologies such as writing or photography). The reason this is important is the second point: Different ways of presenting history create different meanings. That is why I think investigating historical games is worth considering—players are not having history revealed to them, they are experiencing one construction of history.

There are two other game terms that repeatedly appear throughout this article. One is the word *game* itself. The game form (or the idea of *game*) certainly transcends its digital manifestation: Board games, card games, sports games are all called games. Wittgenstein (1958) famously argued that there could be no central definition that joined all these forms together (pp. 31–32). Many have disagreed with him and tried to map that very thing (Caillois, 1961; Huizinga, 1938/1949; Juul, 2003; Salen & Zimmerman, 2004; Suits, 1978). Various definitions sometimes substantially disagree, but most game theorists include something describing games as rule-guided systems of play. In other words, games consist of a set of rules that give structure to playful activity. This is a broad definition, but it is sufficient for the subsequent arguments.

The other important game term for this article is *simulation*. This is not strictly a term limited to gaming. As Frasca (2003) puts it, "To simulate is to model a (source) system through a different system which maintains (for somebody) some of the behaviors of the original system" (p. 223). These models can vary in complexity. High-fidelity simulations strive for accuracy and realism, whereas low-fidelity simulations model only a few significant features (Thiagarajan, 1998). A common example of the latter is chess, which very loosely simulates a medieval battlefield; by contrast, many hobbyist war games strive for as much realism as possible. A wide range of games are in fact simulations, and most historically themed digital games fall into this category. This is not the same thing as saying that historical simulations are historically accurate. Although most games of this type are well researched, like the writers of historical fiction, game makers will bend actual events, appearances, or anything else to make a good and balanced game. In a sense, however, this is irrelevant: Whether the simulation is accurate or not, it effectively models history.

The bias of digital games

This article will analyze four different historically themed game simulation series. The Civilization series (Firaxis Games, 2001, 2005; Microprose Software,

1991, 1996), currently in its fourth iteration, is a grand strategy turn-based game that allows players to guide a culture to world dominance during a 6,000-year timeline. The Total War (Creative Assembly, 2000, 2002, 2004) series, including games set in medieval Japan and Europe and the classical-era Mediterranean, gives the opportunity to shepherd a faction across several centuries of conquest. Sid Meier's Pirates (Firaxis Games, 2004; Microprose Software, 1987, 1993), hereafter referred to simply as Pirates, is a genre-stretching simulation set in the 16th and 17th century Caribbean that, according to the game's slogan, lets the player "live the life" of a privateer. And finally, the Battlefield games (Digital Illusions Canada & Digital Illusions CE AB, 2004; Digital Illusions CE AB, 2002) are first-person shooter games that set the gamer in the action-packed combat zones of World War II or the Vietnam War. There are dozens more games that this analysis could consider. But these four series provide a good cross-section of different game styles set in different historical eras.[6]

Masculine history

Both computers and computer games have a strongly masculine history that still manifests itself in numerous ways. Although it is widely believed that the first computer programmer was a woman—Ada Lovelace is reputed to have written theoretical programs for Charles Babbage's never-constructed Analytical Engine—the roots of the modern computer are in thoroughly masculine contexts, such the cold war–era U.S. military, academic engineering departments of major research universities, and the early hacker culture.[7] Although the gender balance has clearly shifted during the past two or three decades, it is clear that computers are still very male items in many ways (Cassell & Jenkins, 1998). For example, recent statistics from the U.S. Bureau of Labor Statistics (2005) list women as occupying only 27.0% of positions in "computer and mathematical occupations," and a recent survey completed by the International Game Developers Association found that women form only 11.5% of the game industry's total workforce and only 5.0% of its programmers (Gourdin, 2005).

This latter statistic is not a new development: Computer games have also had a very male-dominated history. A few prominent female designers, such as Roberta Williams, have managed to make their mark on game culture, but, by and large, the people who made the digital game industry what it is today were men. A look at any list of credits today shows that although there are ever-greater numbers of women working in the game-making industry, the vast majority are still male. In short, one of the most salient features of the digital game medium—both in terms of computer technology and the game industry itself—is that it is very masculine in nature. It should be clear that there is nothing essentially masculine about either games or computers; nevertheless, a masculine bias has been a major feature of the social construction of the digital game medium throughout its history.[8]

For decades now, critical historians have struggled to counteract the manner in which the standard Western histories of Great White (dead) Men have written marginal social groups out of our cultural historical consciousness. Although the discipline of history has been busy correcting this significant problem, digital games tend to reinscribe it. A kind of masculine slant is exceptionally clear in game presentation of history. For one thing, practically all history in digital games is focused on some combination of politics, economics, and war. For another, all of the historical games examined for this article demonstrate the centrality of aggressive power and/or acquisition. The centrality of these features displays the importance of stereotypical manhood to historical simulations.

The first evidences of this masculine bias are the types of historical focuses of the game simulations. Partly as an attempt to correct the hegemonic bias of traditional historical research, the discipline of history has broadened its scope to include a great diversity of subjects. Social, cultural, and critical histories are particularly valuable for emphasizing the significance of people ignored in the traditional accounts of monarchs, merchants, and military campaigns. Most historical digital games, however, ignore these trends and almost exclusively focus on politics, economics, and war. Strategy games that are historical simulators almost always have an economic component and frequently have a political dimension as well. A major part of Civilization and the Total War games—and, to a lesser extent, Pirates—consists of balancing income and expenses, developing commercial trade, exploiting resources, investing in economic infrastructure, and so on. Another part of these same games is dedicated to developing and maintaining advantageous relationships with other factions or powers in the games (whether they are played by humans or the computer): making and breaking alliances, trading deals, and other diplomatic agreements. Both Civilization and the Total War games have an internal political element as well, requiring the player to keep his or her own population content enough to avoid rebellion.

More blatant than the two themes of economics and politics, however, is the centrality of war. Practically all commercial historical digital games feature some kind of military- or combat-oriented activity, even if it is not the only option available to players. Pirates allows the player to be a peaceful merchant instead of a bloodthirsty privateer, and the Civilization player may win the game without conquering anyone or anything. In both cases, however, it would be extremely challenging to make it all the way through the game without a single battle. In addition, the mechanics of these games, their manuals and even their promotional literature clearly indicate that game makers wish violence and combat to prominently feature in gameplay. In many other historical simulations, war is the raison d'être, as clearly evidenced by the titles of the Total War and Battlefield games. Playing these games in a nonconfrontational or nonviolent way would be to deliberately subvert the games' purposes (which, of course, is possible).

Other kinds of historical focuses certainly do appear in historical representations of the past. All of the games except for the Battlefield series feature broader cultural issues. Civilization has numerous cultural and social technologies such as mysticism or nationalism and buildings such as coliseums or cathedrals. In addition, its encyclopedic descriptions of the various game units, improvements, and concepts give a great deal of historical depth that often moves beyond political, economic, and military considerations. In Pirates, one of the major minigames is the decidedly artistic activity of ballroom dancing. But, as a whole, these social and cultural pictures of history are subservient to the political, economic, and military focuses of the game mechanics: Their game function is to help the player become more politically, economically, and militarily successful. Successful dancing in Pirates, for example, leads the charmed governor's daughter to give gifts or tips about financially rewarding quests.

When culture is apparently autonomous, it ends up functioning in much the same manner as an economic system. In the last two versions of Civilization, a player may win the game by achieving cultural dominance. Buildings such as libraries or theaters produce culture points. These accumulate throughout the game, extending the territory of the player and even leading to enemy cities defecting to a dominant neighboring civilization. If a player's culture is powerful enough, he or she wins the game. Although the game uses the word *culture*, this is obviously misleading: Culture in reality is a complex, particular, multifaceted phenomenon (Barkin, 2002; Chen, 2003). What we are seeing here is currency dressed up as culture points. Even when the game tries to get away from politics, economics, and war, it cannot escape the well-worn pattern.

In fact, Civilization's culture system is also a good illustration of another masculine theme: Games typically present history as a matter of aggressive power. In the Battlefield games, this is particularly clear: The player must kill or be killed—the player's team must physically destroy the opposition with firearms or military vehicles. In the strategy games, the focus can be on this kind of conquest-oriented militaristic power drive, but just as often, the key motive of the game is aggressive acquisition. In Total War, the player tries to get as much territory and as large an army as possible. In Civilization, the player has several options, but whether he or she chooses a military, cultural, or technological route to success, the game consists of trying to get as much stuff as possible, often forcefully. In Pirates, we see the modern suburban dream of acquiring a career, wife, and house with a yard written onto a 17th century Caribbean setting; the player's score is dependent, among a few other things, on the amount of treasure acquired, the amount of land rewarded by grateful governors, and the attractiveness of the wife.[9] Again, the player achieves this primarily via sword fights, ship-to-ship combat, and ground-based invasions.

It is of course important to note that politics, economics, and even war are not inherently male spheres of life, nor that only men desire power or focus on acquisition (or that all men wish for these things). However, all of these themes are stereotypically male; they fit widely publicized, rough masculine ideals of aggressiveness and domination (e.g., Douglas, 1999; Faludi, 1999; Jeffords, 1994). More importantly, these themes crowd out or subvert things that are not stereotypically masculine, especially in the presentation of historical games. Many, including myself, have reasonable hope that this might change. There are a growing number of popular digital games that break the hyper-masculine mold—notably best-sellers SimCity and The Sims—although virtually none take place in historical settings. MIT's "Games-to-Teach" project developed a historical multiplayer role-playing game that also suggests that the representation of history in games is not locked into the stereotypically masculine interests (Squire & Jenkins, 2003). For the moment, however, the bias of the medium is pretty thoroughly in favor of one gender, and it will take work to change that.

Systematic history

Friedman (1999) argues that when we play games we are taught to "think like a computer," to exercise "cyborg consciousness" (pp. 136–138). Computers process symbols in a highly systematic manner, and this clearly shows up in their presentation of history. Several media theorists note that all computerized or digital texts are "procedural"; that is, all programs and the objects within those programs operate according to a series of rules (e.g., Manovich, 2001; Murray, 1997). Without definition of data and instructions on how to handle that data, a computer can do nothing. And, as noted already, whether they are digital or not, games also run according to rules. Try to imagine the board game Monopoly with no rules. It would still be something—a piece art or a toy, maybe—but it would not be a game.

Both computers and games are systematic—computer games are, by implication, inescapably so. What this means is that anything in a computer game either has some kind of game function or is, in game terms, decoration. Decoration is important and is often the reason that players buy games. Imagination can move the player well beyond the literal and mental confines of the game and its system (and authorial intentions). But what the media user plays with (configures)—if he or she is in fact playing the game rather than just looking at it or listening to it—always has a definable part in the game system. In short, then, the digital game medium introduces all the benefits and drawbacks of a structured system. Another way of putting it is this: With other media, if creators can imagine something, their challenge is to find a way to express it. This can be a challenge, especially with visual media such as television or film. But with a game, the bulk of whatever the creators imagine must be both expressed and presented to the player as a working, logical model.

Thus, games can go beyond the representations or explanations of history typically found in older media by modeling history. History can be simulated outside of the computer. For example, a kind of live-action role-playing situation (e.g., those we might see at historic tourist attractions) might allow people to experience or work through historical situations. But this is where the medium makes a difference. A digital game model, because of its requirement to have a systematic structure, has a series of important implications: The people modeled in historical games tend to have highly defined roles, the games tend to present the development of history with a clear chain of cause and effect, and any unavoidable nonsystematic elements of life are rendered as inconsequential or random influences.

We all know from everyday experience that people are not simply classifiable, that a few words or sentences will not be able to sum up a person. Although I am a professor, I could also be a father, a pugilist, a part-time dance instructor, a dog owner, and someone who likes Mel Torme.[10] Even more important, my life may change, I may change direction, I may become a different person. In short, I am nothing like a cog in a machine. This is also true of people throughout history. Napoleon was a general, but he was much more than that! Digital games, however, tend not to be able to present the full fluidity and flexibility of what it means to be human. As far as most historical games are concerned, people are important in terms of the one or two roles they play in society.[11]

In Total War, individuals are known only as soldiers of a specific type: generals, cavalry soldiers, archers, or infantry. The people running around the Battlefield games are just as rigidly defined by the type of weapon kits they possess. In Civilization, the same is mostly true, although when negotiating with other cultures, a window opens that allows the player to enter into prearranged dialogue with a cartoony (animated) leader of that civilization, who is a famous historical figure such as Cleopatra, Mao Zedong, or Catherine the Great. Again, however, although these characters can—in a sense—speak with the player, they are defined by their role of great leader. Likewise, the various people that populate the Caribbean in Pirates are usually capable of menu-option conversation, but they remain stock characters without life beyond their role: the flirtatious barmaid, the mysterious man selling treasures, the magisterial governor, and the villainous Marquis de Montalban. Because digital games are systematic in nature, it is at best very difficult to use them to present humans with agency beyond predefined parameters—or indeed to present very much about the human outside of those predefined parameters. In other words, historical actors are free only to do what the game allows them to do, and what they are allowed to do in most historical games is only what a preset social role defines.[12]

In addition, historical games tend to display a systematic unfolding of time and causality. The two grand strategy game series reviewed for this article (Total War and Civilization) actually present the development of history itself as incremental and sequential, just as a 19th century Darwinian would be likely to chart evolutionary and social progress. These kinds of games frequently break history into stages, usually defined by a level of technological or economic development. Civilization is a classic example of this. Technology develops according to a tree structure, where learning one technology opens up the possibility of learning more advanced related technologies. So, for example, learning polytheism is a prerequisite for developing monotheism (the former, by implication, being simpler and the latter being more complex or developed). The latter versions of the game are split into eras or ages, such as ancient, classical, and medieval, that affect the aesthetic presentation of the buildings in the game; advances in technology allow the player to move to a new stage. Likewise, in the Total War games, certain buildings and units are not available until a community reaches the requisite population level, which grows at a relatively stable percentage rate, barring any catastrophes or military invasions. In other words, historical development can travel down only a limited number of predetermined paths, as societies and cultures are built on top of previous achievements.

Linear development of history, however, is not a strict requirement of the medium. Although programming used to be sequential and procedural, today object-oriented programming, hypertext, and other digital tools easily allow for associative or nonlinear creations. What this means is that history could be presented more as a network and less as a unidirectional timeline. Pirates is a pretty good example of this: The game has less of a sense of a grand narrative and more a sense of emergent narrative (Jenkins, 2002), developed by choices made from a wide array of possibilities available to the player at any give point in time. The player sails from one port to the next without a clear sense of overall direction given by the game. The Battlefield games are even more open ended, allowing the players to run anywhere and do anything that is physically possible in the virtual environment until one side or the other gains victory.

So linearity is not required; a systematic presentation of time and causality, however, is. Although Pirates may not present history as the unfolding of progress, its time is still systematic. What I mean by this is that time is still rule bound. The experience of historical development can occur only at a pace that only the computer game allows. The calendar in a game moves with clockwork efficiency whether there is a sense of narrative trajectory or not. In addition, nothing happens in a game without a clear and traceable cause (more on this below).

Although systematic time and causality still allow for many different variations and possibilities, games are still more limited than analogue media such as print or film. In fact, great systematic flexibility requires great complexity because the system has to accommodate a wider range of variables. In her insightful critique of culture in Civilization III, Barkin (2002) rightly notes that the game is monocultural with a veneer of multiculturalism. That is, you can play the Zulus, Russians, or Aztecs, but all of them essentially have to follow the Western pattern of economic and technological development and conquest. What she fails to note, however, is that presenting greater cultural complexity challenges the bias of the medium: Because various cultures have to be turned into an airtight system of programs and game rules, modeling more than a few truly distinct cultures (even if they are greatly simplified) becomes exceptionally difficult.

A connected point is that although Pirates or the Battlefield games may not have a grand narrative guiding them, they do not have a lot of room for contingency, for the unpredictable accidents of history that have changed its direction. Again, it is difficult to fit such things into a fully predictable system. A simulation is, by necessity, a simplification of something much more complex. In other words, a simulation could not completely capture even systematic elements of life, such as a local government bureaucracy governed by established procedures and composed of people in clearly defined roles. And there are many elements of life that defy practically *any* serious attempt to simulate them. Everyone anticipated that weather would be a major factor in the success or failure of the Allied landings on

D-Day—this can be modeled. Few could have predicted, however, that a lightning storm would have been responsible for Martin Luther becoming a monk. Such unpredictable elements are almost impossible to systematically model, which makes a significant impact on historically themed digital games. Both D-Day and Luther's conversion were phenomenally important historical events, but only one of them can be simulated in a meaningful way. And this limitation in modeling is not related just to unpredictable events but to fundamentally human emotional phenomena such as love, which is amorphous, quotidian, powerful, and typically unsystematic.

Games have a number of ways of dealing with aspects of life that are hard to simulate. Some historical games effectively ignore nonsystematic aspects of life. The Battlefield series is like this. The human body is a machine, our environment is a space governed by physical laws that are perfectly predictable. The only unpredictability in the game results from the player's ignorance of all the relevant details—for example, the computer knows each little nuanced contour of the terrain, but the player cannot. Other games effectively reduce everything to systems, like Pirates, where courting, for example, really is a mechanistic— albeit entertaining—performance of dance routines. However, many history games recognize that not all life is systematic or predictable, and they generally have only one solution for incorporating these features of life: add an element of randomness.

This is most obvious in combat simulation. A perusal of military history will reveal to even the most passing observer that battles are not predictable events. Warriors sometimes fight with complete abandon and at other times run away from apparently certain victory screaming because of a poor omen. Although a historical military simulation such as Total War tries to model battle as a mechanical system (attacking from a higher elevation to a lower is positive, getting attacked on a unit's flanks or rear is negative, etc.), it recognizes that war is not chess. So does Civilization. What this means in practice is that combat strengths are not a measure of effect; they are a measure of probable effect. In Civilization, a weaker unit always has the possibility of beating a stronger unit because although the relative combat strengths are taken into battle-resolution calculations, the deciding factor is a randomly generated number. This is the only way that nonsystematic aspects of life can enter into a system like that of a historical computer game.

Some digital games have attempted to mitigate the most rigidly mechanical nature of computerized people with varying degrees of success. For example, more and more digital games try to create worlds with as few boundaries as possible, allowing the player to break out of preestablished roles; the controversial Grand Theft Auto III (DMA Design, 2001) received numerous accolades for this. However, no matter how open ended the system, it is never completely unbounded. A more promising route is the rise (or perhaps dominance) of multiplayer games. One of the most compelling aspects of the Games-to-Teach Revolution game is the fact that all the historical characters in the game are played by real people (students). This means that instead of talking to robots—even highly intelligent robots—students are encountering historical characters played by other students. Elaborate and well-researched role-playing could certainly lead to compelling presentations and experiences of historical scenarios. But even this has its limits. Multiplayer games clearly free up the social dimension from simplistic systems, but the (virtual) material world of the game still must operate according to the game system. If it remains a game—or even a nongame simulation—it must have rules, and rules usually mean boundaries that do not exist in other mediated forms. This is not inherently wrong, but it is a limitation of the medium.

Historical space rather than historical events

The final feature of digital games worth remarking on is the most difficult to map and most ambiguous in its effect on the presentation of history, yet it is also perhaps the most profound of the three characteristics I discuss in this article. Although computers are able to show movies and books, play recorded music, and speak to us, perhaps the most important ability of computers and video games is the power to create and present virtual, interactive, navigable spaces.

Computers have a series of features that allow them to represent old media in new ways (digital emulation) and add types of experiences not possible or very difficult to have in old media. The computer, as Bolter and Grusin (1999) put it, is a remediation machine: It takes old media forms and re-presents them (to improve on them). In other words, the computer can pretend to be a book, a radio show, a film, a television show, and more. Of course, digital media transform the analogue media being emulated. Although the computer can make a book appear on screen or present text in a scrolling window, these representations are quite obviously not the same as a tangible bound sheaf of papers.

But the computer adds new features that are significantly different from older media: To its emulation capabilities it adds the novelty of easy and powerful interaction. Together, these features allow the computer to create navigable virtual spaces. Old media have been creating imaginary spaces for as long as we have had records. Any narrative (whether fiction or not) can conjure up locations that exist in the mind of the listener, viewer, or reader. Visual media such as film and television move beyond written and aural media by actually showing the imaginary spaces. As emulators, computers can do all these things, but they are able to add interactivity.

Although *interactivity* is an overused term (for a good discussion, see McMahan, 2003), it signifies something very real: Computers invite humans to change texts via their input. This is not something that is strictly limited to computer texts. As Espen Aarseth (1997) points out, cybertexts—texts in which the user actions produce "nontrivial effects"—are actually quite old. Certainly a noncomputerized board game such as chess is interactive. Nevertheless, computers are particularly good at facilitating a wide range of human input and showing a wider range of effects than are possible in other media. It would be difficult, for instance, to imagine the appearance of a player's board game piece in Monopoly changing to reflect how much money the player has—fat and well dressed while winning, emaciated and filthy while losing—but this kind of thing is easily done in a computer game.

In light of this, it is not surprising that the presentation of history changes in the new medium. One of the most interesting and appealing features of historical games is that they invite the player to enter into another world. In fact, all but the most abstract games (e.g., Tetris [AcademySoft, 1986] or Snood [Dobson, 1996]) do this. Again, other media such as books and films do this too, but where these old media are like a glass tour bus—look but do not touch—digital game worlds are tangible, changeable places. This has several profound implications for the way digital games present history. First, it favors a kind of objectivist understanding of history that is present in other media but, I would argue, can be more intense in computer and video games. Second, history in digital games is playable. Finally, computer and video games shift historical attention away from events and on to spaces and societies.

Although the idea of objectivity may or may not predate the photograph, visual representational media are certainly well suited to reinforce the notion. A written text—printed or handwritten—regardless of how precise and detailed it is, always has a certain degree of ambiguity (Sontag, 1977). I can describe a character via statistics (6 feet tall, 180 pounds), meticulous detail (a barely visible mole on the lobe of the left ear), colorful metaphors (hair like the sand from a Caribbean tourist brochure), explanation of disposition (a sunny, uplifting personality), and much more. But no matter how complex the written portrait, if two people were to turn their internal visualization into a photograph or painting, they would almost certainly end up with different pictures.

And therein lies the difference between written words and representational media: We may differently interpret the meaning of a photograph or a film, but the visuals are identical from one viewing to the next. The photograph, as Sontag (1977) and Postman (1985) argue, has always carried the idea of objectivity with it. A photograph captures only what is there, so if it is not doctored, then it is showing reality that nobody can dispute. It implies an objective reality. Of course, historians have long recognized that all historical work involves points of view, even if there are pieces of evidence most people interpret the same way and that many scholars have broad agreement on many events or people in the past. Written texts are clearly not objective, as all writers write from their own point of view. Sontag points out that photographs are really no different—in spite of their appearance, they involve selection and thus a point of view. Nevertheless, historical films and television shows always carry a sense with them that "this is the way it happened" because of their apparent objectivity.

I would argue that the digital game medium in some ways strengthens this notion of an objective history. This is not immediately obvious. Currently, the graphical capabilities of computers for game playing, although impressive in comparison to where they were even 10 years ago, have not reached the level of true photorealism, something that should hamper a sense of objectivity. In addition, the interface necessary for playing—displays and meters, for example—also clearly marks the text as a game, not a transparent recording of something or an actual world with which we can interact. Nevertheless, the creation of a tangible historical space is in some senses a much more convincing case for historical objectivity than any picture might be. Although the battlefields of Total War do not purport to be photographs of the real thing, they are modeled on real geography, and, more importantly, the player can move around them, interact with them, guide his or her soldiers across them, and experience the effects of the terrain (going up hills is more tiring than going down, crossing a bridge or river is a difficult and dangerous thing to do in battle, etc.). If the space does not look real, it feels real. And it feels objective because although the game allows the player to zoom all over as if in a helicopter, the space itself does not change according to the player's perspective.

Another crucial difference between digital game history and history presented in other media is play. Other media give opportunities to play with history—the genre of historical fiction is full of "what if?" questions—but only digital games ask their users to enter historical situations and start interfering with them. This is, in fact, one of the key appeals for most of these games. Civilization asks the player to see if he or she can guide a culture to greater success than it really had. The Battlefield and Total War games allow players to redo famous battle or campaigns and see if history might have had a different outcome. Pirates gives the player the option of redrawing the colonial map of the Caribbean by ousting governors and replacing them with a leader of another nationality.

This results in a very open-ended picture of history. This difference between static and dynamic understandings of the past cannot be stressed enough. In a book, history is completed; the future work of the historian may change history, of course, but not the specific history that the reader is currently engaging. Short of using WiteOut and a pen, print is not likely to change. In a digital game, however, history is never set: The player always has the ability to redo history. If this option is not present, the digital game ceases to become a game and instead becomes some kind of computerized movie. Interestingly, then, historical digital games seem to be a living embodiment of a controversial kind of scholarship called "counterfactual" or "virtual" history (Ferguson, 1997). Although much of this body of writing is effectively fanciful historical fiction, some very serious and careful historians view it as an alternative to the assumed determinism in most accounts of the past. Essentially, this notion of history emphasizes the indeterminacy of events from the perspective of those experiencing them. This is the notion of history that the digital game medium favors, albeit with a caveat. Although the player has freedom to change the course of history, it is only to the degree that the game system allows. You may wish for the Zulus in Civilization to pursue a different technology tree, for instance, but it is not going to happen because it is simply not part of the game. Nevertheless, once the boundaries of the system are established, history in digital games is freed from a predetermined set of occurrences.

In fact, history in computer and video games is far less about events and far more about space. Although events happen in a game session, the play does not emphasize specific instances of activity, which are usually just variations on the same action. There are dozens of similar battles in a typical game of Total War and dozens of similar sword fights in a typical game of Pirates. After a few of these, they are no longer new or need serious investigation. Instead, it is the space and the system of the game that the player explores. This is what Henry Jenkins (2002) describes as "spatial storytelling." That is, a story of this type is less about what happens and more about where it happens. As Jenkins points out, this style of storytelling is not just unique to computer games; certain novels, such as Tolkien's *The Lord of the Rings*, have emphasized space over events. Nevertheless, digital games, because of their proficiency at creating consistent, tangible, navigable space, are particularly well suited to spatial storytelling. The upshot is that history in digital games will tend to be less like a linear narrative of "this happened and then that happened." Instead, the game will be much more about historical places and historical systems (social or otherwise).

It is difficult to sum up what the digital game medium's interactivity does to its presentation of history, and critiquing it is even more challenging.[13] History, in the games I examined, feels tangible (and thus objective) and undetermined. It is less about an account of time and more about an experience of space and people in the past. All of this changes the meaning or the feel of what we understand as history. I am not at all certain that this is an entirely bad thing by the standards of critical history today, especially in the sense that digital games do a good job of portraying the indeterminacy of history. At the same time, educators and players would do well to be aware of the medium's tendencies. The feeling of being able to enter into history is quite profoundly different from reading about it or watching it unfold as a spectator. If players do not recognize this difference, they may not even be aware that their notion of history will profoundly differ from perspectives formed in an old media setting.

Conclusion: what are they good for?

What I have tried to show in this article is that the presentation of history in digital games is likely to be quite different than it would be in other media: Computer and video games are likely to display masculine, systematic, and spatially oriented interactive versions of history. Although the medium does not determine the way game makers will or will not present the past, the facts that it is historically dominated by men and masculine values, that it requires all texts to be systematic in nature, and that it is adept at producing interactive virtual spaces mean that representations of history that step outside of the characteristics listed above will take extra effort.

As this analysis should demonstrate, I believe a consideration of the digital game medium itself should be a part of any complete analysis of games. But like any medium, digital games are complex enough social and technological phenomena that any analysis of it should draw on multiple perspectives. In fact, game studies, as an interdisciplinary field, should broaden its theoretical foundations, drawing as heavily on communication and media studies, sociological theory, and cultural studies as it does on literary formalism. I do not mean to say, however, that the theories and methods employed here should be the favored ones—rather, they provide a limited, but valuable, part of the picture. If I understood this as the final word, I would be ignoring the importance of play and interpretation. It might be that when many or even most gamers actually play digital historical games, they use or understand them in such a way that the tendencies described above are countered or moderated. Even so, the text has some say in the way communication occurs. Although any interpretation (and action on that interpretation) is possible, not all of those interpretations are equally likely. Thus, medium bias is an important thing to keep in mind.

I also want to be clear that although this article is generally critical in tone, I am in no way saying that we should avoid the use of digital games in the teaching of history or that we should avoid playing them. Were we to use that kind of logic, we should not communicate at all! Every medium, including the venerable book (once considered upstart itself), has its strengths and weaknesses. And all cultures make different use of their media to communicate. I think that digital games are a fantastic avenue to immerse students and other kinds of players in historical settings and situations, to give them a sense of the kinds of decisions and pressures that both the patricians and the plebeians faced in different contexts. And, of course, games help educate in a more general cognitive sense, developing strong problem-solving skills. As a teenager, the first version of Pirates taught me the geography of the Caribbean in addition to the logic of colonial development (albeit from a rather uncritical perspective). As an adult, Civilization has allowed me to develop careful, experimental thought processes and has given me an opportunity to critically explore social logics. The list could go on. The point I wish to make is that all tools have their drawbacks. If we were to think of digital games as the way to experience or learn about the past, I think we would end up missing some important aspects of how we should understand history.

It is my hope that innovative and principled game designers continue to push the boundaries of the medium. I have already mentioned several promising developments, such as an increasing popularity of games that break the masculine mold and the huge success of multiplayer games that act as alternative social spaces. But the games industry as it currently exists is not well suited to innovation. Perhaps the rise of indie gaming—the production of digital games by individuals, educational institutions, or small-scale companies outside the mainstream system of production and distribution—will help lead to the development of really unique ways of working through history. Even so, we will always do best to remember that any historical game, no matter how engrossing, immersive, or fun it is, should only ever be a part of our picture of the past. Learning to engage recorded history should never be fully supplanted by user-controlled, systematic, history-themed play. Quintus the Mighty agrees (because I say he does).

Notes

1 Discussions about the educational value of games has actually gone on for a long time (Egenfeldt-Nielsen, 2004; Squire, 2004a). According to Squire (2004a), teaching with games was somewhat in vogue during the 1970s, but these games rarely used computers, and they fell out of favor in the 1980s. What we are seeing now is a renaissance of interest from a distinctively constructivist educational theory viewpoint.

2 Squire's (2006) recent writing, "Videogames as Designed Experience," is an excellent example of a broad ideological critique of the digital game medium. He touches some of the same issues as this article does, but his main focus is on educational ideology—the way game playing and game design encode the character of learners. Another contrast with this piece is that Squire's article spends much more time talking about the performance of gameplay.

3 Much social construction of technology theory recognizes these points, but I feel these clarifications are necessary because the same writings frequently and fervently disavow technological determinism, and *technological determinism* is precisely the label most often applied to media ecology. My point is that when understood properly, the social construction of technology perspective and media ecology are not necessarily incompatible.

4 Again, many cultural studies scholars recognize these points. Yet the not-unusual methodological critique that critical research suffers from an overabundance of textual studies and dearth of audience studies might lead to the impression that anyone accepting many of the tenets of cultural studies should not waste their time studying texts or technology. Again, my point is that media ecology is not incompatible with cultural studies.

5 My thanks to Dr. Robynne Healey of Trinity Western University for this suggested definition.

6 This article does not consider nonsimulation games such as the adventure or puzzle genres. In addition, some kinds of simulation genres, such as flight simulators or classic war games, are only partly represented by the four texts. Nevertheless, I think most of the observations mapped below still apply to a wide variety of digital game genres.

7 Although none of these observations are particularly controversial, a good game-oriented discussion of some of these issues is in *Digital Play* (Kline, Dyer-Witheford, & De Peuter, 2003).

8 Again, for a good discussion of the "militarized masculinity" in games, see *Digital Play* (Kline et al., 2003). Also see Cassell and Jenkins (1998) and Herz (1997).

9 This is actually ranked in the game; the three varieties are "plain," "attractive," and "beautiful."

10 Only the first two are actually true.

11 This line of reasoning might seem to assume a Western individualist mind-set. Of course some societies (e.g., medieval European culture) were (and are) much more collective and tended to think of people first and foremost in terms of the role they played in society. The point is not so much that this way of thinking of people is invalid or incorrect. The point is that this is only one way of thinking about historical actors, and it tends to be the way that games use.

12 A few games feature more rounded and developed characters, but these are not typically historical games. Even so, the development of these characters is arguably nowhere near that found in pulp fiction and popular film.

13 Shoshana Magnet (2006) uses landscape theory and coins the term *gamescape* to explain how ideology is encoded into the spaces of tropical dictator simulator Tropico (PopTop Software, 2001). Although her criticisms are provocative, they are by and large specific to the game more than the medium as a whole.

References

Aarseth, E. J. (1997). *Cybertext: Perspectives on ergodic literature*. Baltimore: Johns Hopkins University Press.

AcademySoft. (1986). Tetris [Computer game]. Moscow: Author.

Barkin, G. (2002, January 15). The culture of Civilization III. Message posted to http://web. archive.org/web/20020201200724/www.joystick101.org/?op=displaystory&sid=2002/ 1/12/222013/422

Bijker, W. (1995a). *Of bicycles, bakelites, and bulbs: Toward a theory of sociotechnical change*. Cambridge, MA: MIT Press.

Bijker, W. (1995b). Sociohistorical technology studies. In S. Jasanoff, G. E. Markle, J. C. Petersen, & T. J. Pinch (Eds.), *Handbook of science and technology studies* (pp. 229–256). London: Sage.

Bolter, J. D., & Grusin, R. (1999). *Remediation: Understanding new media*. Cambridge, MA: MIT Press. Caillois, R. (1961). *Man, play, and games*. New York: Free Press.

Cassell, J., & Jenkins, H. (1998). Chess for girls? feminism and computer games. In J. Cassell & H. Jenkins (Eds.), *From Barbie to Mortal Kombat: Gender and computer games* (pp. 2–45). Cambridge, MA: MIT Press.

Chen, K. (2003). Civilization and its disk contents: Two essays on civilization and Civilization. *Radical Society, 30*(2), 95–107.

Creative Assembly. (2000). Shogun: Total war [Computer game]. Redwood City, CA: Electronic Arts.

Creative Assembly. (2002). Medieval: Total war [Computer game]. Santa Monica, CA: Activision.

Creative Assembly. (2004). Rome: Total war [Computer game]. Santa Monica, CA: Activision.

Digital Illusions Canada, Digital Illusions CE AB. (2004). Battlefield Vietnam [Computer game]. Redwood City, CA: Electronic Arts.

Digital Illusions CE AB. (2002). Battlefield 1942 [Computer game]. Redwood City, CA: Electronic Arts.

DMA Design. (2001). Grand theft auto III [Computer game]. New York: Rockstar Games.

Dobson, D. M. (1996). Snood [Computer game]. Calabasas, CA: Word of Mouse Games.

Douglas, S. (1999). *Listening in: Radio and the imagination, from Amos 'n Andy and Edward R. Murrow to Wolfman Jack and Howard Stern*. New York: Times Books.

Egenfeldt-Nielsen, S. (2004). Practical barriers in using educational computer games. *On the Horizon, 12*(1), 18–21.

Faludi, S. (1999). *Stiffed: The betrayal of the American man*. New York: William Morrow.

Ferguson, N. (Ed.). (1997). *Virtual history: Alternatives and counterfactuals*. London: Picador.

Firaxis Games. (2001). Sid Meier's civilization III [Computer game]. Lyon, France: Infogrames.

Firaxis Games. (2004). Sid Meier's pirates! [Computer game]. New York: Atari.

Firaxis Games. (2005). Sid Meier's civilization IV [Computer game]. New York: 2K Games.

Fiske, J. (1987). *Television culture*. New York: Routledge.

Frasca, G. (2003). Simulation versus narrative: Introduction to ludology. In M. J. P. Wolf & B. Perron (Eds.), *The video game theory reader* (pp. 221–235). New York: Routledge.

Friedman, T. (1999). Civilization and its discontents: Simulation, subjectivity and space. In G. M. Smith (Ed.), *On a silver platter: CD-ROMs and the promises of a new technology* (pp. 132–150). New York: New York University Press.

Gee, J. P. (2003). *What video games have to teach us about learning and literacy*. New York: Palgrave Macmillan.

Gourdin, A. (2005). *Game developer demographics: An exploration of workforce diversity*. San Francisco: International Game Developers Association.

Herz, J. C. (1997). *Joystick nation: How videogames ate our quarters, won our hearts, and rewired our minds*. Boston: Little, Brown.

Huizinga, J. (1949). *Homo ludens: A study of the play-element in culture* (R. F. C. Hull, Trans.). London: Routledge and Kegan Paul. (Original work published 1938)

Innis, H. A. (1951). *The bias of communication*. Toronto, Ontario, Canada: University of Toronto Press.

Innis, H. A. (1972). *Empire and communications*. Toronto, Ontario, Canada: University of Toronto Press. (Original work published 1950)

Jeffords, S. (1994). *Hard bodies: Hollywood masculinity in the Reagan era*. New Brunswick, NJ: Rutgers University Press.

Jenkins, H. (1992). *Textual poachers: Television fans and participatory culture*. New York: Routledge.

Jenkins, H. (2002). Game design as narrative architecture. In N. Wardrip-Fruin & P. Harrigan (Eds.), *First person: New media as story, performance, and game* (pp. 118–130). Cambridge, MA: MIT Press.

Johnson, S. (2005). *Everything bad is good for you: How today's popular culture is actually making us smarter*. New York: Riverhead Books.

Juul, J. (2003). The game, the player, the world: Looking for a heart of gameness. In *Level up: Digital games research conference* (pp. 30–45). Utrecht, the Netherlands: Utrecht University Press.

King, B., & Borland, J. (2003). *Dungeons and dreamers: The rise of computer game culture from geek to chic*. New York: McGraw-Hill/Osborne.

Kline, S., Dyer-Witheford, N., & De Peuter, G. (2003). *Digital play: The interaction of technology, culture, and marketing*. Montreal, Quebec, Canada: McGill-Queen's University Press.

Latour, B. (1996). *Aramis, or the love of technology*. Cambridge, MA: Harvard University Press.

Learning Company. (1997). The Oregon trail (3rd ed.) [Computer game]. San Francisco: Author.

Magnet, S. (2006). Playing at colonization: Interpreting imaginary landscapes in the video game Tropico. *Journal of Communication Inquiry, 30*(2), 142–162.

Manovich, L. (2001). *The language of new media*. Cambridge, MA: MIT Press.

Maxis Software. (1989). SimCity [Computer game]. Eugene, OR: Broderbund.

Maxis Software. (2000). The Sims [Computer game]. Redwood City, CA: Electronic Arts.

McMahan, A. (2003). Immersion, engagement, and presence: A method for analyzing 3-D video games. In M. J. P. Wolf & B. Perron (Eds.), *The video game theory reader* (pp. 67–86). New York: Routledge.

Microprose Software. (1987). Sid Meier's pirates! [Computer game]. Hunt Valley, MD: Author.

Microprose Software. (1991). Sid Meier's civilization [Computer game]. Hunt Valley, MD: Author.

Microprose Software. (1993). Pirates! gold [Computer game]. Hunt Valley, MD: Author.

Microprose Software. (1996). Sid Meier's civilization II [Computer game]. Hunt Valley, MD: Author.

Murray, J. H. (1997). *Hamlet on the holodeck: The future of narrative in cyberspace.* Cambridge, MA: MIT Press.

Nystrom, C. (1973). *Towards a science of media ecology: The formulation of integrated conceptual paradigms for the study of human communication systems.* Unpublished doctoral dissertation, New York University.

PopTop Software. (2001). Tropico [Computer game]. New York: Gathering of Developers.

Postman, N. (1985). *Amusing ourselves to death.* New York: Elizabeth Sifton.

Salen, K., & Zimmerman, E. (2004). *Rules of play: Game design fundamentals.* Cambridge, MA: MIT Press.

Shaffer, D. W., Squire, K. R., Halverson, R., & Gee, J. P. (2005). Video games and the future of learning. *Phi Delta Kappan, 87*(2), 105–111.

Sontag, S. (1977). *On photography.* New York: Farrar, Strauss and Giroux.

Squire, K. (2004a). *Replaying history: Learning world history through playing Civilization III.* Unpublished doctoral dissertation, Indiana University, Bloomington.

Squire, K. (2004b). Review: Sid Meier's civilization III. *Simulation and Gaming, 35*(1), 135–140.

Squire, K. (2005). Changing the game: What happens when video games enter the classroom? *Innovate Journal of Online Education, 1*(6). Retrieved June 8, 2006.

Squire, K. (2006). From content to context: videogames as designed experience. *Educational Researcher, 35*(8), 19–29.

Squire, K., & Jenkins, H. (2003). Harnessing the power of games in education. *Insight, 3,* 5–33.

Starr, P. (1994). Seductions of Sim. *American Prospect, 5*(17). Retrieved July 18, 2006, from http://www.prospect.org/print/V5/17/starr-p.html

Suits, B. (1978). *The grasshopper: Games, life and utopia.* Toronto, Ontario, Canada: University of Toronto Press.

Thiagarajan, S. (1998). The myths and realities of simulations in performance technology. *Educational Technology, 38*(5), 35–41.

Trotter, A. (2004). Digital games bring entertainment into learning realm. *Education Week, 23*(44), 8.

Trotter, A. (2005). Despite allure, using digital games for learning seen as no easy task. *Education Week, 25*(10), 1, 19.

U.S. Bureau of Labor Statistics. (2005). *Women in the labor force: A databook* (Publication No. 985). Retrieved June 12, 2006, from http://www.bls.gov/cps/wlf-databook-2005.pdf

Wittgenstein, L. (1958). *Philosophical investigations* (2nd ed.). Oxford, UK: Basil Blackwell.

Wright, W. (2006, April). Dream machines: Will Wright explains how games are unleashing the human imagination. *Wired, 14*(4), 110–112.

20

MAINFRAME GAMES AND SIMULATIONS

David H. Ahl

Source: Mark J. P. Wolf (ed.), *The Video Game Explosion: A History from PONG to PlayStation and Beyond* (Westport, CT: Greenwood Press, 2007), pp. 31–34.

In the 1950s and 1960s, computer time was both scarce and expensive and writing games for the fun of it was actively discouraged at most computer centers. Nevertheless, there were many other reasons than just plain fun for writing computer games. Common reasons included exploring the power of the computer, improving understanding of human thought processes, producing educational tools for managers or military officers, simulating dangerous environments, and providing the means for discovery learning.

In some sense, the association of computers and games started in 1950 when Alan Turing, a British mathematician often considered the father of modern computer science, proposed his famous *imitation game* in the article "Computing Machinery and Intelligence," published in *Mind* magazine. In the imitation game a human judge engages in a natural language conversation with two other parties, one a human and the other a machine; if the judge cannot reliably tell which is which, then the machine is said to pass the test. Never programmed by Turing himself, a variation of Turing's game called *Eliza* was put in the form of a computer program 13 years later by Joseph Weizenbaum, a professor of computer science at MIT. In this game, the user could "converse" with the computer using real phrases and sentences. The computer would reply with a question to clarify the user's statement gradually learning more and more about the user until it seemed that the computer was actually carrying on an intelligent, human-like conversation.

In 1952, behind a cloak of secrecy, the first military simulation games were programmed by Bob Chapman and others, researchers at Rand Air Defense Lab in Santa Monica. That same year, a number of "formula" games (*Nim*, etc.) and "dictionary look-up" games (*Tic-tac-toe*, etc.) were programmed for several early computers. Also in 1952, a computer was specially designed to play *Hex*, a game with no exact solution, by E.F. Moore and Claude Shannon at Bell Labs in New Jersey.

In 1953, Arthur Samuel, a researcher in artificial intelligence at IBM, first demonstrated his *Checkers* program on the newly unveiled IBM 701 computer at IBM in Poughkeepsie, New York. Later that year, the book *The Complete Strategyst* by J.D. Williams was published by the RAND Corporation (Santa Monica, California). This was the first primer on game theory and provided the theoretical foundation for many early computer game programs.

The first computer game of blackjack was programmed in 1954 for the IBM 701 at the Atomic Energy Laboratory at Los Alamos, New Mexico. Also in 1954, a crude game of pool—perhaps the first nonmilitary game to use a video display— was programmed at the University of Michigan.

The military set the pace for simulation games for many years, and in 1955, *Hutspiel*, the first theater-level war game (NATO vs. USSR) was programmed at the Research Analysis Corporation in McLean, Virginia.

Although Allen Newell, J.C. Shaw, and Herbert Simon, three computer science professors at Carnegie Institute of Technology (now Carnegie-Mellon University) are frequently credited with the first chess game—probably because they stayed at it for over 20 years—the first version of computer chess was actually programmed in 1956 by James Kister, Paul Stein, Stanisław Ulam, William Walden, and Mark Wells on the MANIAC-1 at the Los Alamos Atomic Energy Laboratory. The game was played on a simplified 6 x 6 board and examined all possible moves two levels deep at the rate of 12 moves per minute. It played at a similar level as a human player with about 20 games worth of experience. In contrast, *Deep Thought*, the 1990 computer chess champion, examined about 1.5 million moves per second and used a combination of brute force and intuitive play on a standard board. Although *Deep Thought* was rated at about 2600 on the FIDE system (tournament chess players are rated by the Federation Internationale des Eches, which orders players who participate in international games under strict tournament rules), which places it among the top 40 human players in the world, the program was decisively defeated by Garry Kasparov in a two-game match in October 1989. Except for a small band of enthusiasts, the interest in computer chess has waned somewhat, probably because the computer programs are so good that playing them is discouraging for all but a small handful of championship-level players.

In 1958, a tennis game, *Tennis for Two*, was designed for an analog computer at Brookhaven National Lab by Willy Higinbotham. This game, played on an oscilloscope display, was significant in that it was the first game to permit two players actually to control the direction and motion of the object moving on the screen (the ball). The object of the game was to maintain a volley for as long as possible by hitting the ball with one of the two rackets at each side of the screen. A line down the middle indicated the net; gravity, bounce, and even wind speed were calculated into game play.

In 1959, large-scale simulation games moved into the private sector with the programming of *The Management Game* by Kalman J. Cohen, Richard M. Cyert, and William R. Dill, and others at Carnegie Tech in Pittsburgh. This game simulated competition between three companies in the detergent industry and integrated modules on marketing, production, finance, and research. Modified and updated for newer computers, but still in use at many graduate schools of business today, this game may well have set the record for the longest life of any computer game ever written. In this two-semester-long game, players make decisions about manufacturing, advertising, distribution, finances, personnel research and development, and all the aspects of running a real business over a simulated period of three years. Each week of play corresponds to a calendar quarter of business and the competition is fierce to have the highest profit and market share at the end of three years. (It is interesting to note that the Bendix G-15 computer with its rudimentary high-level GATE language, on and in which this game was initiated, is a direct descendent of the very first electronic digital computer, Colossus, invented by Tommy Flowers in 1943 for codebreaking at Bletchley Park, United Kingdom.)

With the delivery in 1959 of the first Digital Equipment Corporation (DEC) PDP-1 computer with its 15-inch video display, the continuing evolution from text-only games to video games was dramatically hastened with the demonstration at an MIT open house in 1962 of *Spacewar!*, an interactive game written by Stephen R. Russell, J. Martin Graetz, and Alan Kotok. In this game, two crude spaceships orbited around a star that exerted a powerful gravitational pull on each ship. Each opponent controlled his ship and attempted to shoot the other ship while also trying to avoid being pulled into and burned up by the star.

Also in 1962, but in a completely different area, Omar K. Moore at Yale built a device called "The Talking Typewriter" for teaching reading to young children. In the device, built by Edison Electric, a computer controlled a CRT display, slide projector, and audio recorder. In 1964, a more general-purpose computer-assisted instruction (CAI) system using IBM hardware, including a CRT with graphics, light pen, and audio, was developed by Patrick Suppes at Stanford. Military research kept pace, and in 1964 the Bunker-Ramo Corporation demonstrated a CRT display that simultaneously combined computer data with a projected background.

Artists began to realize the potential of the computer in 1964 when A. Michael Noll at Bell Labs produced the first computer art on a CRT display. Many years later, spurred by such companies as Activision, Lucasfilm Games, and Cinemaware, artists began to play a much larger role in the creation of games through computer animation.

Rounding out the landmark year of 1964, the language Basic was developed by John Kemeny and Tom Kurtz on the GE 225 timesharing system at Dartmouth College. Within a few months, the first interactive educational games and simulations began to appear on the Dartmouth system.

Various types of graphics displays from many manufacturers were introduced in the mid-1960s, opening the door to new video effects. Thus, we find a video pool game developed at RCA (1967), a ball-and-paddle game by Ralph Baer at Sanders Associates (1967, later to become the Magnavox Odyssey home video game in 1972), a rocket car simulation by Judah Schwartz at MIT (1968), a graphic flight simulation by the computer firm Evans & Sutherland (1969), a lunar lander game at DEC (1969), and a device to permit computer output and standard television video on the same display at Stanford (1968).

In the October 1970 issue of *Scientific American*, Martin Gardner devoted his "Mathematical Games" column to a description of John Conway's *Game of Life*. Easily programmed, it began to appear on virtually every video computer terminal in the country within weeks. In this game, colonies of figures reproduce, move around, and die off according to certain rules with the object of the game being to devise patterns that can sustain life for as long as possible.

In the late 1960s, the National Science Foundation was attempting to encourage the use of computers in secondary schools to improve science education. One of the notable NSF-funded projects that produced scores of simulation games in science and social studies was the Huntington Computer Project directed by Ludwig Braun at Brooklyn Polytechnic Institute (later at SUNY, Stony Brook). In the project's *Malaria* simulation game, for example, students must try to control an outbreak of malaria in a Central American country using a combination of various pesticides, inoculations, and treatment of the ill—all without bankrupting the country.

Also in the late 1960s, both DEC and Hewlett-Packard started major marketing efforts to sell computers to secondary and elementary schools. As a result, both companies sponsored a number of small-scale projects to write computer games and simulations in various fields, many of which were released in the early 1970s. In DEC's *King* game (later called *Hammurabi*), for example, players must decide how much land to buy, sell, and cultivate each year, how much to feed the people, etc., while dealing with problems of industrial development, pollution, and tourism.

In 1972, William Crowther and Don Woods wrote a game for the DEC PDP-10 timesharing system that they simply called *Adventure*. The game, the first in the interactive role-playing fantasy genre, was unbelievably popular and players consumed vast amounts of timeshared computer time on whatever system it was loaded.

By the mid-1970s, computer games had successfully made the transition to commercial arcade games and the rapidly expanding field of home computers, where their growing popularity helped them become the basis of an industry and a mass medium.

21

VIDEOGAMES IN COMPUTER SPACE

The complex history of Pong

Henry Lowood

Source: *IEEE Annals in the History of Computing*, July–September 2009, 5–19.

Abstract

The earliest digital games emerged out of laboratories and research centers in the 1960s and 1970s. The intertwined histories of Nolan Bushnell's Computer Space and Pong illustrate the transition from these "university games" to accessible entertainment and educational games as well as the complicated historical relationship among the arcade, computer, and videogames.

Computer games such as *Spacewar*! and Adventure were created in institutions, such as the Massachusetts Institute of Technology, BBN, and Stanford University, that defined the main streams of computing research during the 1960s and 1970s.[1] Telling the stories of these games reveals the emergence of "university games" out of laboratories and research centers.[2] The institutional contexts of *Spacewar* and *Adventure* suggest an important, and at times underappreciated, relationship between exploratory work in computer science and the early history of computer games. Both games grew out of the very institutions that played an essential role in defining timeshared and then networked computing in its early days. Games such as these exemplified the technical mastery of programmers and hardware hackers. These links between games and computing recall Brian Sutton-Smith's argument that games are fundamentally "problems in adaptation" and that computer games specifically address the problem that "is the computer."[3]

A success story that marked the early evolution of the videogame, Atari's original *Pong* arcade console betrays few obvious connections to computer technology of the mid-1970s. The prototype's cabinet and circuitry, designed by Al Alcorn, reveal only a modest investment in electronic components, a modified television set, and some ad hoc wiring and parts. Years later, Alcorn made a block diagram of the game's logic for a later generation of computer science students less familiar with tricks of transistor-transistor logic (TTL); it shows the circuitry that generated game control functions as well as video signals to produce the game's images and sounds (see Figure 1). The original game ran not one line of program code. It did not use a microprocessor or a custom integrated circuit; rather, it was a digital logic design made from components familiar to a television engineer who thoroughly understood the various ways pulse waveforms could be generated and manipulated.

Despite being constructed entirely from television technology, Pong is occasionally depicted as a product of the computer age or even as a computer artifact. One of the earliest critical studies of videogames, Geoffrey R. Loftus and Elizabeth F. Loftus' *Mind at Play* described *Pong* as being "entirely under the control of a computer," and their version of the videogame's "family tree" showed arcade games and digital computing as its parents. Michael Malone wrote in his excellent history of Silicon Valley that Pong was put together by a computer programmer.[5] These mischaracterizations of *Pong* reflect a natural, if perhaps careless, assumption about the dawn of the videogame. If much of its past—and, as we now know, its future— was bound to the computer, we are tempted to read these connections into every videogame artifact. Like the theory of pre-formation in the 18th century, this idea leads us to see a fully formed adult in the germ of origin, a little computer inside every game machine.

The relationship of *Pong*'s creators at Atari to computer technology has not yet been investigated in a manner that illuminates the connections, if any, between early computer games and videogames. On the face of it, there would seem to be no particular connection, at least nothing that can be traced in the particular technologies involved; the convergence certainly cannot be found inside the original *Pong* arcade console. The relationship might have played out in other ways, however, that might better be described in terms of influence rather than convergence. The reading of *Pong* as a product of the computer age sidesteps the emergence of the videogame out of TV engineering, but it also calls attention to other factors in the development of the new videogame technology—what the key figures had in mind, their entrepreneurial aspirations, their specific engineering training, and the impact of subsequent litigation on the story.

Pong was an easy game to play, a definite competitive advantage for an arcade game often placed in bars and restaurants where a patron could play with a drink in one hand. Has its simplicity discouraged serious attention to its history? This first success story of the commercial videogame has deflected critical reflection through reduction to a "keep it simple, less is more" narrative. According to this argument, Pong succeeded in a manner that requires little explanation; it was easy to learn and fun to play, providing uncomplicated amusement suited to taverns and arcades.[6] End of story.

Simplified Block Diagram Pong

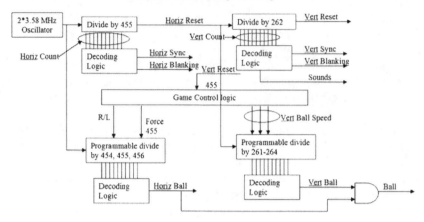

Figure 1 Al Alcorn's simplified block diagram for Pong[4]

But what about the antecedents that set up its success? Nolan Bushnell's guiding vision of an electronic arcade game inspired by computer technology and previous work in TV game technology do not figure much in the explanation that Pong succeeded only because of its design simplicity. Hindsight and the appeal of a good Silicon Valley success story have perhaps postponed deeper investigation of how the earliest commercial videogames were envisioned and built.[7] In fact, *Pong* emerged from a complex of research projects, product design, and business relationships that later figured in heated legal and corporate disputes about intellectual property, priority of invention, and so on through the 1980s.[8]

This history of Pong begins with its problematic connection to computer-based games such as *Spacewar*. These games inspired Bushnell's industrial design project, *Computer Space*. Tracking how that inspiration led to Pong corrects other accounts of the relationship between the TV game console and computer technology. Claims put forward in the courtroom, for example, attempted to portray computer games as a prior art of TV game technology. These disputes usually had little to do with Pong but were about rights and licenses associated with the invention of the television game and the reduction to practice of the relevant technology. In any case, the argument for computer games as prior art failed to make this case persuasively, as evidenced by settlements that benefited the holders for the original Baer/Harrison/Rusch TV game patents, assigned to Sanders Associates [now BAE Systems] and licensed to first Magnavox, and later Philips (pp. 157–161).[9] As for Atari, it is fair to say that no other company of the early videogame era negotiated as many contradictions and convergences of computer and TV technology, which besides developing *Pong* also manufactured arcade games, dedicated home consoles, programmable game machines, and home computers. The path of invention, innovation, and design that led to *Pong* reveals points both of intersection and disconnection between computer and TV technology during the videogame's early development.

Spacewar

The winding path from the computer to *Pong* began with *Spacewar*. Few computer games are linked so tightly with the technical and institutional contexts of digital computing. Steve Russell, Alan Kotok, J. Martin Graetz, and others at MIT created *Spacewar* in February 1962 to demonstrate the new PDP-1 minicomputer and Precision CRT Display Type 30, both donated by the Digital Equipment Corporation (DEC) to the Electrical Engineering Department only months earlier.[10] The *Spacewar* authors were part of the Tech Model Railroad Club (TMRC) on campus, and *Spacewar* became an integral part of that culture. They were unimpressed by the "little pattern-generating programs" that others had made to show off the PDP-1, assuming more could be done with "this display that could do all sorts of good things!"[11]

The group decided that the most interesting demonstration of the computer's capabilities would be "a two-dimensional maneuvering sort of thing, and . . . that naturally the obvious thing to do was spaceships."[11] They were guided by several principles for a good demo program, especially that "it should involve the onlooker in a pleasurable and active way—in short, it should be a game."[12] Russell led the project, influenced by earlier computer programs such as *Tic-Tac-Toe* and Marvin Minsky's Tri-Pos: Three Position Display, better known as the Minskytron. Russell's collaborators contributed code and built control boxes so that players could maneuver virtual spaceships around on the CRT and shoot at their opponents. The code was available to all hackers at MIT, who improved, extended, and modified the game. Peter Samson, offended by the sparse background of empty space, coded "Expensive Planetarium" to portray accurately the stars in the night sky; Dan Edwards worked on gravity calculations; Graetz programmed explosions; and so on. The game superbly showcased the lab's new computer, while stimulating better understanding of new graphics, I/O, and display technology. In April 1962, soon after *Spacewar* was unveiled, J.M. Graetz, the editor of *Decuscope*, wrote that the "use of switches to control apparent motion of displayed objects amply demonstrates the real-time capabilities of the PDP-1." He had visited the computer room and could "verify an excellent performance" for the emerging PDP community.[13]

Spacewar thus demonstrated not only computing technology, but the technical mastery of programmers and hardware hackers as well. It expressed their shared culture and institutional setting. In working out the game, Russell fixed on the popular science fiction novels of Edward Elmer Smith's Lensman series. This was the early Space Age, so it is not surprising that a fan and hacker would place his game in the world of these novels. Smith's writing excelled at portraying action and movement, with spaceships blasting away at each other, so what better homage than a fast-paced shoot'em-up action game?

351

Setting it in outer space only required a visual backdrop of flickering stars that was relatively easy to render graphically because the Type 30's display could directly plot stars as points. Having an essentially dark background and a fantasy setting meant that the game's visual treats, spaceships and missiles, could be set in an appropriate visual space without overburdening the hardware. Russell noted also that,

> by picking a world which people weren't familiar with, we could alter a number of parameters of the world in the interests of making a good game and of making it possible to get it onto a computer.[11]

For example, Edwards' gravity calculations were realistic, but the programmers decreed that "photon torpedoes" ignored gravitational attraction to ease the computational task. Collaboration and design flexibility became the project's defining characteristics, much like the nascent culture of the computer lab.

Spacewar was distinctly a product of MIT computing. Like Whirlwind, the TX-0, and the PDP-1, it exemplified the tradition of what Gordon Bell has called "MIT personal computers."[14] The gift of the PDP-1 established DEC as a provider of equipment for academic research, and *Spacewar* returned the favor. Freely distributed via paper tape in the lab, the game was shipped by DEC with PDP computers as a test program to verify their operation after new installations. *Spacewar* became a fixture in university and industrial laboratories of the 1960s and 1970s.

Figure 2 Spacewar at the Stanford AI Lab. (Courtesy of Stanford University, http://infolab. stanford.edu/pub/voy/museum/pictures/AIlab/list.html.)

A community of programmers and players formed around it as a popular and competitive entertainment, described in Brand's reports of the 1972 *Spacewar* Olympics at Stanford (see Figure 2). Programmers everywhere added elements to the game or tweaked settings and controls in a local version. *Rolling Stone* reported, "within weeks of its invention Spacewar was spreading across the country to other computer research centers [that] began adding their own wrinkles."[11] This convergence of competitive skill, programming wizardry, and collaborative community characterized hacker culture.

Computer Space

How did *Spacewar* extend its influence from the TMRC hackers to the design of products such as arcade consoles? With the growth of a network of research laboratories funded by DARPA, especially its Information Processing Techniques Office (IPTO), a generation of computer science students was introduced to computers such as DEC's PDP series that ran *Spacewar*. One of these laboratories was at the University of Utah, home of a strong program in computer graphics that DARPA generously funded. One historian of computer graphics has remarked that, "almost every influential person in the modern computer-graphics community either passed through the University of Utah or came into contact with it in some way," while DARPA historians have called its program "especially influential in the birth and development of interactive graphics."[15]

Nolan Bushnell graduated in 1968 from the University of Utah with a degree in electrical engineering. While there, he had access to the program's computers, and like many other students, he often played *Spacewar*. He also held a summer job as an amusement park employee, staffing a pinball arcade and other attractions. This unusual exposure to both carnival and computer culture stimulated his notion of creating a new kind of entertainment arcade filled with *Spacewar*-like games.

After graduating, he moved to California to work for Ampex, a leader in the development of magnetic recording, video, and computer storage technologies. He was now in the hotbed of high-technology entrepreneurship, at the southern boundary of the region Don Hoefler began calling "Silicon Valley U.S.A." in 1971.[16] The first big wave of Silicon Valley start-ups crested between 1967 and 1969, with the founding of National Semiconductor, Intel, Advanced Micro Devices, and many more companies. Bushnell's entrepreneurial imagination responded to this environment. Surrounded by first-rate research engineers and product development teams at Ampex, he thought more about his vision of a *Spacewar* arcade. He was in the right place to ponder the impact of component miniaturization and integration. Moreover, located in Redwood City, Ampex was a short drive from a hotbed of *Spacewar* activity in Stanford University's Artificial Intelligence Laboratory (SAIL), an important center for computer science research.[11] Bushnell revived his enthusiasm for the game and pondered how money could be made in the arcade videogame business.

Bushnell's original plan was to create an arcade videogame based on *Spacewar* using a "Data General 1600—to have a minicomputer running multiple games."[17] Having played *Spacewar* and used time-sharing systems at Utah and Stanford, Bushnell started out with the ambitious goal of creating an arcade system that utilized a time-sharing environment to display interactive graphics concurrently on several consoles. Although the concept was understandable, it was not feasible. In terms of cost, DEC's 36-bit, multitasking PDP-10/DEC System-10 had begun shipping to computer science departments in 1968, but a complete system cost well in excess of $100,000—far more with displays, disk storage, printers, and hardware peripherals. Still, Bushnell was determined to create a modestly priced computer arcade game inspired by Spacewar, a commitment underscored by calling this project Computer Space.

Key events related to the story of *Computer Space*—Bushnell's departure from Ampex in March 1971, his partnership with Ted Dabney, the decision to join Nutting & Associates, which acquired and manufactured *Computer Space*, and the founding of Atari (originally called Syzygy) in June 1972—have been well documented.[6,17–21] Less has been written about the technical and cultural contexts of Bushnell and Dabney's work on *Computer Space.*

While still at Ampex, Dabney and Bushnell began to consider how to build an arcade version of the six-figure computing platforms used to play *Spacewar.* In the early 1970s, the steady progress of hardware miniaturization and software innovation sounded the call to deliver computing technology in smaller packages for many applications, so *Computer Space* can be instructively compared to other projects. Microcomputer kits such as the Altair 8800 would not be available for a few years, but digital logic components such as TTL and other ICs had become standard electronics parts.

In November 1971, Intel introduced its first single-chip microprocessor, the 4004. Douglas Engelbart, Ted Nelson, and others had already begun to ponder the impact of computing on human potential. Nelson, for example, called for "computer liberation" in *Computer Lib* and proclaimed that everyone "can and must understand computers NOW."[22] He predicted new applications for a variety of purposes and asked, "Can the public learn, in time, what good and beautiful things are possible" from computer systems (pp. 2–3)?[22] Nelson's manifesto included computer games, for he had observed that "wherever there are graphic displays, there is usually a version of the game Spacewar." Citing the 1972 *Rolling Stone* article,[11] Nelson might have been looking through Bushnell's eyes when he remarked that "games with computer programs are universally enjoyed in the computer community" (p. 48)[22] He discussed computer games at about the same time as Bushnell began working on *Computer Space*, specifically mentioning versions of Conway's The Game of Life[23] and BASIC programs published by the People's Computer Company, an organization near Stanford University (and Ampex) that sought to bring programming power to the people through recreational and educational software. Nelson provided a voice for those who proposed to move advanced text, graphics, networking, and other computer technologies out of academic laboratories to make them available to everyone. Bushnell took the engineer's route as he thought about building a machine on which anyone could play a version of *Spacewar*.[24]

As Bushnell worked on *Computer Space* during 1971, he might have been aware of other projects like his. In 1969, Rick Blomme had written a two-player version of *Spacewar* for the Programmed Logic for Automatic Teaching Operations (PLATO) time-sharing system at the University of Illinois. It was the first multiplayer game hosted by the PLATO project, which during the 1970s became a hotbed for innovative, networked games.[25]

As he was completing *Computer Space*, Bushnell probably heard about a summer project closer to home; a recently graduated SAIL student, Bill Pitts, and his friend Hugh Tuck built a coin-operated (coin-op) computer game, *The Galaxy Game*, for the newly released PDP-11/20, DEC's first 16-bit computer. DEC had fit the PDP-11 into a relatively small box and listed it for a mere $20,000, hoping to open new markets and applications.[26] Pitts and Tuck formed a company called Computer Recreations, bought the low-end version of the PDP-11 for only $13,000, and converted the PDP-10 version of *Spacewar* for this machine. Including a Hewlett-Packard vector display, wooden cabinet, and other parts, their expenses came to roughly $20,000. In September 1971, they installed it in Stanford's student union, where a later version that supported up to four monitors (eight players) could be found until 1979. *The Galaxy Game* was faithful not only to *Spacewar*, but also to the player community (university students and computer engineers) and to the technical configuration (software code, vector displays, time-sharing, and so on) that produced it.[27]

Bushnell started out on the same course of programming a version of *Spacewar*. Like Pitts and Tuck, his first thought was to purchase an inexpensive minicomputer, maybe the new Data General Nova or the SuperNova.[28] Instead of coupling the computer to expensive monitors, he would link up several game stations equipped with cheap, off-the-shelf TV sets using raster, not vector, graphics.[29] At first, Bushnell knew almost nothing about how TV sets might function as monitors, but Dabney brought him up-to-speed quickly on TV signal generation and related topics. Indeed, Dabney showed Bushnell how to modify a TV using TTL components to move an object around on the screen.[30]

This promising union of technologies—the computer from the university lab and the TV from the home—proved impractical, however. There was little chance of getting the design to work with the equipment available, and no chance to do so at an acceptable cost. According to Bushnell, the burden of providing images to multiple TV monitors would bring a computer to its knees; it would be "blindingly slow" even if Dabney and Bushnell were able to tweak monitors and build circuitry to offload processing from the CPU.[17]

Dabney certainly grasped quickly that computers designed to drive vector displays could not be used to produce raster-scan output for analog TV monitors. Bushnell's telling of the story suggests that they were able to lash up parts of a working system, but it is clear that the original concept was abandoned quickly.

According to Al Alcorn, Bushnell's wife was responsible for ordering the computer but considered the price tag for the computer "crazy" and never ordered it.

Frustrated by the likelihood of poor performance and fuzzy images, Bushnell

> designed out the need for the computer, because the computers were so slow at that time . . . So there was this brilliant leap that Nolan made about how he could get rid of just a little bit of logic [and still] do the same thing the computer's going to do, just much, much faster, so he didn't need the computer.[31]

Bushnell and Dabney promptly dumped the stillborn idea of a computer controlling multiple raster-scan displays. They replaced the minicomputer with dedicated circuits based on TV technology that controlled all aspects of the game, from game logic and graphics to player controls. Resetting the project made it possible to finish with a working prototype. After sculpting a futuristic cabinet for the arcade console, Bushnell sold *Computer Space* to Nutting Associates, where the design benefited from the contributions of experienced engineers; Bushnell joined the firm as chief engineer to oversee the final design, manufacturing, and distribution. It was released in August 1971.

Even though Nutting went on to build between 1,500 and 2,300 machines,[6,30] the historical verdict on *Computer Space* has generally been negative, whether with respect to sales, game play, or controls. Videogame historians have written that, besides Bushnell's friends, "the rest of the world didn't show any interest in the game at all" and it "failed," that it was "unsuccessful," a "failure," "lacking in mainframe complexity," and a "colossal commercial flop."[6,17,19,20] Bushnell offers only a weak defense, claiming that it "did okay, but it really didn't do as well as it could have" or that it did "very well on college campuses and in places where the educational value was higher. However, there weren't any arcades as such back then."[17,20]

Computer Space redeemed itself mostly as a negative example for Bushnell and Al Alcorn when they made the next game and as the first step toward the creation of Atari and *Pong*. From his own mistakes and the work with Nutting Associates, Bushnell learned about game console engineering and, especially, the arcade business. On the positive side, Dabney and Bushnell took away $500 in royalties from *Computer Space* to start their new company. On the whole, however, *Computer Space* was the failure that motivated *Pong's* designers to keep things simple the second time around.

Design lessons from *Computer Space*

These assessments of *Computer Space* miss its significance for the videogame as a technological artifact. It provided more than a learning experience: *Computer Space* established a design philosophy and general technical configuration for arcade consoles,[32] and it reduced the laboratory-based computer game to a format that would launch the videogame as a consumer product. When Bushnell noted years later that his engineering friends loved *Computer Space*, even if "the typical guy in the bar" was completely baffled, it is easy to hear echoes of this appreciation in assessments of his technical achievement from engineers, designers, and operators. Most notably, they argued, "The machine is like a historical blueprint of how all arcade games to follow would be made,"[33] and "The brilliance of these machines was that Nolan Bushnell and company took what was computer programming (in *Spacewar*) and translated it into a simpler version of the game (no gravity) using hard-wired logical circuits."[34]

The arcade videogame design defined by *Computer Space* was notable on three counts: (1) packaging, both internal and external; (2) optimization; and (3) despite the daunting complexity of its game play, simplification, especially with respect to service requirements. Because Bushnell's lovingly shaped, futuristic cabinet design was visually memorable, good enough to serve as a prop in Hollywood movies such as *Soylent Green* (1973) and *Jaws* (1975), it is easy to forget that this technical configuration of *Computer Space* would remain essentially unchanged for a generation of coin-op arcade consoles. Bushnell divided his machine into component modules. Nutting's sales flyer, probably authored by Bushnell, crowed that there were "only three assemblies in the entire unit": a modified General Electric black-and-white TV set, the front control panel, and the "computer (brain box)." Circuitry, control, and screen were set into the "beautiful space-age cabinet" with a few other parts, such as a power supply and coin acceptor (see Figure 3).[35]

In Computer Space, physical modules in the form of ICs mounted on three printed circuit boards replaced programs and executed game logic in hardware. Bushnell's original concept of a configuration of several raster displays connected to a computer was a failure, so he and Dabney replaced software with electronic components and ICs such as Texas Instruments' 7400 series of TTL circuits. At Ampex, they had been surrounded by engineers (like Al Alcorn) busy at developing products that utilized TTL technology. It was natural to consider how physical logic elements like flip-flops, counters, and registers could provide the synchronization signals needed to display graphical elements and scores, the creation of on-screen symbols, or execution of game logic.[36] For example, a small number of diode arrays connected to logic gates produced the rotating images of rockets seen on the screen; the rocket images were clearly visible even in the pattern of diodes on one of the PC boards (see Figure 4).

It is tempting to think of these diode arrays as precursors of game ROMs, but this conception reintroduces the notion of program code, exactly what Bushnell and Dabney eliminated from the design. Bushnell's rockets were essentially hardwired bitmaps that could be moved around the screen independently of the background, a crucial innovation that made it possible to produce screen images efficiently. He called these moving images *patches*. The design concept would become part of Atari's shared knowledge; even if "nobody could ever understand Nolan's schematic, . . . it was the idea of taking the bitmap in a little area that could be moved around so that it would not be necessary to redraw an entire

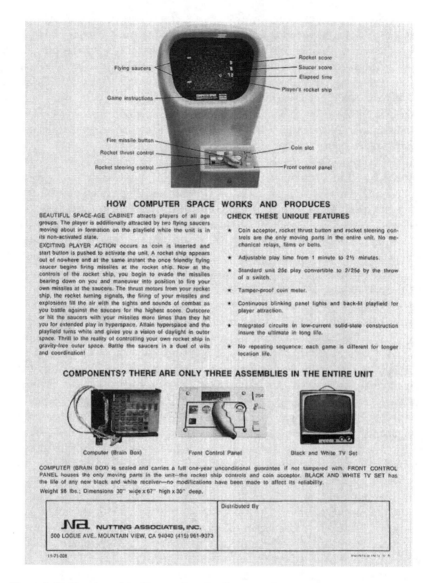

Figure 3 Nutting Associates' instructions for Computer Space

screen every time an image moved" that every Atari engineer understood.[37] Bushnell's patch solution eventually became a staple of game machines and home computers in the form of *sprites*, the term taken from Seymour Papert's briefly popular Logo programming language after a new generation of Texas Instruments graphics chips put it into home computers during the late 1970s.

358

Figure 4 Circuit board, possibly from Computer Space, serial number 1. (Courtesy of http://www.computerspacefan.com/SN1large.htm)

The idea of taking a game design and making it "more efficient in silicon" persisted in the design of dedicated and programmable game machines such as the Atari 2600 VCS, with the Stella custom graphics chip, even after the introduction of microprocessor control and program storage in ROM;[38] sprites were an important feature of home computers such as the Atari 400/800 (as "player/missile graphics" or "motion objects") or the Texas Instruments TI99/4A. The cost of expensive microprocessors could not be justified for home machines as they could for arcade consoles through much of the 1970s. Hence, Atari's original coin-op design philosophy was carried on in the design of home machines, reducing the workload on slow central processors by using specialized graphics hardware.

Because the main criticism leveled at *Computer Space* has been the daunting complexity of game controls and game play, Bushnell's efforts to keep the design of the arcade console as simple as possible have been overlooked.[39] His goal was to ensure reliability and ease servicing of delivered units. As he put it in a sales flyer, it was "our object to create a new standard of reliability using the latest technology. We believe that this goal has been met . . . *Computer Space* requires operators to have no more fear of replacing a bad tube than of replacing a bad relay." Because it was built with solid-state circuits, the manufacturers could boast that *Computer Space* had "no mechanical relays, films, or belts" to repair, the only moving parts being the coin acceptor and player controls. Bushnell reminded operators that the display was an ordinary TV set with "no modifications to affect its reliability." It would be "no harder to adjust than any home receiver."

It is worth noting that he played both ends of the stick by designating the internal hardware circuits mounted on PC boards as the "*computer.*" By doing so, he recalled the origins of the game and created a space age aura around it, but on the other hand, he demarcated the "brain box" as a no-touch zone, a black box, by telling operators that it carried an "unconditional guarantee" only "if not tampered with."[35]

Atari and *Pong*

When it became obvious that *Computer Space* would not be a hit in arcades, Bushnell and Dabney severed their relationship with Nutting and founded Syzygy/Atari in June 1972. Before long, they were joined by another talented Ampex engineer, Al Alcorn, who had studied electrical engineering and computer science at the University of California, Berkeley, and since 1968 refined his skills in video and analog engineering at Ampex.[40] Alcorn was particularly skilled at applying his knowledge of transistor logic and ICs to "analog problems." Busy with the two-player version of *Computer Space*, Bushnell assigned Alcorn the task of designing a simple home-consumer game based on Ping-Pong. He inspired the new employee with a story that Atari had a buyer for the game—General Electric, no less. Bushnell failed to mention that he had almost certainly taken the idea from playing a similar game earlier that year on the new Magnavox Odyssey TV game console.[9,31] Concerned that it was "too big a step for [Alcorn] to go from not knowing what a video game was" to designing a real game, Bushnell's ruse set up a training exercise through which he eased Alcorn into electronic games. So Bushnell came up with "the simplest game I could think of, which was a tennis game." According to Alcorn, he understood the task as simply, "let's just do the most simple game to save time."[31]

In fact, no such contract existed, but Alcorn rose to the challenge and proved his mettle as an engineer. With his previous job experience and training, he was thoroughly familiar with state-of-the-art electronic components such as TTL ICs. The project also demonstrated his mastery of TV electronics. And last but not least, he distilled value from Bushnell's ideas and suggestions, which were as often chaotic as enlightening. Even though he could not decipher the schematics Bushnell showed him of *Computer Space*, Alcorn recalls:

> Nolan had filed a patent on the fundamental trick: . . . how to make a spot appear on a TV screen like Pong without having to do a memory map, a frame buffer, like what you would do today, because there was no memory other than flip flops. And so it was a very, very, very clever trick. I think I perused, glanced at the patent and [learned verbally] from Nolan how it was done; it was really clever. It involved simply making

a . . . television sync generator which had counters to count clock pulses to make a horizontal sync, and then counters to count horizontal sync to make vertical sync, and so you'd get the lines set up. If you had another sync generator and you just had it running at the same time, but not synchronous with it, just the same clock and you decided to take the second sync generator output and make a spot where horizontal and vertical sync happen at the same time, that spot would appear randomly, somewhere on that screen, just by happenstance . . . . it was this happy relationship between using the digital TTL circuits, which are absolutely ones and zeros, to do video which in those days was absolutely analog.[41,42]

Within a few months, Alcorn produced a prototype from a store-bought TV set, a homemade cabinet, about 75 TTL ICs, and some tricks from his bag of analog and television engineering (see Figures 5 and 6).

Figure 5 Pong prototype. (Photographs courtesy of Al Alcorn.)

Figure 6 Atari's coin-op Pong machine

Surprisingly, Alcorn was at first disappointed by his effort because the "criterion then was cost, cost, cost," and he felt that the final chip count was too high. Bushnell and Alcorn named it *Pong* and installed the coin-op prototype in Andy Capp's Tavern, a local bar where eager players lined up to stuff quarters into the game.[5,6,17,18,20,41,43]

As I noted earlier, *Pong's* triumph has been credited to the unrepentant simplicity of its design. Three short sentences on the cabinet's faceplate told players everything they needed to know: put a quarter into the machine, a "ball" will be served; move the paddle to hit the ball back and forth. Alcorn felt instructions were unnecessary altogether, but Bushnell insisted on them, so in a semisarcastic spirit, Alcorn responded by putting on the faceplate a simple summation that became the motto of the new game: "Avoid missing ball for high score."[41] *Pong* owed much of its success to breaking with the complexity of *Computer Space* and *Spacewar* in a manner suited to bar patrons. Unlike *Computer Space's* beautiful fiberglass cabinet, the Pong prototype was set in an ugly square box covered with orange paint and wood veneer, with a simple faceplate for control knobs and instructions. In game play and aesthetics, *Pong* and *Computer Space* were polar opposites.

As an engineering design, however, *Pong* followed *Computer Space* in its modularization and optimization of hardware. Compared to Bushnell, Alcorn was better prepared by experience and inclination to build an efficiently engineered arcade console in three respects:

- He built his game with TV technology from the ground up.
- He deftly used digital components to solve the analog problem of mastering TV output, precisely Alcorn's special domain of engineering knowledge.
- The images required for the game were relatively simple. Unlike the oddly shaped objects such as spaceships in *Computer Space* that required ad hoc memory solutions such as diode arrays, the ball, paddle, and other images in *Pong* were all based on simple rectangles that digital TV circuits could easily generate on the fly.

This last point was especially important. Not a single line of software code was involved in the construction of *Pong*. Like *Computer Space, Pong's* game logic and control operations were paced by synchronization signals for the rasterized TV display, but Alcorn understood more intuitively than Bushnell how to work with these signals during every cycle of the TV circuits. Because every image was based on rectangles, he could generate them by gating counters, even the seven segments of the score display. Alcorn was thus able to build Pong optimally from a modest number of ICs, and he was more obsessed than Bushnell with reducing the parts count. He eliminated unnecessary parts not only to make the game run more efficiently, but also to reduce the final product cost. Bushnell's original assignment for a simple home console game explains Alcorn's concern that the prototype even had 75 TTL circuits "and would cost way too much for a high volume home machine." His singleminded attention to optimization of the electronic circuitry continued the legacy of *Computer Space* and remained in Atari's engineering culture through the 1970s.[37,43,44]

The technology lineage leading from *Spacewar* through *Computer Space* to *Pong* is one way to narrate the complicated historical relationship between the computer and the videogame. *Computer Space* and *Pong* were both TV games in the sense that their designers applied techniques of television engineering to make them, and in fact they required a television to operate. Yet, Bushnell's project emerged from the computer space of academic laboratories and large-scale computers, while *Pong* was cut loose from this mooring. In this telling of the story, arcade consoles, the home game foreshadowed in Alcorn's original *Pong* design, and home consoles created during the mid-1970s—including Atari's home version of *Pong* (1975), General Instruments AY-3-8500 "TV game on a chip" (1976), and the microprocessor- and ROM-based Atari 2600 (1977)—solved Bushnell's problem of reducing the computer game to a configuration suitable for delivery as an entertainment product to mass markets.

Atari never gave up on the computer game, however. When Bushnell first assigned Alcorn to the apocryphal GE project, his long-range goal was still to produce games that were "more complex ... not something simpler" after Alcorn's trial by fire.[20] Atari's misleading advertising encouraged the view that videogames were an ambitious coupling of the computer and TV technology (see Figure 7). The company's early marketing literature characterized games like *Pong* as "video computer games" and claimed to having revolutionized the industry "when we harnessed digital computers and video technology to the amusement game field with Pong."[45]

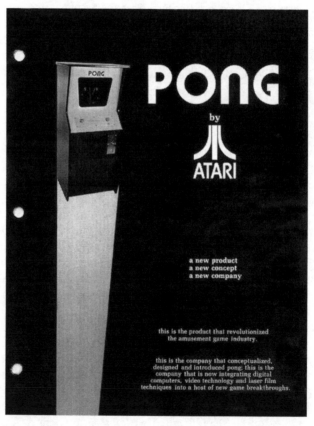

Figure 7 Pong advertising depicting Atari as a high-tech company

Pong as a television game

Narrating the history of Pong as a kind of hyperspace jump from computer space contradicts what has been described as the real story behind videogames and, ironically, as the Pong story. This story begins with the notion of the videogame as "an apparatus that displays games using RASTER VIDEO equipment," not with inspiration from computer games (see http://www.pong-story.com). The inventor of this TV game console was Ralph Baer, a television engineer at the military electronics firm Sanders Associates. Indisputably, in 1966 he designed circuitry to display and control moving dots on a television screen, leading to a simple chase game called *Fox* and *Hounds* based on his original idea for a home television game. After proving the concept by designing several chase and light-gun games, he received permission from Sanders management to continue his TV Game Project. With two coworkers, Baer improved the game system, leading in 1968 to a seventh version called the Brown Box, a solid-state prototype for a videogame console (see Figure 8). The Brown Box offered handball and light-gun shooting games, in addition to the original chase games and a ping-pong game. Sanders licensed the technology and patent rights to Magnavox, and by mid-1971, a working prototype of what would be marketed as the Magnavox Odyssey console was available for consumer testing. Sanders was awarded several US patents for the technology developed by the TV Game Project in 1972, the same year in which Magnavox began selling the Odyssey—the first commercial TV game console for the home.[46]

Bushnell attended a presentation of the Odyssey in Burlingame, California, on 24 May 1972. Working for Nutting at the time, he viewed and played the Odyssey at the demonstration. When he tasked Alcorn with a balland-paddle game, his suggestion must have been influenced by what he had seen from Magnavox (pp. 5–9, 76–82).[9] This version of the Pong story rebuts the construction of the videogame as emerging entirely through Bushnell's engineering of the computer game.

Baer saw the videogame as an enhanced, interactive form of television, a key motivation for his project at Sanders Associates. Baer's inspiration thus differed markedly from Bushnell's encounters with computer games. Situating *Pong* in computer space complicates the "keep it simple" version of its success story. A version of this story that includes Baer's seminal role in TV game technology must

Figure 8 The Brown Box with shooting rifle

take note not only of the connection between the Odyssey and *Pong*, but also of the differences between their approaches to the problem of designing videogames:

> Mr. Bushnell did indeed play the Magnavox Odyssey's Ping-Pong game hands-on. He clearly needed no instructions on how to play that game. On the other hand, his much more elaborate Computer Space game was failing in the marketplace because it was too complicated to play. A light bulb may have gone on in Mr. Bushnell's head the moment he played ping-pong on the Odyssey: "Keep it simple." Complicated games may work for nerds but not for ordinary people. (pp. 5–6)[9]

The failure of *Computer Space* provided the motivation for adopting a design philosophy evident in Baer's "television gaming apparatus." Inspired by computer technology, Bushnell adopted the TV game as the basis for the success of Atari's coin-op console.

After the 1975 Christmas season, a *Business Week* reporter wrote that "at the moment, only two companies are serious factors in consumer electronic games:" Atari and Magnavox.[47] Ten years later, the videogame industry had crashed, burned, and risen again under the new regime of Nintendo's carefully crafted protection of the technical platform, intellectual property, and content of videogames. Nintendo's strategy was zealous control of its technology and products. It staved off competition by using legal, business, and technical means to screen and occasionally block independent software developers from access to its hardware: the Famicom (1983) and its American version, the Nintendo Entertainment System (1985).

Magnavox and Sanders by then were in the habit of tenaciously defending their patents. They had litigated effectively against a virtual who's who of the game industry.[48] A clash was inevitable. As early as 1975, Nintendo had declined Magnavox's offer of a license for TV game technology; a year later in correspondence with Sanders, Nintendo's representative noted a "conflict" with the "concept of Mr. Nolan K. Bushnell," but apparently without knowledge of the licensing agreement that existed between Atari and Magnavox.[49]

More than a decade later, after the introduction of the NES, Nintendo decided to fight the Sanders-Magnavox patents. Conflating the Atari and Baer versions of the *Pong* story, Nintendo's lawyers tried to convince the court that the Sanders patents had been preceded by *Spacewar*. They insisted that the Sanders team must have known about *Spacewar*—a Magnavox patent lawyer had probably seen the game but failed to inform the Patent Office about it, a Sanders engineer had played it at Stanford and later installed a version on a Sanders computer, or they must have read a description of the game in the *Rolling Stone* article or the book II *Cybernetic Frontiers* (Random House, 1974). Nintendo brought in expert witnesses to state that a person "reasonably conversant in the field" would have been able to convert *Spacewar* for a raster-scan display. Nintendo skirted over the difficulties Bushnell encountered in attempting to realize this idea, with its lawyers asserting that the electronic circuitry for a rasterized computer game would have been relatively standard.[50] The dispute was brought before New York Federal District Court Judge Leonard B. Sands, but before the case could be adjudicated, Nintendo realized the futility of its claims against Magnavox and settled out of court in April 1991.[51]

Conclusion

The lesson of *Pong's* historical journey through computer space is that invention stories are never as simple as a game of *Pong*. Nolan Bushnell's *Computer Space* leads to *Pong* as a product inspired by computer technology but practically realized by TV technology. The result was the coin-op videogame console. Baer's TV game apparatus provides a story about who was first to invent the home TV game as a technical, legal, and financial matter (p. 14).[9]

In later years, Bushnell acknowledged the Odyssey, but he unfairly dismissed its significance as being only an analog game. His historical judgment was more accurate when he admitted, "I feel in some way that I didn't invent the video game—I commercialized it. The real digital game was invented by a few guys who programmed PDP-1s at MIT."[52]

Acknowledgments

I thank Ralph Baer, the inventor of the original videogame console, for his comments and suggestions based on an earlier draft of this article, particularly with regard to arguments made in lawsuits related to infringements on the original patents and licenses and how these arguments might have distorted accounts of the early development of the TV console game. I also thank Allan Alcorn, Pong's designer, for reading an early draft of this article and for many conversations about his work and career, including a recent oral history interview.

References and notes

1 I use the more traditional *Spacewar!* on the first reference and then drop the exclamation point thereafter to avoid any awkward sentence punctuation.

2 For example, H. Lowood, "A Brief Biography of Computer Games," *Playing Video Games: Motives, Responses and Consequences*, P. Vorderer and J. Bryant, eds., Lawrence Erlbaum, 2006, pp. 25–41, and P. Ceruzzi, *A History of Modern Computing*, MIT Press, 1998, pp. 207–210.

3 B. Sutton-Smith, *Toys as Culture*, Gardner, 1986, p. 64.

4 A. Alcorn, "Simplified Block Diagram Pong," PowerPoint presentation and lecture, Stanford Univ., 13 Jan. 2005.

5 G.R. Loftus and E.F. Loftus, *Mind at Play: The Psychology of Video Games*, Basic, 1983, pp. 6–7, and M. Malone, *The Big Score: The Billion-Dollar Story of Silicon Valley*, Doubleday, 1985, p. 343.

6 L. Herman, *Phoenix: The Fall and Rise of Videogames*, 3rd ed., Rolenta, 2001, pp. 11–15.

7 Two terms used throughout this article require some clarification. *Videogame* refers to console games produced for display on televisions and early arcade systems, generally

raster-scan displays. Likewise, *video* does not in this article have the general meaning of referring to any signal for any display but rather to the specific analog television signal specifications of the 1960s and 1970s—horizontal and vertical sync, color synchronization, and so forth—and thus pertains to television technology specifically.

8　For a quick summary of the major cases in the business history of videogames, see the Patent Arcade website, http://www.patentarcade.com/2005/05/feature-video-game-lawsuits.html. See especially *Magnavox Co. v. Activision, Inc.*, WL 9496, 1985 (N.D. Cal.).

9　R.H. Baer, *Videogames in the Beginning*, Rolenta, 2005. For a list of patents, see pp. 197–220.

10　K.H. Olsen to P. Elias, "The Story of . . . PDP-1," internal corporate document, Digital Equipment, 15 Sept. 1961; http://research.microsoft.com/~gbell/Digital/timeline/pdp-1story.htm.

11　S. Russell, quoted in: S. Brand, "SPACEWAR: Fanatic Life and Symbolic Death Among the Computer Bums," *Rolling Stone*, 7 Dec. 1972; http://www.wheels.org/spacewar/stone/rolling_stone.html.

12　J.M. Graetz, "The Origin of Spacewar!," *Creative Computing Video & Arcade Games*, vol. 1, no. 1, Spring 1983, pp. 78–85. This was originally published in *Creative Computing*, Aug. 1981.

13　D.J. Edwards and J.M. Graetz, "PDP-1 Plays at Spacewar," *Decuscope*, vol. 1, no. 1, Apr. 1962, pp. 2–4.

14　G. Bell, "Towards a History of (Personal) Computer Workstations (Draft)," Proc. *ACM Conf. History of Personal Workstations*, ACM Press, 1986, pp. 10–11.

15　R. Rivlin, *The Algorithmic Image: Graphic Visions of the Computer Age*, Microsoft Press, 1986; as quoted by the Univ. of Utah, "History of the School of Computing," http://www.cs.utah/dept/history/; A.L. Norberg and J.E. O'Neill, *Transforming Computer Technology: Information Processing for the Pentagon*, 1962–1986, Johns Hopkins Univ. Press, 1986, p. 122.

16　D.C. Hoefler, "Silicon Valley USA," *Electronic News*, 11 Jan. 1971, p. 3.

17　R. DeMaria and J.L. Wilson, *High Score: The Illustrated History of Electronic Games*, McGraw Hill/Osborne, 2002, pp. 16–21.

18　S. Cohen, *Zap! The Rise and Fall of Atari*, McGraw-Hill, 1984, pp. 15–28.

19　S. Bloom, "The First Golden Age," *Digital Deli: The Comprehensive, User-Lovable Menu of Computer Lore, Culture, Lifestyles, and Fancy*, Steve Ditlea, ed., Workman, 1984, pp. 327–332; V. Burnham, *Supercade: A Visual History of the Videogame Age, 1971–1984*, MIT Press, 2001, pp. 64–77.

20　S.L. Kent, *The Ultimate History of Video Games*, Three Rivers Press, 2001, pp. 28–41.

21　D. Sheff, *Game Over: How Nintendo Conquered the World*, GamePress, 1999, pp. 133–140; P.J. Coughlan and D. Freier, "Competitive Dynamics in Home Video Games (A): The Age of Atari," *Harvard Business School Industry and Competitive Strategy Cases*, 9-701-091, 12 June 2001, pp. 1–3.

22　T.H. Nelson, *Computer Lib: You Can and Must Understand Computers Now*, Hugo's Book Service, 1983, title page & pp. 2–3.

23　M. Gardner, "The Fantastic Combinations of John Conway's New Solitaire Game 'Life,'" *Scientific Am.*, vol. 223, no. 4, 1970, pp. 120–123.

24　According to Al Alcorn, the Atari group did not hear about Nelson until the late 1970s, and "lots of people had ideas but no one . . . built any working machines" (email correspondence, Aug. 2005).

25　J. Mulligan, "Talkin' 'bout My . . . Generation," 22 Jan. 2002, http://www.skotos.net/articles/BTH_17.shtml; M. Friedl, *Online Game Interactivity Theory*, Charles River Media, 2003, pp. 4–5.

26　J.P. Pearson, ed., *Digital at Work: Snapshots from the First Thirty-Five Years*, Digital Equipment, 1992, pp. 58, 65.

27 B. Pitts, "The Galaxy Game," 29 Oct. 1997, Computer History Exhibits, Stanford University; http://www-db.stanford.edu/pub/voy/museum/galaxy.html. Al Alcorn saw the Galaxy Game on the Stanford campus with Bushnell while collecting quarters from their Pong machine right next to it. Alcorn remembers that "right next to me was Pitts with his, what do you call it, Galaxy Game. And Nolan—we looked at this thing and my goodness, there was a teletype terminal sitting behind it, and he'd be in there modifying code on this thing. There was a vector scan display, from I think Hewlett-Packard or Tektronics, there was a real mini-computer in there." "Oral History of Al Alcorn. Interviewed by Henry Lowood," Computer History Museum, X4596.2008, transcript 2, Apr. 2008, p. 3.

28 In his book *The Ultimate History of Video Games*, Kent, who interviewed Bushnell, refers to "a new and inexpensive Texas Instruments minicomputer" (p. 31). DeMaria and Wilson's *High Score* reported that Bushnell said, "I originally planned to do it on a Data General 1600," noting that the cost was $4,000 (p. 16). Bushnell probably meant the 16-bit Nova 1200, which cost $3,995 when launched in 1969. Perhaps Kent had in mind Bushnell's use of the TI 7400 series of TTL integrated circuits, such as the 74150 and 74153 multiplexers shown in the design schematics for the board that controlled graphics and motion of in-game rockets, "B-MEMORY 1 or 2 Player, NA 73–103, Computer Space" (29 Jan. 1973), Computer Space Instructions, http://www.arcadedocs.com/vidmanuals/C/ComputerSpace. pdf. According to Alcorn, Bushnell's original idea was to use the Supernova minicomputer, which came out soon after the Nova ("Oral History," transcript 1, p. 9).

29 Atari did not use vector-generated images until 1979, when it developed the Digital Vector Generator for the coin-operated games *Lunar Lander* (like Computer Space, formerly a popular computer game in university labs) and *Asteroids*.

30 L. Herman, "The Untold Atari Story," *Edge*, no. 200, Apr. 2009, pp. 94–99.

31 "Oral History of Al Alcorn. Interviewed by Henry Lowood," Computer History Museum, X4596.2008, transcript, part 1, Apr. 2008, p. 9–11.

32 Burnham appreciates this point in *Supercade*, noting that "the game established the basic system architecture for nearly every arcade game to follow," p. 71.

33 A. Maclean, "Computer Space Restoration"; http://www.ionpool.net/arcade/archuk/computer_space_restoration.html.

34 L. Kerecman, "Computer Space," Arcade History Database; http://www.arcade-history.com/?n=computer-space&page=detail&id=3388.

35 Nutting Associates, "How Computer SpaceWorks and Produces," flyer, Nov. 1971; N.K. Bushnell, "Computer Space Instructions," typescript, Nutting Associates, Feb. 1972.

36 On this point, I am indebted to Ralph Baer's comments on an earlier draft of this article.

37 Videotaped interview with Atari engineers filmed in August 1997: R. Milner and S. Mayer, "Stella at 20: An Atari 2600 Retrospective," video recording, Cyber PuNKS, 2000. See also T.E. Perry and P. Wallich, "Design Case History: The Atari Video Computer System," *IEEE Spectrum*, vol. 20, no. 3, Mar. 1983, pp. 45–51.

38 Atari's Tank (1974) was the first videogame to use ROM for storing game graphics.

39 He eliminated some videos of game play from *Spacewar*, a topic outside this article's scope.

40 Ampex's role as incubator of talented Silicon Valley engineers and entrepreneurs, such as Ray Dolby, Steve Mayer, Steve Bristow, and Lee Felsenstein, deserves study.

41 "Oral History of Al Alcorn. Interviewed by Henry Lowood," Computer History Museum, X4596.2008, transcript 2, Apr. 2008, pp. 2–6.

42 N. Bushnell, *Video Image Positioning Control System for Amusement Device*, US patent 3,793,483, 19 Feb. 1974. The patent was actually filed on 24 Nov. 1972, shortly after Alcorn began work on Pong.

43 Vintage Gaming Network, "Al Alcorn Interview," Vintage Gaming; http://atari.vg-network.com/aainterview.html; D. Owen, "The Second Coming of Nolan Bushnell," *Playboy*, June 1983.

44 Steve Wozniak's reduction of the TTL count for Atari's *Breakout* game provides a famous example. See also O.W. Linzmayer, *Apple Confidential: The Real Story of Apple Computer, Inc.*, No Starch Press, 1999, pp. 17–20.

45 Atari Inc., "Atari Expands Worldwide!" flyer, Arcade Flyer Database, 1972; http://www.arcadeflyers.com/?page=thumbs&db=videodb&id=3303. In the early 1980s, Atari invested heavily in the game machine as home computer in the form of the Atari 400/800.

46 Notably, *Television Gaming Apparatus*, US patent 3,659, 285, filed 21 Aug. 1969. The details of this story can be found in R. Baer's *Videogames*. Baer deserves great credit for the extensive documentation of his activities during the key period of his work at Sanders, both in his book and by donating his significant collection of papers to the Smithsonian Institution's Lemelson Center Archives. See http://invention. smithsonian. org/resources/fa_baer_index.aspx.

47 "TV's Hot New Star: The Electronic Game," *Business Week—Industrial Edition*, 29 Dec. 1975, p. 24.

48 For example, *Magnavox Co. v. Chicago Dynamic Industries*, 201 U.S.P.Q. 25 (N.D. Ill. 1977), and *Magnavox Co. v. Mattel, Inc.*, 216 U.S.P.Q. 28 (N.D. Ill. 1982).

49 *Nintendo v. Magnavox*, US District Court, Southern District of New York, document 100. NARA Central Plains Region, duplicate photocopies of selected records at Stanford University.

50 *Nintendo v. Magnavox*, US District Court, Southern District of New York, document 81, p. 18.

51 *Nintendo v. Magnavox*, "Order of Discontinuance," US District Court, Southern District of New York, document 112.

52 D. Becker, "The Return of King Pong," interview, CNET News.com, 15 Mar. 2005; http://news.com.com/The+return+of+King+Pong/2008-1043_3-5616047.html.

22

BATTLEZONE AND THE ORIGINS OF FIRST-PERSON SHOOTING GAMES

Mark J. P. Wolf

Source: Gerald Voorhees, Joshua Call, and Katie Whitlock (eds), *Guns, Grenades and Grunts: First Person Shooter Games* (New York, NY: Continuum, 2012), pp. 25–40.

Atari's arcade game *BattleZone* (Atari 1980) was not the first shooting game, nor the first to have a first-person perspective, nor even the first to combine the two. But the game does represent the coalescence of the first-person shooter (FPS) genre (or subgenre of the shooting game genre, since not all shooting games are from a first-person perspective), as it brought together all the necessary elements now recognized as being essential to the first-person shooter as it is typically defined today. *BattleZone* combined them into a single game that was commercially available in wide release to the general public, and, as such, became a milestone and turning point in the history of the FPS. The influences, precursors, and development of the elements found in *BattleZone* occurred over more than a century, so it is to these that we must first turn our attention, as we examine how shooting became a game, how shooting games became virtual, and finally how they arrived at the form taken in *BattleZone*.

Shooting becomes a game

If the idea of shooting projectiles developed to allow one to do damage at a distance without putting one's self into harm's way, that is, within reach of whatever was being shot at, it makes sense to assume that increasing one's accuracy would be a good thing. Shooting practice would be the result, and if two or more individuals practiced shooting, it seems natural that it would turn into a competition, and finally, into a kind of game.

Shooting competitions have probably existed for as long as projectile weapons have been around, and were no doubt the inspiration for shooting galleries on carnival fairgrounds from the late 1890s onward, which we might consider the very first first-person shooting games. As a fairground attraction with less dangerous guns, shooting galleries allowed carnival patrons to try their hand at shooting even if they would normally never handle real guns. This reduced possibility of danger helped to enhance the game-like nature of competitive shooting, allowing more concentration on its more playful aspects. Shooting galleries, however, still required safety measures and operators who tended the games, and it would be some time before technology had advanced sufficiently such that these could be eliminated.

Meanwhile, other outdoor games were adapted into indoor versions. For example, croquet was turned into billiards, and during the late 1700s in France the pool table used for billiards was narrowed and posts were added, becoming the game Bagatelle. Players would use cues to send balls up the table and ricochet them off pegs and into holes. During the 1800s, Bagatelle games became smaller, and eventually table-top versions were made. French soldiers brought Bagatelle to America during the Revolutionary War, and the tables became popular in the United States. In 1869, British inventor Montague Redgrave started producing Bagatelle tables in Ohio, but he replaced the pool cues with plungers and glassed over the Bagatelle table, making the game more self-contained. After further innovation and redesign, Bagatelle became known as pinball, which went on to even greater success during the twentieth century, during which time such features as backlights, bumpers, and flippers were added, and the game was electrified.

As pinball began to find success, other fairground games were adapted into electromechanical games, and among them were shooting gallery games. The Mechanical Trading Co. produced the coin-operated *Automatic Shooting Range* in 1895, and the Automatic Sports Company of London, England, produced several coin-operated shooting games for the arcade into the 1920s. Automatic Sports' coin-operated games took place in glass-enclosed cases atop fanciful pedestals designed to bring the games up to the right height for standing players. Electromechanical games further sanitized and automated shooting galleries through the use of easily resettable targets, reusable ammunition, a mounted gun, and an enclosed space that contained all the elements of the game apart from the controls of the gun. Everything stayed within the game cabinet, and targets and guns were automatically reset, so no operator was required, allowing players to play unattended and greater profits to be made. Shooting games became less like shooting with real guns; gone was the noise and recoil of a real gun, and the field of action was miniaturized to only a few feet across, making timing far less important since the short distances eliminated the need to anticipate the movements of targets and compensate one's aim as a result (although some games did attempt to simulate these things, like Chicago Coin's *Pistol* (1947), which advertised "Realistic Recoil and Report Action" on its flyer; and some games also used mirrors within their cabinets to increase the shooting distance). From a design point of view, this meant that moving targets and other elements of difficulty became more important, since the use of distant targets was no longer possible. Overall, however, encased coin-operated games abstracted shooting games to an even greater degree than had fairground shooting galleries, and skills needed for the games no longer translated into the skills needed for the use of real weaponry.

Electromechanical games were the dominant coin-operated arcade games from the late 1930s to the early 1970s, and shooting games released during this time included such games as A. B. T. Manufacturing Corporation's *Challenger* (1939), Chicago Coin's *Pistol* (1947), Genco's *Sky Gunner* (1953), Midway's *Trophy Gun* (1964), and Chicago Coin's *Super Circus Rifle Gallery* (1969) and *Sharp Shooter* (1971). Although today the abilities of electromechanical games seem very limited when compared with possibilities that video games offer, by the time arcade video games appeared in 1971, electromechanical games had become quite advanced, even to the point of offering competitive machine-controlled players. Midway's *Wild Kingdom* (1971), for example, had "Jungle Charlie" who competed against the player; according to pinball and game collector Clay F. Harrell,

Midway's *Wild Kingdom* is a very challenging gun game because the player is shooting against "Jungle Charlie", a 3″ high moving mechanical marksman on the game's playfield. Unlike say *Haunted House* where the player can take their time and shoot as slow as they want, *Wild Kingdom* forces the player to shoot fast. After the first shot is taken, the player is shooting against Jungle Charlie (the first shot is a 'warm up' shot and the player can take as long as they want for the first shot). If the player takes too long to shoot, Jungle Charlie shoots the animal instead causing the animal to retreat, and Jungle Charlie *never* misses. To slow Jungle Charlie, the player can fire his gun – Jungle Charlie can not shoot if the player is shooting (and likewise the player can not shot [*sic*] if Jungle Charlie is shooting). Each game gets 25 shots, with Jungle Charlie shooting out of the 25 shots. If the player is slow he may only get the first shot, and Jungle Charlie will use the other 24 shots! Jungle Charlie's movement speed can be adjusted. If he's adjusted too fast the game is nearly impossible to shoot as Jungle Charlie is too quick. At 3000 points the game automatically speeds up Jungle Charlie too. (Pinrepair.com 2011b)

Although early video games represented a technological novelty, they could not provide some of the kinds of play experiences that electromechanical games could. Eventually, video games improved and surpassed electromechanical games, ending their dominance in the arcade, and video games offered additional benefits for arcade operators as well, especially when it came to repairs.

Whereas electromechanical arcade games did not need constant supervision from a human attendant the way that carnival games did, they still needed frequent maintenance due to their many moving parts and occasional breakdowns. Video games, with far few moving parts (usually only the controllers), were less likely to break down and more reliable, and technologically they were much less idiosyncratic in their design; all used a monitor for their imagery instead of plastic or metal models that had to be painted, assembled, and tested. After *PONG* (Atari 1972) proved that arcade video games could be successful, it was natural that games would begin the transition from electromechanical contraptions to virtual on-screen versions of the same activities. But shooting games had already begun the process of becoming virtual as early as the 1920s.

Shooting games become virtual

The first element of shooting games to become virtual was ammunition. So long as actual physical projectiles of some kind flew through the air between the player's gun and the target, the field of action between the two had to be encased for safety reasons, as well as to recycle the ammunition and keep it from leaving the system. By using a light beam instead of a physical projectile, guns could once again be used in the open air just as in carnival shooting galleries; all that was needed was a way to sense when the beam of light struck its target.

William Gent used an electrical light gun in his *Electric Rifle* game of the 1920s (Pinrepair 2011c), and in 1936 the jukebox manufacturer Seeburg Corporation used the newly invented phototube, a vacuum tube with a light sensor inside it, in a duck shooting arcade game called *Ray-O-Lite* (Pinrepair 2011a). Players held a full-sized rifle which shot a light beam at the moving targets, each of which contained a phototube inside it; when the phototube detected the light beam, the hit was registered and the score increased. The "Ray-O-Lite" technology went on to be used in other Seeburg games like *Shoot the Bear* (1947), and other companies began to use similar light gun-based technologies. Eventually light gun technology became available in a consumer product for home use; in 1970, Nintendo released Gunpei Yokoi's *Beam Gun* toy, a light gun that came with targets with photoelectric cells on them.

The Magnavox Odyssey was the first home video game system with a light gun peripheral (released in 1972, and based on Ralph Baer's prototype of 1968), and reversed the usual hardware configuration by putting the photoelectric cell inside the gun barrel, where it would detect the light of the target on the television screen (though it would also register hits if pointed at a light bulb or any light source). Four Odyssey games used the light gun (*Prehistoric Safari* [1972], *Shooting Gallery* [1972], *Dogfight* [1972], and *Shootout* [1972]), in which the player fired at on-screen targets. The Odyssey's shooting games represented a further advancement of the first-person shooting game into the virtual realm, as both their ammunition and their targets were now virtual.

Virtual shooting found its natural home in the video game, and video games had involved shooting from their very beginning. The first patent for an interactive electronic game, United States patent #2,455,992, "Cathode-Ray Tube Amusement Device," was filed by Thomas T. Goldsmith, Jr. and Estle Ray Mann on January 25, 1947 and issued on December 14, 1948 (it did not involve a video signal, however, and could therefore arguably be denied the status of a "video" game). The description of the proposed device's content describes a scenario with shooting going on:

In carrying out the invention a cathode-ray tube is used upon the face of which the trace of the ray or electron beam can be seen. One or more targets, such as pictures of airplanes, for example, are placed upon the face of the tube and controls are available to the player so that he can manipulate the trace or position of the beam which is automatically caused to move across the face of the tube. This movement of the beam may be periodic and its repetition rate may be varied. Its path is preferably caused to depart from a straight line so as to require an increased amount of skill and care for success in playing the game.

The game can be made more spectacular, and the interest therein both from the player's and the observer's standpoint can be increased, by making a visible explosion of the cathode-ray beam take place when the target is hit. (United States Patent 2,455,992)

Some of the earliest video games, such as the mainframe game *Spacewar!* (1962) and commercial games based on it like *Galaxy Game* (1971) and *Computer Space* (1971), also involved shooting. In these games, the weaponry, the ammunition, and the targets were all virtual; but as these games featured shooting from a third-person perspective, they provided a much different kind of shooting experience than first-person shooting games. The third person perspective required the control of an on-screen avatar, and its top-down or side view was less immersive than a first-person perspective. But a first-person perspective required z-axis depth and a three-dimensional game-space, something that electromechanical games, with their physical game-spaces, could not help providing, but which video games would struggle to simulate during the 1970s.

Video games and first-person perspective

Actual shooting, and shooting games involving a hand-held gun of some sort, naturally make use of the first-person perspective of the player's own vision, since shooting depends greatly on the player's ability to aim while assessing the three-dimensional position of targets, whether they are moving or static. This close connection between shooting and perspective is apparent in the sharp divide that we find between first-person and third-person shooting games; no other genre of video game finds itself so divided according to player point-of-view. For example, racing games are available from both first-person and third-person perspectives, but we do not speak of "first-person racers" as often as we do "first-person shooters" (a Google search performed on April 8, 2011, found 17,100,000 results for "first-person shooter" but only 4,420 results for "first-person racer"; a ratio of more than 3868 to 1).

As video games, shooting games had to wait until the mid-1970s for first-person perspective. The Odyssey's four shooting games had flat graphics, and were little more than the back wall of a shooting gallery, and although it might be argued that the use of the light gun made the games first-person perspective shooting games, such an argument would broaden the sense of the term to the point where the usual distinctions made between perspectives would be lost. One would be able to argue that *Pac-Man* (Namco 1980) had a first-person perspective of someone hovering over the maze and looking down at the figures moving within it; the term "first-person" would come to encompass all third-person points of view as well as the usual meaning of subjective, optical viewpoints located at characters' positions. (It is interesting to note how this problem does not occur in media involving lens-based imaging, like photography, film, and television; every view shown in these media is either from a character's point of view or at the very least a point of view that has a distinct position in the three-dimensional space of the image's diegesis; but the two-dimensional worlds of video games are seen from views from a standpoint outside of their worlds.)

The first two shooting games to use a first-person perspective were both mainframe games; *Maze War* (Colley 1974) on the Imlac PDS-1 (see Figure 1), and *Spasim* (Bowery 1974), which was short for *space simulator*, on the PLATO system. Mainframe games had more processing power and speed than arcade games or home video games of the day, and were the incubators where many genres of video games were born, including the FPS. Both *Maze War* and *Spasim*

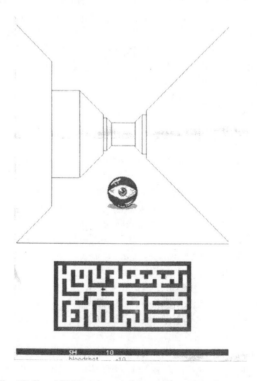

Figure 1 *Maze War* (Colley 1974) was one of the earliest shooting games to feature a first-person perspective

depicted movement through a three-dimensional space, and including the shooting of enemy figures when they were on-screen and positioned in the player's view. In *Spasim*, movement advanced in jumps from one position to another, with time needed in between to render the next view, as opposed to movement and shooting that occurred in real time. In *Maze War*, movement in a straight line down hallways was relatively smooth, but turning was done in 90-degree increments, resulting in potentially confusing graphics as the vanishing point stays the same during 90-degree turns while everything else changes abruptly.

Maze War and *Spasim* were both networked multiplayer games, allowing players to shoot at each other. Thus, unlike almost all shooting games that had gone before them, competitive shooting no longer meant only a competition to see who could hit the most targets or who had the most accurate shooting, but rather who could shoot the other player's avatar first; thus did shooting games go from friendly competition to kill-or-be-killed deathmatches, a move that would set the stage and tone for most of the FPSs that followed. *Maze War* also contained "robots" that would automatically shoot you if they were in line with you down a hallway, so even in a singleplayer game, danger could lurk just around the corner.

But if danger was just around the corner, it could be avoided. Although *Maze War* allowed players to switch between the first-person point of view and an overhead map of the maze (making it also the first game to incorporate both points of view and allow a player to choose between them), the map only showed the player's location in the maze, and not those of the other players. Because it was so easy to turn a corner and suddenly be surprised and shot at, an additional feature allowed the player to peek around a corner without being seen, momentarily disconnecting the first-person view from the player's actual location ("The Maze War 30 Year Retrospective at the DigiBarn", Digibarn Computer Museum website), a feature prefiguring the separation of point-of-view from movement.

Another new twist introduced in *Maze War* was the possibility of getting shot at and killed from behind, without ever even seeing your attacker. Instead of the fixed and unchanging point of view found in a shooting gallery, *Maze War* required you to change your view as well as keep watch on the space all around you. Unlike all other video games up to this point, one did not merely watch the game's world from some point outside it, but rather from within the world, and there was a sense of off-screen space surrounding the player and events that were occurring unseen in those spaces.

Both *Maze War* and *Spasim* used vector graphics to display their views (raster versions of *Maze War* appeared later). Since lines of perspective extending to a vanishing point are almost always diagonal lines, vector graphics had an advantage over early raster graphics in creating a first-person perspective. Raster graphics could only roughly approximate diagonal lines, by linking blocks corner to corner diagonally, or spacing them apart like the pylons in Atari's *Night Driver* (1976). Vector graphics, drawn on the screen one line at a time in any direction, could produce a stronger sense of lines converging at a vanishing point. Vector graphics came to the arcade with Cinematronics's release of *Space Wars* (1977), and another of the company's games, *Speed Freak* (1978) featured the first real-time rendered three-dimensional computer animation in an arcade video game, an explosion of car parts when the player crashed.

Yet although they both represented advances in the genre, what *Maze War* and *Spasim* lacked was the kind of aiming and shooting that players enjoyed in third-person perspective shooting games. In both games, shooting was done with a keystroke, and aiming was limited to facing in the right direction, due to the limitations of the positioning of the player's point-of-view, like the 90-degree incremental turns in *Maze War*.

The following year, another multiplayer shooting game on PLATO advanced the genre a step further. John Edo Haefeli's tank simulator *Panther* (1975) was even more complex, with an entire screen listing the game's features and their keyboard shortcuts. The tank and its turret could be turned independently of each other, there were gross, coarse, and fine adjustments for turret positioning, the player's view could be zoomed in and out, and the controls allowed the player to determine the distance to targets, fire shells, deploy mines, and move ammunition and fuel from one player's tank to another. Whereas *Maze War* allowed the player to switch between a first-person view and an overhead map of the game's space, *Panther* had an overhead view of the tank (showing the direction that the tank and its gun turret was facing) that appeared in the corner of the first-person view, splitting the player's attention between the two different views. The game also had hidden line removal, and simulated the physics of shooting along a trajectory, accounting for source and target speeds, and even the curvature of the earth. Two years later, an updated version of *Panther* with better graphics, known as *Panzer* (1977), was produced by Northwestern University along with the US Army Armor School at Fort Knox. (For other takes on militarism in FPS games, see the essays by Voorhees, Miller, and Moore in this volume.)

The games on PLATO were far more advanced than the simpler and more streamlined games of the arcade, and, as networked games, sometimes slower in their operation as well. They were operated entirely by keyboard, and could take time to learn, due to all their features and commands. That *PONG* (1972) was so much more successful than *Computer Space* (Nutting Associates 1971) demonstrated that simplified controls were needed to reach a mass audience at the arcade, where shorter game times meant more money and steep learning curves were bad for business. While *Panther* enjoyed a following of technology-savvy users on mainframe computers, it would take another first-person tank game to break through to the mass commercial market of the arcades: *BattleZone* (1980).

The arrival of *BattleZone*

Atari's *BattleZone* was a three-dimensional vector graphics game and the first arcade video game to feature a computationally true three-dimensional environment. Its green vector graphics depicted a barren landscape with cubical and pyramidal obstacles and mountains on the horizon (including an erupting volcano), and enemy tanks (and a UFO) that came at the player's tank from any direction on the plane, forcing the player to watch the radar scope that revealed enemy positions within a short radius. Above the action were red vector graphics (the screen used a color overlay) displaying the score, high score, tanks remaining, and the radar scope. Released the same year as *Pac-Man* (1980) and *Defender* (Williams 1980), *BattleZone* joined the ranks of the most popular arcade video games to appear during the Golden Age of the arcade.

Because *BattleZone* is both a tank game and a vector graphics game, it is often compared to *Panther*, which is assumed to be its inspiration. But apart from the tank theme and vector graphics, the games differ in many ways, and a more likely candidate for *BattleZone*'s inspiration can be found in an earlier tank arcade game from Atari; *Tank!* (1974), the groundbreaking and influential game which was the first arcade game to use read-only memory (ROM) and which inspired *Combat* (1977), the cartridge packaged with the Atari VCS 2600.

Unlike *Panther*, which used a computer keyboard, *BattleZone*'s controls were, like *Tank!*, a pair of joysticks and a fire button which allowed the player to move forward, move backward, right turn, left turn, and fire. Firing was done only in the direction the tank was facing, meaning you could not fire and run away at the same time (as you could in *Panther*); *BattleZone* was almost like a first-person version of *Tank!* since both tanks were operated in a similar fashion. Both games were also designed at Atari, as commercial arcade games. Finally, there is the admission from Ed Rotberg, the designer of *BattleZone*, that *Tank!* was more of an influence than *Panther*:

> Actually it wasn't based on *Panther*. It may have inspired whoever originally suggested the idea at the brainstorming meeting where it was proposed, but I seriously doubt it. It was more a matter of the success of the original, top-down *Tank* game Atari did and the advent of the vector generator. There is only so much you can do with vectors, a tank concept, and somewhat limited processor power. While I did play on PLATO, I don't ever remember playing *Panther*, though I was aware of it. The design of *BattleZone* was primarily mine. (Ed Rotberg, e-mail to the author, April 12, 2011)

BattleZone combined shooting with a first-person shooting perspective, a three-dimensional environment, a mobile viewpoint, computer-controlled enemies, smooth movement in all directions, and simple controls with a shallow learning curve, and made them available to a mass audience as an arcade video game.

For many people, *BattleZone* was their first encounter with an FPS video game (and with interactive three-dimensional computer graphics, for that matter), and it is no wonder that it became one of the most popular and influential games of the 1980s. *BattleZone* was ported to other game systems, including the Atari 2600 in 1983, and Atarisoft released home computer versions of *BattleZone* for the Apple II, the Commodore 64, and MS-DOS in 1983, the Sinclair ZX Spectrum in 1984,

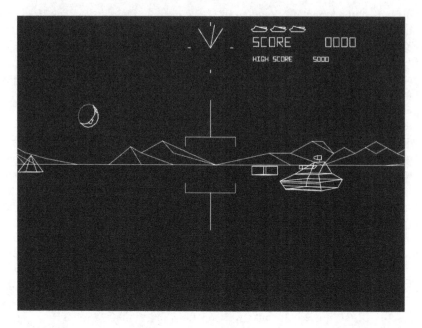

Figure 2 BattleZone (Atari 1980) was the first FPS to become available to a general public audience

the Atari ST in 1986, the Atari XE in 1987, the Nintendo Game Boy in 1996, and the PlayStation Portable in 2006. Updated versions of *BattleZone* include the four-player networked *BattleZone 2000* (1995) for the Atari Lynx, a 1996 Java version that can be played online, a 3D remake in 1998, Pandemic Studios's *BattleZone II: Combat Commander* (1999), a high-definition version for Xbox Live Arcade in 2008, and a download for Microsoft's Game Room service for the Xbox 360 in 2010. A host of *BattleZone* clones also appeared, for various consoles and computers, including Atari's own *Red Baron* (1980), which used the same hardware but depicted dogfights between biplanes instead of tanks. In 1981, a more advanced version of *BattleZone* known as the "Bradley Trainer" was also developed for the US military for tank training, but only two prototypes were ever produced.

Eventually the FPS would undergo other refinements, most notably in the relationship between *looking* and *aiming*. Just as the later, more advanced version of *Panther* allowed one to aim in a different direction than the direction of movement (a feature not found in *BattleZone*), later FPS games would make the direction of one's aim less dependent on the direction of one's view. Whereas in *BattleZone* the gunsight is always centered in the player's point of view, making "looking" and "aiming" the same thing, these games allowed the gunsight to be moved around freely within the player's point of view, limited only by the edges of the screen. Although earlier games, like Taito's *Interceptor* (1976) and Atari's *Missile Command* (1980), had gunsights that could move around the screen, the

380

player's point-of-view itself was fixed and immovable. Such a feature could have been incorporated into *BattleZone*, but it would not have made sense due to the vehicular nature of the player's avatar, since the aiming of a tank is much less flexible than that of standing and aiming a pistol with one's own arm. During the mid to late 1990s, however, "free looking," also known as "mouselooking," would become a standard feature of the FPS.

Although *BattleZone* significantly shaped the development of the FPS, many of its features had already appeared in one form or another in earlier games, so it was the combination of these in a single game, and, most importantly, the game's availability to a wide audience, that was its main contribution to the genre. In this sense, *BattleZone* helped the FPS coalesce into a full-fledged subgenre of the shooting game genre (or, as some would have it, a genre all its own); and *BattleZone*'s iconic status as a video game and widespread popularity set a standard that helped make certain elements seem indispensable to the FPS, even if it was not the first game to introduce those elements. As such, *BattleZone* was both a milestone in the development of the FPS and one of the main games to promote it to the public, and it will always be remembered along with the great games of the video arcade game's Golden Age.

References

Digibarn Computer Museum. 2011. "The Maze War 30 Year Retrospective at the DigiBarn" http://www.digibarn.com/collections/games/xerox-maze-war/index.html#started.

Goldsmith, Thomas T. and Estle Ray Mann. 1948. "Cathode-Ray Tube Amusement Device." United States Patent 2,455,992, filed January 25, 1947 and issued December 14, 1948.

International Arcade Museum. 2012. "Automatic Shooting Range." http://www.arcade-museum.com/game_detail.php?game_id=704.

Nintendoland.com. 2011. "Toys & Arcades – (1969–82)." http://nintendoland.com/History/Hist2.php.

Pinrepair.com. 2011a. "1936 Seeburg Ray-O-Lite." http://www.pinrepair.com/arcade/rayolit.htm.

—2011b. "Wild Kingdom." http://www.pinrepair.com/arcade/wildkin.htm.

—2011c. "William Gent Mfg Electric Rifle." http://www.pinrepair.com/arcade/gent.htm.

Games

A. B. T. Manufacturing Corp. *Challenger* [arcade]. A. B. T. Manufacturing Corp., 1939.

Atari. 1972. *PONG* [arcade]. Atari.

—1974. *Tank!* [arcade]. Atari.

—1976. *Night Driver* [arcade]. Atari.

—1977. *Combat* [Atari VCS 2600]. Atari.

—1980. *BattleZone* [arcade]. Atari.

—1980. *Missile Command* [arcade]. Atari.

—1980. *Red Baron* [arcade]. Atari.

—1995. *BattleZone 2000* [Atari Lynx]. Atari.

Bowery, Jim. 1974. *Spasim* [PLATO System]. Bowery.

Chicago Coin. 1947. *Pistol* [arcade]. Chicago Coin.

—1969. *Super Circus Rifle Gallery* [arcade]. Chicago Coin.

—1971. *Sharp Shooter* [arcade]. Chicago Coin.

Cinematronics. 1977. *Space Wars* [arcade]. Cinematronics.

—1978. *Speed Freak* [arcade]. Cinematronics.

Colley, Steve. 1974. *Maze War* [Imlac PDS-1]. Colley.

Genco. 1953. *Sky Gunner* [arcade]. Genco.

Haefeli, John Edo. 1975. *Panther* [PLATO System]. Haefeli.

—1977. *Panzer* [PLATO System]. Haefeli.

Maganvox. 1972. *Dogfight* [Magnavox Odyssey]. Magnavox.

—1972. *Prehistoric Safari* [Magnavox Odyssey]. Magnavox.

—1972. *Shooting Gallery* [Magnavox Odyssey]. Magnavox.

—1972. *Shootout* [Magnavox Odyssey]. Magnavox.

Mechanical Trading Co. 1895. *Automatic Shooting Range* [arcade]. Mechanical Trading Co.

Midway. 1964. *Trophy Gun* [arcade]. Midway.

—1971. *Wild Kingdom* [arcade]. Midway.

Namco. 1980. *Pac-Man* [arcade]. Midway.

Nutting Associates. 1971. *Computer Space* [arcade]. Nutting Associates.

Pandemic Studios. 1999. *BattleZone II: Combat Commander* [Microsoft Windows]. Activision.

Pitts, Bill and Hugh Tuck. 1971. *Galaxy Game* [DEC PDP-11/20]. Pitts and Tuck.

Russell, Steve, et al. 1962. *Spacewar!* [PDP-1]. Russell.

Seeburg Corporation. 1936. *Ray-O-Lite* [arcade]. Seeburg Corporation.

—1947. *Shoot the Bear* [arcade]. Seeburg Corporation.

Taito. 1976. *Interceptor* [arcade]. Taito.

William Gent. circa 1920s. *Electric Rifle* [arcade]. William Gent.

Williams. 1980. *Defender* [arcade]. Williams.